Eye Movement Desensitization and Reprocessing

EMDR Therapy

Scripted Protocols and Summary Sheets

TREATING TRAUMA- AND STRESSOR-RELATED CONDITIONS

Marilyn Luber, PhD, is a licensed clinical psychologist and has a general private practice in Center City, Philadelphia, Pennsylvania, working with adolescents, adults, and couples, especially with complex posttraumatic stress disorder (C-PTSD), trauma and related issues, and dissociative disorders. She has worked as a Primary Consultant for the FBI field division in Philadelphia.

In 1992, Dr. Francine Shapiro trained her in Eye Movement Desensitization and Reprocessing (EMDR). She was on the Founding Board of Directors of the EMDR International Association (EMDRIA) and served as the Chairman of the International Committee until June 1999. Also, she was a member of the EMDR Task Force for Dissociative Disorders. She conducts facilitator and consultation trainings and teaches other EMDR-related subjects both nationally and internationally. Since 1997, she has coordinated trainings in EMDR-related fields in the greater Philadelphia area. In 2014, she was a member of the Scientific Committee for the EMDR Europe Edinburgh Conference. Currently, she is a facilitator for the EMDR Global Alliance to support upholding the standard of EMDR Therapy worldwide.

In 1997, Dr. Luber was given a Humanitarian Services Award by the EMDR Humanitarian Association. Later, in 2003, she was presented with the EMDR International Association's award "For Outstanding Contribution and Service to EMDRIA" and in 2005, she was awarded "The Francine Shapiro Award for Outstanding Contribution and Service to EMDR."

In 2001, through EMDR HAP (Humanitarian Assistance Programs), she published, *Handbook for EMDR Clients,* which has been translated into eight languages; the proceeds from sales of the handbook go to EMDR HAP organizations worldwide. She has written the "Around the World" and "In the Spotlight" articles for the EMDRIA Newsletter, four times a year since 1997. In 2009, she edited *Eye Movement Desensitization and Reprocessing (EMDR) Scripted Protocols: Basics and Special Situations* (Springer) and *Eye Movement Desensitization and Reprocessing (EMDR) Scripted Protocols: Special Populations* (Springer). She interviewed Francine Shapiro and co-authored the interview with Dr. Shapiro for the *Journal of EMDR Practice and Research* (Luber & Shapiro, 2009) and later wrote the entry about Dr. Shapiro for E. S. Neukrug's, *The SAGE Encyclopedia of Theory in Counseling and Psychotherapy* (2015). Several years later, in 2012, she edited Springer's first CD-ROM books: *Eye Movement Desensitization and Reprocessing (EMDR) Scripted Protocols With Summary Sheets CD-ROM Version: Basics and Special Situations* and *Eye Movement Desensitization and Reprocessing (EMDR) Scripted Protocols With Summary Sheets CD-ROM Version: Special Populations.* In 2014, she edited, *Implementing EMDR Early Mental Health Interventions for Man-Made and Natural Disasters: Models, Scripted Protocols, and Summary Sheets.* In 2015, three ebooks were published that supplied protocols taken from *Implementing EMDR Early Mental Health Interventions for Man-Made and Natural Disasters: Models, Scripted Protocols, and Summary Sheets: EMDR Therapy With First Responders* (ebook only), *EMDR Therapy and Emergency Response* (ebook only), and *EMDR Therapy for Clinician Self-Care* (ebook only). The text, *Eye Movement Desensitization and Reprocessing (EMDR) Therapy Scripted Protocols and Summary Sheets: Treating Anxiety, Obsessive-Compulsive and Mood-Related Conditions* will be released in 2015. Currently, she is working on *Eye Movement Desensitization and Reprocessing (EMDR) Therapy Scripted Protocols and Summary Sheets: Treating Medical-Related Conditions.*

Eye Movement Desensitization and Reprocessing
EMDR Therapy
Scripted Protocols and Summary Sheets

TREATING TRAUMA- AND STRESSOR-RELATED CONDITIONS

Edited by

Marilyn Luber, PhD

SPRINGER PUBLISHING COMPANY
NEW YORK

Copyright © 2016 Springer Publishing Company, LLC

All rights reserved.

No part of this publication may be reproduced, stored in a retrieval system, or transmitted in any form or by any means, electronic, mechanical, photocopying, recording, or otherwise, without the prior permission of Springer Publishing Company, LLC, or authorization through payment of the appropriate fees to the Copyright Clearance Center, Inc., 222 Rosewood Drive, Danvers, MA 01923, 978-750-8400, fax 978-646-8600, info@copyright.com or on the Web at www.copyright.com.

Springer Publishing Company, LLC
11 West 42nd Street
New York, NY 10036
www.springerpub.com

Acquisitions Editor: Sheri W. Sussman
Composition: Newgen KnowledgeWorks

ISBN: 978-0-8261-3164-5
e-book ISBN: 978-0-8261-3165-2
CD-ROM ISBN: 978-0-8261-3166-9

15 16 17 18 / 5 4 3 2 1

The author and the publisher of this Work have made every effort to use sources believed to be reliable to provide information that is accurate and compatible with the standards generally accepted at the time of publication. The author and publisher shall not be liable for any special, consequential, or exemplary damages resulting, in whole or in part, from the readers' use of, or reliance on, the information contained in this book. The publisher has no responsibility for the persistence or accuracy of URLs for external or third-party Internet websites referred to in this publication and does not guarantee that any content on such websites is, or will remain, accurate or appropriate.

Library of Congress Cataloging-in-Publication Data
Luber, Marilyn, editor, author.
 Eye movement desensitization and reprocessing (EMDR) therapy scripted protocols and summary sheets. Treating trauma- and stressor-related conditions / Marilyn Luber.
  p. ; cm.
 Treating trauma- and stressor-related conditions
 Includes bibliographical references.
 ISBN 978-0-8261-3164-5
 I. Title. II. Title: Treating trauma- and stressor-related conditions.
 [DNLM: 1. Eye Movement Desensitization Reprocessing—methods—Handbooks. 2. Eye Movement Desensitization Reprocessing—methods—Practice Guideline. 3. Interview, Psychological—methods—Handbooks. 4. Interview, Psychological—methods—Practice Guideline. 5. Medical History Taking—methods—Handbooks. 6. Medical History Taking—methods—Practice Guideline. 7. Stress Disorders, Traumatic—therapy—Handbooks. 8. Stress Disorders, Traumatic—therapy—Practice Guideline. WM 34]
 RC489.E98
 616.85'210651—dc23   2015013758

Special discounts on bulk quantities of our books are available to corporations, professional associations, pharmaceutical companies, health care organizations, and other qualifying groups.

If you are interested in a custom book, including chapters from more than one of our titles, we can provide that service as well.

For details, please contact:
Special Sales Department, Springer Publishing Company, LLC
11 West 42nd Street, 15th Floor, New York, NY 10036-8002
Phone: 877-687-7476 or 212-431-4370; Fax: 212-941-7842
E-mail: sales@springerpub.com

Printed in the United States of America by Bradford & Bigelow.

To my extraordinary companion and therapy dog, Emmy Luber,
a true wonder of nature and
sweet loving presence,
my heart.

The wound is the place where the Light enters you.

—Rumi

Contents

Contributors xi
Preface xvii
Acknowledgments xxv

PART I
EMDR Therapy and Trauma- and Stressor-Related Conditions

Reactive Attachment Disorders

Chapter 1   **Child Attachment Trauma Protocol.** 9
Debra Wesselmann, Cathy Schweitzer, and Stefanie Armstrong

                Summary Sheet: Child Attachment Trauma Protocol 37
Marilyn Luber

Chapter 2   **Working on Attachment Issues With EMDR Therapy:**
The Attachment Protocol 45
Anna Rita Verardo and Maria Zaccagnino

                Summary Sheet: Working on Attachment Issues With EMDR Therapy:
The Attachment Protocol 83
Marilyn Luber

Posttraumatic Stress Disorder

Chapter 3   **EMDR Therapy for Traumatized Patients With Psychosis** 97
Berber van der Vleugel, David van den Berg, Paul de Bont, Tonnie Staring, and Ad de Jongh

                Summary Sheet: EMDR Therapy for Traumatized Patients With Psychosis 149
Marilyn Luber

Chapter 4   **EMDR Integrative Group Treatment Protocol© Adapted for Adolescents**
(14–17 Years) and Adults Living With Ongoing Traumatic Stress 169
Ignacio Jarero and Lucina Artigas

                Summary Sheet: EMDR Integrative Group Treatment Protocol© Adapted for
Adolescents (14–17 Years) and Adults Living With Ongoing Traumatic Stress 181
Marilyn Luber

Acute Stress Disorder

Chapter 5   Reaching the Unseen First Responder With EMDR Therapy:
Treating 911 Trauma in Emergency Telecommunicators.................... 185
Jim Marshall and Sara G. Gilman

Summary Sheet: Reaching the Unseen First Responder With EMDR Therapy:
Treating 911 Trauma in Emergency Telecommunicators..................... 217
Marilyn Luber

PART II
EMDR Therapy and Grief and Mourning

Grief and Mourning

Chapter 6   EMDR Therapy and Grief and Mourning.................................... 231
Roger M. Solomon and Therese A. Rando

Summary Sheet: EMDR Therapy and Grief and Mourning...................... 253
Marilyn Luber

PART III
Self-Care for Clinicians

Chapter 7   Healer, Heal Thyself: A Commonsense Look at the
Prevention of Compassion Fatigue.. 269
Catherine M. Butler

Summary Sheet: Healer, Heal Thyself: A Commonsense Look
at the Prevention of Compassion Fatigue 285
Marilyn Luber

Appendix A: Worksheets 293

Appendix B: EMDR Therapy Summary Sheet and EMDR Therapy Session Form..... 313

Contributors

Stefanie Armstrong, MS, LIMHP, specializes in treating trauma resolution and attachment problems in children and adolescents. Before she cofounded The Attachment and Trauma Center of Nebraska, she spent 10 years working in the public school system as a school counselor. She is EMDR certified and is an EMDR consultant providing training and consultation as part of The Attachment and Trauma Center Institute consultation team. Ms. Armstrong is part of the team that created the EMDR and Family Therapy Integrative Protocol for the treatment of attachment trauma in children. She is a coauthor of a book on EMDR treatment for attachment trauma in children and a parenting book related to attachment trauma. She has presented her expertise nationally to numerous parent and professional groups. Ms. Armstrong is a trainer for The Attachment and Trauma Center Institute, training clinicians in the Family Therapy and EMDR Integrative Team Treatment and training parents in the Integrative Parenting Approach. Ms. Armstrong has been invited to present at numerous professional conferences and workshops around the country and has also trained public school personnel in the area of trauma and attachment.

Lucina Artigas, MA, MT, who specialized in Humanitarian Programs for early EMDR Therapy intervention with children and adolescents, has provided field services in Latin America, the Caribbean, and Spain to natural or human-provoked disaster victims, family members of those deceased, and first responders. She is an EMDR Institute and EMDR-Iberoamerica Senior Trainer of Trainers for Latin America and the Caribbean and has received the EMDRIA Creative Innovation Award for the Butterfly Hug method for bilateral stimulation and the EMDR-Iberoamerica Francine Shapiro Award. Lucina is a coauthor of *The EMDR Protocol for Recent Critical Incidents (EMDR-PRECI)*, *The EMDR Individual Protocol for Paraprofessionals Use in Acute Trauma Situations (EMDR-PROPARA)*, and *The EMDR Integrative Group Treatment Protocol*, which have been applied worldwide for natural or human-provoked disaster survivors. She has conducted trainings, seminars, and workshops around the world and coauthored articles on topics of EMDR Therapy, trauma, resilience, crisis intervention, and cancer-related posttraumatic stress disorder (PTSD) treated with EMDR Therapy in group format. She is the cofounder of EMDR Mexico; cofounder and executive director of International Center of Psychotraumatology; and cofounder and executive director of the Mexican Association for Mental Health Support in Crisis (AMAMECRISIS, NGO). She has presented workshops in United States, Latin America, and Europe, and has published articles on EMDR, crisis intervention, and compassion fatigue.

Catherine M. Butler, EdD, LMFT, is a clinician in private practice in San Diego, California. Her practice focuses on the impact of PTSD on first responders and veterans. The area of compassion fatigue and burnout has been of interest for several years and she trains extensively in the San Diego area for agencies, volunteer groups, and organizations that face increasing demands for their services and dwindling resources. She is a member of the San Diego EMDR Trauma Recovery Network (TRN) and works to assist the community after critical incidents, as well as supporting the first responder network as they meet emergent needs. Promoting strength, resilience, and compassion within the treatment and first-responder community is the focus of her work and passion.

Paul A. J. M. de Bont, MSc, is a clinical psychologist. He is a member of the Dutch EMDR Association (Vereniging EMDR Nederland) and scientist–practitioner at the Mental Health Organization GGZ Oost Brabant, the Netherlands. He works with severely mentally ill psychiatric patients in an outpatient setting for assertive community services. He is a researcher and PhD student in the RCT Treating Trauma in Psychosis (TTIP). He is author and coauthor on several TTIP-related studies and protocols concerning the application of guidelines of psychological treatment (EMDR and prolonged exposure) for PTSD in patients with psychosis. He received the European EMDR Francine Shapiro Award in 2014.

Ad de Jongh, PhD, is both a clinical psychologist and dentist. He is professor of anxiety and behavior disorders at the Behavioural Science department of the Academic Centre for Dentistry (ACTA) in Amsterdam, the Netherlands, a collaboration of the University of Amsterdam and Vrije University. He is also an honorary professor at the School of Health Sciences of Salford University in Manchester, UK. He is involved in research investigating the efficacy of evidence-based treatments for the consequences of traumatic events in a variety of target populations, including children, people with intellectual disabilities, and people with complex psychiatric conditions, including psychosis and schizophrenia. He (co)authored more than 250 scientific articles–book chapters on anxiety disorders, and their treatment (including five books), and provides lectures and courses in his field of expertise, both in the Netherlands and abroad. He is an EMDR Europe–accredited trainer. In 2011, he received the outstanding EMDR Research Award from the EMDR International Association.

Sara G. Gilman, MS, LMFT, is the founder and president of Coherence Associates, Inc., a professional individual and family counseling corporation. Coherence Associates is dedicated to expanding human potential through the coherence of mind, body, and spirit, and is located in Encinitas, California. Ms. Gilman is a licensed marriage and family therapist, and specializes in the areas of performance enhancement, trauma, and addictions. She graduated in 1983 from California State University, Fullerton, with a masters of science degree in clinical psychology. She is a diplomate in forensic traumatology and holds a fellowship status with the American Academy of Experts in Traumatic Stress. She is certified in NLP, hypnotherapy, and HeartMath; is an EMDR consultant; and is the past president of the EMDR International Association. As a former firefighter/EMT, she has a passion for working with first responders, is CISM certified, and supports agencies with their peer support teams. She has brought EMDR to first responders of all kinds, speaks nationally on this topic, and serves on the 911 Wellness Foundation (911WF) board of directors.

Ignacio Jarero, PhD, EdD, specializes in humanitarian programs for early EMDR Therapy intervention and has provided field services in Latin America, the Caribbean, Spain, and South Asia to natural or human-provoked disasters victims, family members of those deceased, and first responders. Dr. Jarero is an EMDR Institute & EMDR-Iberoamerica Senior Trainer of Trainers for Latin America and the Caribbean and has received the EMDR-Iberoamerica Francine Shapiro Award; the International Critical Incident Stress Foundation International Crisis Response Leadership Award; the EMDR Colombia Jaibaná Award for Humanitarian Work; and the Argentinean Society of Psychotrauma (ISTSS affiliate) Psychotrauma Trajectory Award. He is a coauthor of *The EMDR Protocol for Recent Critical Incidents* (*EMDR-PRECI*), *The EMDR Individual Protocol for Paraprofessionals Use in Acute Trauma Situations* (*EMDR-PROPARA*), and *The EMDR Integrative Group Treatment Protocol*, which have been applied worldwide for natural or human-provoked disaster survivors. He is a mental health adviser for the Mexican Department of Defense and Air Force, Navy, National Human Rights Commission, and World Vision International. He has conducted trainings, seminars, and workshops around the world and authored articles on topics of EMDR Therapy, trauma, resilience, crisis intervention, and cancer-related PTSD treated with EMDR Therapy in a group format. Dr. Jarero is the cofounder of EMDR Mexico; founder and president of Latin American and Caribbean Foundation for Psychological Trauma Research (Francine Shapiro Award Winner); cofounder and president of the International Center of Psychotraumatology; cofounder and editor in chief of *Iberoamerican Journal of*

Psychotraumatology and Dissociation; and cofounder and president of the Mexican Association for Mental Health Support in Crisis (AMAMECRISIS, NGO).

Jim Marshall, MA, is the president of MasterCare Institute and a certified EMDR Therapist, specializing in treatment of traumatic stress and its impact on relationships. The brother of a 911 telecommunicator, he recognized emergency telecommunicators to be an underserved population at high risk of PTSD and became embedded in the 911 community as an emergency mental health educator and policy advocate. As director of the 911 Training Institute, he has created and delivers curricula preparing 911 professionals to prevent stress-related illnesses and boost peak performance through personal resilience and mastery of emergency calls involving mental illness and suicidality. He is a regular contributor to 911 industry journals and conferences and is founding chief executive officer (CEO) and chair of the 911WF, a nonprofit organization devoted to fostering optimal health and performance of public safety telecommunicators through research, education, policy, and intervention. He served as a cochair of the National Emergency Number Association Working Group and coauthored the industry's first *Standard on 911 Acute, Traumatic, and Chronic Stress Management*. With past EMDRIA president Sara Gilman, he is developing the National Registry of EMDR Therapists for 911, assuring access to this evidence-based treatment for all emergency telecommunicators.

Therese A. Rando, PhD, BCETS, BCBT, is a clinical psychologist in Warwick, Rhode Island, USA. She founded The Institute for the Study and Treatment of Loss, which provides mental health services through psychotherapy, training, supervision, and consultation, and specializes in loss and grief; traumatic stress; and the psychosocial care of persons impacted by chronic, life-threatening, or terminal illness. A recipient of numerous awards for her accomplishments in thanatology, she has consulted; conducted research; provided therapy; written; provided expert witness legal testimony; and lectured internationally in areas related to loss, grief, illness, dying, and trauma. Current professional foci include treatment of complicated mourning, loss of a child, the interface between posttraumatic stress and grief, anticipatory mourning, and specialized intervention techniques for traumatic bereavement. Dr. Rando has written more than 80 works pertaining to the clinical aspects of thanatology and is a national media resource expert in dying, death, loss, and trauma for the American Psychological Association.

Cathy Schweitzer, MS, LMHP, specializes in treating trauma resolution and attachment problems in children and adolescents. She is a cofounder of the Attachment and Trauma Center of Nebraska in Omaha, Nebraska. She is part of the treatment team that created the EMDR and Family Integrative Protocol for the treatment of attachment trauma in children and the coauthor of a book on EMDR treatment for attachment trauma and children and a parenting book related to trauma-informed parenting. Ms. Schweitzer is also the cofounder of the Attachment and Trauma Training Center Institute, an organization dedicated to training clinicians in the EMDR and Family Therapy Integrative Team Treatment, as well as training parents in the Integrative Parenting Approach. She is a certified EMDR Therapist and consultant and provides consultation to professionals across the country. Ms. Schweitzer has also been invited to present at numerous professional conferences and workshops around the country and has participated in training public school personnel in the area of trauma and attachment. Ms. Schweitzer spent 15 years in both private and public school settings as a school counselor.

Roger M. Solomon, PhD, is a psychologist and psychotherapist specializing in the areas of trauma and grief. He is on the senior faculty of the EMDR (Eye Movement Desensitization and Reprocessing) Institute and provides basic and advanced EMDR training internationally. He also provides advanced specialty trainings in the areas of grief, emergency psychology, and complex trauma. He currently consults with the U.S. Senate, the National Aeronautics and Space Administration (NASA), and several law enforcement agencies. As a police psychologist with the South Carolina Department of Public Safety, he is the clinical director of the Post Critical Incident Seminar (PCIS), a 3-day posttrauma program that draws on psychological first aid, peer support, and EMDR Therapy. Working with the South Carolina Army National Guard, he is the clinical director of the Post Deployment Seminar, a 3-day program for war veterans. He has provided clinical services and training to the FBI; Secret Service; U.S. State Department, Diplomatic Security; Bureau of Alcohol, Tobacco, and Firearms; U.S. Department of Justice (U.S. attorneys); and numerous state and local law enforcement organizations. Internationally, he consults with the Polizia di Stato in Italy and also provides a posttrauma program for the police in Finland. Dr. Solomon has planned critical incident programs, provided training for peer support teams, and has provided direct services following tragedies, such as Hurricane Katrina, the September 11 terrorist attacks, the loss of the space shuttle *Columbia*, and the Oklahoma City bombing. He has authored or coauthored 34 articles and book chapters pertaining to EMDR, trauma, grief, and law enforcement stress.

Tonnie Staring, PhD, is a clinical psychologist, psychotherapist, CBT supervisor, and EMDR Therapist. He works at Altrecht Psychiatric Institute for young people with psychosis, and the Early Detection and Intervention (EDI) team. He got his PhD at the Erasmus Medical Center in the area of psychological interventions for psychosis. He worked as a guest teacher and supervisor for various Dutch institutes, and occasionally for the WHO and the NIMH. He is a board member of the psychosis section of the Dutch Association for Behavioural and Cognitive Therapy, as well as the Cognition and Psychosis Foundation. He participates in various research projects in the treatment of psychosis and anxiety. He has published various books, and more than 40 national and international articles and chapters.

David van den Berg, MSc, is a clinical psychologist at Parnassia Psychiatric Institute, the Hague, the Netherlands. He has specialized in CBT for psychosis, PTSD, and ultra-high risk for psychosis patients and has coauthored treatment protocols, books, and scientific articles on these topics. He is conducting a PhD study into the feasibility and safety of EMDR and prolonged exposure on patients with psychotic disorders and chronic PTSD (www.ttip.nl). He is a member of the Dutch Association for Behavioural and Cognitive Therapy and the Dutch Association for EMDR. David leads several innovative projects, in which he collaborates with industrial design engineers and service users. In 2013, he received the outstanding EMDR Research award from the EMDR International Association and, in 2014, he won the Rotterdam Designers Award for an app for people who hear voices.

Berber van der Vleugel, MSc, is employed at the Community Mental Health Service GGZ Noord-Holland Noord in the Netherlands. She works as a therapist in a Flexible Assertive Community Treatment (FACT) team, offering treatment to patients with severe mental illnesses, and is the coordinator of scientific research in this population. She is a PhD candidate on agents of change in the Dutch multisite randomized clinical trial TTIP. She is a member of the board of the Psychosis Section and trainer and supervisor of the Dutch Association for Behavioural and Cognitive Therapy. She is a registered member of the Dutch Association for EMDR and, in 2013, she received the first Research Award that was given out by the VEN. She has coauthored several articles and book chapters on treatment for psychosis and assertive outreach.

Anna Rita Verardo, PsyD, is a psychologist and psychotherapist and an EMDR Europe–approved trainer and supervisor. She is a member of the Italian EMDR Association board and coordinator of the EMDR Child and Adolescents Committee. She is also a member of the European EMDR Child Board. Her main area of intervention is childhood and adolescence, and she has conducted numerous workshops on the use of EMDR in children, in particular regarding loss and mourning and adopted children. She has published a number of articles and books on EMDR and she coordinates research, in collaboration with CNR and Tor Vergata University, in Italy. Since 2001, she has been involved in humanitarian projects in Italy.

Debra Wesselmann, MS, LIMHP, has specialized in treating trauma resolution and attachment problems in adults, children, and families for the past 25 years. She is cofounder and member of the treatment team at The Attachment and Trauma Center of Nebraska in Omaha, Nebraska. She is part of the team that developed the EMDR and Family Therapy Integrative Protocol for the treatment of attachment trauma in children and the Integrative Parenting method for raising traumatized children. She is a co-trainer for professionals and parents associated with The Attachment and Trauma Center Institute. Ms. Wesselmann has been on the faculty at the University of Nebraska at Omaha and collaborates with faculty at the University of Nebraska at Lincoln for research and development of effective trauma treatment methods. She is an EMDR consultant and has been on the faculty of the EMDR Institute since 1998. She is a coauthor of a book on EMDR treatment for attachment trauma in children, two books related to parenting, and a number of chapters and articles related to trauma and attachment. Ms. Wesselmann has been invited to present or deliver keynote addresses for numerous professional conferences and workshops nationally and internationally, including invited presentations at the Menninger Clinic, EMDRIA, and conferences in Rome, Amsterdam, Hamburg, Cologne, Madrid, the Netherlands, Hong Kong, and Costa Rica.

Maria Zaccagnino, PhD, is a clinical psychologist and psychotherapist with a cognitive evolutionary approach. She is an EMDR Europe–approved supervisor and she works in particular in the field of attachment theory and eating disorders, where she has achieved remarkable results in both clinical and research contexts. She coordinates several studies concerning these areas of EMDR application for the Italian EMDR association and she has also presented workshops. She has published articles regarding the application of EMDR treatment in the context of parenting problems.

treatment for the veterans when compared to exposure therapy. Other controlled studies in that era had a variety of methodological problems, such as treatment integrity issues (Jensen, 1994; Pitman et al., 1993; Sanderson & Carpenter, 1992); limited or unusual populations (Boudewyns et al., 1993; Jensen, 1994; Pitman et al., 1993; Sanderson & Carpenter, 1992); or small sample sizes (Boudewyns et al., 1993; Jensen, 1994; Pitman et al., 1993). Although the progress of EMDR Therapy research has been slow and hampered by many difficulties, over the years, the studies are increasing. See the EMDR Institute's website (www.emdr.com) or EMDR International Association's (EMDRIA) website (www.emdria.org) for the current status of randomized controlled trials.

The work with EMDR and clinical applications, as seen in the chapters in this text, is based on the adaptive information-processing model (AIP) as explained by Dr. Shapiro (2001, 2002, 2006, 2007). This model is used to guide our clinical practice and show EMDR Therapy's clinical effects. The idea is that the direct reprocessing of the stored memories of the first and other events connected with the problem—as well as any other experiential contributors—has a positive effect on clients' presenting problems. The results of case studies and open trials with various diagnostic categories give support to this prediction. In fact, many experts have taken the basic standard EMDR protocols reported by Shapiro in *Eye Movement Desensitization and Reprocessing (EMDR): Basic Principles, Protocols and Procedures* (1995, 2001) and adapted them to meet the particular needs of their clients while maintaining the integrity of EMDR Therapy.

Furthermore, the AIP model is in keeping with the important findings of Vincent J. Felitti and Robert F. Anda in the Adverse Childhood Experiences (ACE) Study. The ACE study was conducted with more than 17,000 Kaiser Permanente members, who voluntarily participated in a study with the purpose of finding out the effects of stressful and traumatic experiences during childhood on adult health (acestudy.org website, 2015). They learned that 63% of the participants in the study had at least one childhood trauma, while 20% experienced at least three or more categories of trauma, which were labeled adverse childhood experiences, such as emotional abuse (11%), physical abuse (28%), sexual abuse (21%), emotional neglect (15%), physical neglect (10%), witnessing their mothers treated violently (13%), growing up with someone in the household using alcohol and/or drugs (27%), growing up with a mentally ill person in the household (19%), losing a parent due to separation or divorce (23%), and/or growing up with a household member in jail or prison (5%). They found that the more categories of trauma a person experienced in childhood, the greater the likelihood of experiencing the following: alcoholism and alcohol abuse, chronic obstructive pulmonary disease (COPD), depression, fetal death, hallucinations, illicit drug use, ischemic heart disease (IHD), liver disease, risk of intimate partner violence, multiple sexual partners, obesity, poor health-related quality of life, PTSD, sexually transmitted diseases (STDs), smoking, suicide attempts, and/or unintended pregnancies. These are important findings that inform our work as EMDR practitioners.

Felitti and Anda (2009, pp. 77–87) in their chapter, "The Relationship of Adverse Childhood Experiences to Adult Medical Disease, Psychiatric Disorders, and Sexual Behavior: Implications for Healthcare," concluded the following concerning adverse childhood experiences:

> The influence of childhood experience, including often-unrecognized traumatic events, is as powerful as Freud and his colleagues originally described it to be. These influences are long lasting, and neuroscientists are now describing the intermediary mechanisms that develop as a result of these stressors. Unfortunately, and in spite of these findings, the biopsychosocial model and the bio-medical model of psychiatry remain at odds rather than taking advantage of the new discoveries to reinforce each other.
>
> Many of our most intractable public health problems are the result of compensatory behaviors like smoking, overeating, and alcohol and drug use which provide immediate partial relief from the emotional problems caused by traumatic childhood experiences. The chronic life stress of these developmental experiences is generally unrecognized and hence unappreciated as a second etiologic mechanism. These experiences are lost in time and concealed by shame, secrecy, and social taboo against the exploration of certain topics of human experience.

The findings of the Adverse Childhood Experiences (ACE) Study provide a credible basis for a new paradigm of medical, public health, and social service practice that would start with comprehensive biopsychosocial evaluation of all patients at the outset of ongoing medical care.

A number of EMDR clinical applications are mainly case studies or open trials that show promise; however, they are in need of further investigation. To see examples of EMDR clinical applications, go to the EMDR International Association website: www.emdria.org, or the EMDR Institute website: www.emdr.com.

As a result of the growing research, many organizations have recognized the efficacy of EMDR Therapy as a treatment for PTSD by including it in their treatment guidelines beginning with the Clinical Division of the American Psychological Association (Chambless et al., 1998) and most recently the WHO Guidelines for the management of conditions specifically related to stress (WHO, 2013). For the complete list, check the EMDR Institute website (www.emdr.com).

With the understanding of the importance of randomized controlled studies, several groups have made it their mission to support EMDR research. Since 2011, the EMDR Research Committee of the EMDR Europe Association has been granting monetary rewards for research to further the understanding of the mechanisms involved during the various steps of EMDR Therapy, the application to many psychological disorders related to stress and anxiety, and the efficacy of the standard protocol as well as adapted protocols. Our European colleagues have truly set a high bar for the work that they are doing through their encouragement of the gold standard in research. For further information, see EMDR Europe's website: www.emdr-europe.org.

From the United States, a group of concerned EMDR practitioners (Wendy Freitag, Jim Gach, and Rosalie Thomas) founded the EMDR Research Foundation (ERF; www.emdrresearchfoundation.org) in 2006 as a 501(c)(3) nonprofit organization dedicated to the promotion of quality, unbiased research in EMDR Therapy, and the only funding agency dedicated solely to support EMDR Therapy research worldwide. Its mission is to "promote health and growth of human beings through the support of quality research, evidence-based practice and compassionate, well-informed clinicians." Since 2010, ERF has offered research grants, dissertation grants, consultation awards, and research dissemination travel awards. ERF also offers nonfinancial support to both researchers and clinicians via the two monthly clinical newsletters, the "Translating Research Into Practice" article published in the *Journal of EMDR Research and Practice*, and the *Researcher's Resource Directory*. Currently, it is possible to sign up for the *EMDR Early Intervention Researcher's Toolkit* on their website.

This is the fifth in a series of texts dedicated to the better understanding of EMDR Therapy and how the Standard EMDR principles, protocols, and procedures form the basis for the work that we do as EMDR Therapy clinicians. To understand any subject matter deeply, the rule of thumb is to know the basics, so that if a departure from the structure is needed, it is done in an informed manner. The purpose of *Eye Movement Desensitization and Reprocessing (EMDR) Scripted Protocols: Basics and Special Situations* (Luber, 2009a) was to support the structure in Dr. Shapiro's (1995, 2001) earlier texts by showing each step in detail. *Eye Movement Desensitization and Reprocessing (EMDR) Scripted Protocols: Special Populations* (Luber, 2009b) was built on that structure and showcased how many experts use the EMDR principles, protocols, and procedures to adapt to their specific populations, such as children; couples; and patients with dissociative disorders, complex PTSD, addictive behaviors, pain, and specific fears. The next book would have been: *Eye Movement Desensitization and Reprocessing (EMDR) Scripted Protocols and Summary Sheets: Anxiety, Depression and Medical-Related Issues* to continue to show how expert clinicians are working with EMDR Therapy clients with anxiety disorders, depression, and medical-related issues. However, in 2011, man-made and natural disasters were impacting our colleagues experiencing the Tōhoku earthquake and tsunami in Japan; floods in China, the Philippines, Thailand, Pakistan, Cambodia, India, and Brazil; earthquakes in Turkey and New Zealand; droughts and consecutive famines affecting Ethiopia, Kenya, and Somalia; storms in the United States; and so on. In consultation with Springer and EMDR colleagues in the EMDR Humanitarian Assistance Programs worldwide, the decision was made to move up the publication of

Implementing EMDR Early Mental Health Interventions for Man-Made and Natural Disasters, in book, CD, and e-book formats. It was published in 2014 as an up-to-date collection of the current EMDR Therapy–related responses and protocols for recent trauma events.

In 2012, *Eye Movement Desensitization and Reprocessing (EMDR) Scripted Protocols and Summary Sheets: Anxiety, Depression and Medical-Related Issues* was slated to appear and was originally conceptualized with the *Diagnostic and Statistical Manual of Mental Disorders, 4th Edition, Text Revision* (*DSM-4-TR*; American Psychiatric Association, 2000) in mind; however, as the publication time approached, *DSM-5* had become the standard. This entailed some reorganization, resulting in *Eye Movement Desensitization and Reprocessing (EMDR) Therapy Scripted Protocols and Summary Sheets: Treating Trauma, Anxiety and Mood-Related Conditions*. However, there was so much material involved that it was decided to create three books instead of one. This is the second of this trio—*Eye Movement Desensitization and Reprocessing (EMDR) Therapy Scripted Protocols and Summary Sheets: Treating Trauma- and Stressor-Related Conditions*—with the choice of book, CD, and/or e-book formats. Anxiety-, obsessive–compulsive-, and mood-related issues were separated from this current text and will appear as *Eye Movement Desensitization and Reprocessing (EMDR) Therapy Scripted Protocols and Summary Sheets: Treating Anxiety, Obsessive–Compulsive, and Mood-Related Conditions* (Luber, in press [b]) in 2016. Medical-related issues, as well, were separated from this current text and will appear as *Eye Movement Desensitization and Reprocessing (EMDR) Therapy Scripted Protocols and Summary Sheets: Treating Medical-Related Conditions* (Luber, in press [a]) in 2016.

The following description from *Eye Movement Desensitization and Reprocessing (EMDR) Scripted Protocols: Basics and Special Situations* gives a clear understanding of the evolution and importance of this format:

Eye Movement Desensitization and Reprocessing (EMDR) Scripted Protocols: Basics and Special Situations grew out of a perceived need that trained mental health practitioners could be served by a place to access both traditional and newly developed protocols in a way that adheres to best clinical practices incorporating the Standard EMDR Protocol that includes working on the past, present, and future issues (the 3-Pronged Protocol) related to the problem and the 11-Step Standard Procedure that includes attention to the following steps: image, negative cognition (NC), positive cognition (PC), validity of cognition (VoC), emotion, subjective units of disturbance (SUD), and location of body sensation, desensitization, installation, body scan, and closure. Often, EMDR texts embed the protocols in a great deal of explanatory material that is essential in the process of learning EMDR. However, sometimes, as a result, practitioners move away from the basic importance of maintaining the integrity of the Standard EMDR Protocol and keeping adaptive information processing in mind when conceptualizing the course of treatment for a patient. It is in this way that the efficacy of this powerful methodology is lost.

"Scripting" becomes a way not only to inform and remind the EMDR practitioner of the component parts, sequence, and language used to create an effective outcome, but it also creates a template for practitioners and researchers to use for reliability and/or a common denominator so that the form of working with EMDR is consistent. The concept that has motivated this work was conceived within the context of assisting EMDR clinicians in accessing the scripts of the full protocols in one place and to profit from the creativity of other EMDR clinicians who have kept the spirit of EMDR but have also taken into consideration the needs of the population with whom they work or the situations that they encounter. *Reading a script is by no means a substitute for adequate training, competence, clinical acumen, and integrity; if you are not a trained EMDR therapist and/or you are not knowledgeable in the field for which you wish to use the script, these scripts are not for you.*

As EMDR is a fairly complicated process, and indeed, has intimidated some from integrating it into their daily approach to therapy, this book provides step-by-step scripts that will enable beginning practitioners to enhance their expertise more quickly. It will also appeal to seasoned EMDR clinicians, trainers and consultants because it brings together the many facets of the eight phases of EMDR and how clinicians are using this framework to work with a variety of therapeutic difficulties and modalities, while maintaining the integrity of the AIP model. Although there are a large number of resources, procedures and protocols in this book, they do not constitute the universe of protocols that are potentially useful and worthy of further study and use.

These scripted protocols are intended for clinicians who have read Shapiro's text (2001) and received EMDR training from an EMDR-accredited trainer. An EMDR trainer is a licensed mental health practitioner who has been approved by the association active in the clinician's country of practice. (Luber, 2009a, p. xxi)

In 2012, the CD-ROM versions of the original 2009 books were published in a different format. Included in the CD-ROM were just the protocols and summary sheets (the notes were not included and are available in the 2009 texts in book form). As explained in the preface of *Eye Movement Desensitization and Reprocessing (EMDR) Scripted Protocols With Summary Sheets (CD-ROM Version): Basics and Special Situations* (Luber, 2012a):

> The idea for *Eye Movement Desensitization and Reprocessing (EMDR) Scripted Protocols: Summary Sheets for Basics and Special Situations* grew out of the day-to-day work with the protocols that allowed for a deeper understanding of case conceptualization from an EMDR perspective. While using the scripted protocols and acquiring a greater familiarity with the use of the content, the idea of placing the information in a summarized format grew. This book of scripted protocols and summary sheets was undertaken so that clinicians could easily use the material in *Eye Movement Desensitization and Reprocessing (EMDR) Scripted Protocols: Basics and Special Situations*. While working on the summary sheets, the interest in brevity collided with the thought that clinicians could also use these summary sheets to remind themselves of the steps in the process clarified in the scripted protocols. The original goal to be a summary of the necessary data gathered from the protocol was transformed into this new creation of data summary and memory tickler for the protocol itself! Alas, the summary sheets have become a bit longer than originally anticipated. Nonetheless, they are shorter—for the most part—than the protocols themselves and do summarize the data in an easily readable format...
>
> The format for this book is also innovative. The scripts and summary sheets are available in an expandable, downloadable format for easy digital access. Because EMDR is a fairly complicated process, and often intimidating, these scripted protocols with their accompanying summary sheets can be helpful in a number of ways. To begin with, by facilitating the gathering of important data from the protocol about the client, the scripted protocol and/or summary sheet then can be inserted into the client's chart as documentation. The summary sheet can assist the clinician in formulating a concise and clear treatment plan with clients and can be used to support quick retrieval of the essential issues and experiences during the course of treatment. Practitioners can enhance their expertise more quickly by having a place that instructs and reminds them of the essential parts of EMDR practice. By having these fill-in PDF forms, clinicians can easily tailor the scripted protocols and summary sheets to the needs of their clients, their consultees/supervisees and themselves by editing and saving the protocol scripts and summary sheets. The script and summary sheet forms are available as a digital download or on a CD-ROM, and will work with any computer or device that supports a PDF format.
>
> Consultants/supervisors will find these scripted protocols and summary sheets useful while working with consultees/supervisees in their consultation/supervision groups. These works bring together many ways of handling current, important issues in psychotherapy and EMDR treatment. They also include a helpful way to organize the data collected that is key to case consultation and the incorporation of EMDR into newly-trained practitioners' practices. (Luber, 2012a, p. iv)

This book is divided into three parts with seven chapters that comprise *Trauma- and Stressor-Related Conditions*, including Reactive Attachment Disorders, Posttraumatic Stress Disorder, and Acute Stress Disorder; *Grief and Mourning*; and *Self-Care for Clinicians*. To address the specific needs of their populations or issues, authors were asked to include the types of questions relevant for history taking, helpful resources and explanations needed in the preparation phase, particular negative and positive cognitions that were frequent in the assessment phase and for cognitive interweaves, other concerns during phases 4 (desensitization) through 8 (reevaluation), a section on case conceptualization and treatment planning, and any pertinent research on their work.

Part I is devoted to "Trauma- and Stressor-Related Disorders," with chapters on how EMDR Therapy is used for a range of these disorders. In the area of "Reactive Attachment Disorders," Debra Wesselman, Cathy Schweitzer, and Stefanie Armstrong present some of their innovative work at The Attachment and Trauma Center of Nebraska in their "Child Attachment Trauma Protocol." Anna Rita Verardo and Maria Zaccagnino's (from Italy) "Working on Attachment Issues With EMDR Therapy: The Attachment Protocol," uses their wide range of knowledge concerning children, adolescents, parenting, and attachment theory to craft their own way to address attachment trauma for adults. Both chapters have research showing that the processing of attachment-related memories with EMDR Therapy results in a positive effect on participants' attachment status. The groundbreaking work on "EMDR for Traumatized Patients With Psychosis" by the Dutch team of Berber van der Vleugel, David van den Berg, Paul de Bont, Tonnie Staring, and Ad de Jongh, is one of a series of articles and chapters this team has brought to our community to address this population's many traumas. Ignacio Jarero and Lucina Artigas extend their idea of working in a group with the Integrative Group Treatment Protocol to its use with ongoing traumatic stress, in the chapter, "EMDR Integrative Group Treatment Protocol Adapted for Adolescents (14–17 Years) and Adults Living With Ongoing Traumatic Stress." In the section on "Acute Stress Disorder," Jim Marshall's knowledge of 911 telecommunicators intrigued Sara Gilman with her expertise in working with other groups of first responders and EMDR, and, together, they crafted "Reaching the Unseen First Responder With EMDR: Treating 911 Trauma in Emergency Telecommunicators," "a true gift to our community and the underserved 911 Telecommunicators."

In the section on Grief and Mourning, Therese Rando paired her extensive knowledge about complicated mourning with Roger Solomon's EMDR expertise and working in the field with grief-related issues to put together an excellent approach to this subject, "EMDR Therapy and Grief and Mourning."

The idea of "Self-Care for Clinicians" has been underlined in all of the *Eye Movement Desensitization and Reprocessing (EMDR) Scripted Protocol* books (Luber, 2009a, 2009b, 2012, 2014) and should be at the core of all of our work. Too often we focus on our clients at the expense of ourselves. Catherine Butler's chapter, "Healer, Heal Thyself: A Commonsense Look at the Prevention of Compassion Fatigue," is an important reminder about how essential it is for us to practice the self-modulating techniques that we teach to our clients and look out for the signs and signals that let us know we are in need of help ourselves.

Appendix A includes the scripts for the 3-Pronged Protocol that includes past memories, present triggers, and future templates. This section helps clinicians remember the important components of the Standard EMDR Protocol to ensure fidelity to the model. Furthermore, it allows practitioners to copy the protocols and put personalized copies in clients' charts. Appendix B contains an updated version of this author's "EMDR Summary Sheet" (Luber, 2009a) and the "EMDR Session Form" to assist in easy retrieval of important client information and the important components of EMDR sessions. A summary sheet for each of these chapters serves as a checklist showing the important steps needed in these protocols, with a CD-version format also available to provide mobile access.

Eye Movement Desensitization and Reprocessing (EMDR) Therapy Scripted Protocols and Summary Sheets: Treating Trauma- and Stressor-Related Conditions, with the choice of book, CD, and/or e-book formats, in the manner of its predecessors, offers EMDR practitioners and researchers a window into the treatment rooms of experts in the fields of trauma- and stress-related conditions. This book is in no way a compendium of all that is being done with EMDR in this field, but points us to the possibilities of EMDR Therapy. It is designed to apply what we are learning through research and to support the increasing knowledge and capabilities of clinicians in the method of EMDR Therapy.

References

Acestudy.org website, 2015.

American Psychiatric Association. (2000). *Diagnostic and statistical manual of mental disorders* (4th ed., text rev.). Washington, DC: Author.

American Psychiatric Association. (2013). *Diagnostic and statistical manual of mental disorders* (5th ed.). Arlington, VA: American Psychiatric Publishing.

Boudewyns, P. A., & Hyer, L. A. (1996). Eye movement desensitization and reprocessing (EMDR) as treatment for post-traumatic stress disorder (PTSD). *Clinical Psychology and Psychotherapy, 3*, 185–195.

Boudewyns, P. A., Stwertka, S. A., Hyer, L. A., Albrecht, J. W., & Sperr, E. V. (1993). Eye movement desensitization and reprocessing (EMDR): A pilot study. *Behavior Study, 16,* 30–33.

Chambless, D. L., Baker, M. J., Baucom, D. H., Beutler, L. E., Calhoun, K. S., Cris-Christoph, P.,...Woody, S. R. (1998). Update on empirically validated therapies, II. *The Clinical Psychologist, 51,* 3–16.

EMDR Europe's website: www.emdr-europe.org

EMDR Institute website, www.emdr.com

EMDR International Association website, www.emdria.org

EMDR Research Foundation website, www.emdrresearchfoundation.org

Felitti, V. J., & Anda, R. F. (2009). The relationship of adverse childhood experiences to adult medical disease and psychiatric disorders, and sexual behavior: Implications for healthcare. In R. Lanius, E. Vermetten, & C. Pain (Eds.), *The hidden epidemic: The impact of early life trauma on health and disease* (pp. 77–87). Cambridge, England: Cambridge University Press.

Jensen, J. A. (1994). An investigation of eye movement desensitization and reprocessing (EMD/R) as a treatment for posttraumatic stress disorder (PTSD) symptoms of Vietnam combat veterans. *Behavior Therapy, 25,* 311–325.

Lang, P. J. (1977). Imagery in therapy: An information processing analysis of fear. *Behavior Therapist, 10,* 224, 242.

Lang, P. J. (1979). A bioinformational theory of emotional imagery. *Psychophysiology, 16,* 495–512.

Luber, M. (Ed.). (2009a). *Eye movement desensitization and reprocessing (EMDR) therapy scripted protocols: Basics and special situations.* New York, NY: Springer.

Luber, M. (Ed.). (2009b). *Eye movement desensitization and reprocessing (EMDR) therapy scripted protocols: Special populations.* New York, NY: Springer.

Luber, M. (Ed.). (2012a). *Eye movement desensitization and reprocessing (EMDR) therapy scripted protocols with summary sheets (CD ROM version): Basics and special situations.* New York, NY: Springer.

Luber, M. (Ed.). (2012b). *Eye movement desensitization and reprocessing (EMDR) therapy scripted protocols with summary sheets (CD ROM version): Special populations.* New York, NY: Springer.

Luber, M. (Ed.). (2014). *Implementing EMDR early mental health interventions for man-made and natural disasters: Models, scripted protocols and summary sheets.* New York, NY: Springer.

Luber, M. (Ed.). (In press [a]). *Eye movement desensitization and reprocessing (EMDR) therapy scripted protocols and summary sheets: Treating medical-related conditions.* New York, NY: Springer.

Luber, M. (Ed.). (In press [b]). *Eye movement desensitization and reprocessing (EMDR) therapy scripted protocols and summary sheets: Treating anxiety, obsessive-compulsive, and mood-related conditions.* New York, NY: Springer.

Luber, M., & Shapiro, F. (2009). Interview with Francine Shapiro: Historical overview, present issues, and future directions of EMDR. *Journal of EMDR Practice and Research, 3*(4), 217–231.

Pavlov, I. P. (1927). *Conditioned reflexes.* New York, NY: Liveright.

Pitman, R. K., Orr, S. P., Altman, B., Longpre, R. E., Poire, R. E., & Lasko, N. B. (1993, May). *A controlled study of EMDR treatment for post-traumatic stress disorder.* Paper presented at the 146th annual meeting of the American Psychiatric Association, Washington, DC.

Sanderson, A., & Carpenter, R. (1992). Eye movement desensitization versus image confrontation: A single session crossover study of 58 phobic subjects. *Journal of Behavior Therapy and Experimental Psychiatry, 23,* 269–275.

Shapiro, F. (1989a). Efficacy of the eye movement desensitization procedure in the treatment of traumatic memories. *Journal of Traumatic Stress, 2,* 199–223.

Shapiro, F. (1989b). Eye movement desensitization: A new treatment for post-traumatic stress disorder. *Journal of Behavior Therapy and Experimental Psychiatry, 20,* 211–217.

Shapiro, F. (1995). *Eye movement desensitization and reprocessing: Basic principles, protocols and procedures.* New York, NY: Guilford Press.

Shapiro, F. (2001). *Eye movement desensitization and reprocessing: Basic principles, protocols and procedures* (2nd ed.). New York, NY: Guilford Press.

Shapiro, F. (2002). *EMDR as an integrative psychotherapy approach: Experts of diverse orientations explore the paradigm prism.* Washington, DC: American Psychological Association Press.

Shapiro, F. (2006). *EMDR: New notes on adaptive information processing with case formulation principles, forms, scripts and worksheets.* Watsonville, CA: EMDR Institute.

Shapiro, F. (2007). *EMDR: Part 1 training manual.* Watsonville, CA: EMDR Institute, Inc.

World Health Organization. (2013). *World Health Organization's guidelines for the management of conditions specifically related to stress.* Geneva, Switzerland: Author.

EMDR Therapy and Trauma- and Stressor-Related Conditions

I

When Dr. Shapiro was looking for a population to work with Eye Movement Desensitization (EMD) for her dissertation research in 1987, she recognized that the people most troubled by old memories were trauma victims, rape victims, and so on. At the time, she did not know if EMD would work with a diagnosed population and so she contacted a veterans' outreach. She was allowed to demonstrate EMD with a counselor who was also a Vietnam vet with a troubling memory from the war that still bothered him. After several moments of EMD, the memory changed, faded, and was resolved. EMD worked and Dr. Shapiro did the first controlled study with a group mainly consisting of sexual assault victims and veterans still troubled by old memories; it was published in the *Journal of Traumatic Stress* (*JTS*; 1989).

In 1980, the diagnosis of posttraumatic stress disorder (PTSD) was accepted into the *Diagnostic and Statistical Manual of Mental Disorders* (Third Edition [DSM-III], American Psychiatric Association, 1980); however, there were no validated treatments for trauma then. Peniston (1986) was the first to publish a randomized study ($N = 8$) with combat veterans evaluating biofeedback-assisted desensitization. By the year 1989, when Dr. Shapiro's study appeared in *JTS*, several other studies have been published and probably began the field of trauma treatment. According to Dr. Shapiro (Luber & Shapiro, 2009), there were very few treatment outcome studies then (Brom, Kleber, & Defares, 1989; Keane et al., 1989; Kinzie, 1989; Lindy, 1989). One of the 1989 studies used exposure therapy with in-patient combat veterans. Even though there was only a 30% success rate and a 30% dropout rate, clinicians appreciated anything that could help with this difficult-to-treat population. In spring 1990, the *PTSD Research Quarterly* was published by the National Center for Post-Traumatic Stress Disorder. Matthew J. Friedman's article "1989: The Year's Work in PTSD" appeared in it, and he gave an overview of 18 papers demonstrating the breadth and diversity of the PTSD publications (e.g., articles on assessment and diagnosis of PTSD; biological research and treatment; the importance of trauma itself versus pretraumatic factors for predicting subsequent psychiatric symptoms in military cohorts; risk factors for developing posttraumatic symptomatology following disasters; treatment of PTSD; an article on "Janet" that offered the first systematic understanding of how the mind can dissociate in the face of overwhelming threat); and an additional 27 citations in an annotated bibliography. The diagnosis of PTSD and the need for treatment were becoming more familiar.

By 1998, the APA Division 12 Task Force (Chambless et al.) looked at the field in order to figure out what treatments had been validated for different disorders. They gave two distinctions: "fully validated" and "probably efficacious." A treatment was fully validated when it had two comparative studies from different research teams. Although there were hundreds of treatments for the various disorders, they identified only 12 treatments that were on the empirically validated list, such as exposure therapy for specific phobias and another for headaches. For the treatment of PTSD, eye movement desensitization and reprocessing (EMDR) and exposure therapy appeared on the list of "probably efficacious." At this time, the field was not working with validated procedures and there was little funding for treatment outcome studies, mainly because these studies were hard to conduct. In the same year, Carlson et al. did a randomized study investigating the effectiveness of two psychotherapeutic interventions for PTSD that were compared in a randomized controlled outcome group design. Treatment comprised 12 sessions of biofeedback-assisted relaxation, 12 sessions of EMDR or routine clinical care as a control with a combat veteran population; on completion, EMDR showed significant treatment effects when posttreatment results on measures were compared. In contrast to the other treatment group, effects were generally maintained at a 3-month follow-up.

Since then, meta-analyses comparing EMDR Therapy to numerous exposure therapies with and without cognitive therapy techniques have found that both methods are equally efficacious (Bisson, Roberts, Andrew, Cooper, & Lewis, 2013; Bradley, Greene, Russ, Dutra, & Westen, 2005; Davidson & Parker, 2001; Lee & Cuijpers, 2013; Maxfield & Hyer, 2002; Rodenburg, Benjamin, de Roos, Meijer, & Stams, 2009; Seidler & Wagner, 2006). It is important to note that in EMDR's favor, exposure therapy uses 1 to 2 hours of daily homework and EMDR uses none (retrieved from the EMDR Institute website: www.emdr.com, 2015).

After Dr. Shapiro's pivotal study in 1989, randomized clinical trials have been slowly appearing in the literature: *1994* (Vaughan et al.); *1995* (Wilson, Becker, & Tinker); *1997* (Marcus, Marquis, & Sakai; Rothbaum; Wilson, Becker, & Tinker); *1998* (Carlson, Chemtob, Rusnak, Hedlund, & Muraoka; Scheck, Schaeffer, & Gillette); *1999* (Edmond, Rubin, & Wambach); *2002* (Chemtob, Nakashima, Hamada, & Carlson; Ironson, Freund, Strauss, & Williams; Lee, Gavriel, Drummond, Richards, & Greenwald; Power et al.); *2003* (Taylor et al.); *2004* Jaberghaderi, Greenwald, Rubin, Dolatabadim, & Zand; Marcus, Marquis, & Sakai); *2007* (Abbasnejad, Mahani, & Zamyad; Ahmad, Larsson, & Sundelin-Wahlsten; Högberg et al.; van der Kolk et al.); *2008* (Cvetek; Högberg et al.; Wanders, Serra, & de Jongh); *2010* (Kemp, Drummond, & McDermott); *2011* (Arabia, Manca, & Solomon; de Roos; Jarero, Artigas, & Luber; Ter Heide et al.); *2012* (Nijdam, Gersons, Reitsma, de Jongh, & Olff); *2013* (Capezzani et al.; Doering, Ohlmeier, de Jongh, Hofmann, & Bisping); *2014* (Diehle, Opmeer, Boer, Mannarino, & Lindauer) and *2015* (van den Berg et al.). However, more research is needed to guarantee acceptance of EMDR Therapy throughout the world.

Since the 1998 APA Division Task Force's classifying EMDR Therapy as one of the "probably efficacious treatments" for the treatment of PTSD (Chambless et al., 1998), the following countries and organizations have mandated EMDR as a recommended treatment for patients suffering from trauma:

- Cities and Countries: *Australia*, Australian Centre for Posttraumatic Mental Health, 2007; *France*, INSERM, 2004; *Israel*, Bleich, Kotler, Kutz, & Shalev, 2002; *London, England*, National Collaborating Centre for Mental Health, 2005; *The Netherlands*, Dutch National Steering Committee Guidelines Mental Health Care, 2003; *Northern Ireland*, CREST, 2003; *Stockholm, Sweden*, Sjöblom et al., 2003; *United Kingdom*, Department of Health, 2001
- Organizations: *American Psychiatric Association*, 2004; *California Evidence-Based Clearinghouse for Child Welfare*, 2010; *Department of Veterans Affairs and Department of Defense*, 2004; *The Substance Abuse and Mental Health Services Administration* (SAMHSA), 2011; *Therapy Advisor*, 2004–2007; *International Society for Traumatic Stress Studies*, Foa, Keane, Friedman, & Cohen, 2009.

In 2013, the World Health Organization (WHO) published its *Guidelines for the Management of Conditions Specifically Related to Stress* and stated: "Trauma-focused CBT and EMDR are the only psychotherapies recommended for children, adolescents and adults with PTSD."

The chapters in this section on "EMDR and Trauma- and Stressor-Related Disorders" are divided into three categories: Reactive Attachment Disorder, Posttraumatic Stress Disorder, and Acute Stress Disorder.

Reactive Attachment Disorder

In 2002, reactive attachment was first discussed in the EMDR Therapy literature when R. J. Taylor published an article on the treatment of a family with an 8-year-old child with reactive attachment disorder and the qualitative evaluation observed by the parents concerning the child's instant change of attitude. There have also been case studies to support the positive effect of EMDR with children who have attachment trauma (Madrid, Skolek, & Shapiro, 2006; Robredo, 2011). Since 2007, Wesselmann (2007, 2009, 2010, 2013a, 2013b) has been writing and presenting on the innovative work that she and her colleagues, Cathy Schweitzer and Stefanie Armstrong, are doing at *The Attachment and Trauma Center of Nebraska* to make sure that children affected by attachment trauma and their families can work through these difficulties. Their approach includes an integrative treatment team that highlights the importance of the incorporation of parents into treatment with their child (Wesselmann et al., 2014a, 2014b). The authors' research showed that there is distinct improvement in behavioral and attachment measures after using EMDR and conjoint therapy (Attachment and Trauma Center of Nebraska, 2011; Wesselmann, 2013a, 2013b; Wesselmann & Shapiro, 2013a, 2013b; Wesselmann et al., 2012). In the section on Reactive Attachment Disorder, "Child Attachment Trauma Protocol" is Wesselmann, Schweitzer, and Armstrong's contribution to support EMDR clinicians in furthering their understanding and treatment of this important topic.

The authors Anna Rita Verardo and Maria Zaccagnino, from Italy, wrote the chapter, "Working on Attachment Issues with EMDR Therapy: The Attachment Protocol." They used John Bowlby's theoretical framework (1969, 1973, 1980) to guide their work and were interested in helping clients change their internal representation, or Internal Working Models, that they were unworthy of care to one where they felt worthy and worthwhile to be cared for. These clinicians used the Adult Attachment Interview (George, Kaplan, & Main, 1985) to understand the client's early experience and state of mind regarding attachment relationships and Grice's conversational maxims (1989) to evaluate and understand the attachment style further. In their preliminary study, they saw significant changes in attachment patterns using the EMDR Attachment Protocol during treatment. Their innovative "Parent as Child" exercise at the end of the protocol is particularly helpful.

Posttraumatic Stress Disorder

The next section, on posttraumatic stress disorder (PTSD), is but a small representation of the many ways in which EMDR Therapy is used with a wide range of populations and situations. One of Dr. Shapiro's six basic protocols, "Single Traumatic Event Protocol," which shows the basic structure for working on single traumatic events with the Standard EMDR Protocol and the 3-Pronged Protocol (Luber, 2009, 2012).

Berber van der Vleugel, David van den Berg, Paul de Bont, Tonnie Staring, and Ad de Jongh broke new ground when they began working with traumatized patients with psychosis. Their chapter, "EMDR Therapy for Traumatized Patients with Psychosis," introduces us to their innovative ways of working with patients diagnosed with psychosis and opens up a whole new possibility of work with this population. They create a comprehensive treatment program that includes a multidisciplinary team, and EMDR Therapy is part of this program. They have stepped carefully into this treatment by doing an open study (van den Berg & van der Gaag, 2012) from which they found significant improvements; another group did a within-subjects controlled case study model (de Bont, van Minnen, & de Jongh, 2013), with both EMDR Therapy and Prolonged Exposure, showing positive results for both modalities. Then, they did a randomized clinical trial applying EMDR Therapy and Prolonged Exposure for PTSD for patients with psychosis in addition to treatment as usual (de Bont, van den Berg, et al., 2013) and again the eight-session treatment was shown to be "feasible, effective and safe" (van den Berg et al., 2015). The effects for both treatments were maintained 6 months later. What they are finding is that using standardized treatment protocols is possible with minor adaptations and is effective in treating comorbid PTSD with this population. Their approach is the Dutch Two Method Approach (de Jongh, ten Broeke, & Meijer, 2010), a structured approach in Phase 2 to select target memories that need to be processed for symptom relief. They include a Third Method (also called flashforwards) to deal with the unrealistic expectations or negative imagery related to psychosis.

Note: Only well-trained clinicians who are familiar with psychosis and part of a multidisciplinary team should use this protocol.

Ignacio Jarero and Lucina Artigas's chapter, "EMDR Integrative Group Treatment Protocol for Adolescents (14–17 years) and Adults Living With Ongoing Traumatic Stress," is an adaptation of their EMDR Integrative Group Treatment Protocol (EMDR-IGTP; Artigas, Jarero, Alcalá, & López Cano, 2009, 2014). The EMDR-IGTP was originally used in response to the need to address the large numbers of victims of Hurricane Pauline in 1997. The addition here is to take into consideration patients who have been traumatized and then lack a posttrauma safety period for memory consolidation. They observed that six applications of this protocol were necessary in an intensive treatment format (twice a day for 3 consecutive days) to resolve the traumas.

Acute Stress Disorder

For the Acute Stress Disorder section, Jim Marshall and Sara Gilman introduce us to the world of 911 emergency telecommunicators (911 TCs) through their chapter "Reaching the Unseen First Responder with EMDR Therapy: Treating 911 Trauma in Emergency Telecommunicators." Through Marshall's access to his brother—a 911 TC—and his brother's 911 TC colleagues, he recognized the vulnerability of these "very first responders" who are often not seen as being in the line of fire. He took on the responsibility of serving this underserved group by creating the 911 Institute and establishing a nonprofit organization, 911 Wellness Foundation, devoted to the health and safety of this population through research, education, policy, and intervention. Gilman brings her expertise in EMDR Therapy and knowledge as a first responder herself. They introduce us to the 911 TCs and educate us about what we need to do to treat them competently, effectively, and respectfully.

References

Abbasnejad, M., Mahani, K. N., & Zamyad, A. (2007). Efficacy of "eye movement desensitization and reprocessing" in reducing anxiety and unpleasant feelings due to earthquake experience. *Psychological Research, 9,* 104–117.

Ahmad, A., Larsson, B., & Sundelin-Wahlsten, V. (2007). EMDR treatment for children with PTSD: Results of a randomized controlled trial. *Nordic Journal of Psychiatry, 61,* 349–354.

American Psychiatric Association. (1980). *Diagnostic and statistical manual of mental disorders, third edition (DSM-III)*. Washington, DC: American Psychiatric Association Practice Guidelines.

American Psychiatric Association. (2004). *Practice guideline for the treatment of patients with acute stress disorder and posttraumatic stress disorder*. Arlington, VA: American Psychiatric Association Practice Guidelines.

Arabia, E., Manca, M. L., & Solomon, R. M. (2011). EMDR for survivors of life-threatening cardiac events: Results of a pilot study. *Journal of EMDR Practice and Research, 5,* 2–13.

Artigas, L., Jarero, I., Alcalá, N., & López Cano, T. (2009). The EMDR Integrative Group Treatment Protocol (IGTP). In M. Luber (Ed.), *Eye movement desensitization and reprocessing (EMDR) scripted protocols: Basics and special situations* (pp. 279–288). New York, NY: Springer Publishing.

Artigas, L., Jarero, I., Alcalá, N., & López Cano, T. (2014). The EMDR Integrative Group Treatment Protocol (IGTP) for children. In M. Luber (Ed.), *Implementing EMDR early interventions for man-made and natural disasters* (pp. 237–251). New York, NY: Springer Publishing.

Attachment and Trauma Center of Nebraska. (2011). *EMDR integrative team treatment for attachment trauma in children: Treatment manual*. Omaha, NE: Author.

Australian Centre for Posttraumatic Mental Health. (2007). *Australian Guidelines for the treatment of adults with acute stress disorder and posttraumatic stress disorder*. Melbourne, Victoria: ACPMH.

Bisson, J., Roberts, N. P., Andrew, M., Cooper, R., & Lewis, C. (2013). Psychological therapies for chronic post-traumatic stress disorder (PTSD) in adults [review]. *Cochrane Database of Systematic Reviews, 2013*. doi:10.1002/14651858.CD003388.pub4

Bleich, A., Kotler, M., Kutz, I., & Shalev, A. (2002). *A position paper of the (Israeli) National Council for Mental Health: Guidelines for the assessment and professional intervention with terror victims in the hospital and in the community*. Jerusalem, Israel: National Council for Mental Health.

Bowlby, J. (1969). *Attachment and loss: Vol 1. Attachment*. New York, NY: Basic Books.

Bowlby, J. (1973). *Attachment and loss, Vol. 2: Separation*. New York, NY: Basic Books.

Bowlby, J. (1980). *Attachment and loss, Vol. 3: Loss, sadness and depression*. New York, NY: Basic Books.

Bradley, R., Greene, J., Russ, E., Dutra, L., & Westen, D. (2005). A multidimensional meta-analysis of psychotherapy for PTSD. *American Journal of Psychiatry, 162*, 214–227.

Brom, D., Kleber, R. J., & Defares, P. B. (1989). Brief psychotherapy for posttraumatic stress disorders. *Journal of Consulting and Clinical Psychology, 57*, 607–612.

California Evidence-Based Clearinghouse for Child Welfare. (2010). *Trauma treatment for children*. Retrieved from http://www.cebc4cw.org

Capezzani, L., Ostacoli, L., Cavallo, M., Carletto, S., Feranandez, I., Solomon, R., . . . Cantelmi, T. (2013). EMDR and CBT for cancer patients: Comparative study of effects on PTSD, anxiety, and depression. *Journal of EMDR Practice and Research, 5*, 2–13.

Carlson, J. G., Chemtob, C. M., Rusnak, K., Hedlund, N. L., & Muraoka, M. Y. (1998). Eye movement desensitization and reprocessing treatment for combat related posttraumatic stress disorder. *Journal of Traumatic Stress, 11*, 3–24.

Chambless, D. L., Baker, M. J., Baucom, D. H., Beutler, L. E., Calhoun, K. S., Crits-Christoph, P., . . . McCurry, S. (1998). Update on empirically validated therapies. *The Clinical Psychologist, 51*, 3–16.

Chemtob, C. M., Nakashima, J., Hamada, R. S., & Carlson, J. G. (2002). Brief-treatment for elementary school children with disaster-related posttraumatic stress disorder: A field study. *Journal of Clinical Psychology, 58*, 99–112.

Clinical Resource Efficiency Support Team (CREST). (2003). *The management of post-traumatic stress disorder in adults*. A publication of the Clinical Resource Efficiency Support Team of the Northern Ireland Department of Health, Social Services and Public Safety, Belfast.

Cvetek, R. (2008). EMDR treatment of distressful experiences that fail to meet the criteria for PTSD. *Journal of EMDR Practice and Research, 2*, 2–14.

Davidson, P. R., & Parker, K. C. H. (2001). Eye movement desensitization and reprocessing (EMDR): A meta-analysis. *Journal of Consulting and Clinical Psychology, 69*, 305–316.

de Bont, P. A. J. M., van den Berg, D. P. G., van der Vleugel, B. M., de Roos, C., Mulder, C. L., Becker, E. S., . . . van Minnen, A. (2013). A multi-site single blind clinical study to compare prolonged exposure, eye movement desensitization and reprocessing and waiting list on patients with a current diagnosis of psychosis and co-morbid post-traumatic stress disorder: Study protocol for the randomized controlled trial Treating Trauma in Psychosis. *Trials, 14*, 151.

de Bont, P. A. J. M., van Minnen, A., & de Jongh, A. (2013). Treating PTSD in patients with psychosis: A within-group controlled feasibility study examining the efficacy and safety of evidence-based PE and EMDR protocols. *Behavior Therapy, 44*(4), 717–730. doi:10.1016/j.beth.2013.07.002

de Jongh, A., ten Broeke, E., & Meijer, S. (2010). Two method approach: A case conceptualization model in the context of EMDR. *Journal of EMDR Practice and Research, 4*, 12–21.

Department of Veterans Affairs & Department of Defense. (2004). *VA/DoD clinical practice guideline for the management of post-traumatic stress*. Washington, DC. Retrieved from http://www.oqp.med.va.gov/cpg/PTSD/PTSD_cpg/frameset.htm

de Roos, C. (2011). A randomized comparison of cognitive behavioral therapy (CBT) and eye movement desensitization and reprocessing (EMDR) in disaster exposed children. *European Journal of Psychotraumatology, 2*, 5694. doi:10.3402/ejpt.v2i0.5694

Diehle, J., Opmeer, B. C., Boer, F., Mannarino, A. P., & Lindauer, R. J. (2014). Trauma-focused cognitive behavioral therapy or eye movement desensitization and reprocessing: What works in children with posttraumatic stress symptoms? A randomized controlled trial. *European Child & Adolescent Psychiatry*, 24/2(227–236), 1018–8827.

Doering, S., Ohlmeier, M.-C., de Jongh, A., Hofmann, A., & Bisping, V. (2013). Efficacy of a trauma-focused treatment approach for dental phobia: A randomized clinical trial. *European Journal of Oral Sciences, 121*, 584–593.

Dutch National Steering Committee Guidelines Mental Health Care. (2003). *Multidisciplinary guideline anxiety disorders*. Utrecht, The Netherlands: Quality Institute Heath Care CBO/Trimbos Institute.

Edmond, T., Rubin, A., & Wambach, K. G. (1999). The effectiveness of EMDR with adult female survivors of childhood sexual abuse. *Social Work Research, 23*, 103–116.

Foa, E. B., Keane, T. M., Friedman, M. J., & Cohen, J. A. (2009). *Effective treatments for PTSD: Practice guidelines of the International Society for Traumatic Stress Studies.* New York, NY: Guilford Press.

Friedman, M. J. (1989). 1989: The year's work in PTSD. *PTSD Research Quarterly, 1,* 2–7.

George, C., Kaplan, N., & Main, M. (1985). *Adult attachment interview* (unpublished manuscript). Department of Psychology, University of California, Berkeley, CA.

Grice, H. P. (1989). *Studies in the way of words.* Cambridge, MA: Harvard University Press.

Högberg, G., Pagani, M., Sundin, O., Soares, J., Aberg-Wistedt, A., Tarnell, B.,...Hallstrom, T. (2007). On treatment with eye movement desensitization and reprocessing of chronic post-traumatic stress disorder in public transportation workers—A randomized controlled trial. *Nordic Journal of Psychiatry, 61,* 54–61.

Högberg, G., Pagani, M., Sundin, O., Soares, J., Aberg-Wistedt, A., Tarnell, B., & Hallstrom, T. (2008). Treatment of post-traumatic stress disorder with eye movement desensitization and reprocessing: Outcome is stable in 35-month follow-up. *Psychiatry Research, 159,* 101–108.

INSERM. (2004). *Psychotherapy: An evaluation of three approaches.* Paris, France: French National Institute of Health and Medical Research.

Ironson, G. I., Freund, B., Strauss, J. L., & Williams, J. (2002). Comparison of two treatments for traumatic stress: A community-based study of EMDR and prolonged exposure. *Journal of Clinical Psychology, 58,* 113–128.

Jaberghaderi, N., Greenwald, R., Rubin, A., Dolatabadim, S., & Zand, S. O. (2004). A comparison of CBT and EMDR for sexually abused Iranian girls. *Clinical Psychology and Psychotherapy, 11,* 358–368.

Jarero, I., Artigas, L., & Luber, M. (2011). The EMDR protocol for recent critical incidents: Application in a disaster mental health continuum of care context. *Journal of EMDR Practice and Research, 5,* 82–94.

Keane, T. M., Fairbank, J. A., Caddell, J. M., Zimering, R. T., Taylor, K. L., & Mora, C. A. (1989). Clinical evaluation of a measure to assess combat exposure. *Psychological Assessment: A Journal of Consulting and Clinical Psychology, 1,* 53–55.

Kemp, M., Drummond, P., & McDermott, B. (2010). A wait-list controlled pilot study of eye movement desensitization and reprocessing (EMDR) for children with post-traumatic stress disorder (PTSD) symptoms from motor vehicle accidents. *Clinical Child Psychology and Psychiatry, 15,* 5–25.

Kinzie, J. D. (1989). Therapeutic approaches to traumatized Cambodian refugees. *Journal of Traumatic Stress, 2,* 75–91.

Lee, C., Gavriel, H., Drummond, P., Richards, J., & Greenwald, R. (2002). Treatment of PTSD: Stress inoculation training with prolonged exposure compared to EMDR. *Journal of Clinical Psychology, 58,* 1071–1089.

Lee, C. W., & Cuijpers, P. (2013). A meta-analysis of the contribution of eye movements in processing emotional memories. *Journal of Behavior Therapy & Experimental Psychiatry, 44,* 231–239.

Lindy, J. D. (1989). Transference and post-traumatic stress disorder. *Journal of the American Academy of Psychoanalysis, 17,* 397–413.

Luber, M., & Shapiro, F. (2009). Interview with Francine Shapiro: Historical overview, present issues, and future directions of EMDR. *Journal of EMDR Practice and Research, 3*(4), 217–231.

Madrid, A., Skolek, S., & Shapiro, F. (2006). Repairing failures in bonding through EMDR. *Clinical Case Studies, 5,* 271–286.

Marcus, S., Marquis, P., & Sakai, C. (2004). Three- and 6-month follow-up of EMDR treatment of PTSD in an HMO setting. *International Journal of Stress Management, 11,* 195–208.

Marcus, S. V., Marquis, P., & Saki, C. (1997). Controlled study of treatment of PTSD using EMDR in an HMO setting. *Psychotherapy, 34,* 307–315.

Maxfield, L., & Hyer, L. A. (2002). The relationship between efficacy and methodology in studies investigating EMDR treatment of PTSD. *Journal of Clinical Psychology, 58,* 23–41.

National Collaborating Centre for Mental Health. (2005). *Post traumatic stress disorder (PTSD): The management of adults and children in primary and secondary care.* London, UK: National Institute for Clinical Excellence.

Nijdam, M. J., Gersons, B. P. R., Reitsma, J. B., de Jongh, A., & Olff, M. (2012). Brief eclectic psychotherapy v. eye movement desensitization and reprocessing therapy in the treatment of post-traumatic stress disorder: Randomized controlled trial. *British Journal of Psychiatry, 200,* 224–231.

Peniston, G. E. (1986). EMG biofeedback-assisted desensitization treatment for Vietnam combat veterans post-traumatic stress disorder. *Clinical Biofeedback Health, 9,* 35–41.

Power, K. G., McGoldrick, T., Brown, K., Buchanan, R., Sharp, D., Swanson, V., & Karatzias, A. (2002). A controlled comparison of eye movement desensitization and reprocessing versus exposure plus cognitive restructuring, versus waiting list in the treatment of post-traumatic stress disorder. *Journal of Clinical Psychology and Psychotherapy, 9,* 299–318.

Rando, T. A. (1993). *Treatment of complicated mourning.* Champaign, IL: Research Press.

Robredo, J. (2011, June). *EMDR and gender violence: Brief and intensive treatment for children exposed to gender violence.* Paper presented at the annual meeting of the EMDR Europe Association, Vienna, Austria.

Rodenburg, R., Benjamin, A., de Roos, C, Meijer, A. M., & Stams, G. J. (2009). Efficacy of EMDR in children: A meta-analysis. *Clinical Psychology Review, 29*, 599–606.

Rothbaum, B. O. (1997). A controlled study of eye movement desensitization and reprocessing for posttraumatic stress disordered sexual assault victims. *Bulletin of the Menninger Clinic, 61*, 317–334.

SAMHSA's National Registry of Evidence-based Programs and Practices. (2011). Retrieved from http://nrepp.samhsa.gov/ViewIntervention.aspx?id=199. [The Substance Abuse and Mental Health Services Administration (SAMHSA) is an agency of the U.S. Department of Health and Human Services (HHS)].

Scheck, M. M., Schaeffer, J. A., & Gillette, C. S. (1998). Brief psychological intervention with traumatized young women: The efficacy of eye movement desensitization and reprocessing. *Journal of Traumatic Stress, 11*, 25–44.

Seidler, G. H., & Wagner, F. E. (2006). Comparing the efficacy of EMDR and trauma-focused cognitive-behavioral therapy in the treatment of PTSD: A meta-analytic study. *Psychological Medicine, 36*, 1515–1522.

Shapiro, F. (1989). Efficacy of the eye movement desensitization procedure in the treatment of traumatic memories. *Journal of Traumatic Stress Studies, 2*, 199–223.

Sjöblom, P. O., Andréewitch, S., Bejerot, S., Mörtberg, E., Brinck, U., Ruck, C., & Körlin, D. (2003). *Regional treatment recommendation for anxiety disorders*. Stockholm, Sweden: Medical Program Committee/Stockholm City Council.

Taylor, R. J. (2002, September). Family unification with reactive attachment disorder: A brief treatment. *Contemporary Family Therapy, 24*, 475–481. doi:10.1023/A%3A1019867317042

Taylor, S., Thordarson, D. S., Maxfield, L., Fedoroff, I. C., Lovell, K., & Ogrodniczuk, J. (2003). Comparative efficacy, speed, and adverse effects of three PTSD treatments: Exposure therapy, EMDR, and relaxation training. *Journal of Consulting and Clinical Psychology, 71*, 330–338.

Therapy Advisor. (2004–2007). Retrieved from http://www.therapyadvisor.com

United Kingdom Department of Health. (2001). *Treatment choice in psychological therapies and counselling evidence based clinical practice guideline*. London, England: Her Majesty's Stationery Office.

van den Berg, D. P. G., de Bont, P. A. J. M., van der Vleugel, B. M., de Roos, C., de Jongh, A., van Minnen, A., & van der Gaag, M. (2015). Prolonged exposure versus eye movement desensitization and reprocessing versus waiting list for posttraumatic stress disorder in patients with a psychotic disorder: A randomized clinical trial. *JAMA Psychiatry 72*(3), 259–267. Online First. doi:10.1001/jamapsychiatry.2014.2637

van den Berg, D. P. G., & van der Gaag, M. (2012). Treating trauma in psychosis with EMDR: A pilot study. *Journal of Behavior Therapy and Experimental Psychiatry, 43*, 664–671.

van der Kolk, B., Spinazzola, J., Blaustein, M., Hopper, J., Hopper, E., Korn, D., & Simpson, W. (2007). A randomized clinical trial of EMDR, fluoxetine and pill placebo in the treatment of PTSD: Treatment effects and long-term maintenance. *Journal of Clinical Psychiatry, 68*, 37–46.

Vaughan, K., Armstrong, M. F., Gold, R., O'Connor, N., Jenneke, W., & Tarrier, N. (1994). A trial of eye movement desensitization compared to image habituation training and applied muscle relaxation in post-traumatic stress disorder. *Journal of Behavior Therapy and Experimental Psychiatry, 25*, 283–291.

Wanders, F., Serra, M., & de Jongh, A. (2008). EMDR versus CBT for children with self-esteem and behavioral problems: A randomized controlled trial. *Journal of EMDR Practice and Research, 2*, 180–189.

Wesselmann, D. (2007). Treating attachment issues through EMDR and a family systems approach. In F. Shaprio, F. W. Kaslow, & L. Maxfield (Eds.), *Handbook of EMDR and family therapy processes* (pp. 113–130). Hoboken, NJ: John Wiley.

Wesselmann, D. (2009, August). *Adapting EMDR for children with reactive attachment disorder behaviors*. Presentation at the 14th EMDR International Association Conference, Atlanta, GA.

Wesselmann, D. (2010, June). *Adapting EMDR for children with reactive attachment disorder behaviors*. Preconference presentation at the 11th EMDR Europe Association Conference, Hamburg, Germany.

Wesselmann, D. (2013a). Healing trauma and creating secure attachments with EMDR. In M. Solomon & D. S. Siegel (Eds.), *Healing moments in psychotherapy: Mindful awareness, neural integration, and therapeutic presence* (pp. 115–128). New York, NY: Norton.

Wesselmann, D. (2013b, April). *Changing the lives of children with reactive attachment disorder behaviors through EMDR treatment*. Keynote presented at the Congress EMDR Vereniging EMDR Nederland, Nijmegen, the Netherlands.

Wesselmann, D., Schweitzer, C., & Armstrong, S. (2014a). *Integrative team treatment for attachment trauma: Family therapy and EMDR*. New York, NY: W.W. Norton.

Wesselmann, D., Schweitzer, C., & Armstrong, S. (2014b). *Integrative parenting: Strategies for raising children affected by attachment trauma*. New York, NY: W.W. Norton.

Wesselmann, D., & Shapiro, F. (2013). EMDR and the treatment of complex trauma in children and adolescents. In J. Ford & C. Courtois (Eds.), *Treating complex traumatic stress disorders in children and adolescents* (pp. 203–224). New York, NY: Guilford Press.

Wesselmann, S., Davidson, M., Armstrong, S., Schweitzer, C., Bruckner, D., & Potter, A. (2012). EMDR as a treatment for improving attachment status in adults and children. *European Review of Applied Psychology, 62*, 223–230.

Wilson, S. A., Becker, L. A., & Tinker, R. H. (1995). Eye movement desensitization and reprocessing (EMDR) treatment for psychologically traumatized individuals. *Journal of Consulting and Clinical Psychology, 63,* 928–937.

Wilson, S. A., Becker, L. A., & Tinker, R. H. (1997). Fifteen-month follow-up of eye movement desensitization and reprocessing (EMDR) treatment for PTSD and psychological trauma. *Journal of Consulting and Clinical Psychology, 65,* 1047–1056.

World Health Organization. (2013). *Guidelines for the management of conditions specifically related to stress.* Geneva, Switzerland: World Health Organization Press.

REACTIVE ATTACHMENT DISORDERS

Child Attachment Trauma Protocol | 1

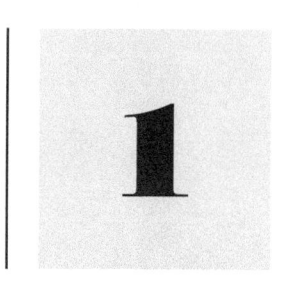

Debra Wesselmann, Cathy Schweitzer, and Stefanie Armstrong

Introduction

Children who have experienced neglect, abuse, attachment losses, or some other form of attachment trauma frequently exhibit severe behaviors, even when they are placed in a stable environment (Wesselmann, Schweitzer, & Armstrong, 2014a). The stored, unprocessed attachment trauma drives reactivity and mistrust of caregivers and other adults (Ide & Paez, 2000; van der Kolk, 2005; van der Kolk et al., 1996). Behaviors may include aggression, stealing, lying, defiance, food and elimination problems, and sexualized behaviors.

Team Collaboration for Challenging Cases

In order to address the traumatic roots related to their inability to trust and be close, children need the support of parents or other caregivers. Yet, the parent–child relationship may be fraught with conflict due to the parents' feelings of frustration and anger regarding the children's behaviors. In the most challenging cases, we recommend that the Eye Movement Desensitization and Reprocessing (EMDR) therapist collaborate with a family therapist to address the parent–child relationship and lay the groundwork for the EMDR Therapy session each week, increasing the efficiency with which the EMDR Therapy is conducted.

The EMDR therapist treating a complex child case can develop a two-person team by approaching another therapist who is like-minded regarding the etiology of the child's behaviors and who is willing to collaborate and work with the family. Although, logistically, it is helpful to work with someone who has an office in the same physical location, it is not a prerequisite. Therapists working in different nearby settings can communicate via phone or email between sessions. Prior to the EMDR session, the family therapist communicates discoveries to the EMDR therapist regarding the child's recent triggers, identified memories, or future template needs.

If there is no opportunity for a two-person collaboration, one therapist can perform both the family therapist and the EMDR therapist roles by designating one session as the family therapy session and the next as the EMDR Therapy session, and so on. The intent should be made clear to the child and family so expectations for the respective sessions are clear.

The Family Therapist

The family therapist strengthens attachment security by helping the parents understand the traumatic roots of the children's behaviors and respond to their children's emotions with greater sensitivity (Wesselmann, Schweitzer, & Armstrong, 2014b). Early attachment trauma interferes with the typical developmental trajectory, leaving children with immature social, emotional, and cognitive skills. The family therapist coaches the child in identifying, managing, and expressing feelings, listening, following directions, and improving peer and sibling relationships. The family therapist addresses current crises and identifies related triggers, cognitions, and memories, and subsequently provides the information to the EMDR therapist, who follows up with EMDR Therapy as soon as possible. The work of the family therapist allows the EMDR therapist to implement EMDR Therapy every week, accelerating the rate of healing and recovery for suffering children and their families.

The EMDR Therapist

The EMDR therapist implements EMDR Therapy resource development exercises to strengthen attachment security and self-regulation (see later) and addresses memories, triggers, and future templates, depending on the insights discovered and communicated by the family therapist. Because the family therapist devotes an hour to the time-consuming work of identifying triggers, emotions, cognitions, touchstone events, and future templates with the child and parents, the EMDR therapist is able to implement EMDR Therapy weekly. The EMDR therapist typically begins processing current triggers and developing future templates prior to memory work. As the child develops skills for self-regulation and the parent–child relationship is strengthened, past events are targeted and reprocessed.

Research

Case studies have shown EMDR Therapy to improve symptomology and attachment in adults with complex trauma (Potter, Davidson, & Wesselmann, 2013; Wesselmann & Potter, 2009). Case studies have demonstrated that EMDR has a positive effect on symptoms and parent–child attachment in children with a history of attachment trauma (Madrid, Skolek, & Shapiro, 2006; Robredo, 2011; Taylor, 2002). In our ongoing research with children with a history of attachment trauma, children have shown marked improvement on behavioral and attachment measures following EMDR and conjoint family therapy (Attachment and Trauma Center of Nebraska, 2011; Wesselmann, 2013; Wesselmann & Shapiro, 2013; Wesselmann et al., 2012).

Randomized treatment control studies are needed to further appraise the impact of integrative EMDR and family therapy on attachment security and other disorders in children related to early relational traumas.

Treating Attachment Trauma in Children Protocol Script Notes

Phase One: History Taking

The history taking helps the therapist identify likely past, present, and future targets for EMDR Therapy and helps increase parental attunement and compassion related to the child's challenging behaviors. History taking begins initially with an interview with the parents and can be conducted by the EMDR therapist or the family therapist when using the collaborative approach. The psychosocial history should include identification of the following:

- *Past symptoms, behaviors, and traumatic events*: Identify the child's problem symptoms and behaviors and all traumatic events in the child's past.
- *Current and recent triggers*: The therapist asks the parents to consider the child's symptoms/behaviors and identify the present-day situations (current and recent triggers) that tend to precede the child's symptoms.
- *Negative thoughts/cognitions*: Finally, the therapist asks the parents to assist in brainstorming and hypothesizing the negative thoughts/cognitions (NCs) that might be

driving the child's behaviors, taking into consideration the child's traumatic experiences and current triggers. Common NCs related to attachment trauma are as follows:
- Defectiveness (e.g., I am not good enough)
- Responsibility (e.g., I deserved to be abandoned/abused)
- Safety (e.g., I am not safe)
- Control (e.g., I must be in charge of getting what I want and need)
- Parents/others (e.g., Parents are mean)
- Love/belongingness (e.g., I do not belong).

Case Conceptualization

When using a team approach, the EMDR therapist and family therapist look at the child's history together and write down the following:

- Potential EMDR Therapy targets
- Current triggers that seem to precipitate aggression, defiance, or other symptoms or behaviors; hypothesized NCs associated with the child's traumas and triggers
- Needed skills related to self-awareness, self-regulation, socialization, and communication. The skills list is a working plan for psychoeducation and skills work that can be conducted by the family therapist and reinforced by the EMDR therapist through future templates.

Phase 2: Preparation

Attachment Resource Development

These are the exercises used to develop attachment resources:

1. "Playing Baby" Exercise
2. "Lollipop" Game
3. "Magical Cord of Love" Exercise
4. "Circle of Caring" Exercise
5. "Safe Place for the Little One" Exercise
6. Songs for younger children

Children who do not trust or feel close to their attachment figures naturally dissociate or use other defenses to protect themselves from vulnerable emotions. Parents are integral to attachment resource development (ARD), as the therapist facilitates experiences of emotional and physical closeness between the parent and child and then reinforces the child's positive affect with bilateral stimulation (BLS; Wesselmann et al., 2014a). Therapists can prepare parents by explaining the process in advance. The therapist disarms the child initially by pointing out that his parent(s) will be doing all the work during this exercise, while he gets to sit back and take it easy. The therapist should use clinical judgment in order to avoid pressuring the child or parent to move into a position that involves more physical touch than one or both can tolerate with a reasonable level of comfort.

Note: Although ARD is part of the Preparation Phase, it is helpful to repeat ARD exercises regularly throughout the course of treatment to help maintain the positive feelings of connection.

BLS DURING RESOURCE DEVELOPMENT

Children should be introduced to the various forms of BLS prior to commencing the exercises. During the resource work, it is helpful to use tactile BLS, at a relatively slow speed, because it reinforces positive affect and enhances feelings of relaxation. Many children seem to enjoy the bilateral tactile pulsars, as a form of BLS. These can be conveniently placed in the children's hands, shoes, socks, or pockets, allowing children the freedom to position themselves in any way they feel comfortable. The therapist holds the control and can easily keep one hand free to take notes.

It is recommended to continue the tactile BLS while the therapist or parent is guiding the child's thoughts through the positive messages or imagery and to discontinue the BLS when the dialogue stops. This helps ensure that the child's thoughts and affect remain positive throughout the exercises.

Note: Scripts for the following exercises can be found in the next section.

MESSAGES OF LOVE EXERCISE

During this exercise, the therapist creates an experience of closeness and connection between the child and the parent(s). Through a series of questions, the therapist encourages the parent to talk about traits the parent loves about the child, positive early memories with the child, activities the parent enjoys doing with the child, and the parent's hopes and dreams for the child. BLS is implemented to reinforce the child's feelings of closeness, warmth, and security created through the physical closeness and the parent's loving words. The exercise is conducted with one parent at a time.

PLAYING BABY EXERCISE

This exercise is very applicable to children 7 and younger, although some older children may also enjoy the exercise. The therapist should use clinical judgment regarding its appropriateness and then implement the exercise in a playful manner. The therapist reinforces the child's feelings of shared pleasure and closeness with the parent(s) using BLS. The exercise is conducted with one parent at a time.

"LOLLIPOP" GAME

This adaptation to the authors' Playing Baby Exercise was developed by Lovett (2009). The "Lollipop" Game is another playful exercise designed to help the child experience feelings of closeness and to view the parent(s) as safe, attuned, and responsive to his needs. BLS reinforces the child's feelings of trust and comfort. The exercise is conducted with one parent at a time.

MAGICAL CORD OF LOVE EXERCISE

Children with insecure attachment do not trust love to be continuous. They are often concrete thinkers, and from their perspective, they are unloved and alone when a parent is not present and interacting with them. Children who are unable to hold onto a feeling of the parent's love commonly develop maladaptive methods for seeking attention. The positive image of connection through the cord of love is reinforced with BLS to assist the child with insecure attachment in trusting that the parent's love is always present.

CIRCLE OF CARING EXERCISE

Attachment trauma, changes in caregivers, and moves to new homes teach children that they are outsiders who do not really belong anywhere. The Circle of Caring Exercise heightens the child's awareness of the people who love and care about him in his present-day life, and BLS reinforces associated feelings of safety, security, and belonging. This exercise can be conducted easily with children and adolescents who are residing in nonpermanent foster care or residential placements.

SAFE PLACE FOR THE INNER CHILD EXERCISE

Children with a history of attachment trauma often exhibit quick changes in affect state, especially when traumatic material is consciously or subconsciously triggered. One way to help parents understand this is by explaining the sudden fearful or aggressive behaviors as stemming from feelings associated with a younger age at which the child was traumatized. Parents and children of all ages and developmental levels seem to intuitively understand the concept of the "smaller child within."

The exercise for working with "the smaller child within" involves creating a safe or comfortable place for the inner child and prompting parents to describe how they imagine caring for the inner child there in the safe place. The exercise helps create inner feelings of safety and helps stabilize children with varying degrees of dissociation. The therapist normalizes the concept by bringing out a set of nesting dolls and allowing the child to take them apart, while explaining that everyone carries the thoughts and feelings they experienced as a young child somewhere inside themselves. After completing the exercise, the imagery can be accessed whenever needed to reinforce feelings of safety and nurturance for the inner child.

SONGS FOR YOUNGER CHILDREN

Younger children are soothed by music, rhythm, and rocking with their parents. Music and rhythm can be combined with bilateral movement to reinforce feelings of pleasure, safety, and security between children and their parents. Parents and therapists can make up lyrics that provide the positive messages children need to hear.

Self-Regulation Development and Installation

Whereas ARD reinforces the child's sense of connection with parents, Self-Regulation Development and Installation (S-RDI) is resource work specifically intended to reinforce the child's experience of self-efficacy in moving from a dysregulated state to a regulated state (Wesselmann et al., 2014a). A good time to implement this protocol is when a child becomes anxious for the session to be over, irritated over some small annoyance, or compelled to pick at his skin or bite his nails. The therapist reinforces the parents' role as expert and coach by asking for parents' opinions and encouraging them to join the therapist in demonstrating skills.

Phase 3: Assessment

When a past trauma has been identified and the child has been adequately prepared for EMDR, the therapist takes the child through the assessment phase, using child-friendly language and assisting the child as needed. It is often easier for the child to identify the emotion associated with the image prior to identification of the NC. The identified emotion can then be used to lead the child to the associated negative thoughts. Parents can be prompted to talk about the feelings and thoughts they might have experienced as children in order to encourage openness and to assist their child with self-awareness.

Phases 4 to 8: Desensitization, Installation, Body Scan, Closure, and Reevaluation

Keeping Parents Present

Keeping the parent present for the child during EMDR processing naturally increases the parent's level of empathy and compassion for all the difficulties and traumas the child has endured. Additionally, the presence of a supportive parent or trusted adult can provide the vulnerable child with a sense of protection and safety, giving the child courage to feel his feelings and address his traumatic past with EMDR. The presence of attuned parents can help the child stay present and regulated as memories, thoughts, emotions, and sensations are accessed during reprocessing.

Adult clients can find empowerment through the integration of the child and adult perspective regarding childhood traumas, while the child client lacks a store of adult adaptive information. Interactive interweaves involve feedback from parents, prompted by the therapist, that help provide adult perspective as well as newfound awareness of parents' empathy and support. Parents can be utilized for assistance during any of the eight phases of EMDR, reinforcing parents' role as expert and caregiver in the eyes of the child.

BLS During Desensitization and Reprocessing

There are many ways in which BLS can be implemented with children during desensitization and reprocessing. The therapist may move the child's eyes bilaterally by simply asking the child to watch her hand or fingers move from side to side. To help keep the child's attention, the therapist may hold a wand, puppet, or other toy or use an electronic eye scan machine. During reprocessing, the stimulation should be applied as rapidly as the child can comfortably manage. Attune to the child's preferences for modality and speed. Bilateral tactile stimulation through tapping on the child's hands or knees, use of tactile pulsars, or use of headphones that provide bilateral tones are alternative methods of BLS. The therapist should be prepared to change direction, speed, or modality of stimulation as a possible means of accessing new associations when processing seems stuck.

The Rescue Interweave

The rescue interweave is an interactive interweave, utilizing the parent to describe an imaginary rescue of the child from an earlier traumatic event. The parent may describe removing the child from the scene and taking the child to a safe place, protecting the child in some other way, or removing or intervening with the perpetrator figure. The therapist can implement BLS throughout the parent's dialogue. This type of interweave provides the parent with an opportunity to demonstrate his or her dedication to protection of the child (Wesselmann et al., 2014a). The child develops a feeling of empowerment through envisioning the scenario in which he is protected.

Separating Present-Day Triggers From the Past Through Inner Child Interweaves

The child often lacks adequate adaptive information for spontaneous reprocessing, and it is frequently helpful to utilize interweaves to help him separate the present triggers from the past traumas. Interweaves prompting both the parent and the child to dialogue with the inner, smaller child part help the child step into the more mature affect state and establish the difference between past and present. By utilizing the parents as a resource during the interweave, the therapist helps the child see the parent as an expert and a supporter (Wesselmann et al., 2014a).

Future Template

The future template should always follow EMDR processing of current triggers, and may be conducted at any time a skills deficit becomes apparent. Due to the effects of attachment trauma on emotional and cognitive development, children with a history of attachment trauma typically are lacking many behavioral and coping skills, such as assertiveness and communication skills, friendship skills, responding to directions or redirection, and coping with frustration. The family therapist gives specific behavioral instructions and demonstrations, freeing the EMDR therapist to reinforce the new skill with an EMDR future template. The EMDR future template can be effectively reinforced by a more hands-on method of role–play versus an imagined rehearsal.

Treating Attachment Trauma in Children Protocol Script

Phase 1: Client History

Say to the parent, *"Let's make a list of your child's behaviors and symptoms that are problematic."*

"To the best of your ability, please tell me everything you can about your child. I would like to know about _____ (his/her) strengths as well as _____ (his/her) problems and symptoms. Include any behavioral problems at home or school, academic functioning, social functioning, fears, sleep, food, and bathroom issues. I'm going to take extensive notes, because it is all going to be important to understanding what is going on."

_____

_____

_____

_____

_____

_____

Say, *"Tell me what you know about your child's 'story.' I especially need to know about any distressing or traumatic events that your child has experienced, even if those events took place when _____ (he/she) was a baby. You may or may not know everything that has happened to your child, but please try to identify the events that are known to you. This would include any physical, sexual, or emotional abuse; neglect, losses, and major changes; witnessing of domestic abuse or drug or alcohol abuse by parents; accidents, medical interventions; changes in caregivers."*

_____

_____

Say, *"Were there any prenatal or postnatal issues such as prenatal drug exposure, domestic violence during pregnancy, or postpartum depression?"*

_____

_____

Together with the parent, make a list of hypothesized NCs. Themes include defectiveness, responsibility, safety, control, parents/other, and love/belongingness.

Say, *"Your child experienced multiple traumatic events during the period of _____ (his/her) development in which _____ (he/she) was formulating foundational beliefs about self and others. Instead of learning that _____ (he/she) was loved and lovable, that _____ (he/she) could trust and depend upon _____ (his/her) caregivers to love and care for _____ (him/her), your child was learning to believe the opposite. Look again at this list of your child's problems and triggers. Let's brainstorm together and see if we can come up with a list of negative beliefs about self and others that might be clouding _____ (his/her) judgment and impacting* _____ (his/her) *ability to accept love and guidance from you."*

___
___

Say, *"Tell me about any previous therapeutic or psychiatric treatment and the outcome."*

___
___

Say, *"Does your child have any health concerns or have there been health concerns in the past?"*

___
___

Say, *"Please list your child's current medications, including any over-the-counter medications."*

___
___

Say, *"Raising children who exhibit these kinds of problems can be very stressful. How are you coping in the face of all of this?"*

___
___

Say, *"Tell me about your child's strengths, and the traits you most enjoy about your child."*

___
___

Say, *"What are the positive attitudes and behaviors you hope your child will be able to adopt in the future?"*

___
___

Phase Two: Preparation Phase: ARD

If either the child or parent becomes significantly uncomfortable during these exercises, gently move out of the exercises by introducing a game or another playful activity. In this case, ARD can be conducted for a very short time each session until the child and parent become more comfortable.

"Messages of Love" Script

Although both parents may be in the room, this exercise is conducted with one parent at a time. The therapist first meets with the parent(s) without the child in the room.

Explain the exercise to the parent(s) by saying the following:

Note: Alternative wording, depending on the presence of one or both parents, is provided.

> Say to the parent(s), *"We are going to do an exercise today that will help create and reinforce feelings of closeness and connection between you and your child. Remember that increasing your child's sense of security and connection with you will help calm _____ (his/her) nervous system and increase _____ (his/her) capacity to listen and cooperate at home and school."*

> *"When your child joins us, if you don't mind, I will suggest that your child sit physically close to _____ (you/one of you), or as close as possible while remaining relatively comfortable."*

If both parents are in the room say the following:

> Say, *"We will conduct the exercise with one of you and then the other. I will then prompt you to talk about things that will help your child experience positive feelings of closeness and connection with you. For example, I will invite you to talk about things you enjoy about your child, times you have felt proud of your child, and positive early memories with your child. Let's brainstorm and make sure _____ (you/each of you) feel prepared with some positive thoughts and memories. I will make notes to which you can refer, if needed, during the exercise."*

_____

_____

Note: Many parents identify positive thoughts and memories with little assistance, while other parents welcome ideas and suggestions from the therapist.

> Say to the parent(s), *"If there is anything during the ARD exercise that begins creating a high level of distress for _____ (you/either one of you), give me a small signal* (show parent how to lift a finger to give a signal) *and I will find a way to comfortably close it down for today."*

Invite the child to join you and the parent(s) in your office.

> Say to the child, *"Today, you get to sit back and relax. Your _____ (mom/dad) will be doing all of the work! But first, I would like to invite you and your _____ (mom/dad) to sit close to each other today. Perhaps your _____ (mom/dad) can put an arm around you, if you are comfortable.*

> Say to the child, *"During this exercise, if it is OK, I would like you to hold the buzzers* (tactile pulsars) *or place them in your pockets, whichever you prefer. Is it OK?"*

_____

If the tactile pulsars are not an option, say the following:

> Say to the child, *"During this exercise, if it is OK, I would like to tap lightly on your hands or knees, whichever you prefer. Which would you prefer?"*

_____

_____

Ask the parent to talk about the things he or she enjoys about the child.

Say to the parent, *"I would like to know about all of the things you enjoy about _____ (state child's name). First, what are the strengths and positive traits that you appreciate about _____ (state child's name)?"*

Implement slow, tactile BLS for the duration of the parent's dialogue.

_____

_____

Say to the parent, *"Tell me about the activities you enjoy doing with your child."*

Implement slow, tactile BLS for the duration of the parent's dialogue.

_____

_____

Say to the parent, *"Describe the ways in which the two of you are alike. For instance, do you like any of the same foods or have any of the same habits?"*

Implement slow, tactile BLS for the duration of the parent's dialogue.

_____

_____

Say to the parent, *"Tell me about some times that you felt proud of _____ (state child's name), recently, or in the past."*

Implement slow, tactile BLS for the duration of the parent's dialogue.

_____

_____

Say to the parent, *"Describe your memory of when you first set eyes on _____ (state child's name) or even when you first learned about _____ (state child's name) and how you felt."*

Implement slow, tactile BLS for the duration of the parent's dialogue.

_____

_____

Say to the parent, *"Tell me about some of your favorite early memories of _____ (state child's name)."*

Implement slow, tactile BLS for the duration of the parent's dialogue.

_____

_____

Say to the parent, *"Please talk about your positive hopes and dreams for _____ (state child's name) and for your relationship."*

Implement slow, tactile BLS for the duration of the parent's dialogue.

_____

_____

Implement slow, tactile BLS as you direct the child to notice the positive feelings.

If the parent(s) and child appear to be enjoying feeling close and relaxed, give them some quiet time together. In the case of a younger child, the therapist can turn on lullaby music or play a heartbeat sound and offer a soft blanket.

> Say to the child, *"Just notice the feelings of closeness between you and your _____ (mom/dad) right now, and notice the feelings of calm and comfort in your body. Notice the feelings of warmth and connection."*

Repeat the above for the other parent.

"Playing Baby" Script

This exercise is best conducted with one parent at a time.

> Meet with the parent(s) first and say, *"If you are comfortable with it, I would like to do a fun activity today that allows your child to pretend _____ (he/she) is a baby on your lap. I'll conduct the exercise with one of you and then the other. It provides an opportunity for your child to get some of _____ (his/her) earlier unmet needs met through imagination and play, and we will use bilateral stimulation to reinforce feelings of trust and closeness. Does this feel do-able for _____ (you/both of you) if your child is also receptive?"*

Invite the child to join you and the parent(s) in your office.

> Say to the parent, *"_____ (Mom/Dad), if _____ (child's name) were a baby again, just for a day, what would that be like for you?"*

_____

_____

> Say to the child, *"Let's just pretend for a few minutes that you are a baby again. Maybe you could get right up on _____ (mom's/dad's) lap!*

> Say to the parent, *"_____ (Mom/Dad), what position would feel most comfortable for you?"* Help the child and parent arrange pillows and create a comfortable position for both of them.

_____

_____

If using tactile pulsars, say, *"May I place these tappers in your shoes or pockets?"*

_____

If tactile pulsars are not an option, say, *"Is it all right if I sit near you and do a little tapping on your legs once in awhile?"*

_____

_____

> Say to the parent, *"_____ (Mom/Dad), what do you think about this little baby _____ (child's name) on your lap?"*

_____

_____

Add bilateral stimulation by tapping slowly on the child's legs or running the tactile pulsars at a relatively slow speed throughout the parent's discourse.

Say to the parent, *"I'll bet you would be stroking* _____ (his/her) *hair, looking at* _____ (his/her) *little fingers, tracing with your fingers around* _____(his/her) *face, mouth, and eyes, and feeling* _____ (his/her) *soft baby skin."*

_____

_____

Say to the child, *"Notice how comfy you feel right now."*

_____

Tap slowly on the child's legs or run the tactile pulsars at a relatively slow speed for a short time.

Say to the parent, *"*_____ (Mom/Dad), *what other things would you be doing with this lovable little baby?"*

_____

_____

Tap on the child's legs slowly or run the tactile pulsars slowly throughout the parent's discourse.
If the other parent is present, do the above exercise again with this parent.

The "Lollipop Game" Script

This exercise is best conducted with one parent at a time.

Meet with the parent(s) first and say, *"I would like to do another fun activity designed to help children learn that it can be safe and even enjoyable to allow the parent/s to be in charge. The parent holds a lollipop during the activity and the child signals to the parent when* _____ (he/she) *wants the lollipop or doesn't want the lollipop. We will want to stay positive and playful and just have fun with it. I'll handle the logistics. Which one of you would like to do the activity with your child today? Does this activity feel relatively comfortable for you?"*

_____

Say to the child, *"We're going to do a fun activity today that involves a lollipop. First, you get to show me which flavor you want."*
The therapist offers two or three flavors and allows the child to pick one.

_____

_____

Say to the child, *"Now, your* _____ (mom/dad) *is going to hold the lollipop, but don't worry.* _____ (He/She) *will make sure you get to suck on the lollipop just as much as you want. Your job will be to signal your* _____ (mom/dad) *with your mouth and eyes when you want the lollipop in your mouth and when you want it out. Your* _____ (mom's/dad's) *job is to watch carefully and read your signals. Now, let's help you get situated, right on your* _____ (mom's/dad's) *lap, nice and comfy."*

Help the child get situated with pillows and a comfortable position.

Say, *"Can we place these tappers inside your pockets or shoes?"* (Or if tactile pulsars are not an option, say, *"Is it OK if I sit nearby and tap a little sometimes on your feet or knees?"*)

_____

_____

Say to the child, *"OK, you can signal your _____ (mom/dad) with your mouth and your eyes when you want to suck on that lollipop! You can signal, too, when you don't want to take a break from the lollipop. _____ (Mom/Dad) is going to pay close attention."*

Sit silently for a minute or two while the parent and child play the game.

Then say to the child, *"Notice how comfortable it is to let your _____ (mom/dad) be in charge of the lollipop. You can trust _____ (him/her) to know what you need. If you were a baby, you could trust your _____ (mom/dad) to read your signals and take good care of you. _____ (She/He) would give you a bottle as soon as you needed one. _____ (She/He) would rock you, hold you, change you, and provide whatever you needed to feel safe and comfortable."*

Tap slowly or run the tactile pulsars slowly as you say these words. Allow the parent and child to continue with the game until the lollipop is gone or the child tires of the game.

If the other parent is present, do the above exercise again with this parent.

The "Magical Cord of Love" Script

This exercise can be conducted with one or both parents at the same time. Alternate wording for two parents is provided in parentheses.

Say to the child, *"None of us can see love, but we all know it exists. If you could see love, what color would it be? There is no right or wrong answer, it is whatever color you choose."*

_____

_____

Say to the child, *"So if we could see the love that is streaming from your _____ (mom's/dad's/parents') heart/s into your heart, we would see a beautiful, shimmery, _____ (child's chosen color) cord of light—a "magical cord of love."*

Say to the child and parent(s), *"This would be a good time to sit close or snuggle."* Help arrange pillows as needed so both child and parent(s) will be comfortable.

Say to the child, *"If it's OK, I'm going to ask you to place the buzzers* (tactile pulsars) *in your shoes or pockets, and I will be turning them on a little and then off a little. Is it OK?"*

_____

Alternatively, say, *"If it's OK, I'm going to tap on your legs a little now and a little more later. Is it OK?"*

_____

Say to the child and parent(s), *"Let's all close our eyes and picture this magical cord of love together. See the beautiful, shimmery,* _____ *(child's chosen color) cord of light, pouring from* _____ *(mom's/dad's/parents') heart/s into your heart. This cord is magical because it stretches and stretches, so you are always connected, and the love never stops. Even if* _____ *(mom/dad/mom and dad) are on the moon or in Australia, the love can stretch and stretch and you are still connected, heart-to-heart, every second, every minute, every hour, everyday."*

Reinforce with slow BLS as you guide the child's thoughts with the mental imagery.

Say to the parent(s), "_____ *(Mom/Dad/Mom and dad), when you can't see* _____ *(child's name) because you are at work and* _____ *(he/she) is at school, is* _____ *(he/she) gone from your heart and from your mind? Or is* _____ *(he/she) still in your mind and heart? Do you love* _____ *(him/her) just the same?"*

___
___

Tap on the child's legs slowly or run the tactile pulsars slowly throughout the parent's (each parent's) discourse.

Say to the parent(s), _____ *(Mom/Dad/Mom and dad), "What happens if you get busy? For example, what happens to the cord of love if you are tending to another child's needs, or if you are on the phone talking with someone else? When you are not paying attention to* _____ *(child's name), does your love for him/her still exist?"*

___
___

Tap on the child's legs slowly or run the tactile pulsars slowly throughout the parent's discourse.

*Say to the parent, "*_____ *(Mom/Dad/Mom and dad), what about if you are frustrated or angry with* _____ *(child's name)? Can you be angry and love* _____ *(him/her) at the same time? Do you stop loving* _____ *(him/her) when you are upset with* _____ *(him/her)?"*

___
___

Tap on the child's legs slowly or run the tactile pulsars slowly throughout the parent's discourse.

Say to the child, *"The magical cord of love stretches and still connects you with your* _____ *(mom/dad/mom and dad) all of the time, no matter what. If your* _____ *(mom/dad/parents) can't see you, or if your* _____ *(mom/dad/parents)* _____ *(is/are) busy, paying attention to another child, or paying attention to someone else, the magical cord of love stretches and stretches so that you and your* _____ *(mom/dad/parents)* _____ *(is/are) still connected, heart to heart. Even when* _____ *(mom/dad/mom and dad) is upset,* _____ *(mom/dad/mom and dad) still love/s you, and you are still connected, heart-to-heart."*

Tap on the child's legs slowly or run the tactile pulsars slowly throughout the guided imagery.

"Circle of Caring" Script

Say to the child, *"I am going to make a list of all of the people in your life who care about you. This list includes adults and children, relatives, nonrelatives, neighbors, and professional helpers. Your list may also include pets. I will write down all of the names on this piece of paper."*

Say to the parent, *"You may contribute names that come to you, as well. Please tell me the list."*

Write down the list of names.

_____

_____

_____

_____

_____

_____

Say to the child, *"Now, I am going to read through your list, and I want you to picture all of these people here in this room, surrounding you with their love. You can see how much they care about you by the beautiful, shimmery, _____ (child's chosen color for love) light, all around you, like sparkly floating glitter in the air."*

Tap on the child's legs slowly or run the tactile pulsars slowly throughout the guided imagery.

"Safe Place for the Inner Child" Script

Bring out a set of nesting dolls.

Say to the child, *"We are all a little like these nesting dolls. Each one of us still holds feelings deep inside from when we were much younger. We call this the 'inner child' or the 'smaller child inside.' I have an inner child, your _____ (mom/dad/parents) _____ (has/have) an inner child, and you have an inner child. You have feelings and thoughts you carry inside from when you were just a preschooler, a toddler, and even from when you were a baby. Let's look at these nesting dolls again. If this bigger one is your bigger self, see if you can pick ages for the smaller dolls."*

_____

_____

Say to the child, *"Pick one doll that you think is your most hurt little one."*

_____

_____

Say to the child, *"What do grown-ups need to do to help little children feel safe and loved?"*

The therapist writes down any ideas offered by the child. All ideas should be accepted unless they are unsafe or unhealthy.

Say to the child, *"We want to begin helping this littler one inside your heart to feel safe and loved."*

Say to the parent(s), *"_____(Mom/Dad/Mom and dad), you will have an important role in helping to make the smaller child inside feel safe and loved today."*

Say to the child, *"The smaller you needs a nice, comfortable, safe place. What kind of place do you think this should be? What kind of items should be in this place to help the little you feel happy and safe?*

_____

_____

Say to the parent(s), *"Do you have any suggestions about what might make this little one feel happy and safe?"*

_____

_____

Say to the child, *"Do I have permission to add your _____ (mom's/dad's/parents') suggestions to the list?"*

_____

_____

Say, *"Would you like to draw a picture of this safe place for the little one?"*

_____

_____

If the child agrees, offer paper and crayons or any other preferred medium.

Say, *"Here are some _____ (state the preferred medium)."*

If the child asks for help, the parent and therapist and child can all work together to draw the picture.

Say, *"If you like, we can all work together to draw the picture."*

_____

Alternatively, a picture can be made in a sand tray.

Say, *"If you like, you can make your picture in the sand tray."*

Say, *"All little ones need parents to take care of them. _____ (Mom/Dad/Mom and dad) will need to take care of this little one inside the safe place."*

Allow time for the child to draw his or her parent(s) into the picture. If the child has made a visual representation, say the following:

Say, *"Where could you add _____ (mom/dad/mom and dad) to the picture, taking care of the little one?"*

_____

_____

Encourage the parent and child to be physically close, if it is comfortable for both of them. Sometimes younger children will sit on their parent's lap.

> Say to the child, *"I would like you to relax now with your _____ (mom/dad/parents)."*
>
> Say to the child, *"You may place the buzzers in your hands, socks, or pockets. What would you prefer?"*

_____

Alternatively, say to the child, *"Is it OK if I tap on your hands or on your knees? Which would you prefer?"*

_____

_____

> Say to the child, *"Picture the smaller you in this wonderful safe, calm, enjoyable place and _____ (describe the details of the created safe place)."*

Implement slow, tactile BLS through the duration of your verbal description.

_____

_____

> Say to the parent(s), *"_____ (Mom/Dad/Mom and dad), can you picture yourself, there, with the littler _____ (state child's name) in the safe place today? Tell us what you are doing there, for the little _____ (state child's name) today."*

Implement slow, tactile BLS throughout the parent's description of his or her nurturing actions in the inner child's safe place.

_____

_____

If the parent(s) give(s) a short answer, continue to probe and ask questions to elicit more description.

> Say to the parent(s), *"What will you do if the littler _____ (state child's name) feels uncomfortable or distressed?"*

Implement slow, tactile BLS throughout the parent's description.

_____

_____

> Say to the parent(s), *"What will you do to have fun with the smaller _____ (state child's name)?"*

Implement slow, tactile BLS throughout the parent's description.

_____

_____

> Say to the parent(s), *"What will you do when the littler _____ (state child's name) gets tired?"*

Implement slow, tactile BLS throughout the parent's description.

_____

_____

Say to the child, *"Notice the feelings of closeness and the feelings of calm inside your body right now. Notice the feelings of connection, warmth, and safety."*

Implement slow, tactile BLS as the therapist guides the child's thoughts.

_____

_____

Songs for Younger Children Script

Initially talk with the parent(s) individually while the young child plays or draws on the floor.

Say, *"Song, rhythm, and movement are soothing and regulating for the developing nervous system of young children. When children are soothed by their parents, their sense of security and connection with their parents grows. Furthermore, right–left stimulation, an important component of EMDR Therapy, assists with integration of the emotional and cognitive regions of the brain. We are going to combine both today to help your child. An easy and fun way to do this is through simple tunes that we all know and love along with simple lyrics that will help your child feel loved. A good way for you to engage your child in the song and provide bilateral stimulation is to place your child on your lap facing me, swaying side-to-side with him in rhythm with the song. I'll lead the song and you can join in. Often children will catch on and join in as well."*

Say to the child, *"_____ (child's name), we're going to sing a fun song today. Feel free to bring the _____ (stuffed animal or other toy) to hold while we sing. Come up on your _____ (mom's/dad's) lap. OK, here we go!"*

Sample lyrics to the tune of "Wheels on the Bus":

Say,
*"Mommy and Daddy love you so, love you so, love you so,
Mommy and Daddy love you so, each and every day.
Mommy and Daddy keep you safe, keep you safe, keep you safe,
Mommy and Daddy keep you safe, each and every day.
Mommy and Daddy give you hugs, give you hugs, give you hugs,
Mommy and Daddy give you hugs, each and every day."*

Say to the parent, *"You can sing and sway with your child at home as much as you like. Feel free to make up a variety of lyrics with your own favorite tunes. Young children need repeated experiences of soothing and closeness over time to develop a calm and regulated nervous system and feelings of security and connection with parents."*

Self-Regulation Development and Installation

S-RDI Script

The EMDR therapist or family therapist can best prepare the child for S-RDI by teaching "belly breath" when the child is calm.

Say, *"I'm going to teach you and your parents a way to calm your body and your brain. We call this method 'belly breath.' The more any of us practices belly breath, the easier it is to keep our bodies and our brains calm. Let's all lie back comfortably together and put a hand on our bellies like this. As you take a breath, let your belly fill up with air. You can feel it with your hand. Let it go, and now feel the air leave your belly. Continue breathing in this way, and let your body relax."*

Therapist, parent, and child all begin taking slow breaths, filling the diaphragm with air on the inhale and blowing it out slowly on the exhale.

The EMDR therapist implements S-RDI when children become irritable or fidgety.

Say, *"I notice that you are getting fidgety/irritable. Can you tell me what is going on?"*

_____

_____

Say, *"OK, this gives us an opportunity to help you practice finding your calm feelings."*

Hand the child the tactile pulsars or get positioned to tap on the child's legs or feet.

Say, *"The tapping will help your body learn and remember the feeling of going from fidgety/irritable to calm. One of the first things I do when I get fidgety/irritable is take big belly breaths."*

Say to the parent(s), *"Do belly breaths help you when you get fidgety?"*

_____

_____

Say, *"Let's all take five big belly breaths together. Notice what happens in your body with five big belly breaths. Remember, breathe in and fill your belly with air like a big balloon."*

Implement BLS throughout your discourse while you say the following:

Say, *"I can see your body is relaxing. Pay attention to how it feels in your body as you continue taking big breaths. You are helping your body go from an upset/fidgety feeling to a more relaxed feeling. That's right, continue to breathe nice and slow with me, in, and out."*

Stop the BLS.

Say, *"Are you completely relaxed, or is there still some upset/wiggly feeling there?"*

_____

_____

If the child remains slightly dysregulated, say the following:

Say, *"Another important way for you to relax is by talking to your brain. This is sometimes called self-talk. For instance, when I get the 'I can't wait' feelings and get fidgety, I tell my brain, 'It's OK, this will be done soon. I can handle it.'"*

Say to the parent/s, "_____ (Mom/Dad/Mom and dad), *what do you say to your brain to help when you get fidgety?"*

_____

_____

Say to the child, *"What can you say to your brain right now that might help?"*

_____

_____

Implement the BLS throughout while you say the following:

Say, *"Excellent. Talk to your brain right now and notice what happens. Tell your brain* _____ (remind the child what he/she can say to his/her brain). *Notice how it feels in your body and your brain, as your brain slows down, your body slows down, and you feel more relaxed. That's right, keep breathing, all the way into your belly. Talk to your brain. Notice how good it feels as your body relaxes."*

Phase Three: Assessment

Say, *"When you remember what happened, what is the most upsetting part?"*

_____

_____

Say, *"What is the picture that is stuck in your brain?"*

_____

_____

It is sometimes easier for children to identify their emotions before identifying the NC. Show the child a list of feelings or pictures of feelings faces.

Say, *"Look at these faces and point to any faces that match the way you feel when you see that picture in your brain."*

_____

_____

If the child still has difficulty, say the following:

Say to the parent(s), "_____ (Mom/Dad/Mom and dad), *what would you feel if this had happened to you when you were a child?"*

_____

_____

Say to the child, *"Could this be a feeling you have inside?"*

_____

_____

Identify the NC.

Say, *"What is the _____ (state the sad/mad/scared/confused, etc.) thought that goes with that feeling?"*

_____

_____

If the child still has difficulty,

Say to the parent(s), *"_____ (Mom/Dad/Mom and Dad), what would you think if you were a child and you had gone through something like this?"*

_____

_____

Say, *"Do you have a thought like that?"*

_____

_____

Identify the PC:

Say, *"Let's come up with a thought that would be more helpful. Can you think of one? Even though it might not feel very true to you right now, see if you can come up with something that is opposite to your upset thought."*

_____

_____

If the child needs some extra assistance, say the following:

Say to the parent, *"_____ (Mom/Dad/Mom and Dad), what thought would you want _____ (state child's name) to have instead of the upset thought?"*

_____

_____

Say to the child, *"Would that be a helpful thought? Remember, it's OK if it doesn't feel true to you, right now."*

_____

_____

Say, *"Let's check how true it feels right now. When you see that picture in your brain, how true does it seem to you, down inside, to say _____ (repeat PC)?"*

"Completely true?" (Therapist spreads hands wide.)

"Pretty true?" (Therapist moves hands closer together.)

"Just a little true?" (Therapist holds hands close together.)

_____

_____

Say, *"Right now when you think of the picture and the upset thought _____ (repeat the NC), how big is the upset feeling?"*

"The biggest upset feeling ever?" (Therapist spreads hands wide.)

"Pretty big?" (Therapist moves hands closer together.)

"Just a little upset feeling?" (Therapist holds hands closer together.)

_____

_____

Say, *"Where do you notice the upset in your body? Let's look for it together. Pay attention to how it feels in your head, face, jaw, neck, and gradually notice all the way down your body."*

_____

_____

If the child is not aware of any feelings in his body and he is sitting near the parent, say the following:

Say to the parent(s), *"If it's OK with you both, I would like you to put your arm around your child. As you do so, notice if there is any tension in _____ (his/her) back, shoulders, or neck. What do you notice?"*

_____

_____

Phase 4: Desensitization

Say, *"Remember, you are safe here with your _____ (mom/dad/parents) and me, and you can have any feelings or thoughts today and be OK. It's normal to want to push those feelings and thoughts away, but then they stay stuck inside. If you can just let your feelings and thoughts pop up without pushing them away, as you watch my fingers, we can help those feelings and thoughts get better so they aren't stuck anymore. Bring up the picture and your upset thought _____ (repeat the NC). Also notice that place in your body. Now follow my fingers."*

Alternatively, say, *"I am going to run the buzzers/tap."*
Add BLS.

"Take a breath, now let it go. What is there? Is there anything in your brain or in your body?"

_____

_____

Desensitizing Early Traumatic Memories: The Rescue Interweave

An appropriate time to implement the rescue interweave is during the Desensitization Phase when the child is experiencing sudden intense feelings of helplessness or fear that does not shift with further eye movements or changes in direction or speed.

Say to the parent(s), *"If right this minute, you could jump into a time machine that would take you back in time, and you could land right in the middle of this situation, what would you do? You have permission to help in any way you wish."*

_____
_____

Note: Typically, the parent describes rescuing the child and taking the child to a safe place, protecting the child in some other way, or removing or intervening with the perpetrator figure. Implement BLS as the parent describes the rescue.

_____
_____

Say to the child, *"Take a breath and let it go. What is there now? Is there something in your brain or in your body?"*

_____
_____

Say, *"Go with that."*

Resume BLS and continue reprocessing. When the child's SUD is 0 or 1, or slightly higher, if deemed ecological, begin installation. See Phase 5: Installation.

Desensitizing Present Triggers: Interweaves to Separate the Present From the Past

An appropriate time to implement this interweave is when a child is stuck and looping in the feelings and negative beliefs associated with a present-day trigger during EMDR desensitization.

After another set of BLS, say the following:

Say to the child, *"Do you think this feeling* _____ (repeat child's feeling) *and this upset thought* _____ (repeat the NC) *might be stuck in your brain from those earlier experiences we talked about?"*

_____
_____

If the child agrees, say the following:

Say to the child, *"The little you inside may not understand that the past is over, even though the bigger you does understand. How is your* _____ (life/parent/home) *today different from your* _____ (life/parent/home) *in the past?"*

_____
_____

Say, *"What could you say to the smaller child inside to help* _____ (him/her) *understand?"*

_____
_____

Say, *"Go with that."* Resume eye movements.

Turn to the parent(s) and say, *"What do you want the littler _____ (state child's name) to know?"*

_____
_____

Say, *"Go with that."* Continue the Standard EMDR Protocol to desensitize the current trigger.

_____
_____

Phase 5: Installation

To begin installation, the EMDR therapist checks on the appropriateness of the PC, using child-friendly language.

Say, *"Remember the helpful thought, _____ (repeat the PC). Is that still the best thought, or do you think there might be a better thought?"*

_____
_____

If the child indicates that he might prefer a different thought, say the following:

Say, *"What would be a more helpful thought? It might be a thought you had during our work today."*

_____
_____

Say, *"When you think of what happened, how true does _____ (repeat the PC) feel right now?"*

"Completely true?" (Therapist spreads hands wide.)

"Pretty true?" (Therapist moves hands closer together.)

"Just a little true?" (Therapist holds hands close together.)

_____
_____

Say, *"Hold the thought with the memory and watch my fingers."*

_____
_____

Continue with installation until the PC feels completely true to the child.

Phase 6: Body Scan

Say, *"Keep the helpful thought in your mind with the memory, and let's check your body for any uncomfortable feelings. Let's start with your head, move down into your face, your jaw, and your neck. Notice your shoulders, your chest, your stomach, your arms, and your hands. Did you find anything?"*

_____

_____

If the child notices any disturbing residual body sensations, resume eye movements until the sensations are eliminated.

If the child notices any pleasant sensations, repeat a set of BLS to reinforce the positive sensation.

Phase 7: Closure

If the session is incomplete, say the following:

Say, *"What is the most helpful idea that you have had about this memory so far?"*

_____

_____

Say, *"Just hold that thought in mind while you watch my fingers one more time."* Implement one set of slow eye movements to reinforce the helpful idea.

If the session is complete or incomplete, say the following:

Say, *"You worked hard today. Remember that there is no need to continue to think about today's session. You are free to go home and play and learn and have a good week. Leave this and any upsetting past memories here in the _____ (use any container image that is useful for the child, such as a file cabinet). But let your parent/s know if anything bothers you this week."*

Additionally, the child can be asked to bring up a safe place or other resource, or the therapist can invite the child and parent to play a short game to help reinforce feelings of safety and connection.

Say, *"If you would like, bring up _____ (remind child of safe place or other resource)."*

_____

Phase 8: Reevaluation

In the follow-up session, begin without the child in the room.

Say to the parent, *"Was there any indication from your child's behaviors this last week that _____ (he/she) was experiencing any thoughts or feelings related to the last session?"*

_____

_____

If the session from the previous week was left incomplete, or the parent's observations indicate the child may have continued processing the material, the EMDR therapist says the following:

Say, *"I would like you to think back on the memory we worked on last week. Today, when you think about what happened, what feelings do you notice?"*

_____

_____

Say, *"How big are your feelings today? Show me with your hands—big* (hands held wide), *medium, or small* (moving hands closer together).*"*

_____
_____

Say, *"Do you notice any upset inside your body? Start at the top of your head, then check your face, neck, shoulders, chest, stomach, arms, hands."*

_____
_____

Say to the parent(s), *"If it's OK with you both, I'd like you to put your arm around your child and see if you observe any tension in* _____ (his/her) *back, shoulders, or neck."*

_____
_____

Say to the child, *"Bring up the picture, notice the feelings and that place in your body, and follow my fingers."*
Resume reprocessing from desensitization through closure.

Future Template

Future Template Role-Play

Say to the child, *"Let's think back on the incident that triggered those big feelings. I think you might need the skill of* _____ (name a skill such as cooperation, following directions, assertiveness, staying calm, saying no, asking for what you need) *to better handle that situation the next time. I am going to pretend to be you, and I will demonstrate how I would have handled the situation, using this skill."*

Say to the parent(s), *"_____(Mom/Dad/Mom and dad), would you help me role-play so I can demonstrate?"*

_____

Act out the incident with the help of the child's parent, demonstrating an appropriate skill for handling the situation.

Say to the child, *"Now it's your turn to try it. See if you can respond to _____ (Mom/Dad/Mom and dad) the way I just did. The tappers* (handing child the tactile pulsars) *will help your brain remember how to do this."*

Alternatively, say, *"If it's OK, I would like to tap on your ____ (knees/shoulders) to help your brain remember how to do this."*

Add relatively slow, bilateral, tactile stimulation throughout the child's demonstration of the skill.

Say, *"You acted so grown-up just now. How do you feel inside right now?"*

_____
_____

Say, *"Just notice those great feelings."*

Repeat the slow bilateral tactile stimulation.

Summary

Children who have suffered attachment trauma due to maltreatment, neglect, separations, losses, and caregiver changes have difficulty trusting adults, accepting comfort, recognizing and managing their feelings, and managing their behaviors. They carry deep-seated negative beliefs about themselves, others, and their world. Relationships are natural triggers for mistrust and fear. Parents are frequently overwhelmed by the child's behaviors, and they may resort to punitive disciplinary tactics, which only escalate the child's emotional and behavioral dysregulation. Families are frequently desperate for help.

The Integrative Team Treatment approach is designed to improve the child's behaviors and relationship in the most efficient way possible. Creating a two-therapist team allows the EMDR therapist to implement EMDR Therapy weekly, while a family therapist coaches parents and children in new skills and patterns of interaction. ARD and S-RDI with parent involvement during the preparation stage increase the child's sense of security and capacity for self-regulation. Involving parents during work with memories, triggers, and templates helps children move from feelings of loneliness, mistrust, and fear to feelings of connection, security, and safety.

References

Attachment and Trauma Center of Nebraska. (2011). *EMDR integrative team treatment for attachment trauma in children: Treatment manual.* Omaha, NE: Author.

Ide, N., & Paez, A. (2000). Complex PTSD: A review of current issues. *International Journal of Emergency Mental Health, 2,* 43–49.

Lovett, J. (2009, October). *Using EMDR to treat trauma and attachment in children and adults.* Paper presented at the Attachment and Trauma Center of Nebraska, EMDR Specialty Workshop by Joan Lovett and Debra Wesselmann, Omaha, NE.

Madrid, A., Skolek, S., & Shapiro, F. (2006). Repairing failures in bonding through EMDR. *Clinical Case Studies, 5,* 271–286.

Potter, A., Davidson, M., & Wesselmann, D. (2013). Utilizing dialectical behavior therapy and eye movement desensitization and reprocessing as phase-based trauma treatment: A case study series. In L. C. Stewart (Ed.), Eye movement: Developmental perspectives, dysfunctions, and disorders in humans (pp. 49–72). New York, NY: Nova Publishers.

Robredo, J. (2011, June). *EMDR and gender violence: Brief and intensive treatment for children exposed to gender violence.* Paper presented at the annual meeting of the EMDR Europe Association, Vienna, Austria.

Taylor, R. J. (2002). Family unification with reactive attachment disorder: A brief treatment. *Contemporary Family Therapy: An International Journal, 24,* 475–481.

van der Kolk, B. (2005). Developmental trauma disorder: Toward a rational diagnosis for children with complex trauma histories. *Psychiatric Annals, 35*(5), 401–408.

van der Kolk, B. A., Pelcovitz, D., Roth, S., Mandel, F. S., McFarlane, A. C., & Herman, J. L. (1996). Dissociation, somatization, and affect regulation: The complexity of adaptation to trauma. *American Journal of Psychiatry, 153*(7), 83–93.

Wesselmann, D. (2013). Healing trauma and creating secure attachments with EMDR. In M. Solomon & D. S. Siegel (Eds.), *Healing moments in psychotherapy: Mindful awarenss, neural integration, and therapeutic presence* (pp. 115–128). New York, NY: Norton.

Wesselmann, D., Schweitzer, C., & Armstrong, S. (2014a). *Integrative team treatment for attachment trauma: Family therapy and EMDR.* New York, NY: W.W. Norton.

Wesselmann, D., Schweitzer, C., & Armstrong, S. (2014b). *Integrative parenting: Strategies for raising children affected by attachment trauma.* New York, NY: W.W. Norton.

Wesselmann, D., & Shapiro, F. (2013). EMDR and the treatment of complex trauma in children and adolescents. In J. Ford & C. Courtois (Eds.), *Treating complex traumatic stress disorders in children and adolescents* (pp. 203–224). New York, NY: Guilford Press.

Wesselmann, D., & Potter, A. E. (2009). Change in adult attachment status following treatment with EMDR: Three case studies. *Journal of EMDR Practice and Research, 3,* 178–191.

Wesselmann, S., Davidson, M., Armstrong, S., Schweitzer, C., Bruckner, D., & Potter, A. (2012). EMDR as a treatment for improving attachment status in adults and children. *European Review of Applied Psychology, 62,* 223–230.

SUMMARY SHEET:
Child Attachment Trauma Protocol

Debra Wesselmann, Cathy Schweitzer,
and Stefanie Armstrong
SUMMARY SHEET BY MARILYN LUBER

Name: _____ Diagnosis: _____

Medications: _____

Test Results: _____

☑ Check when task is completed, response has changed, or to indicate symptoms.

Note: This material is meant as a checklist for your response. Please keep in mind that it is only a reminder of different tasks that may or may not apply to your incident.

Treating Attachment Trauma in Children Protocol Script

Phase 1: Client History

Child's problematic behaviors and symptoms: _____

_____

_____

_____

_____

Child's strengths: _____

_____

_____

_____

Child's distressing or traumatic events (physical, sexual, or emotional abuse; neglect, losses, and major changes; witnessing of domestic abuse or drug or alcohol abuse by parents; accidents, medical interventions, or changes in caregivers): _____

_____

_____

_____

_____

Prenatal/postnatal issues (drug exposure, domestic violence during pregnancy/postpartum depression): _____

_____

_____

List of hypothesized NCs (defectiveness, responsibility, safety, control, parents/other, and love/belongingness): _____

_____

_____

Previous therapeutic/psychiatric treatment and outcome: _____

_____

_____

_____

Health concerns now or in past: _____

_____

_____

_____

Current medications including OTC meds: _____

_____

_____

_____

How parent(s) is coping: _____

_____

_____

_____

Traits parent(s) enjoy about child: _____

_____

_____

_____

Positive attitudes and behaviors parent(s) want for child: _____

_____

_____

_____

Case Conceptualization

The EMDR therapist and family therapist write down the following from the child's history:

- ☐ Potential EMDR targets
- ☐ Current triggers that seem to precipitate aggression, defiance, or other symptoms or behaviors. Hypothesized NCs associated with the child's traumas and triggers
- ☐ Identify needed skills related to self-awareness, self-regulation, socializing, and communicating. The skills list is a working plan for psycho-education and skills work that can be conducted by the family therapist and reinforced by the EMDR therapist through future templates

Phase 2: Preparation Phase: Attachment Resource Development

☐ *Messages of Love Script*—to create an experience of closeness and connection between child and parents

Note the positive messages: _____

_____

☐ *Playing Baby Exercise*—(usually 7 and younger) therapist reinforces child's feelings of shared pleasure and closeness with parents using BLS.

Note child's and parents' responses to the exercise: _____

_____

☐ *Magical Cord of Love Exercise*—positive image of connection through the cord of love is reinforced with BLS to assist the child with insecure attachment in trusting that the parent's love is always present.

Note child's description of the cord: _____

_____

☐ *Circle of Caring Exercise*—heightens the child's awareness of the people who love and care about him in his present-day life, and BLS reinforces associated feelings of safety, security, and belonging. Can be conducted easily with children and adolescents who are residing in nonpermanent foster care or residential placements.

Note names of individuals in the child's circle: _____

_____

☐ *Safe Place for the Inner Child Script*—for working with "the smaller child within." Involves creating a safe or comfortable place for the inner child and prompting parents to describe how they imagine caring for the inner child there in the safe place. The exercise helps create inner feelings of safety and helps stabilize children with varying degrees of dissociation. Show nesting dolls while explaining that everyone carries the thoughts and feelings they experienced as a young child somewhere inside themselves. Later access imagery whenever needed to reinforce feelings of safety and nurturance for the inner child.

Note the child's description of the place: _____

_____

☐ *Songs for Younger Children*—combine music and rhythm with BLS to reinforce feelings of pleasure, safety, and security between children and their parents. Make up lyrics that provide the positive messages children need to hear.

Note tunes or words: _____

_____

☐ *Self-Regulation Development and Installation*—resource work specifically intended to reinforce the child's experience of self-efficacy in moving from a dysregulated state to a regulated state. Helpful when a child becomes anxious for the session to be over, irritated over some small annoyance, or compelled to pick at his skin or bite his nails.

Note child's response: _____

_____

Phase 3 Assessment

Note: Get emotion before cognition

☐ Target: _____

Picture/Image: _____

Emotions: *"Look at these faces and point to any faces that match the way you feel when you see that picture in your brain"* _____

If there is difficulty, ask parent(s) how they would feel if this happened to him/her when a child.

Negative Cognition: _____

If there is difficulty, ask parent(s) how they would think if this happened to him/her when a child.

Positive Cognition: _____

Validity of Cognition:
    ☐ Completely true? (Spread hands wide)
    ☐ Pretty true? (Hands closer)
    ☐ Just a little true? (Hands close together)

Subjective Units of Disturbance:
    ☐ The biggest feeling ever? (Spread hands wide)
    ☐ Pretty big? (Hands closer)
    ☐ Just a little upset feeling? (Hands close together)

Location of Body Sensation: _____

If there is difficulty, ask parent(s) to put arm around child and notice if tension is in back, shoulders, or neck.

Phase 4: Desensitization

To child: *"Remember, you are safe here with your* _____ (mom/dad/parents) *and me, and you can have any feelings or thoughts today and be OK. It's normal to want to push those feelings and thoughts away, but then they stay stuck inside. If you can just let your feelings and thoughts pop up without pushing them away, as you watch my fingers, we can help those feelings and thoughts get better so they aren't stuck anymore. Bring up the picture and your upset thought* _____ (repeat the NC). *Also notice that place in your body. Now follow my fingers."*

Desensitizing Early Traumatic Memories: The Rescue Interweave

Use when child is experiencing sudden intense feelings of helplessness or fear that do not shift with further eye movements or changes in direction or speed.

To parent(s): *"If right this minute, you could jump into a time machine that would take you back in time, and you could land right in the middle of this situation, what would you do? You have permission to help in any way you wish."*

Parent describes rescuing the child and taking the child to a safe place, protecting the child in some other way, or removing or intervening with the perpetrator figure. Implement BLS as the parent describes the rescue.

Desensitizing Present Triggers: Interweaves to Separate the Present From the Past

Use when a child is stuck and looping in the feelings and negative beliefs associated with a present-day trigger

"Do you think this feeling _____ (repeat child's feeling) *and this upset thought* _____ (repeat the NC) *might be stuck in your brain from those earlier experiences we talked about?"*

If child agrees: *"The little you inside may not understand that the past is over, even though the bigger you does understand. How is your* _____ (life/parent/home) *today different from your* _____ (life/parent/home) *in the past?"*

To child: *"What could you say to the smaller child inside to help* _____ (him/her) *understand?"* Add BLS.

To parent(s): *"What do you want the littler* _____ (state child's name) *to know?"*

Add BLS.

Phase 5: Installation

PC: ☐ Completed

New PC (if new one is better): _____

Validity of Cognition:
    ☐ Completely true? (Spread hands wide)
    ☐ Pretty true? (Hands closer)
    ☐ Just a little true? (Hands close together)

Incident + PC + BLS

Continue Installation with BLS until material becomes and feels completely true to the child.

Phase 6: Body Scan ☐ Completed

> *"Keep the helpful thought in your mind with the memory, and let's check your body for any uncomfortable feelings. Let's start with your head, move down into your face, your jaw, and your neck. Notice your shoulders, your chest, your stomach, your arms, and your hands. Did you find anything?"*

Note: If child reports any disturbing body sensations, resume BLS. If notices pleasant sensations, repeat a set of BLS.

Phase 7: Closure ☐ Completed

Most helpful idea about this memory: _____

_____

+ BLS

> *"You worked hard today. Remember that there is no need to continue to think about today's session. You are free to go home and play and learn and have a good week. Leave this and any upsetting past memories here in my _____ (use any container image that is useful for the child, such as a file cabinet). But let your parent(s) know if anything bothers you this week."*

Bring up Safe Place or other resource as needed.

Phase 8: Reevaluation ☐ Completed

Parent's report of child's behaviors related to last session: _____

_____

_____

If incomplete session, ask what is noticed: _____

_____

Subjective Units of Disturbance:

☐ The biggest feeling ever? (Spread hands wide)

☐ Pretty big? (Hands closer)

☐ Just a little upset feeling? (Hands close together)

Location of Body Sensation: _____

If there is difficulty, ask parent(s) to put arm around child and notice if tension is in back, shoulders, or neck.

Future Template

Future Template Role Play

Script: *"Let's think back on the incident that triggered those big feelings. I think you might need the skill of _____ (name a skill such as cooperation, following directions, assertiveness, staying calm, saying no, asking for what you need) to better handle that situation the next time. I am going to pretend to be you, and I will demonstrate how I would have handled the situation, using this skill."*

To parent(s) _____ (mom/dad/mom and dad), *"would you help me role-play so I can demonstrate?"*

Act out the incident with the help of the child's parent, demonstrating an appropriate skill for handling the situation

To the child, *"Now it's your turn to try it. See if you can respond to _____ (mom/dad/mom and dad) the way I just did. The tappers (handing child the tactile pulsars) will help your brain remember how to do this."*

Alternatively, say, *"If it's OK, I would like to tap on your _____ (knees/shoulders) to help your brain remember how to do this."*

Use slow BLS.

To child: *"You acted so grown-up just now. How do you feel inside right now?"*

Then: *"Just notice those great feelings."*

Repeat BLS

Working on Attachment Issues With EMDR Therapy: The Attachment Protocol

Anna Rita Verardo and Maria Zaccagnino

Introduction and Theoretical Background

The Attachment and Caregiving Systems

The theoretical framework that guides this protocol is John Bowlby's *Attachment Theory*. Bowlby (1969, 1973, 1980) stresses that attachment is an innate predisposition that moves children to seek protective closeness of their attachment figure in response to real or perceived stress or danger. Furthermore, Bowlby proposed that, in parallel with *the attachment system*, the parent(s) develop *the caregiving system*. The goals of the caregiving system are to provide protection to children; promote the closeness and well-being of children; and comfort children in moments of difficulty, distress, or danger. The two systems operate in a balanced dynamic: When separation from the attachment figure becomes excessive (in terms of time and/or distance), the attachment system is activated and children seek to obtain sufficient closeness with their attachment figure. In this condition, children show different attachment behaviors in order to activate the caregiver system in the parent(s) and ensure protective closeness with them. The deactivation of the attachment system promotes the activation of *the exploratory system* (Cassidy & Shaver, 2008). According to Bowlby (1969), attachment behaviors are ultimately guided at a cognitive level by internal representation, or Internal Working Models (IWMs), based on the generalization and differentiation of children's experiences, which will then extend to later social interactions. The development of the IWM, therefore, is intimately linked to children's experiences of interaction with the attachment figures; they are based on the sensitivity, responsiveness, stability, and attention that the adult supplies in response to children's requests. The quality of attachment that an infant develops with a specific caregiver, therefore, is largely determined by the caregiver's response to the infant when the infant's attachment system is "activated."

The theory emphasizes the fact that a child's emotional, cognitive, and social development is largely influenced by the quality of his early relationships with caregivers (Cassidy & Shaver, 2008; Main, 1995). Bowlby (1980) suggests that a sensitive and prompt response by the caregiver is linked to the possibility of the child developing a positive representation of self, other, and self-with-others relationship. The child goes on to internalize a representation of himself as being worthy of love, and a representation of the other (the attachment figure) as a person who is accessible in moments of difficulty. In contrast, children whose primary attachment figures fail to respond in an empathic way to their needs tend to perceive themselves as unworthy of care. Main and Hesse (1990) hypothesize that an attachment figure, who has experienced negative life events (such as a loss or trauma), might behave in ways that show the child that the caregiver is either frightened or frightening.

This can result in the dysregulation of the infant in relation to the caregiver, leading to disorganization of the infant's attachment strategy.

Patterns of Attachment

Mary Ainsworth (Ainsworth, Blehar, Waters, & Wall, 1978) addressed the issue of the attachment construct through the use of the Strange Situation Procedure. She identified three main patterns of attachment:

- *Secure style:* In relation to the caregiver, the child experiences a warm, affectionate, and sensitive interaction. Both share an emotional closeness, where the parent understands all the child's cues and responds in a consistent and appropriate manner. Children who have this kind of experience will develop a sense of themselves as being worthy of love, and an image of the caregiver as being willing and able to help in difficult moments. Their relationship will be cooperative and satisfying to both of them. A secure relationship will make it possible for the child to build a perception of the world as a place where it is possible to find caring people to whom he can turn in moments of difficulty.
- *Avoidant style:* These children have experienced interaction with their attachment figures in which their requests were easily ignored. As a result, they have learned that the only strategy for survival is to deactivate their attachment behavior. These children show strong features of independence, even at a very early age, and they tend to be strongly oriented toward exploration.
- *Ambivalent style:* The interaction between children with this pattern of attachment and their caregivers is characterized by an extreme closeness with the attachment figure, a strong anxiety in times of separation, and difficulty in being comforted. These children have learned from the very beginning that the presence of the caregiver is inconsistent and unpredictable, so they overactivate the attachment system in an attempt to catch the caregiver's attention and guarantee as much closeness as possible. They have difficulty in activating the exploration system and they stay very close to their parents.

A fourth model, identified later by Main and Solomon (1990), is defined as disorganized:

- *Disorganized style*: It is used to describe the disorganization of the strategies and attachment behavior seen in a considerable minority of children during the Strange Situation Procedure (Ainsworth et al., 1978). This category consists of children who do not seem to have an organized strategy to deal with the stress of separation and reunion with their attachment figure during the procedure. They behave in inconsistent and contradictory ways (like freezing, for example), which do not seem intended to achieve any particular goal. Liotti (1992, 2004) hypothesized that the experience of being cared for by a frightened/frightening parent could result in a tendency to build multiple and mutually incompatible representations of self-with-other relationship, leading to the drama triangle representations of "rescuer," "persecutor," and "victim."

The Adult Attachment Interview and the Parental State of Mind

The Adult Attachment Interview (AAI; George, Kaplan, & Main, 1985) is a semi-structured interview whose purpose is to assess the representations of the parent in relation to his or her own earliest attachment experiences (Hesse, 1999). Questions are asked about infant–parent relationship; moments of vulnerability, like illness, physical hurts, or emotional upsets; possible major separation; experiences of rejection; significant loss; and possible episodes of abuse. Other questions are asked to help subjects to reflect on the influences that early infancy experiences may have had on their adult personality, on which experiences may have constituted obstacles to growth, and, finally, on what the subjects think might have caused their parents to behave in the way they did.

Main, Kaplan, and Cassidy (1985) identified five categories that reflect the state of mind with regard to attachment relationships during infancy: *secure/autonomous, dismissing, entangled/preoccupied, unresolved,* and *cannot classify.*

- *Secure/autonomous*: The first group includes those subjects whose narrative is sufficiently *consistent*, whether or not the subject is able to describe both positive and negative experiences. The memories are concrete and fit into context, showing a capacity for free exploration of their own thoughts and feelings throughout the interview (Hesse, 1999).
- *Dismissing:* The second group, the *dismissing* ones, is characterized by an idealizing narrative, which is in contrast to negative memories and episodes described in the course of the interview—or with recourse to generalization in the absence of specific memories. So, in reference to attachment, members of this group tend to show a state of mind that is centered on an attempt to affirm their *independence*, minimizing any possible negative effects of their early experiences (Main, Kaplan, & Cassidy, 1985). There is continuous violation of Grice's maxims (1989, see subsequently), especially with regard to quantity and quality.
- *Preoccupied*: The third category, the *preoccupied*, consists of subjects whose narrative is inconsistent and often irrelevant, indicating that the IWMs oscillate between positive and negative representations of the attachment emotions regarding themselves and others. Overall, they appear to still be involved with the dynamics of attachment: they appear angry, passive, or frightened in their initial relationships, and these experiences have an effect on the quality of their narrative—which in turn shows frequent violation of Grice's maxims (particularly in terms of relation, manner, and quantity; see later).
- *Unresolved:* Those subjects who display an *unresolved* state of mind, bringing up potentially traumatic memories, for instance, mourning, fail to monitor their discourse or their reasoning; for example, they might refer to a dead person as if the person were still alive.
- *Cannot classify*: Finally, the *cannot classify* category refers to those subjects whose representations are incompatible and contradictory. This last group is often associated with stories of violence, abuse, and psychiatric disturbances (Hesse, 1999).

Grice's Conversational Maxims

Herbert Paul Grice was a philosopher of language who was interested in the nature of meaning. He was interested in the idea of *coherence*, which is ordinarily identified as a connectedness of thought such that different parts of the discourse are clearly related, form a logical unit, and are congruent and adapted to the context. However, Grice (1989) provided a more formal definition of the requirements of coherence of the discourse and formulated a general principle (called the Cooperative Principle) that guides participants involved in a conversation. From this comprehensive Cooperative Principle emerge four maxims: quantity, quality, relation, and manner.

Because the AAI could be viewed as a discourse, Grice's (1989) conversational maxims can be helpful in providing more detailed comprehension of the coherence of the narrative or clients' responses to the AAI. Following are some examples of violation of coherence that can be found within narratives that can be useful in understanding the nature of a person's attachment style:

- *The maxim of quantity*: "Provide the information that is necessary; neither too much nor too little."

Examples of violation of the quantity maxim: Speakers who give far more information than is necessary and appear to be lost in their own memories often have a *preoccupied* style that is observed in their texts.

Another example of this maxim is when an interviewee chooses to or cannot answer a specific question and responds by saying, "I don't remember." This response illustrates a *dismissing* style.

- *The maxim of quality:* "*Be sincere; tell the truth as you see it.*"
Example of violation of the quality maxim: When there is a contradiction between the abstract or semantic description of attachment figures and descriptions of specific episodes involving those persons (e.g., a speaker states that the mother was "very loving," but reports episodes of rejection or maltreatment). This is often a characteristic of speakers with *dismissing* styles.
- *The maxim of relation:* "*Be pertinent.*"
Example of violation of the relation maxim: The speaker departs from interview topic, for example, by using free associations. This violation is typical of speakers with *preoccupied* styles.
- *The maxim of manner:* "*Be clear.*"
Example of violation of the maxim of manner: When the speaker uses quotations from others without making it clear that a quotation is about to be offered or has the tendency to start a sentence and does not finish it. This violation is typical of speakers with *preoccupied* styles.

Intergenerational Transmission of Attachment

From the point of view of attachment theory, the mother's ability to form consistent, positive, and flexible representations of her child, of their relationship, and of their feelings develops within the mother–child dynamic (Fonagy & Target, 2001; George & Solomon, 1996). This capacity, called *Reflective Function* (RF), is the ability of the adult to mentalize and to understand that behavior—everyone's behavior—is a reflection of underlying mental states, like feelings, desires, thoughts, and intentions (Fonagy, Target, Steele, & Steele, 1998). Maternal RF plays a central role in the development of the child's attachment and, in this regard, can be considered a central mechanism in the intergenerational transmission of attachment (Fonagy, Gergely, Jurist, & Target, 2002; Fonagy et al., 1995). Research has shown a clear correlation between the mental representations of the parent (assessed through the AAI) and the attachment IWM of the child (assessed through the Strange Situation Procedure) (Hesse, 1999; van IJzendoorn, 1992, 1995).

Researchers who have studied intergenerational transmission of attachment have further discovered that the effects of trauma also are transmitted in the course of the affective and communicative contacts within the parent–child relationship. The manner in which the parent cares for the child is linked to the implicit traces of past traumas, and, by means of this mechanism, these will be transmitted to the child as well.

Measures

In order to assess multidimensional information about the client's life history, questions are drawn from the following instruments:

- *The AAI* (see earlier discussion).
- *The Parent Development Interview* (PDI; Aber, Slade, Berger, Bresgi, & Kaplan, 1985; Slade, Grienenberger, Bernbach, Levy, & Locker, 2005). This is a semi-structured clinical interview that consists of 45 items, designed to evaluate the IWM of the caregivers, the relations with the children, and the parental role. In other words, it reveals the types of representations parents build of themselves as caregivers, of

the child, and of their relationship. In the course of the interview, the subjects are asked to focus on the present, to describe their modalities of response to the child's cues, and to describe how they see themselves in their roles as parents and what emotions they feel. They are also asked about the relationship, with particular attention paid to the moments of joy, moments of difficulties, moments of harmony, and moments of conflict. Then, parents are asked to tell about the child's reactions to normal separations, to changes of habits, or to the unavailability of the parent, and to imagine how the child might be feeling in these situations (Fonagy et al., 1998). The parents' capacity to think reflectively about their children can be assessed using the Reflective-Functioning (RF) Scale when reviewing the transcripts of the AAI and PDI. The RF Scale is operationalized using the range 1 to 9: the higher the number, the more advanced the mentalizing. Moderate to high RF might include characteristics such as the following:

1. An awareness of the nature of mental states
2. An explicit effort to tease out mental state underlying behavior
3. Recognition of the developmental aspects of mental states
4. Recognition of the mental states of the interviewer

Low RF might include characteristics such as the following:

1. The rejection of mental states
2. Unintegrated, bizarre, or inappropriate awareness of mental states
3. Distorted or self-serving understanding of mental states
4. Naïve or simplistic awareness of mental states
5. Overly analytical or hyperactive usage of RF

The RF Scale was studied for use in the PDI as well. It was designed to evaluate the caregiver's ability to openly reflect on complex and often uncomfortable mental states without the overintrusion or the breakdown of defensive processes.

- *Adverse Childhood Experiences (ACE) Scale* (Dube, Felitti, & Rishi, 2013): The fundamental concept behind this instrument is that stressful or traumatic events experienced in the first 18 years of life can have negative effects on the social, emotional, and cognitive aspects of a person's adolescence and adulthood. The questionnaire includes 10 negative life experiences and calculates the score by assigning a score of 1 to each of the client's negative life experiences. The sum of the categories to which a score of 1 has been assigned is the total ACE score.
- *Dissociative Experience Scale* (DES; Bernstein & Putnam, 1986): This is a self-administered scale of 28 items that asks clients to score a range of dissociative experiences they may have had on a scale of 0% to 100%.
- *Difficulties in Emotion Regulation Scale* (DERS; Gratz & Roemer, 2004): This is a 36-item scale evaluating the clients' difficulties in regulating their emotions.

Research

The Efficacy of Eye Movement Desensitization and Reprocessing (EMDR) on the IWM of Attachment: Preliminary Data

According to the Attachment Theory (Bowlby, 1969, 1973, 1980) and Adaptive Information Processing (AIP) (Shapiro, 1995, 2001), negative beliefs, emotions, and sensations related to the numerous and repeated traumatic events experienced by children (such as maltreatment; physical, sexual, or psychological abuse; episodes of rejection and neglect) may be dysfunctionally stored in the brain in memory networks. These images, feelings, and sensations may, in turn, affect the person's behavior and, in particular, the quality of parenting and the subsequent possibility of forming a secure and positive attachment relationship. This mechanism, which is well demonstrated in the attachment literature, is the basis of the intergenerational transmission of attachment and trauma (Fonagy et al., 2002, 1995). Given the devastating effects that the transmission of implicit memories of traumatic events can have on attachment issues, it is important to deeply understand the mechanism influencing the continuity/discontinuity of the IWM and the mechanisms connected to how the cycle of trauma can be broken and how survivors of childhood adversities can move toward good health (Dube et al., 2013).

Research in the attachment field stresses that the possibility of developing a later secure attachment relationship with alternative attachment figures (such as the therapeutic relationship) within an emotional, sensitive, and responsive context may facilitate the development of positive representations of self and others (Saunders, Jacobvitz, Zaccagnino, Loch, & Hazen, 2006; Zaccagnino, Cussino, Saunders, Jacobvitz, & Veglia, 2012) and may help to create a more coherent narrative of the traumatic events that occurred during life (Jacobvitz, Leon, & Hazen, 2006; Egeland, Jacobvitz, & Sroufe, 1988; Fonagy & Target, 2001; Saunders et al., 2006). From this perspective, clients who were categorized as *unresolved* in the AAI and who may have experienced negative life events, such as loss or abuse, may gradually process their personal traumatic memories and change their categorization with respect to their attachment style.

How is it possible to impact and transform these traumatic memories and stop the intergenerational transmission of trauma?

EMDR Therapy is an approach designed to address blockages in the natural information processing system by connecting the dysfunctionally stored traumatic memory(ies) with more adaptive information from other memory networks. In the process of this work, the intergenerational transmission of traumatic and dysfunctional behaviors that affect caregiving representations is interrupted, influencing the future generations in a positive direction.

In light of the literature reported about the importance of attachment-related issues, the primary aim of this pilot study was to explore the role of EMDR Therapy on IWMs of attachment in terms of increased coherence and reflective competences regarding attachment representations through the processing of past traumatic experiences. The objective of this research, therefore, was to examine the use of the EMDR Attachment Protocol developed as the primary treatment modality with 20 clients, who were selected for their primary or secondary *unresolved/disorganized* status of attachment, as measured by the AAI. The AAI transcripts may be classified as primary or secondary unresolved, according to the ratings given to unresolved responses to loss or abuse indices. An adult unresolved attachment status is also assigned in conjunction with a "best fitting alternative" category (F, Ds, or E). Through the use of the AAI, it was possible to identify the state of mind of these clients and verify any posttreatment changes.

The RF Scale was also applied to the AAI transcripts in order to evaluate how a person was able to reflect on his own and others' mental states, and the level of complexity of the person's model of mind(s). Over the span of 1 year, each client was given 10 to 15 sessions, using the EMDR Attachment Protocol.

Results

The results of this study show significant changes in attachment patterns during the course of EMDR treatment with the EMDR Attachment Protocol. In posttreatment, there was a decrease in the number of clients previously classified as primary or secondary unresolved attachment ($n = 13, 65\%$, vs. $n = 0$). The paired *t*-test revealed that this difference between pre- and posttreatment was significant ($t = 3.83, p < .01$). Furthermore, before EMDR treatment, no clients were classified as secure; however, a large percentage (60%, 12 clients) had a secure attachment status after treatment for an alternative preoccupied or dismissing classification, showing a significant difference ($\chi^2 = 7.88, p < .05$). The alternative classification is preserved in order to maintain information present in the transcripts regarding E or D characteristics. Posttreatment scores on the RF Scale show the impact of EMDR treatment on the quality of narrative coherence and the RF of these clients, because these scores, during the posttreatment, were higher than those during the first assessment.

Discussion

The results of this study are in line with the Wesselmann and Potter (2009) study, where there was a significant change in the classification of the participants in this four-way coding system (secure, dismissing, entangled, and unresolved) proposed by Main and Hesse (1990) and Main and Goldwyn (1991). The data reveal that the reprocessing of attachment-related memories with EMDR treatment has a positive effect on attachment status, as assessed by the Adult Attachment Inventory (AAI). These findings support the idea that, by using EMDR Therapy, clients with histories of traumatic experiences and insecure attachment status may be able to reprocess early memory(ies) associated with adverse events, resulting in storing these memories in a more adaptive way. In particular, through the use of the AAI (George et al., 1985) and the RF Scale (Fonagy et al., 1998), it is possible for clinicians to verify how the specific indicators of linguistic disorganization (e.g., lapses in the monitoring of discourse or reasoning, which are not monitored by the subject during the discussion of abuse or loss) disappear after the reprocessing of attachment-related memories with the consequent reduction of attachment-related problems.

Clinical experience, as well as the results of the research regarding the application of the EMDR Attachment Protocol, highlights its strong effectiveness in the reprocessing of traumatic memories related to attachment issues. The main objective of this protocol, therefore, was to provide a theoretical background and guidelines for clinical practice that permit the clinician to deal with these clients and reduce their suffering. Given the positive results obtained by using the Attachment Protocol with these clients, the next step would be to conduct follow-up studies with larger samples of experimental and control subjects, in order to determine validity and consistency of positive effects on the attachment status following EMDR treatment.

The Attachment Protocol Script Notes

Phase 1

Client History Taking

The main objective in Phase 1: Client History Taking is to collect information about the client's life history and his present functioning.

- *Client problems/disturbance*: Problems described by the client are looked at in depth, in an attempt to understand the behavior, the emotions, the somatic sensations, and the negative cognitions associated with them.
- *Stressful life events*: It is necessary to evaluate those stressful life events that may have contributed to the development of the problem.
- *Effect of disorder in present life*: Ask questions about living conditions, working conditions, social life, and health conditions, in order to get an idea of the degree to which the subject's present life is affected by the disorder.
- *Family background*: Specific information is gathered about the subject's family background.
- *Attachment history*: Ask questions about the following: the subject's present state of mind with reference to past attachment relationships, and episodes regarding relationships with the significant figures during his early life.

   Note: Attention is paid to the subject's ability to supply descriptions of the relationship with his reference figure that are both *semantic* (in terms of general knowledge, meanings, symbols, and their interconnections) and *episodic* (in terms of information and specific events in their temporal context and in relation to the identity of the subject). These are descriptions of significant episodes touching on areas of physical and emotional vulnerability, separation from parents, feelings of rejection, and so on.

- *Losses and traumatic episodes*: One section is devoted specifically to a detailed account of the presence of losses and episodes that the client considers to have been traumatic.

    Note. It is of utmost importance to ask the client to talk about these topics because it is only through this method that it is possible to identify any indicators of *irresolution or the AAI's unresolved state of mind*, as discussed in the coding system of Main, Kaplan, and Cassidy (1985). As explained earlier, when a client is absorbed in unprocessed memories of mourning or of traumatic events, this is reflected in his ability to recount the events in a coherent and consistent manner.
- *Caregiving behavior*: It is particularly useful to focus on the dynamics of activation of the client's caregiving system; in order to discern this, it is important to use some of the questions contained in the PDI, asking, for example, about periods of parent–child separation, in order to verify the exploratory system dynamics. It is also important to ask about experiences of hopelessness and hostility connected with the activation of the caregiving system.
- *Other measures:* In order to gather the most complete information possible about the psychological state of the client and the significant events in his life, it is useful to employ other measures: the DERS, the ACE Questionnaire, and the DES (see "Measures" section).

Case Conceptualization, Treatment Planning, Target Identification, and Target Selection for Attachment Issues

For target identification, the present–past–future order is used to underline the importance of beginning the inquiry into dysfunctional behaviors in the present and then using the Floatback Technique to find the related target in the past history. Furthermore, it is useful to investigate the past experiences of attachment and caregiving activation in order to find other targets to reprocess. However, for the treatment plan, the past–present–future order is used.

ATTACHMENT STATE OF MIND, LINGUISTIC STYLE, AND EMDR

The clients' attachment states of mind can be ascertained through paying attention to the words that they use and how they describe their past attachment experiences. Knowing the attachment state of mind (by using some of the AAI questioning) can inform clinicians on how to proceed with their EMDR case conceptualization and treatment planning. The material that follows shows clinicians what to look for concerning clients' narratives and what types of violations of Grice's maxims they are making, so as to inform their choices when moving into how to proceed with treatment. The EMDR Therapy section makes suggestions for treatment planning and targeting of incidents.

Secure or Autonomous State of Mind
Narrative: Describes both positive and negative experiences that are consistent, with concrete memories, and fit into context. Shows the capacity for free exploration of thoughts and feelings. Demonstrates awareness of the effects of past experiences upon present state of mind. Shows a strong sense of identity and awareness of the importance of attachment relationships and experiences. Even when describing difficult, dramatic, or traumatic events, one can maintain balance, a high level of coherence in answers, good RF, and use of compassion and humor. In the clinical setting, such clients are collaborative and able to rethink past experiences and see them from a different viewpoint. Difficulties in their discourse are confined to the unprocessed upsetting event. Pay particular attention to those questions that have to do with loss and/or abuse. Work on those experiences; this is often assisted by transcribing the client's answers in order to be able to identify the indices of irresolution as previously defined.
Grice's maxim violation: Little and/or not relevant violations of all the maxims.

EMDR Therapy: Focus work on traumatic experiences and help reprocess these events and support internal and external resources and resilience. Traumatic memories from past experiences can be reactivated when caring for their own children. Reactivation can generate feelings of confusion and alarm and can lead to disorganization in the attachment of children. Intervening appropriately with EMDR Therapy in those issues makes it possible to interrupt the dysfunctional cycle of intergenerational transmission of the trauma.

Dismissing State of Mind

Narrative: Uses an idealizing narrative in contrast to negative memories, such as "My mother was always there; always loving," which is not supported by concrete evidence confirming such a positive description. A narrative is spare, often provides too little information, and generalizes in the absence of specific memories. It tries to limit attention to attachment relationships or experiences, and to affirm independence. It minimizes negative effects of early experiences (Subjective Units of Disturbance or SUDs will be very low or zero) and attempts to portray attachment-related experiences in a positive light. When asked about issues or past history, one will respond with phrases like "I don't remember; anyway, it's over now," or "It was a long time ago."

Grice's maxim violation: Quantity and quality.

EMDR Therapy: In dismissing cases, the Standard EMDR Protocol is *not* applicable, as it is not a question of blocked memories that require unblocking through reprocessing, it is that there are no memories at all. Therefore, it is necessary to activate the networks in such a way that the information they hold is connected and integrated in an adaptive manner. In order to activate recall and the emotions related to the traumatic event, stimulate the mnestic networks. This helps to resynchronize the hemispheres, by reducing the predominance of the cognitive aspect—which is more active in dismissing clients—and encourages connection with the emotional experience (Pagani et al., 2012). Can use photographs and tell family stories to gain access to the mnestic network.

Presents completely contradictory and incompatible images of the representation; therefore, work on episodes of idealization and on the generic representations (semantic memory) relative to the attachment figures presented. Using long sets of bilateral stimulation (BLS) stimulates the memories needed to work on these defensive strategies. It is only when the memories start to emerge that the clinician can begin to work on them, taking them as targets and applying the Standard EMDR Protocol. This type of work often requires a very long time. To stimulate these memories, ask about the image of the parental figure and the positive words used by the client, such as "She was always there," and then use BLS.

Entangled or Preoccupied

Narrative: These subjects show IWMs that oscillate between positive and negative representations of the attachment emotions concerning themselves and others. A narrative is inconsistent, not pertinent, and often contains irrelevant or vague details and/or too much information. The subjects appear angry, passive, or preoccupied with early attachment or attachment-related experiences. During the discussion of past experiences, the subject often slips into the present tense and highlights that these issues still generate discomfort and anger at the present time; departs from the interview topic, for example, by using free association; uses quotations from others, but does not make it clear that it is a quotation; and has a tendency to start a sentence but not finish it.

Grice's maxim violation: Relation, manner, and quantity.

EMDR Therapy: Focus on episodes regarding past traumatic experiences in the context of attachment relationships and explore. In particular, explore episodes of anger and rejections. In Phases 1 and 2, focus on the client's resources to enhance empowerment and activate the cooperative system.

Unresolved
- *Narrative*: Lapses in the monitoring of reasoning are indicated when clients imply that they have doubts or cannot really believe that a beloved person has died. Clues are as follows: Clients speak of the dead person as if he were still alive, in the present tense, such as "My father [who died years earlier] says that I shouldn't act like that"; clients report that they are the cause of the death of the loved one or feel that they are the cause of the abuse and deserved it, such as "I'm afraid that he died because I forgot to pray for him"; and there is disorientation with respect to time, for example, while telling the story of the death of the loved one, clients get the dates wrong—often by many years, such as, "My mother died when I was 6," and then later in the interview says, "My mother died when I was 10"—or, when clients describe having undergone episodes of abuse, and then, subsequently, try to deny or minimize the event.

    Lapses in the monitoring of the discourse occur when clients recount experiences of loss or abuse, and employ a distinctly *different type of language* from what they normally use in recounting other types of experiences. Examples are as follows: When describing the incident, clients are unusually *attentive to details*, with a strong sensory component (visual, tactile, and olfactory), such as when referring to father, they say, "His feet, his hard feet"; or clients use a particularly eulogistic or poetic language, such as "And, then, like a flower torn from the ground at its moment of splendor, she was taken from us." This category also includes *prolonged silences* in the course of the story, and the tendency to *move away from the topic* when asked direct questions about the loss or, contrariwise, a *tendency to speak of the loss even while describing other apparently unrelated episodes*, without mentioning any connection. As to experiences of abuse, this category also includes situations where clients are *unable to name the traumatic experience*: "When my father did it [when referring to the abuse]."

    Other specific indices of irresolution can occur through behavioral reactions, such as reporting extreme behavior (such as attempted suicide, prolonged depression, development of alcoholism or other substance abuse) after a past traumatic episode. It is important to understand the severity of clients' reactions; one must get the sense that the clients are not yet able to reorganize themselves after the event, and that they continue to experience terrible pain, which interferes with their ability to function.
- *Grice's maxim violation*: Quality, quantity, manner, and relation.
- *EMDR Therapy*: Focus on episodes of loss and abuse and try to identify indices of irresolution in narratives in order to verify if the event has been reprocessed or not. Use unprocessed memories as target(s) and apply the Standard EMDR Protocol.

Cannot Classify
- *Narrative:* Representations that are incompatible and contradictory. They are usually associated with stories of violence, abuse, and psychiatric disturbances. In their narratives, they reflect these contradictions, because it is not possible to identify any predominant state of mind with respect to attachment.
- *Grice's maxim violation*: Quality, quantity, manner, and relation.
- *EMDR Therapy*: Start with episodes of anger that still have their focus in the present and that generate discomfort and suffering in the current attachment relationships of the patient (which can occur in relation to one parent). After this, work on generalizations and semantic memories reported by the patient (which can occur in relation to the other parent). To do this, follow the suggestions regarding dismissing patients.

PRESENT

It is necessary to identify the dysfunctional behavior in the management of the activation of the attachment and caregiving systems. While investigating the present conditions and the people or situations that evoke the problem, help the client recognize each of the factors that will be necessary to reprocess. After this, look at the present-day reactions to the activation of the caregiving system within the client's most significant relationships (e.g., with his partner). The client is asked to concentrate on negative or irrational thoughts, the most salient emotions, and somatic sensations that accompany the difficult situations he has described. Then, look at other problem situations linked to the same negative belief.

PAST MEMORIES

The job of the clinician here is to uncover the client's history of attachment with the significant people in his life and the type of caregiving his nuclear family gave him. By understanding how his parents responded to him when he was distressed or requested comfort and reassurance, the clinician learns about the nature of his childhood attachment experiences and the types of targets that will be meaningful for the client. Often, by identifying current attachment issues, with particular attention paid to the emotional experience, the dysfunctional cognitive schema, and the physical sensations present during episodes of this sort, the clinician can use the Floatback or Affect Bridge Technique to find the earlier precursors to his present difficulties; this underlines the connection between his current problems and earlier experiences. Many of these episodes will already have been stimulated through the AAI questioning.

For identification of the specific targets relating to the activation of the attachment system, it is useful to pay particular attention to certain *dynamics* within the client's description of the episodes:

- *Rejection*: Episodes in which the client remembers feeling actively rejected by his own attachment figures.
- *Neglect*: Episodes in which the client remembers having the parent physically present but absorbed in his own thoughts and therefore emotionally unavailable.
- *Pressure to achieve*: Experiences when the client remembers feeling particularly pressured to achieve in school or athletics, accompanied by a considerable anxiety about failure.
- *Role reversal*: Episodes in which the client remembers feeling like he was "taking care of" his parents, or a memory where one of the parents was treating the child as a wife or a husband.

- **Note**: With dismissing clients, it is often difficult to get to specific memories, as they have a tendency to generalize or to insist on their lack of memory. In this case, photographs are useful, or the telling of family stories, to gain access to the mnestic network.

FUTURE

Inquire about the client's concerns about the future and his hoped-for state of behavior. The clinician talks about that behavior and the abilities the client would like to achieve, that is, the new goals to aim for. More specifically, ask the client to imagine the next time he will feel the need for help (e.g., when feeling alone, sad, tired, ill, or in danger), and to focus on the abilities he will require in order to achieve his objectives.

Identification of Resources

After identifying the presented problem, it is helpful to ask the client what are the skills/resources he would need to address the issue(s) and that would give him a sense of self-efficacy. For example, ask the client to remember a time when he felt worthy enough to ask for help and concentrate on the positive emotions, thoughts, and physical sensations associated with the memory. If the client is unable to remember any memories of positive interactions, ask him to focus on how he would have liked to be cared for or what he would have most needed then.

Once the targets of the client's history have been identified, the treatment planning is established, setting down the therapeutic goals and organizing the identified targets in a past–present–future sequence.

Phase 2: Preparation

In Phase 2: Preparation, the client is supplied with all the information necessary to proceed to the successive phases of EMDR Therapy.

The Therapeutic Relationship

To begin EMDR treatment, it is important to establish a client–clinician alliance based on trust, by creating a climate of security within the therapeutic relationship. This allows the client to feel safe and strong enough to explore his memories, while maintaining that double focus of one foot in the past and one foot in the present.

The therapeutic relationship begins at the first moment of contact between the client and the clinician, that is, when the client calls to set up an appointment. It is important that the clinician respond appropriately to this request, by considering the importance of the appeal for help that has been addressed to her.

Explanation of the Method—Psychoeducation

In this phase, the clinician explains the subtleties of the relational problems the client has described. It is important to make sure the dynamics of activation and deactivation of the attachment and caregiving systems are fully understood. The role of any past traumatic events in the development of subsequent difficulties must be made clear. Psychoeducation is essential for enabling the client to increase his self-awareness, to better understand his own IWMs, and to bring him closer to the exploration and enactment of new and appropriate coping strategies in the management of disturbing events.

Then, EMDR Therapy is explained. It is important that the client have a clear understanding of what is involved in an EMDR session, and have his expectations clarified. By helping the client to become familiar with the mechanics of BLS, the clinician helps him to feel more at ease with the method. It is also helpful to use a metaphor to explain how the clinician and the client together can regulate the emotional intensity that occurs during the reprocessing: "In order to help you 'just notice' the experience, imagine riding on a train and the feelings, thoughts, etc. are just the scenery going by," and specifying that, at any point in the course of reprocessing, should the client feel the need to stop the process, all he has to do is make a *stop* signal with his hand and the clinician will stop the BLS.

Resources

The aim of the Safe Base Exercise, a modified version of the Safe Place Exercise, is to familiarize the client with the EMDR method by using positive material to make the processing of subsequent material quicker and simpler. In addition, this exercise can help the client to develop his ability to manage the stress generated by incomplete sessions, as a deactivating technique at the end of each EMDR session. The Secure Base Exercise enables the client to focus on a past memory and the emotions and sensations associated with it, including an adult figure who was receptive and cared about him, providing help and satisfying a need, even if it was just a material one. It is important to proceed with the installation of the Secure Base with short sets of BLS, in order to reinforce the associated positive images, sensations, and emotions evoked. If the client is unable to recall episodes from his childhood, ask him to think of some occasion in his adult life when a significant figure was receptive and provided help.

For resource installation, go back to the resources identified in Phase 1 of the protocol that related to those moments when the client was able to ask for help and feel worthy of receiving it and install these as resources.

Phase 3: Assessment

Once the targets in the relational history of the client have been identified, the clinician continues with the phases of the Standard EMDR Protocol. At the beginning, focus on the targets from the client's past history; then it is necessary to proceed with present-day triggers, and, at the end, with future scenario. It is essential to approach each target memory in a structured way, measuring the primary aspects of each: the most disturbing or representative image connected to the event; the negative cognition the client has of himself; the self-referring positive cognition; the validity of cognition (VoC; i.e., how true the client feels the positive cognition is *now*); the emotions associated with the target event; the SUD; and where he feels it in his body.

Phase 4: Desensitization

During Phase 4: Desensitization, according to the treatment plan, reprocess the targets relating to the past and linked to the present disturbance, for each trigger in the present and for the future scenario.

Phases 5 to 7: Installation, Body Scan, Closure

Phases 5 to 7 are in accordance with the Standard EMDR Protocol.

Phase 8: Reevaluation

For Phase 8: Reevaluation, at the conclusion of the EMDR Therapy, it is necessary to revisit the questions asked in Phase 1 of the protocol—questions about the client's history of attachment and caregiving. This evaluation is important in seeing what changes may have occurred in terms of the subject's narrative consistency and RF.

At the end of the EMDR work with Attachment Protocol, the clinician must proceed with the "Parent as Child" exercise. In the "Parent as Child" exercise, ask the client to imagine a meeting between his adult self and his mother or father as a child. This step is of *fundamental* importance. Through the family narratives, he has internalized the knowledge that he has acquired over a lifetime, and, when the client imagines the response of the child–parent, he can access the history of his parents' early traumas. As is known, the unprocessed traumas of the parents are implicitly transmitted to the children. In addition, this exercise can help the clinician to identify possible vicarious traumatization that the client has undergone in his relations with his parents, which can then be used as EMDR targets. As the adult client has developed resources by processing past memory targets, he is ready now to enter into a dialogue with his parents as children. This can help him access a feeling of compassion for his parents and his earlier life; often, this is an insight that develops during the processing. Use a brief set of BLS to reinforce these images, the feeling, and the positive belief(s).

The Attachment Protocol Script

Phase 1: History Taking

Client History-Taking Questions

Here are the questions relative to Phase 1 of the Protocol:

THE DISTURBANCE

Say, *"What is the problem in question?"*

_____
_____
_____

Say, *"What are its characteristics?"*

_____
_____
_____

Say, *"When did it begin?"*

_____
_____
_____

Say, *"What event/s triggered it? What was happening when it all began?"*
LIST TRIGGERING EVENTS

_____
_____
_____

EFFECT OF DISORDER ON PRESENT LIFE

Say, *"How have your present living conditions been affected by this problem?"*

_____
_____
_____

Say, *"How have your working conditions been affected by this problem?"*

_____
_____
_____

Say, *"How has your social life been affected by this problem?"*

_____
_____
_____

Say, *"How has your health been affected by this problem?"*

_____
_____
_____

FAMILY BACKGROUND

Say, *"How have your family relationships been affected by this problem?"*

_____
_____
_____

ATTACHMENT HISTORY

Say, *"I'd like to ask you to choose five adjectives or words that reflect your relationship with your mother/father starting from as far back as you can remember in early childhood."*

_____
_____
_____

Say, *"Can you think of a memory or an incident that would illustrate why you choose to describe your relationship as _____ (insert adjective chosen by client)?"*

_____
_____
_____

Say, *"When you were upset or worried, and/or in emotional difficulty as a child, what would you do? And how did your parent react? Can you tell me about some specific incident?"*

_____
_____
_____

Say, *"When you got hurt physically, what would happen? Can you think of any particular incident?"*

_____

_____

_____

Say, *"Do you remember the first time you were separated from your parents? How did you react? And, how did they react? Can you think of other significant separations?"*

_____

_____

_____

Say, *"Did you ever feel rejected as a child? How old were you when you had that feeling and what did you do then?"*

LIST OF TIMES FEELING REJECTED AS CHILD

_____

_____

_____

Say, *"Why do you think your parents behaved like that? Do you think they realized how you felt?"*

_____

_____

_____

Say, *"Do you remember any times when your parent/s was/were physically present but absorbed in his/her own thoughts and therefore emotionally unavailable?"*

LIST OF EVENTS WHERE PARENT WAS PHYSICALLY PRESENT BUT ABSORBED IN OWN THOUGHTS AND EMOTIONALLY UNAVAILABLE

_____

_____

_____

Say, *"Do you remember experiences where you felt pressured to achieve in school or athletics that resulted in considerable anxiety about failure?"*

LIST OF TIMES PRESSURED TO ACHIEVE IN SCHOOL OR ATHLETICS

_____

_____

_____

_____

_____

_____

Say, *"Do you remember times when you felt you were 'taking care of' your parent or parents or where one of your parents was treating you as their spouse?"*

LIST OF TIMES TAKING CARE OF YOUR PARENT(S) OR PARENTS TREATING YOU AS THEIR SPOUSE

_____

_____

_____

_____

_____

_____

Note: If dismissing clients are generalizing or unable to get to specific memories, ask them to bring in photographs or tell some family stories.

Say, *"Could you bring in some photographs of your early family life?"*

_____

_____

_____

Or say, *"Help me understand your family by telling me some of the old family stories."*

_____

_____

_____

MOURNING AND/OR TRAUMATIC EXPERIENCES

Other questions are asked, including those relating to losses and traumatic events during childhood and later life.

Say, "Did you experience the loss of a parent or other close loved one while you were a young child?"

LIST LOSSES

_____
_____
_____

Ask the following questions about each memory on the list:

Say, "Could you tell me about the circumstances?"

_____
_____
_____

Say, "How old were you at the time?"

_____
_____
_____

Say, "How did you react at the time?"

_____
_____
_____

Say, "Was this death sudden or was it expected?"

_____
_____
_____

Say, "Can you remember your feelings at the time? Have they changed since then?"

_____
_____
_____

Say, "Are there any other experiences that you consider might have been traumatic?"

_____
_____
_____

CAREGIVING BEHAVIOR TO CHILDREN AND/OR SIGNIFICANT OTHERS

Ask questions about caregiving behavior to child. See below for significant other. Say, *"Can you describe yourself as a parent?"*

_____

_____

_____

Say, *"What is it that gives you the most pleasure in being _____ (state the child's name)'s parent? What causes you the most difficulty or pain in being _____ (state the child's name)'s parent?"*

Say, *"Has anything ever happened that caused a setback in your relationship with _____ (state child's name)?"*

Say, *"What happens after you have been separated from _____ (state child's name) for a period of time?"*

_____

_____

Say, *"Are there times when you experience a sense of hopelessness when parenting _____ (state child's name)?"*

_____

_____

_____

Say, *"Are there times when you experience a sense of hostility when parenting _____ (state child's name)?"*

If not a parent, ask about another relationship with a significant person in the client's life.

Say, *"Can you describe yourself as a significant partner in a relationship?"*

_____

_____

Say, *"What is it that gives you the most pleasure in the relationship with _____ (state the significant other's name)? What is the most difficult part in the relationship with _____ (state the significant other's name)?"*

_____

_____

_____

Say, *"Has anything ever happened that caused a setback in your relationship with _____ (state significant other's name)?"*

_____

_____

_____

Say, *"What happens after you have been separated from _____ (state child's name) for a period of time?"*

Or say, *"What happens after you have been separated from _____ (state significant other's name) for a period of time?"*

_____
_____
_____

Say, *"Are there times when you experience a sense of hopelessness in your relationship with _____ (state significant other)?"*

_____
_____
_____

Say, *"Are there times when you experience a sense of hostility in your relationship with _____ (state significant other)?"*

_____
_____
_____

Identification of Resources

On the subject of the problem that brought him to seek help, the client is asked to think of the moments in his life when he activated coping strategies to achieve this goal, and felt a sense of self-efficacy.

Say, *"Think of the moments in your life when you were able to achieve _____ (state client's goal)."*

_____
_____
_____

The client may be asked to focus on a memory of an episode where he was able to ask for help, feeling worthy enough to do it. He must try to concentrate on the emotions, the thoughts, and the physical sensations associated with this memory.

Say, *"Think of a memory of an episode where you were able to ask for help and felt worthy enough to do it. Please concentrate and express the emotions, thoughts, and the physical sensations associated with this memory."*

_____
_____
_____

If the client is not able to remember any memory of positive interaction, it is possible to focus on the question of how he would have liked to be cared for.

Say, *"When you think of this situation, what is it that you would have most needed then?"*

_____

_____

_____

Or say, *"Recall a time when you felt able to ask for help and worthy enough to do it. Focus on this experience and try to concentrate on the emotions, the thoughts, and the physical sensations associated with this memory."*

_____

_____

_____

Target Identification and Target Selection for Attachment Issues

Present

It is necessary to identify the dysfunctional behavior in the management of the activation of the attachment and caregiving systems. While investigating the present conditions and the people or situations that evoke the problem, help the client recognize each of the factors that is necessary to reprocess.

Say, *"Try to think of some situations where you felt you needed help. What were they?"*

LIST SITUATIONS WHERE YOU FELT YOU NEEDED HELP

_____

_____

_____

For each situation, ask the following questions:

Say, *"What did you do?"*

_____

_____

_____

Say, *"How did you ask for help?"*

_____

_____

_____

Or say, *"What do you do when you feel you are all alone and you are afraid?"*

_____
_____
_____

Say, *"What happens if you ask for help?"*

_____
_____
_____

Say, *"How do you react when somebody responds to your request for help?"*

_____
_____
_____

Say, *"What do you feel emotionally?"*

_____
_____
_____

After these triggers are elicited, look at the present-day reactions to activation of the caregiving system within the client's most significant relationships (e.g., with his partner).

Say, *"What happens when you are asked to do something for _____ (state name of partner)?"*

_____
_____
_____

Say, *"What happens when _____ (state name of partner) does something for you?"*

_____
_____
_____

Say, *"What happens when _____ (state name of partner) and you are away from each other for a bit of time?"*

_____
_____
_____

The client is asked to concentrate on any particularly negative or irrational thoughts, on the most salient emotions, and on the somatic sensations that accompany the difficult situations he has described.

> Say, *"When you think of _____ (state the situation from above), concentrate on any particularly negative or irrational thoughts, on the most salient emotions, and on the somatic sensations that accompany this difficult situation."*

_____
_____
_____

Then it is useful to try to look into possible problematic situations linked to the same negative belief.

> Say, *"When you think of _____ (state the negative belief), are there any problem situations linked to it?"*

_____
_____
_____

Past Memories

To work with past memories, it is important to identify the targets in the client's past history; therefore, use the Floatback or Affect Bridge Techniques starting from dysfunctional behavior reported in present-day life.

> Say, *"What is the earliest memory you have of feeling _____ (list the feeling reported by client)?"*

_____

> Or say, *"When was the first time you realized, learned _____ (state what client has realized or learned)?"*

_____
_____

Note: With dismissing clients, it is often difficult to get to specific memories, as they have a tendency to generalize or to insist on their lack of memory. In this sort of case, photographs are useful, or the telling of family stories, to gain access to the amnestic network.

Future Issues/Template

The future template is to identify the client's hoped-for state of future behavior.

> Say, *"Try to imagine the next time you will feel the need for help _____ (state an example, as when the client feels alone, sad, tired, ill, or in danger). What would be the abilities that you would need more of to handle this situation?"*

_____
_____

TREATMENT PLANNING

Once the targets of the client's history have been identified, the treatment planning is established, setting down the therapeutic goals and organizing the identified targets in a past–present–future sequence. It is important to remember that the goals of the treatment must be clear and that both the clinician and the client must be in agreement about them. As a matter of fact, the client must be in charge of defining his own goals. It is useful to ask the client to imagine himself in such a situation, in as much detail as possible. In order to help the clients to think clearly about them, the clinician can ask questions like the following:

Say, *"What are your goals for our work together?"*

 LIST GOALS:

_____

_____

_____

Say, *"How would that benefit you?"*

_____

_____

_____

Say, *"How would you know that you had achieved that?"*

_____

_____

_____

Say, *"What would you see once you have accomplished your goal/s?"*

_____

_____

_____

Say, *"What would you hear once you have accomplished your goal/s?"*

_____

_____

_____

Say, *"What would you feel once you have accomplished your goal/s?"*

_____

_____

_____

continued

Say, *"Are there any other indications that would let you know that you have accomplished your goal/s?"*

_____
_____
_____

Organize the identified targets in a past–present–future sequence:

Say, *"Please list the past memories we have been speaking about in the order of the first one you want us to process to the last."*

LIST PAST MEMORIES

_____
_____
_____

Say, *"Please list the current triggers we have been speaking about in the order of the first one you want us to process to the last."*

LIST PRESENT TRIGGERS

_____
_____
_____

Say, *"Please list the future issues we have been speaking about in the order of the first one you want us to work with to the last."*

LIST FUTURE ISSUES

_____
_____
_____

Phase 2: Preparation

Give the client all the information necessary to proceed with the successive phases of EMDR Therapy.

Explanation of the Relational Problem Dynamics

In this phase, the clinician explains the subtleties of the relational problems the client has described.

Make sure the dynamics of activation and deactivation of the attachment and caregiving systems are fully understood.

Say, *"Let me explain to you how your attachment and caregiving systems work. When a child feels sad or upset, his/her attachment system is activated and he/she seeks closeness with the caregiver (secure base) to be comforted. Only*

> *after that, when the child feels safe, the attachment system can be deactivated and the child can return to explore. These mechanisms are present in every person throughout the entire lifespan."*
>
> *"When a loved one seeks your help, instead of activating the attachment system, you are activating another behavioral system, called the caregiving system. The caregiving system allows you to take care of your child (or significant other) and respond in a prompt and warm manner to his/her cues. Also, this system is innate and present in every person."*

_____

_____

_____

> Say, *"These are the dynamics of the relational problems that you have described. _____ (state the dynamics of the client's relational problem)."*

Psychoeducation is essential for enabling the client to increase his self-awareness, to better understand his own IWMs, and to bring him closer to the exploration and enactment of new and appropriate coping strategies in the management of disturbing events.

> Say, *"By understanding how your attachment and caregiving systems work and the role of traumatic events in the onset of your difficulties, you will learn how they work and/or don't work for you and bring you closer to new and more helpful coping strategies for managing disturbing events."*

Explanation of EMDR Therapy

It is important that the client have a clear understanding of what is involved in an EMDR session, and that his expectations be clarified. By helping the client to become familiar with the mechanics of BLS, the clinician helps him feel more at ease with the method.

> Say, *"When a trauma occurs, it seems to be locked in the nervous system with the original picture, sounds, thoughts, and feelings. The eye movements we use in EMDR seem to unlock the nervous system and allow the brain to process the experience. That may be what is happening in REM or dream sleep—the eye movements may help to process the unconscious material. It is important to remember that it is your own brain that will be doing the healing and you are the one in control. With your permission, I'm going to _____ (state the type of BLS used)."*

> Say, *"Now I'll show you the procedure in order to decide which is the best distance for you and if you feel comfortable both with eye stimulation and tapping. Feel free to tell me if you don't feel comfortable and try to relax and be calm."*

_____

_____

It has proven useful to reassure the client about the emotional intensity that the reprocessing can generate, using the train metaphor, and specifying that, at any point in the course of reprocessing, should the client feel the need to stop the process, all he has to do is make a *stop* signal with his hand.

> Say, *"In order to help you just notice the experience and handle the intensity of the emotions, you can imagine riding on a train and the feelings and thoughts are just the scenery going by. If during the processing you have a problem or you feel you have to stop, please raise your hand and we will stop."*

Resources

SAFE BASE EXERCISE

> Say, *"Recall a past memory when an adult figure was receptive and cared about you, providing help and satisfying your needs, even if it was just a material need. Try also to focus on the emotions and sensations associated with this memory. What are you remembering?"*

_____

_____

_____

Do short sets of BLS (10 seconds) in order to install the Safe Base and reinforce the associated positive images, sensations, and emotions evoked.

> Say, *"Please focus on the Safe Base you have remembered and the associated positive images, sensations, and emotions evoked and _____ (state BLS being used)."*

If the client is unable to recall any episodes from his childhood, the clinician can ask him to think of some occasion in his adult life when a significant figure was receptive and provided help.

> Say, *"Perhaps there is a time you can recall in your adult life when a significant person was receptive and provided you with help. Please tell me about it."*

_____

_____

_____

> Say, *"Please focus on that time that you have remembered and the associated positive images, sensations, and emotions evoked and _____ (state BLS being used)."*

RESOURCE INSTALLATION

For Resource Installation, go back to the resources identified in Phase 1 of the protocol that related to those moments when the client was able to ask for help and felt worthy of receiving it and install these as resources, focusing only on the positive connections.

> Say, *"Remember the resources we identified earlier concerning those moments when you were able to ask for help and feel worthy of receiving it. Here is the list_____ (state the resources identified earlier).*

LIST RESOURCES OF CLIENT ASKING FOR HELP AND FEELING WORTHY

_____

_____

_____

Say, *"Which one would you like to use?"*

_____
_____
_____

Say, *"Okay, now think about that time when you felt able to ask for help and worthy enough to do it. Focus on this experience and try to concentrate on the emotions, the thoughts, and the physical sensations associated with this memory. Go with that."*

Therapist gives short and slow BLS (10 seconds BLS) and then inquires about the feelings, thoughts, and sensations evoked.

Say, *"Stop and take a breath. Please tell me about the feelings, thoughts, and sensations that the memory evoked."*

_____
_____
_____

Say, *"Go with that."*
Elicit cue word.

Say, *"Now, please choose a name, a word, or a sentence that will be a cue for this experience. What seems to fit for you?"*

_____
_____
_____

Do BLS and install the cue word.

Phase 3: Assessment

Assessment is done according to the Standard EMDR Protocol.

Incident

Say, *"With which concern would you like to begin?"*

_____
_____
_____

Say, *"What happens when you think of _____ (state the issue)?"*

_____
_____
_____

Or say, *"When you think of _____ (state the issue), what do you get?"*

___
___
___

Picture

Say, *"What picture represents the entire _____ (state the issue)?"*

___
___

Say, *"What picture represents the most traumatic part of _____ (state the issue)?"*

___
___

Negative Cognition

Say, *"What words best go with the picture that express your negative belief about yourself now?"*

___
___

Positive Cognition

Say, *"When you bring up that picture or _____ (state the issue), what would you like to believe about yourself, now?"*

___
___

Validity of Cognition

Say, *"When you think of _____ (state the issue, or picture), how true do those words _____ (repeat the PC) feel to you now on a scale of 1 to 7, where 1 feels completely false and 7 feels completely true?"*

    1   2   3   4   5   6   7

(completely false)   (completely true)

Sometimes, it is necessary to explain further.

Say, *"Remember, sometimes we know something with our head, but it feels differently in our gut. In this case, what is the gut-level feeling of the truth of _____ (state the PC), from 1 (completely false) to 7 (completely true)?"*

1   2   3   4   5   6   7
(completely false)   (completely true)

Emotions

Say, "When you bring up the picture or _____ (state the issue) and those words _____ (state the NC), what emotion do you feel now?"

_____

_____

Subjective Units of Disturbance

Say, "On a scale of 0 to 10, where 0 is no disturbance or neutral and 10 is the highest disturbance you can imagine, how disturbing does it feel now?"

0   1   2   3   4   5   6   7   8   9   10

(no disturbance)   (highest disturbance)

Location of Body Sensation

Say, "Where do you feel it (the disturbance) in your body?"

_____

_____

Say, "Now, remember, it is your own brain that is doing the healing and you are the one in control. I will ask you to mentally focus on the target and to follow my fingers (or any other BLS you are using). Just let whatever happens, happen, and we will talk at the end of the set. Just tell me what comes up, and don't discard anything as unimportant. Any new information that comes to mind is connected in some way. If you want to stop, just raise your hand."

Then say, "Bring up the picture and the words _____ (repeat the NC) and notice where you feel it in your body. Now follow my fingers with your eyes (or other BLS)." See below in desensitization.

Note: Dismissing clients could report a very low SUD, often as low as zero. When working with these clients, it is necessary to focus on their episodes of idealization, generalization, and lack of memory relative to the attachment figures. In these cases, do not apply the Standard EMDR Protocol. Rather, to stimulate these memories, use long sets of BLS to work on these defensive strategies. It is only once the memories start to emerge that the clinician can begin to work on them, taking them as targets and applying the Standard EMDR Protocol. This type of work often requires a very long time.

For example, the therapist could say the following:

Say, "Think of the image of your _____ (state name of significant caregiver) and of the words you used _____ (state the client's words, for example, the generalization, 'She was always there') and follow my fingers."

Do BLS.

Say, "What do you notice?"

_____

_____

Note: With *Secure* clients who may have encountered particularly dramatic or traumatic experiences in their lives that have not been reprocessed, apply the Standard EMDR Protocol on these memories.

Phase 4: Desensitization

The work in Phase 4 follows the Standard EMDR Protocol.

To begin, say the following:

> Say, *"Now, remember, it is your own brain that is doing the healing and you are the one in control. I will ask you to mentally focus on the target and to _____ (state BLS you are using). Just let whatever happens, happen, and we will talk at the end of the set. Just tell me what comes up, and don't discard anything as unimportant. Any new information that comes to mind is connected in some way. If you want to stop, just raise your hand."*

The client is asked to focus on the image, the NC, and the bodily sensation of each of the target events, after which the clinician must proceed with the BLS (eye movements or other).

> Say, *"Bring up the picture and the words _____ (repeat the NC) and notice where you feel it in your body. Now follow _____ (state BLS)."*

_____

_____

It is important to reprocess all of the associative channels involved in the network. After each set of BLS, say the following:

Say, *"What do you notice?"*

_____

_____

Then, on the basis of the client's reply, say, *"Good. Go with that."*
Proceed with another set of BLS.
If the material that emerges from each set is neutral—or no other material emerges—it is necessary to ask the client to return to the target and check the SUD.

> Say, *"On a scale of 0 to 10, where 0 is no disturbance or neutral and 10 is the highest disturbance you can imagine, how disturbing does it feel now?"*
>
> 0   1   2   3   4   5   6   7   8   9   10
>
> (no disturbance)   (highest disturbance)

Repeat the procedure until SUDs = 0. Next, install the PC. Each traumatic event associated with the problem that is not reprocessed during the normal course of the first target needs to be processed using the above protocol until the SUDs reach an ecological 1 or 0 and the PC is installed. In this way, the memory will no longer appear isolated, but will be integrated into the broader network and thus assimilated in a more adaptive and functional manner.

Phase 5: Installation

The client is asked to concentrate on the original memory and to pay attention to all parts of his body, to see if there are any residual tensions, rigidity, or strange sensations. If there are, proceed with eye movements until the discomfort completely disappears. If there are any pleasant sensations, proceed with brief sets of BLS in order to reinforce them.

The work in Phase 5 follows the Standard EMDR Protocol.

Say, *"How does _____ (repeat the PC) sound?"*

_____

_____

Say, *"Do the words _____ (repeat the PC) still fit, or is there another positive statement that feels better?"*

_____

_____

If the client accepts the original PC, the clinician should ask for a VoC rating to see if it has improved:

Say, *"As you think of the incident, how do the words feel, from 1 (completely false) to 7 (completely true)?"*

1   2   3   4   5   6   7

(completely false)   (completely true)

Say, *"Think of the event and hold it together with the words _____ (repeat the PC)."*

Do a long set of BLS to see if there is more processing to be done.

Phase 6: Body Scan

The work in Phase 6 follows the Standard EMDR Protocol.

Say, *"Close your eyes and keep in mind the original memory and the positive cognition. Then bring your attention to the different parts of your body, starting with your head and working downward. Any place you find any tension, tightness, or unusual sensation, tell me."*

_____

_____

Phase 7: Closure

At the closing of every session, it is necessary to refocus the client's attention from the targets he has been confronted with, and to help him access the mnestic network that is more neutral and positive. To achieve this, the client is always asked to think back to the Safe Base exercise; this is then reinforced through a brief set of BLS.

Say, *"Think back to the Safe Base Exercise. Go with that."*

_____

_____

The client is also reminded that processing can continue even after the session is over, and that he may find new insights, thoughts, memories, physical sensations, or dreams. In these cases, it is useful for the client to write down whatever emerges and to talk about it with the therapist in the next session or call the therapist if necessary.

Say, *"Things may come up or they may not. If they do, great. Write it down and it can be a target for next time. You can use a log to write down triggers, images, thoughts or cognitions, emotions, and sensations; you can rate them on our 0-to-10 scale where 0 is no disturbance or neutral and 10 is the worst disturbance. Please write down the positive experiences, too."*

Say, *"If you get any new memories, dreams, or situations that disturb you, just take a good snapshot. It isn't necessary to give a lot of detail. Just put down enough to remind you so we can target it next time. The same thing goes for any positive dreams or situations. If negative feelings do come up, try not to make them significant. Remember, it's still just the old stuff. Just write it down for next time. Then use the tape or the Safe Base exercise to let go of as much of the disturbance as possible. Even if nothing comes up, make sure to use the tape every day and give me a call if you need to."*

Phase 8: Reevaluation

At the beginning of each successive session, it is necessary to go back to the target of the previous session and to monitor any residual discomfort, checking the maintenance of the earlier SUD and VoC. Any new elements that the client has noted in the meantime are also addressed, as well as any progress achieved. The work in Phase 8 follows the Standard EMDR Protocol.

Say, *"When you think of _____ (state the issue, or picture), how true do those words _____ (clinician repeats the PC) feel to you now on a scale of 1 to 7, where 1 feels completely false and 7 feels completely true?"*

1   2   3   4   5   6   7

(completely false)   (completely true)

_____

_____

Say, *"On a scale of 0 to 10, where 0 is no disturbance or neutral and 10 is the highest disturbance you can imagine, how disturbing does it feel now?"*

0   1   2   3   4   5   6   7   8   9   10

(no disturbance)   (highest disturbance)

At the end of the EMDR work with Attachment Protocol, the clinician must proceed with the "Parent as Child" exercise and ask the client to imagine a meeting between his adult self and his mother or father as a child. The client is welcome to share the dialogue between his adult part and the parent as a child or not.

Say, *"Try to imagine yourself as you are now, meeting your _____ (state name of caregiver) as a child. Try to focus on how you imagine it; on how old _____ (he/she) is, what _____ (he/she) is wearing, and on all the details that can help you bring more clarity to the image."*

_____

_____

Say, *"Pretend you are standing in front of _____ (him/her) and ask how _____ (he/she) is feeling. Concentrate on the emotions you, the adult, are feeling in that moment."*

_____

_____

Say, *"Ask your child's ____ (state mother/father) what has happened?"*

_____
_____

Say, *"Why is _____ (he/she) feeling like that?"*

_____
_____

Say, *"Why did____ (he/she) act like that towards you?"*

_____
_____

Say, *"Try to ask your child's _____ (state mother/father) what you can do to help."*

_____
_____

Proceed with the installation of the images, feeling, and sensations through brief sets of BLS.

Say, *"Bring up the image, feelings, and sensations and _____ (state BLS being used)."*

_____
_____

As a result of this "Parent as Child" exercise, possible vicarious traumatization can be elicited that can be used as targets:

Say, *"I think that this _____ (state the incident described above) would be a good target for us to use with EMDR Therapy. Would you be willing to target this incident?"*

_____
_____

If the answer is yes, reprocess the target using the Standard EMDR Protocol.
If the answer is no, investigate the reasons (perhaps the client is afraid that something could happen), then proceed with the Floatback Technique.
If the adult client—who has the benefit of the earlier resources and the processing of the targets connected with the past—can imagine entering into a dialogue with his parents as children, ultimately, it could help him access a feeling of compassion for his parents, himself, and his past life.

Say, *"Imagine your parent as a child. How old is your _____ (state which parent)?"*

_____
_____

Say, *"What does* _____ *(he/she) look like?"*

Say, *"What is* _____ *(he/she) doing?"*

Say, *"What has happened to* _____ *(him/her)? Do you know* _____ *(his/her) history?"*

Say, *"What do you think* _____ *(he/she) would say to you if you asked* ____ *(him/her) about what happened to* _____ *(him/her)?"*

Say, *"Can you go toward* _____ *(him/her) and talk with* _____ *(him/her)?"*

Introduce BLS.

Say, *"Go with that."*

If yes, the clinician does a brief set of stimulation to reinforce these images, the feeling, and the positive belief(s).

At the conclusion of EMDR Therapy, it is necessary to revisit the questions asked in Phase 1 of the protocol—questions about the client's history of attachment and caregiving. This evaluation is important in seeing what changes may have occurred in terms of the subject's narrative consistency and reflective function.

Say, *"During this time you have done a lot of work and you have achieved many therapeutic goals. Now I will ask you the same questions I asked you at the beginning of the therapy so that we can understand the changes that have occurred."*

Summary

The theoretical background of this protocol is Bowlby's Attachment Theory (1969, 1973, 1980). His most relevant concepts concern the attachment relationship, caregiving behavior, and the IWMs. Ainsworth's (Ainsworth et al., 1978) Strange Situation Procedure and three patterns of attachment (secure, avoidant, and ambivalent), as well as Main and Solomon's (1990) disorganized style, are discussed. The AAI and the parental state of mind regarding past attachment relationships (secure, dismissing, preoccupied, unresolved, and cannot classify) are described. Grice's maxims are also explored in order to make clear the concept of coherence of the narrative and to help identify the indices of irresolution in the client's narrative. The importance of intergenerational transmission of attachment is presented as well as the RF. The results of a pilot study to explore the role of EMDR on IWMs of attachment in terms of increased coherence and reflective competences regarding attachment presentation through the processing of past traumatic experiences point in the direction that using EMDR Therapy to reprocess attachment-related memories has a positive effect on the attachment status as assessed by the AAI.

The Attachment Protocol and script were explained according to the eight EMDR phases.

References

Aber, J., Slade, A., Berger, B., Bresgi, I., & Kaplan, M. (1985). *The Parent Development Interview.* Unpublished manuscript. Barnard College, Columbia University, New York, NY.

Ainsworth, M. D. S., Blehar, M. C., Waters, E., & Wall, S. (1978). *Patterns of attachment: A psychological study of the strange situation.* Hillsdale, NJ: Lawrence Erlbaum.

Bernstein, E. M., & Putnam, F. W. (1986). Development, reliability, and validity of a dissociation scale. *Journal of Nervous and Mental Disease, 174*(12), 727–735.

Bowlby, J. (1969). *Attachment and loss: Vol. 1. Attachment.* New York, NY: Basic Books.

Bowlby, J. (1973). *Attachment and loss: Vol. 2. Separation.* New York, NY: Basic Books.

Bowlby, J. (1980). *Attachment and loss: Vol. 3. Loss, sadness and depression.* New York, NY: Basic Books.

Cassidy, J., & Shaver, P. R. (Eds.). (2008). *Handbook of attachment: Theory, research, and clinical applications* (2nd ed.). New York, NY: Guilford Press.

Dube, S. R., Felitti, V. J., & Rishi, S. (2013). Moving beyond childhood adversity: Associations between salutogenic factors and subjective well-being among adult survivors of trauma. In M. Linden & K. Rutkowski (Eds.), *Hurting memories and beneficial forgetting: Posttraumatic stress disorders, biographical developments and social conflicts* (pp. 139–152). Waltham, MA: Elsevier.

Egeland, B., Jacobvitz, D., & Sroufe, L. A. (1988). Breaking the cycle of abuse. *Child Development, 59*(4), 1080–1088. doi:10.2307/1130274

Fonagy, P., Gergely, G., Jurist, E., & Target, M. (2002). *Affect regulation, mentalization, and the development of the self.* New York, NY: Other Books.

Fonagy, P., Steele, M., Steele, H., Leigh, T., Kennedy, R., Mattoon, G., & Target, M. (1995). Attachment, the reflective self, and borderline states: The predictive specificity of the Adult Attachment Interview and pathological emotional development. In S. Goldberg, R. Muir, & J. Kerr. (Eds.), *Attachment theory: Social, developmental and clinical perspectives* (pp. 223–279). Hillsdale, NJ: Analytic Press.

Fonagy, P., & Target, M. (2001). Attaccamento e funzione riflessiva: Selected papers of Peter Fonagy and Mary Target. In V. Lingiardi (Ed.), *Attaccamento e funzione riflessiva: Selected papers of Peter Fonagy and Mary Target.* Milan, IT: Raffaello Cortina.

Fonagy, P., Target, M., Steele, M., & Steele, H. (1998). *Reflective-functioning manual version 5 for application to Adult Attachment Interviews.* London, England: University College London.

George, C., Kaplan, N., & Main, M. (1985). *Adult Attachment Interview.* Unpublished manuscript, Department of Psychology, University of California, Berkeley, CA.

George, C., & Solomon, J. (1996). Representational models of relationships: Links between caregiving and attachment. *Infant Mental Health Journal, 17,* 198–216.

Gratz, K. L., & Roemer, L. (2004). Multidimensional assessment of emotion regulation and dysregulation: Development, factor structure, and initial validation of the difficulties in emotion regulation scale. *Journal of Psychopathology & Behavioral Assessment, 26*(1), 41–54.

Grice, H. P. (1989). *Studies in the way of words.* Cambridge, MA: Harvard University Press.

Hesse, E. (1999). The Adult Attachment Interview: Historical and current perspectives. In J. Cassidy & P. R. Shaver (Eds.), *Handbook of attachment: Theory, research, and clinical applications* (pp. 395–433). New York, NY: Guilford Press.

Jacobvitz, D., Leon, K., & Hazen, N. (2006). Does expectant mothers' unresolved trauma predict frightened/frightening maternal behavior? Risk and protective factors. *Development and Psychopathology, 18*(2), 363–379.

Liotti, G. (1992). Disorganized/disoriented attachment in the etiology of the dissociative disorders. *Dissociation, 5,* 196–204.

Liotti, G. (2004). Trauma, dissociation, and disorganized attachment: Three strands of a single braid. *Psychotherapy: Theory, Research, Practice, Training, 41*(4), 472–486. doi:10.1037/0033-3204.41.4.472

Main, M. (1995). Attachment: Overview, with implications for clinical work. In S. Goldberg, R. Muir, & J. Kerr (Eds.), *Attachment theory: Social, developmental and clinical perspectives* (pp. 223–279). Hillsdale, NJ: Analytic Press.

Main, M., & Hesse, E. (1990). Parents' unresolved traumatic experiences are related to infant disorganized attachment status: Is frightened and/or frightening parental behavior the linking mechanism? In M. Greenberg, D. Cicchetti, & E. M. Cummings (Eds.), *Attachment in the preschool years: Theory, research and intervention* (pp. 161–184). Chicago, IL: University of Chicago Press.

Main, M., & Goldwyn, R. (1991). *Adult attachment classification system.* Unpublished manuscript, University of California, Berkeley, CA.

Main, M., Kaplan, N., & Cassidy, J. (1985). Security in infancy, childhood, and adulthood: A move to the level of representation. *Monographs of the Society for Research in Child Development, 50*(1/2), 66–104.

Main, M., & Solomon, J. (1990). Procedures for identifying infants as disorganized/disoriented during the Ainsworth Strange Situation. In M. T. Greenberg, D. Cicchetti, & E. M. Cummings (Eds.), *Attachment during the preschool years: Theory, research and intervention* (pp. 121–160). Chicago, IL: University of Chicago Press.

Pagani, M., Di Lorenzo, G., Verardo, A. R., Nicolais, G., Monaco, L., Lauretti, G., & Siracusano, A. (2012). Neurobiological correlates of EMDR monitoring—An EEG study. *PloS ONE, 7*(9), e45753. doi:10.1371/journal.pone.0045753

Saunders, R., Jacobvitz, D., Zaccagnino, M., Loch, L., & Hazen, N. (2006). Pathways to earned security: The role of alternative support figures. Presented at 15th biennial conference of the SRHD, Fort Worth, TX.

Shapiro, F. (1995). *Eye movement desensitization and reprocessing: Basic principles, protocols, and procedures.* New York, NY: Guilford Press.

Shapiro, F. (2001). *Eye movement desensitization and reprocessing: Basic principles, protocols and procedures* (2nd ed.). New York, NY: Guilford Press.

Slade, A., Grienenberger, J., Bernbach, E., Levy, D., & Locker, A. (2005). Maternal reflective functioning, attachment, and the transmission gap: A preliminary study. *Attachment & Human Development, 7*(3), 283–298. doi:10.1080/14616730500245880

van Ijzendoorn, M. H. (1992). Intergenerational transmission of parenting: A review of studies in nonclinical populations. *Developmental Review, 12,* 76–99.

van Ijzendoorn, M. H. (1995). Adult attachment representations, parental responsiveness, and infant attachment: A meta-analysis on the predictive validity of the Adult Attachment Interview. *Psychological Bulletin, 117*(3), 387–403. doi:10.1037/0033-2909.117.3.387

Wesselmann, D., & Potter, A. E. (2009). Change in adult attachment status following treatment with EMDR: Three case studies. *Journal of EMDR Practice and Research, 3*(3), 178–191. doi:10.1891/1933-3196.3.3.178

Zaccagnino, M., Cussino, M., Saunders, R., Jacobvitz, D., & Veglia, F. (2012). Alternative caregiving figures and their role on adult attachment representations. *Clinical Psychology & Psychotherapy.* Online Ver. doi:10.1002/cpp.1828

SUMMARY SHEET: Working on Attachment Issues With EMDR Therapy: The Attachment Protocol

2A

Anna Rita Verardo and Maria Zaccagnino
SUMMARY SHEET BY MARILYN LUBER

Name: _____ Diagnosis: _____

☑ Check when task is completed, response has changed, or to indicate symptoms or diagnosis.

Note: This material is meant as a checklist for your response. Please keep in mind that it is only a reminder of different tasks that may or may not apply to your client.

Theoretical Background

The Attachment and Caregiving Systems

Bowlby's Attachment Theory: Important Concepts

The Attachment System: An innate predisposition moving children to seek protective closeness of their attachment figure in response to real or perceived stress or danger.

The Caregiving System: To provide protection to children, promote the closeness and well-being of children, and comfort them in moments of difficulty, distress, or danger.

Internal Working Models (IWMs): Attachment behaviors are ultimately guided at a cognitive level by internal representation, or IWMs, based on the generalization and differentiation of children's experiences, which will then extend to later social interactions.

Prompt Response by Caregiver = Possibility of the child developing a positive representation of self, others, and self-with-others relationship.

Failure of Caregiver to Respond Empathically = Children perceiving themselves as unworthy of care.

Patterns of Attachment

Mary Ainsworth's Three Patterns of Attachment and the Strange Situation Procedure

☐ *Secure Style*: The interaction with the caretaker is warm, affectionate, and sensitive, and children feel worthy of love and develop an image of the caregiver as willing and able to help in times of difficulty or danger.

☐ *Avoidant Style*: When the caregiver ignores children's requests, they deactivate their attachment behavior and are independent and oriented toward exploration.

- *Ambivalent Style*: When the caregiver is inconsistent and unpredictable, children overactivate the attachment system to catch the caregiver's attention and have difficulty activating the exploration system and stay very close to their parents.

Main and Solomon's Fourth Model

- It was hypothesized that a frightened/frightening caretaker leads to a disorganization in the attachment pattern of the child. In this case, the child is not able to display an organized strategy to deal with the stress of separation and reunion moments with his or her attached figure.

The Adult Attachment Interview and the Parental State of Mind

The Adult Attachment Interview is a semi-structured interview whose purpose is to assess the representations of the parent in relation to his own earliest attachment experiences.

Kaplan and Cassidy's Five Categories of State of Mind Regarding Attachment Relationships During Infancy

- *Secure/Autonomous:* Describe positive and negative experiences.
  Narrative: Consistent, memories concrete, and fit into context; capacity for free exploration of thoughts and feelings.
  Violation of Grice's maxims: None.
- *Dismissing*: Idealizing narrative in contrast to negative memories; attempt to affirm independence and minimize negative effects of early experiences.
  Narrative: Often providing too much or too little information and generalizing in the absence of specific memories.
  Violation of Grice's maxims: Quantity and quality.
- *Entangled/Preoccupied:* Narrative inconsistent and often irrelevant; IWM oscillates between positive and negative representations of the attachment emotions concerning themselves and others. Appear angry, passive, or frightened in initial relationships.
  Narrative: Often inconsistent, not pertinent, not clear, and give too much or too little information.
  Violation of Grice's maxims: relation, manner, and quantity.
- *Unresolved*: Unresolved state of mind and bring up traumatic memories.
  Narrative: Fail to monitor their discourse of reasoning; for example, will refer to a dead person as living.
  Violation of Grice's maxims: Quality.
- *Cannot Classify*: Representations are incompatible and contradictory. Usually associated with stories of violence, abuse, and psychiatric disturbances.
  Narrative: Fail to monitor their discourse of reasoning; for example, will refer to a dead person as living.
  Violation of Grice's maxims: Quality.

Grice's Conversational Maxims

- *The Maxim of Quantity*: "Provide the information that is necessary; neither too much nor too little."
  Examples of Violation of the Quantity Maxim: Speakers who give far more information than is necessary and appear to be lost in their own memories often have a *preoccupied* style, which is observed in their texts. Another example of this maxim is when an interviewee chooses to or cannot answer a specific question and responds by saying, "I don't remember." This response illustrates a *dismissing* style.
- *The Maxim of Quality*: "Be sincere; tell the truth as you see it."
  Example of Violation of the Quality Maxim: A contradiction between the abstract or semantic description of attachment figures and descriptions of specific episodes involving those persons (e.g., a speaker states that the mother was "very loving"

but reports episodes of rejection or maltreatment). This is often a characteristic of speakers with *dismissing* styles.
- ☐ *The Maxim of Relation*: "Be pertinent."
  Example of Violation of the Relation Maxim: The speaker departs from interview topic; for example, by using free associations. This violation is typical of speakers with *preoccupied* styles.
- ☐ *The Maxim of Manner*: "Be clear."
  Example of Violation of the Maxim of Manner: The speaker uses quotations from others without making it clear that a quotation is about to be offered or has the tendency to start a sentence but not finish it. This violation is typical of speakers with *preoccupied* styles.

Intergenerational Transmission of Attachment

Reflective Function (RF) is the ability of the adult to mentalize and to understand that behavior—everyone's behavior—is a reflection of underlying mental states, like feelings, desires, thoughts, and intentions. It plays a central role in the development of the child's attachment and, in this regard, can be considered a central mechanism in the intergenerational transmission of attachment. The RF Scale is applied to the Parent Development Interview (PDI) transcripts.

- ☐ Moderate to high RF might include characteristics such as the following:
  - An awareness of the nature of mental states
  - An explicit effort to tease out mental states underlying behavior
  - Recognizing developmental aspects of mental states
  - Recognizing mental states of the interviewer
- ☐ Low RF might include characteristics such as the following:
  - The rejection of mental states
  - Unintegrated, bizarre, or inappropriate awareness of mental states
  - Distorted or self-serving understanding of mental states
  - Naïve or simplistic awareness of mental states
  - Overly analytical or hyperactive usage of RF

Measures

- ☐ *The Adult Attachment Interview* (see earlier discussion)
- ☐ *The PDI* (Aber, Slade, Berger, Bresgi, & Kaplan, 1985; Slade et al., 2005)
- ☐ *Adverse Childhood Experiences Scale* (Dube, Felitti, & Rishi, 2013)
- ☐ *Dissociative Experience Scale* (DES; Bernstein & Putnam, 1986)
- ☐ *Difficulties in Emotion Regulation Scale* (DERS; Gratz & Roemer, 2004)

The Attachment Protocol Script

Phase 1: History Taking

Client History–Taking Questions

THE DISTURBANCE

Problem: _____

_____

Characteristics: _____

_____

Onset: _____

_____

List Triggering Events: _____

_____

EFFECT OF DISORDER ON PRESENT LIFE

Effect on present living conditions: _____

_____

Effect on working conditions: _____

_____

Effect on social life conditions: _____

_____

Effect on health: _____

_____

FAMILY HISTORY

Effect on family relations: _____

_____

ATTACHMENT HISTORY

Five adjectives reflecting relationship with your mother/father from as far back as you remember: _____

_____

Memory illustrating adjective: _____

_____

When upset as child, parental response: _____

_____

When hurt as child, parental response: _____

_____

When separated from parents, your response and parental response: _____
_____
_____

Other significant separations: _____
_____

List times felt rejected as child, age, and what parent(s) did: _____
_____
_____

List times parents physically present but emotionally unavailable: _____
_____
_____

List times pressured to achieve in school/athletics: _____
_____
_____

List times taking care of parent(s) or parents treating you as their spouse: _____
_____
_____

For dismissive clients often unable to get to specific memories:
Bring photos of early family life/tell old family stories: _____
_____
_____

MOURNING AND/OR TRAUMATIC EXPERIENCES

List losses of parent or other close loved ones when a child: _____
_____
_____

For each memory ask:
Circumstances, age, and reaction(s): _____
_____
_____
_____

Death, sudden or expected: _____

_____

Feelings at the time and whether they have changed. _____

_____

Other traumatic experiences: _____

_____

CAREGIVING BEHAVIOR

Describe self as parent: _____

_____

Most pleasurable part of relationship: _____

_____

Most difficult part of relationship: _____

_____

Cause of any setbacks in relationship: _____

_____

Any sense of hopelessness when parenting: _____

_____

Any sense of hostility when parenting: _____

_____

Describe self as partner: _____

_____

Most pleasurable part of relationship: _____

_____

Most difficult part of relationship: _____

_____

Cause of any setbacks in relationship: _____

_____

Summary Sheet: Working on Attachment Issues With EMDR Therapy

Any sense of hopelessness with significant other: _____
_____

Any sense of hostility with significant other: _____
_____

Identification of Resources

Identify the memory when able to achieve goal: _____
_____
_____

Identify memory when felt worthy to ask for help with emotions, thoughts, and sensations: _____
_____
_____

Or, what was needed to cope with the situation: _____
_____
_____

Case Conceptualization, Treatment Planning, Target Identification, and Target Selection for Attachment Issues

---

Target Identification and Target Selection for Attachment Issues

Attachment State of Mind, Linguistic Style, and EMDR

☐ *Secure/autonomous*
☐ *Dismissing*
☐ *Entangled/preoccupied*
☐ *Unresolved*
☐ *Cannot classify*

Grice's Conversational Maxims

☐ *The Maxim of Quantity: "Provide the information that is necessary; neither too much nor too little."*
☐ *The Maxim of Quality: "Be sincere; tell the truth as you see it."*
☐ *The Maxim of Relation: "Be pertinent."*
☐ *The Maxim of Manner: "Be clear."*

Resources When You Could Ask For Help

_____
_____

Present

LIST SITUATIONS WHERE YOU FELT YOU NEEDED HELP _____
_____
_____

For each situation:

What you did: _____
_____

How you asked for help: _____
_____

What you do when alone and afraid: _____
_____

What happens when you ask for help: _____
_____

How you react when somebody responds to your request for help: _____
_____

continued

What you feel emotionally: _____

_____

Present-day reactions to activation of caregiving system within client's most significant relationship:

What happens when you are asked to do something for partner: _____

_____

What happens when partner does something for you: _____

_____

NC, emotions, and somatic sensations and this situation: _____

_____

Problems connected with NC: _____

_____

Past Memories

TARGETS RELATED TO ACTIVATION OF ATTACHMENT SYSTEM CONCERNING CERTAIN DYNAMICS
- ☐ Rejection
- ☐ Neglect
- ☐ Pressure to achieve
- ☐ Role reversal

Use Floatback and/or Affect Bridge

Earliest memory of target: _____

_____

FUTURE TEMPLATE (hoped-for future behavior)

Imagine next time you feel the need for help + what are the abilities needed to handle the situation: _____

_____

Treatment Planning

LIST GOALS (benefits, how you know you achieved it; when goals accomplished—what you would see, hear, and feel)

_____

_____

_____

continued

List memories elicited from above in order of most distressing:

Past Memories

_____
_____
_____
_____

Present Triggers

_____
_____
_____
_____

Future Issues

_____
_____
_____
_____

Phase 2: Preparation

☐ *Explanation of the Relational Problem Dynamics*
"Let me explain to you how your attachment and caregiving systems work. When a child feels sad or upset, his or her attachment system is activated and he or she seeks closeness with the caregiver (secure base) to be comforted. Only after that, when the child feels safe, the attachment system can be deactivated and the child can return to explore. These mechanisms are present in every person throughout the entire lifespan. When a loved one seeks your help, instead of activating the attachment system, you are activating another behavioral system, called the caregiving system. The caregiving system allows you to take care of your child (or significant other) and respond in a prompt and warm manner to his or her cues. Also, this system is innate and present in every person."

☐ *Explanation of the Method—Psychoeducation*
"By understanding how your attachment and caregiving systems work and the role of traumatic events in the onset of your difficulties, you will learn how they work and/or do not work for you and bring you closer to new and more helpful coping strategies in the managing of disturbing events."

☐ *Explanation of EMDR Therapy*
"When a trauma occurs, it seems to be locked in the nervous system with the original picture, sounds, thoughts, and feelings. The eye movements we use in EMDR seem to unlock the nervous system and allow the brain to process the experience. That may be what is happening in REM or dream sleep—the eye movements may help to process the unconscious material. It is important to remember that it is your own brain that will be doing the healing and you are the one in control. With your permission, I'm going to _____ (state the type of BLS used). Now I'll show you the procedure in order to decide which is the best distance for you and if you feel comfortable both with eye stimulation and tapping. Feel free to tell me if you don't feel comfortable and try to relax and be calm."

"In order to help you just notice the experience and handle the intensity of the emotions, you can imagine riding on a train and the feelings and thoughts are just the scenery going by. If during the processing you have a problem or you feel you have to stop, please raise your hand and we will stop."

Resources

☐ SAFE BASE EXERCISE

Try to recall a past memory when an adult figure was receptive and cared about you, providing help and satisfying your need, even just a material need. Try also to focus on the emotions and sensations associated with this memory. _____

_____

+ BLS

Then: Safe Base + Positive Images + Sensations + Emotions + BLS

Time in adult life when a significant person was receptive and provided help: _____

_____

Significant Person Receptive + Positive Images + Sensations + Emotions + BLS

Resource Installation

Recall a time (see earlier) when you felt able to ask for help and worthy enough to do it + Emotions + Thoughts + Physical Sensations + BLS. Reinforce with BLS.
Cue word _____ + BLS

Phase 3: Assessment

Target: _____

Picture/Image: _____

NC: _____

Note: If in difficulty: *"In your worst moments, when you are remembering some aspect of the event, what thoughts or negative beliefs do you have about yourself?"*

PC: _____

VoC: _____ /7

Emotions: _____

SUD: _____ /10

Location of Body Sensation: _____

Note: For dismissing clients with low SUD or = 0: Do not use the Standard EMDR Protocol. Focus on episodes when they idealize, generalize, or do not remember episodes with attachment figures and use long sets of BLS to work on these defensive strategies. When memories start to emerge, use as targets for the Standard EMDR Protocol.

Image of Significant Caretaker + Words (idealizing, generalizing, or not remembering) + BLS

Phase 4: Desensitization

Introduce according to the EMDR Standard Protocol. *"Now, remember, it is your own brain that is doing the healing and you are the one in control. I will ask you to mentally focus on the target and to _____ _____ (state BLS you are using). Just let whatever happens, happen, and we will talk at the end of the set. Just tell me what comes up, and don't discard anything as unimportant. Any new information that comes to mind is connected in some way. If you want to stop, just raise your hand."*

Image + NC and Sensations + BLS
    If SUD = 1 or more, continue processing.
    If SUD continues to be 0 after two sets of BLS, go to the Installation Phase.

Phase 5: Installation

PC: ☐ Completed

New PC (if new one is better): _____

VoC: _____ /7

Incident + PC + BLS

Continue Installation with BLS until material becomes increasingly adaptive. If VoC = 6 or less, check and see if there is a limiting belief: *"Which thoughts or concerns prevent you from feeling those words as completely true?"* _____

Note: If the limiting belief is not resolved quickly, explore to see whether there are any limiting beliefs or unidentified/unprocessed memory(ies)/networks that are causing this difficulty.

The session is then considered incomplete; therefore, return to the incomplete target and continue the installation process in the next session.

Phase completed   ☐ Yes   ☐ No

Phase 6: Body Scan   ☐ Completed

"Close your eyes, and keep in mind the original memory and the words _____ (state the positive belief). Then bring your attention to different parts of your body, starting with your head and working downward. Any place you find any tension, tightness, or any unusual feeling, let me know."

Note: If the client reports any negative feeling, do a set of BLS until it disappears. If the client reports positive feelings, continue with BLS in order to strengthen them.

Phase 7: Closure   ☐ Completed

Access more neutral and positive memory networks: Safe Base + BLS

"Things may come up or they may not. If they do, great. Write it down and it can be a target for next time. You can use a log to write down triggers, images, thoughts or cognitions, emotions, and sensations; you can rate them on our 0 to 10 scale, where 0 is no disturbance or neutral and 10 is the worst disturbance. Please write down the positive experiences, too."

"If you get any new memories, dreams, or situations that disturb you, just take a good snapshot. It is not necessary to give a lot of detail. Just put down enough to remind you so we can target it next time. The same thing goes for any positive dreams or situations. If negative feelings do come up, try not to make them significant. Remember, it is still just the old stuff. Just write it down for next time. Then use the tape or the Safe Place exercise to let as much

of the disturbance go as possible. Even if nothing comes up, make sure to use the tape every day and give me a call if you need to."

Phase 8: Reevaluation ☐ Completed

☐ Check target from last session: VoC: _____ /7 SUDs: _____ /10

Use "Parent as Child" exercise after the Attachment Protocol is completed.

☐ *"Parent as Child" Exercise:* ☐ Completed

Imagine a meeting between your adult self and your mother or father as a child

+ Imagine how old the parent is, what he or she is wearing, and all the details of the image _____

_____

+ As you stand in front of parent, ask how he or she is feeling _____

_____

+ Concentrate on emotions you are feeling as an adult _____

_____

+ Ask your child mother or father what is happening _____

_____

+ Why he or she is feeling like that _____

_____

+ Why he or she acted like that toward you _____

_____

+ Ask child mother or father what you can do to help _____

_____

☐ If vicarious trauma is elicited, use the Standard EMDR target with it if okay with the patient. If not okay, use the Floatback and target that.

☐ Ask the adult client to enter into dialogue with parents as children.
If yes, do BLS to reinforce the positive. If no, check for the block.

☐ Review questions from Phase 1 to underline the changes especially concerning the client's narrative consistency and reflective function.

References

Aber, J., Slade, A., Berger, B., Bresgi, I., & Kaplan, M. (1985). *The parent development interview.* Unpublished manuscript. Barnard College, Columbia University, New York, NY.
Bernstein, E. M., & Putnam, F. W. (1986). Development, reliability, and validity of a dissociation scale. *Journal of Nervous and Mental Disease, 174*(12), 727–735.

Dube, S. R., Felitti, V. J., & Rishi, S. (2013). Moving beyond childhood adversity: Association between salutogenic factors and subjective well-being among adult survivors of trauma. In M. Linden & K. Rutkowski (Eds.), *Hurting memories and beneficial forgetting: Posttraumatic stress disorders, biographical developments and social conflicts* (pp. 139-152). Waltham, MA: Elsevier.

Gratz, K. L., & Roemer, L. (2004). Multidimensional assessment of emotion regulation and dysregulation: Development, factor structure, and initial validation of the difficulties in emotion regulation scale. *Journal of Psychopathology & Behavioral Assessment, 26*(1), 41-54.

Slade, A., Bernbach, E., Grienenberger, J., Levy, D., & Locker, A. (2005). Addendum to fonagy, target, steele, and steele reflective functioning scoring manual for use with the Parent Development Interview, Version 2.0. Unpublished manuscript, The City College and Graduate Center of the City University of New York, New York, NY.

EMDR Therapy for Traumatized Patients With Psychosis

Berber van der Vleugel, David van den Berg, Paul de Bont, Tonnie Staring, and Ad de Jongh

Introduction

The most prominent psychotic symptoms are hallucinations and delusions. *Hallucinations* are perceptual experiences without the corresponding external visual, auditory, olfactory, gustatory, or tactile source. Auditory verbal hallucinations are voices that often say negative things; for example, commands (*"Kill yourself"*), comments (*"He's a moron"*), or threats (*"Let's get rid of him"*). Hallucinations are common in psychotic disorders like schizophrenia, but also occur in other disorders, such as borderline personality disorder (Kingdon et al., 2010), bipolar disorder (Hammersley, Taylor, McGovern, & Kinderman, 2010), depression (Gaudiano, Young, Chelminski, & Zimmerman, 2008), posttraumatic stress disorder (PTSD), and dissociative disorders. In the healthy population, especially in children and adolescents, hearing voices is also a relatively frequent phenomenon (Kelleher et al., 2012).

Delusions are strong convictions that are uncommon in a cultural context and that are maintained despite evidence to the contrary. The delusional content varies widely, but the most prevalent delusion is paranoia (Garety & Hemsley, 1987; Stompe et al., 1999). Paranoia is characterized by threat appraisals in which others are thought to have malevolent intentions. For instance, a patient may think that others are spying on him or are out to get him. Delusions can arise as explanations for anomalous or unsettling experiences, like hallucinations. Although some paranoid thinking exists harmlessly in the healthy population (Freeman et al., 2005), in patients it is usually accompanied with preoccupation, anxiety, and safety behaviors. Paranoid delusions are common in psychotic disorders, and frequent in affective disorders (Goodwin & Jamison, 1990; Haltenhof, Ulrich, & Blanenburg, 1999).

A psychotic disorder is often accompanied by at least one comorbid disorder, such as PTSD, depressive disorder, social phobia, substance abuse and dependence, or obsessive–compulsive disorder (Braga, Mendlowicz, Marrocos, & Figueira, 2005; Buckley, Miller, Lehrer, & Castle, 2009; Grech, van Os, Jones, Lewis, & Murray, 2005). With or without comorbidity, a psychotic condition is usually very disruptive. Patients often experience difficulties with their day-to-day functioning. A comprehensive treatment program offered by a multidisciplinary team is recommended (e.g., NICE Clinical Guidelines for Schizophrenia, 2009). This includes pharmacotherapy, case management, cognitive behavioral therapy (CBT), supported employment, family interventions, and peer support. It is within this comprehensive context that eye movement desensitization and reprocessing (EMDR) can be applied.

Trauma and Psychosis Are Related

Trauma and psychosis may interact in three different ways (Morrison, Frame, & Larkin, 2003).

- First, even with distinct onsets, PTSD can exert a negative influence on psychotic symptoms and vice versa (Mueser, Rosenberg, Goodman, & Trumbetta, 2002).
- Second, the experience of psychotic symptoms can be traumatic and lead to PTSD (Shaw, McFarlane, & Bookless, 1997).
- Third, trauma is a substantial risk factor for the development of psychosis (Matheson, Shepherd, Pinchbeck, Laurens, & Carr, 2013; Varese et al., 2012).

Thus, assessing traumatic life experiences is crucial for creating an individual case formulation within the treatment of psychotic symptoms. Ascertaining the links between trauma, PTSD, and psychosis in patients—by evaluating their occurrence, onset, content, and course—enhances insight and reveals relevant targets for treatment. In this chapter, we will elaborate on these interactions and provide a rationale for the EMDR treatment of these symptoms.

Psychosis and Comorbid PTSD

The prevalence of comorbid PTSD in patients with psychoses is high (12.4–29%; Achim et al., 2011; Buckley et al., 2009; de Bont et al., 2015) compared to the general population (less than 5%) (Kessler, Chiu, Demler, & Walters, 2005; Mueser et al., 1998; Perkonigg, Kessler, Storz, & Wittchen, 2000). Psychotic disorders and PTSD may sometimes even be difficult to disentangle, as both disorders are characterized by intrusive experiences, negative symptoms, and avoidance behaviors (Stampfer, 1990).

Psychosis and PTSD may have independent origins (e.g., a person diagnosed with schizophrenia is involved in a car crash and develops PTSD). One disorder may also cause the other, as is the case in "Post-Psychotic PTSD"; about half of the patients reported PTSD symptoms related to a psychotic episode or admission, directly after dismissal from a psychiatric ward (Shaw et al., 1997). It has been found that although these symptoms spontaneously remit in some patients, a year after dismissal one third of the patients still experienced PTSD symptoms related to their first episode of psychosis (McGorry et al., 1991).

PTSD may contribute to psychotic symptoms and increase relapse rates in psychosis (Mueser et al., 2002). The mechanisms for this include PTSD's high stress levels, sleeping problems, difficulties in coping with situations, and low self-esteem. Furthermore, PTSD is associated with substance abuse and retraumatization. Mueser and his colleagues found that in patients with psychosis, those with comorbid PTSD experience more severe delusions, as well as lower functioning in daily life (Mueser, Lu, Rosenberg, & Wolfe, 2010).

Trauma and Psychosis

More than two thirds of the women and more than half of the men with psychosis report sexual or physical abuse as a child (Read, van Os, Morrison, & Ross, 2005). A meta-analysis found that being traumatized as a child almost triples the chance of developing psychosis in adulthood (Varese et al., 2012). Another meta-analysis showed that people with schizophrenia are 3.6 times more likely than those with other psychiatric disorders and nonpsychiatric controls to have experienced severe childhood trauma (Matheson et al., 2013). Almost all studies found a dose–response relationship: the more severe the trauma, the greater the risk of developing psychosis and the worse the prognosis. Trauma exerts direct and indirect influences on the development of psychotic symptoms. Each route requires its own conceptualization, after which the Standard EMDR Protocol can be applied to achieve symptom reduction or relief.

The Direct Route

Similar to other psychopathology, psychotic symptoms often have their origin in real-life experiences. Direct temporal associations may exist between the stressful or emotional life event and the onset of psychotic symptoms. An example is the development of paranoia after being threatened in a pub (Freeman et al., 2013). In a Dutch study, 70% of the patients who heard voices stated that their voices started after an emotional or traumatic experience (Romme & Escher, 1989).

Even in the absence of a clear temporal association, the content or theme of the psychotic symptom may be meaningfully associated with certain life events. It has been found that auditory verbal hallucinations are directly related to actual life experiences in a significant minority of people hearing voices (Hardy et al., 2005; McCarthy-Jones et al., 2012).

The Indirect Route

Basic assumptions about oneself, others, and the world are included in most cognitive models of psychotic symptoms, for they are thought to be important factors in the development and maintenance of these symptoms (e.g., Garety, Kuipers, Fowler, Freeman, & Bebbington, 2001). Negative core beliefs about oneself (e.g., "I am guilty, weak, defenseless"), and others (e.g., "Other people are dangerous, untrustworthy, bad") can form a cognitive link between traumatic life experiences and psychosis (Fowler et al., 2006; Gracie et al., 2007). Basic assumptions may determine the nature of a delusion, as in "Bad me," or "Poor me" paranoia (Trower & Chadwick, 1995). Similarly, negative responses to critical voices have been found to be associated with negative self-esteem, depression, and early life experiences of maltreatment (Birchwood & Chadwick, 1997). Because traumatized voice hearers view themselves as inferior or powerless, they are also inclined to adopt this submissive stance when relating to their voices. This, in turn, increases the intensity and frequency of the voices, as well as the distress they cause (Birchwood & Chadwick, 1997; Vaughan & Fowler, 2004).

Imagery in Psychosis

Mental imagery appears to be an important factor in the onset and persistence of emotional disorders (Beck, 1970; Hackmann, Surawy, & Clark, 1998). Emerging research shows that mental imagery is also highly prevalent in psychosis. About three quarters of the patients with psychosis report visual imagery related to their delusions or hallucinations (Lockett et al., 2012; Morrison et al., 2002; Schulze, Freeman, Green, & Kuipers, 2013). Morrison et al. (2002) found the following three types of imagery to be most dominant in psychosis:

- Images of feared catastrophes (often in paranoia)
- Visualizations of the perceived origin or content of a symptom (often in voices)
- Images of negative life experiences that are somehow related to the psychotic symptoms (actual memories)

Research

Because people with severe mental illnesses are usually excluded from treatment studies, data on the feasibility of standardized treatment protocols for comorbid psychopathology in this population are rare (Bradley, Greene, Russ, Dutra, & Westen, 2005). Many therapists fear that trauma-focused therapy is dangerous for patients with psychosis, and as a consequence a psychotic disorder has long been an exclusion criterion in almost all PTSD treatment studies (Spinazzola, Blaustein, & van der Kolk, 2005). In fact, psychosis is the most frequently applied exclusion criterion in trials on effectiveness of PTSD treatment (Ronconi, Shiner, & Watts, 2014).

However, times are changing and some studies have shown that it is safe to use trauma-focused approaches for patients with psychosis and comorbid PTSD (Frueh et al., 2009;

Mueser et al., 2008). In a within-subjects controlled case study ($N = 10$; de Bont, van Minnen, & de Jongh, 2013), EMDR and Prolonged Exposure (standardized treatment manual by Foa, Hembree, & Rothbaum, 2007) were both effective in reducing PTSD symptoms (12 sessions, 90 minutes). These effects were maintained at 3-month follow-up. Dropout was 20% and no serious adverse events were found.

In an open study, outpatients with a lifetime diagnosis of psychosis and comorbid PTSD received six EMDR sessions of 90 minutes each ($N = 27$; van den Berg & van der Gaag, 2012). Significant improvements were found on PTSD symptoms, depression, anxiety, hallucinations, and self-esteem. The dropout rate was relatively low: 18.5%. One patient had a one-time relapse in drug use; this was the only adverse event. To further test safety, effectiveness, and mechanisms of change, a randomized clinical trial—applying EMDR and Prolonged Exposure for PTSD in patients with psychosis in addition to treatment as usual—was conducted in the Netherlands (de Bont, van den Berg, et al., 2013). Results showed that an eight-session treatment using standard protocols was feasible, effective, and safe (van den Berg et al., 2015). Subjects receiving therapy showed greater reduction in PTSD symptoms and were more likely to achieve loss of diagnosis during treatment than those on the waiting list. The effects were maintained at 6-month follow-up for both treatment conditions. There were no differences in serious adverse events between conditions. Prolonged Exposure and EMDR Therapy showed no difference on any of the outcomes and no difference in dropout (24.5% and 20.0%, respectively).

The only published study thus far that applied EMDR to target psychotic symptoms is a randomized clinical trial in a hospital setting ($N = 45$; Kim et al., 2010). All patients were admitted for an acute psychotic episode and received extensive treatment, including pharmacotherapy. Three sessions—of either EMDR or relaxation exercises—were added to the treatment as usual. Both groups improved; but as a consequence of the design, the improvements should probably be attributed to the effects of the treatment as usual. No significant differences between EMDR and relaxation were found. Yet, this study demonstrated that EMDR may be accepted by patients with psychosis, and can be applied safely.

Recently, Croes et al. (2014) published three case reports on psychotic outpatients, who received an average of six sessions of EMDR on psychosis-related mental imagery. Results were promising and suggest that it is possible to diminish negative affect related to psychotic imagery. Depressive symptoms subsided and patients reported less safety behaviors and increased cognitive insight. Noteworthy is that these patients reported most profound effects after treatment of mental imagery resembling worst-case scenarios (i.e., flashforwards).

According to these findings, standardized treatment protocols are feasible without adaptations and are effective in treating comorbid PTSD. Serious adverse effects do not appear to occur.

EMDR Therapy for Traumatized Patients With Psychosis Script Notes

Considering the diversity and severity of psychotic symptoms and problems in daily life, one should not expect EMDR Therapy to solve all problems. Patients with a severe mental illness, such as schizophrenia, will usually not be cured by EMDR Therapy. Clearly though, EMDR is a powerful intervention for reducing anxiety levels, delusional preoccupation, or the impact of hallucinations on self-esteem. This is especially the case when EMDR Therapy is embedded in a more comprehensive (cognitive behavioral) treatment approach. In order to intervene efficaciously with EMDR Therapy, one should first select the targeted symptom and then look for meaningful life experiences that caused or contributed to its onset. Merely shooting from the hip will not lead to a better clinical outcome. Rather, therapist and patient should behave like snipers.

In order to enhance diagnostic reliability, the use of validated, standardized measures is recommended. Its purpose is to assess symptoms and problematic functioning, construct a case formulation, and evaluate treatment effects. For instance:

- Mini-International Neuropsychiatric Interview-Plus (M.I.N.I.-Plus; Sheehan et al., 1998); it is suitable for diagnosing Axis-1 disorders and reduces the chance of overlooking relevant comorbidity.
- Clinician-Administered PTSD Scale (CAPS; Blake et al., 1995); it is the gold standard in diagnosing PTSD.
- Positive and Negative Syndrome Scale (PANSS; Kay, Fiszbein, & Opler, 1987); it is a semi-structured interview to determine the range and severity of symptoms related to psychosis.
- The Psychotic Symptom Rating Scale (PSYRATS; Haddock, McCarron, Tarrier, & Faragher, 1999); it includes the Auditory Hallucinations Rating Scale (AHRS) and Delusion Rating Scale (DRS), and is an excellent instrument for the evaluation of treatment effects.

For practical reasons, the most relevant questions are listed in the script in Phase 1.

Case Conceptualization Methods

Case conceptualization refers to the process of gathering information about a patient and integrating this information with a theory on mechanisms that may be causing or maintaining symptoms. A case conceptualization organizes information and guides the process of therapy. It offers insight on what is needed to bring about change and it helps to tailor therapeutic interventions to the individual. We distinguish three different ways of conceptualizing in EMDR treatment, depending on the goal of treatment (summarized in Table 3.1 in the Scripted Protocol). Once the target memory is selected, the Standard Protocol of EMDR can be used.

For case conceptualizations in the context of EMDR, we strongly recommend the use of the First and Second Methods (de Jongh, ten Broeke, & Meijer, 2010; see Figure 3.1). This so-called Two-Method Approach offers a clear rationale for a treatment plan for problems other than PTSD per se (see de Jongh et al., 2010, for a detailed description). It is a highly structured procedure for questioning the patient in the Preparation Phase (Phase 2), in order to select the target memories that need to be processed to achieve symptom relief. In addition, the authors have had positive experiences with adding a Third Method—an expansion of the Two-Method Approach—that deals with unrealistic expectations or negative imagery related to psychosis. First, each of these three case conceptualization methods is briefly described and explained. They are summarized in Figure 3.2. The questions to be asked are all scripted in Phases 2 and 3 of the Scripted Protocol.

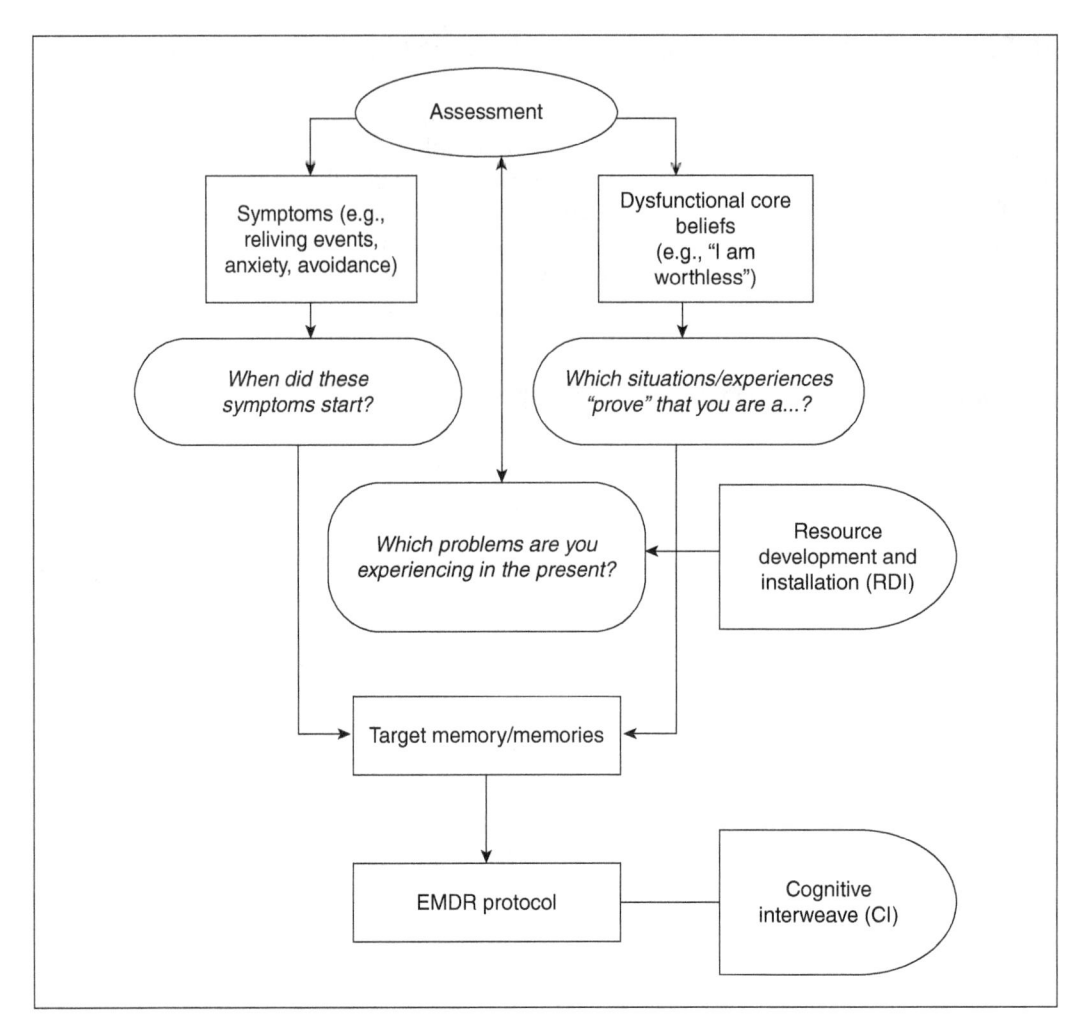

Figure 3.1 Two-method model of EMDR.
De Jongh et al. (2010).

The First Method

The First Method is primarily aimed at conceptualizing EMDR Therapy in the treatment of *Diagnostic and Statistical Manual of Mental Disorders, Fifth Edition* (*DSM-5*) disorders (which in earlier versions of the *DSM* were referred to as Axis-I disorders), including PTSD. The starting point is the selection of the target *symptom* (or cluster of symptoms), after which etiological and subsequent aggravating events are identified and visually summarized on a timeline (de Jongh, ten Broeke, & Meijer, 2010). This First Method is applicable for psychotic symptoms that can be directly related to certain life events (see The Direct Route section). Prompts may include:

- *"From your point of view, which events are responsible for the current symptoms?"*
- *"Which event(s) led to these symptoms?"*
- *"Which event(s) might have worsened these symptoms?"*

The course of the symptoms is then plotted on the timeline. Memories of experiences that are strongly related to the onset and aggravation of the selected symptoms are processed chronologically to achieve symptom reduction.

The Second Method

The Second Method is used to identify memories that underlie dysfunctional basic assumptions. This method is primarily used in complex psychopathology and personality disorders, where dysfunctional basic assumptions exert their influence. The starting point in the Second Method is the negative dysfunctional basic assumption(s) that is/are associated with the patient's problems. This method should be used if negative core beliefs form a cognitive link between life experiences and psychosis (see The Indirect Route section). Target images of experiences that have led to the formation of negative beliefs about oneself, others, and the world (the so-called proof/evidence) are identified. An analogy that describes the search strategy is that of a Google search, with the learning history of the patient being the World Wide Web and the core belief being the keyword entered. The memories that are most relevant to the credibility of the core belief are selected for processing. Using this Second Method, prompts are as follows:

- *"What caused you to start believing/believe that you are (a) _____ (state the core belief)?"*
- *"What 'taught' you that you are (a) _____ (state the core belief)?"*
- *"Which early situations currently still 'prove' to you emotionally, so to speak, that you are (a) _____ (state the core belief)?"*
- *"Think of a more recent situation that shows you that you are (a) _____ (state the core belief)."*

These pieces of evidence are then ranked in a hierarchy (from strong to weak "proof") and processed with the Standard EMDR Protocol. This is done to deactivate the negative schemas and decrease their credibility.

The Third Method

The Third Method is added to identify the unrealistic and terrifying expectations or negative imageries that are related to psychosis. In some patients, imagery may even be the actual internal activating event that triggers paranoid ideation or rumination about voices. Reprocessing such imagery using EMDR Therapy, and in that way removing the trigger for rumination, may reduce patients' symptoms. Many patients experience intrusive imagery that is related to their psychotic symptoms (Morrison et al., 2002). Imagery can be so frightening (e.g., the mental image of getting murdered in the context of paranoid fears, or imagining the voices like horrific creatures) that it results in extensive avoidance behaviors. Processing the worst-case scenario using EMDR can substantially decrease anxiety. EMDR focused on intrusive psychosis imagery or worst-case scenarios can be conceptualized as flashforwards (Engelhard et al., 2011; Engelhard, van den Hout, Janssen, & van der Beek, 2010; Logie & de Jongh, 2014). If the patient has a still image of the worst moment of his catastrophic ideation in mind, he is asked to make it as detailed as possible. Next, the Negative Cognition (NC), Positive Cognition (PC), Validity of Cognition (VoC), emotions, Subjective Units of Disturbance (SUD), and bodily location are elicited in the usual way to process the target. Since patients generally experience a lack of control when bringing up their flashforwards, they are, in fact, powerless against the—by definition—intrusive image. Therefore, when using EMDR aimed at patients' flashforwards, it usually works best to use the NC, "I am powerless," as the default NC; "I am in control [of the flashforward]" or "I can handle it" (i.e., the flashforward, not the feared event actually happening) should then be used as the standard PC. Next, all the remaining phases of the Eight-Phase Protocol (Shapiro, 2001) need to be executed until a SUD of 0 and a VoC of 7 have been reached. After this is done successfully, patients can more easily be motivated to expose themselves to feared stimuli or execute behavioral experiments that they feared beforehand.

	Key Question
First Method	When did the psychotic symptoms start or worsen? Use the timeline to ascertain the event after which the psychotic symptoms started and when the symptoms grew worse.
Second Method	Which experiences emotionally still "prove" that you are ____? Establish the dysfunctional, problematic beliefs. Google-like approach for target selection based on dysfunctional, problematic beliefs. Look for the "evidence" for the dysfunctional, problematic beliefs.
Third Method	What is the intrusive thought or image that you fear may happen in the future? Look for sheer disaster fantasies or worst-case scenarios. Look for visualization of perceived origin or content of psychotic symptoms.

Figure 3.2 Summary of methods for case conceptualization.

Obstacles and Related Treatment Strategies

Clinical experience is that standard EMDR procedures can be followed, although some remarks and caveats need to be made.

Adaptations to the EMDR Standard Protocol

Especially when cognitive impairments are present or patients' thoughts and feelings are disorganized, it is important that sessions be highly structured and instructions clearly formulated in short sentences. Some formulations in this protocol may thus be stated somewhat differently than in the Standard Protocol.

- *Content of Phases 1 and 2*: Phase 1 is a general inventory of current symptoms and problems. This information is used to get an agreement on the goals of treatment and leads to a decision on what method to use for conceptualization (e.g., First, Second, or Third Method). The actual conceptualization is then beyond the scope of an intake assessment and is an in-therapy assessment, preparing the processing, thus Phase 2. In Phase 2 a structured search strategy is used, leading to testable hypotheses about how experiences and symptoms are connected.
- *Keeping focus*: To assist patients in keeping some focus, in Phase 4 (Desensitization) we prefer instructions like: "Stay with that," or "Concentrate on that," over "Go with that."
- *Back to target adaptation*: When applying EMDR with psychotic patients, we recommend a minor adaptation for going Back to Target. Rather than going back to the *incident*, patients are asked to recall the initial *image* that was used to establish the NC/PC (as it is represented in the mind now, if it has changed during processing). In this way, the image is used as the portal to the memory. It is our experience that this strategy helps patients maintain a straight focus on the memory that is being worked on. Using a clear focus on the aspects of the target image that trigger the affect not only appears to be practically helpful (for instance, when asking to rate the SUD),

but also facilitates connecting of the nodes in the fear network that still need to be processed.
- *Distinction between self-esteem and responsibility*: Another adaptation from the Standard Protocol is in the formulation of the NC and PC. Restricting the categories by a distinction between the cognitive domains of self-esteem (e.g., "I am weak" or "I am a bad person") and responsibility (e.g., "I am guilty") is preferred.
- *Positive lessons*: At the end of every session patients are asked for positive lessons learned during the session ("positive closure"), to consolidate changes and improvements that have occurred.

Ongoing Traumatization by Psychotic Experiences

Patients may be unable to feel safe at all (in spite of using the Resource Development and Installation procedure) when they are continuously being threatened by voices or when they are convinced that every hour may be their last. SUD scores will be high and will not drop, irrespective of the selected target or distracting stimulus. A Cognitive Interweave can be used on this type of "blocking belief," but more cognitive interventions may be needed to challenge attributions and patients' delusional convictions. As soon as there is at least some doubt about delusional ideas or preoccupation, EMDR can be used by directly targeting patients' imagery (Third Method). Almost always, this needs to be followed up with behavioral experiments and exposure assignments, as is described in the end of Phase 8 of this Scripted Protocol.

Cognitive Impairments

Poor concentration and working memory deficits are often present in psychotic disorders (Bora, Yucel, & Pantelis, 2009). Hallucinations can make it even harder to concentrate. Patients may have difficulty remembering EMDR instructions or following the distracting stimulus with their eyes. The therapist continues in the usual way, repeating the instructions.

The working memory theory (Andrade, Kavanagh, & Baddeley, 1997) states that in order to keep a visual memory representation in the visuospatial sketchpad (VSSP) of the working memory, it is constantly retrieved from and reconsolidated in the visual long-term memory. This refreshment procedure requires working memory resources that are limited in everyone, and even more limited in many patients with a psychotic disorder. Simultaneously performing a dual task that taxes working memory (for instance, following the therapist's fingers or listening to beeps) is an extra effort. The dual task competes with the refreshment procedure for the limited resources. This may result in a decrease of the vividness and emotionality of the memory representation. In accordance with this working memory explanation of EMDR (see Gunter & Bodner, 2008), the decline in vividness and emotionality of a memory is indeed related to the degree of taxing of the working memory by the dual (distracting) task (van den Hout et al., 2010). While research shows it is good clinical practice to apply eye movements as the first choice of modality when using EMDR (de Jongh, Ernst, Marques, & Hornsveld, 2013), eye movements at a usual pace may be too demanding for some patients with a psychotic disorder. Yet, enough working memory load is required to compete with the refreshment procedure. This dual processing may require individual fine-tuning. The taxing of working memory can be adjusted by speeding up or slowing down the passes when eliciting eye movements, or switching to tasks that require less working memory capacity such as beeps.

Difficulty With Eye Movements

Saccadic eye movements are the directional movements over a large angle that eyes make in order to construct a three-dimensional view of the surrounding world. Schizophrenia is associated with impaired saccadic eye movements (Krebs et al., 2010). Saccadic eye movements can be slower or impaired by involuntary movements; this may be connected to prefrontal impairments in motor inhibition. However, it is the authors' opinion that saccadic impairments are unlikely to be an obstacle for EMDR, since the results of a wide array of experimental studies suggest that rather than the eye movements themselves, it is the taxing of the working memory during recall of aversive memories that is the agent of change (van den Hout et al., 2010). Nevertheless, other tasks may be used, for instance, bilateral auditory beeps, tapping, drawing, simple games, and so on.

Antipsychotic Medications

EMDR may work because it activates the cholinergic system in the brain, associated with learning, memory, and attention (Elofsson, von Schèele, Theorell, & Söndergaard, 2008). Both antipsychotic medications and medication preventing motor side effects of antipsychotics (e.g., hydrochloride) can affect cholinergic receptors. It is uncertain whether EMDR is less effective when patients are on these medications, but it might be the case. If a patient is not responding and, at the same time, is heavily medicated, consider lowering the dosage.

Low Affective Expression

It can be difficult to judge the distress that a patient experiences during EMDR, due to some of the negative symptoms of schizophrenia (e.g., apathy, anhedonia, and affective flattening). Research findings suggest that affective flattening is limited to less emotional *expression*, while the subjective emotional experience remains unaffected (Foussias & Remington, 2010). Therefore, when patients report high SUD scores, while at the same time their facial expressions show no signs of distress, discuss the subjective scale of SUDs with patients to ascertain what is (un)bearable. Engaging patients in this manner is useful in helping them stay within the "optimal arousal zone" or "window of tolerance" (Ogden & Pain, 2006).

Unusual Side Effects and Destabilization

As in other populations, unusual reactions or abreactions may occur. Most patients with serious mental illnesses have a relapse prevention or coping plan that they have established with their caretakers. It is a good thing to discuss this plan, and, if needed, actualize it, before treatment starts.

Psychotic symptoms may increase temporarily in or between sessions. It is recommended to suggest this possibility so patients will not be surprised, and precautions or an action plan can be created together. It is helpful to normalize these types of reactions when they occur (e.g., "Good, this is an indication we are treating the right target because the voices are responding to it") and continue treatment. Also, it is useful to educate patients' social support systems and to improve coping strategies if necessary.

Dissociation is a possible response as well. If this is a familiar response, patients often know what works well for them, if it occurs. Therapists can discuss beforehand what can be done to help stop dissociating. Although uncomfortable, and sometimes exhausting, the dissociative response is always temporary. In our opinion, dissociation is a biopsychological coping mechanism to deal with very high stress levels, and therapists can explain this perspective in the following way:

> *Your stress level rose too high. We'll just wait until the stress is manageable again. Please take your time and do what you have to do to regain control. I'll stay here, with you. Take your time.*

It can be useful to help the patient focus on the here and now, for example, by naming objects in the room or touching things.

Occasionally, other uncommon reactions occur. For instance, one patient kept hearing the beeps that were used as auditory bilateral distracting stimuli for several days after a treatment session. Again, a normalizing attitude is probably best, for these effects have, thus far, always disappeared again.

Therapeutic Stance

The disclosure of traumas, negative schemas, and delusional thinking can cause discomfort. As always, the therapist should be empathic and goal oriented. An inquisitive and self-confident attitude is the ideal combination. For example, when treating arachnophobia, it is important not to show your fear of spiders, and it is preferable that first-aid doctors look unaffected emotionally by blood. It is the same with EMDR and treating patients with psychosis: it is important for therapists to transmit to patients that addressing trauma may be burdensome but harmless. For instance:

> *I am sorry that you experienced such terrible things. While these things are in the past, you are still experiencing memories of them. Memories can be very unsettling, but they cannot really harm you (give an example such as, "Your father used to hit you; but the memory of your father cannot"). In treatment, we will work through some of your worst memories to help you experience that you have the strength and resilience to cope. I am confident that you will succeed.*

EMDR Therapy for Traumatized Patients With Psychosis Scripted Protocol

Phase 1: Symptom Selection

Current and Future Concerns

Say, *"Do you experience any psychological problems at the moment? What worries you? Which kinds of things are upsetting you?"*

_____
_____
_____
_____

Say, *"What do you think may happen in the future?"*

_____
_____

Say, *"What triggers these thoughts?"*

_____
_____

Say, *"What are the images you have about what may happen in the future?"*

_____
_____

Say, *"What triggers these images?"*

_____
_____

Say, *"How do you feel as a result of these thoughts and images?"*

_____
_____

Say, *"What is happening in your body as a result of these thoughts and images?"*

_____
_____

Say, *"What do you do because of these thoughts and images?"*

_____
_____

Say, *"What is your worst-case scenario?"*

_____
_____

Say, *"What is the most likely scenario?"*

_____
_____

Posttraumatic Stress Symptoms

Say, *"In short, what has your life been like so far? Tell me some of the highs and some lows."*

_____
_____
_____

Say, *"Have you experienced, witnessed, or were you confronted with an event or events that involved actual or threatened death or serious injury, or a threat to the physical integrity of yourself or others?"*

_____
_____
_____
_____
_____
_____

If so, say, *"At the time, did you feel terror, helplessness, or horror?"*

_____
_____

The following questions concern present time (last week or month):

Say, *"Do you often think about or reexperience vivid memories of what happened to you in the past? Are those memories intrusive?"*

_____

Say, *"Do you have recurrent and intrusive dreams of the event?"*

_____

Say, *"Do you sometimes act or feel as if the event were recurring?"*

_____

Say, *"Are you distressed when exposed to situations or symbols that resemble the traumatic event (psychologically/physiologically)?"*

_____

Say, *"Do you try to avoid thoughts, feelings, activities, places, or people that are associated with the incident?"*

_____

Say, *"Are you unable to recall an important part of the incident?"*

_____

Say, *"Do you have a pronounced decreased interest in activities that were once important to you?"*

_____

Say, *"Are you feeling detached or estranged from others?"*

_____

Say, *"Are you feeling flat or down?"*

_____

Say, *"Do you have a sense that your future will be short?"*

_____

Say, *"Have you had problems falling or staying asleep?"*

_____

Say, *"Have you felt especially irritable or showed strong feelings of anger?"*

_____

Say, *"Have you found it difficult to concentrate on what you were doing or on things going on around you?"*

_____

Say, *"Have you been especially alert or watchful, even when there was no real need to be?"*

_____

Say, *"Have you had any strong startle reactions?"*

_____

For all of the above symptoms, if an answer is positive, ask the following questions with regard to that symptom:

a. Examples: Say, *"What is that like?"*

_____
_____

Frequency: Say, *"How much of the time in the past week/month did you feel that way?"*

_____

b. Intensity: Say, *"How difficult was that for you? How much does that interfere with your everyday life at the moment?"*

_____
_____

Based on this information, is there an indication for the treatment of frequent and disturbing trauma-related symptom(s)?   ☐ Yes   ☐ No

Symptom(s): _____

Onset: Say, *"When did you first start experiencing this/these symptom/s?"*

_____
_____

Psychotic Symptoms—Delusional Ideas

Say, *"Do you ever feel that others cannot be trusted?"*

_____
_____

Say, *"Do you ever think that others are after you, are spying on you, or want to harm you in any way?"*

_____

_____

Say, *"Are you convinced others can read your mind or hear your thoughts? Or the other way around?"*

_____

_____

Say, *"Have you had the experience that someone is putting ideas in your mind? Or is controlling you in some way?"*

_____

_____

Say, *"Do you receive messages (on TV, radio, or in newspapers) that are expressed/transmitted especially for you?"*

_____

_____

Say, *"Are you special in some way? Do you have any special gifts?"*

_____

_____

For all of the above symptoms, if an answer is positive, ask the following questions with regard to the symptom(s):

Say, *"Tell me about it. What is it like?"*

_____

_____

Say, *"How often does this happen?"*

_____

_____

Say, *"How disturbing is this for you?"*

_____

_____

Based on this information, is there an indication for the treatment of frequent and disturbing delusional ideas?   ☐ Yes   ☐ No

Delusion(s): _____

Onset: Say, *"When did you start having these thoughts?"*

_____
_____

Psychotic Symptoms—Auditory Verbal Hallucinations

Say, *"Do you hear voices or other sounds other people cannot hear?"*

_____

If the answer is positive, ask the following:

Say, *"What kind of things do they say?"*

_____
_____

Say, *"What do you think of them?"*

_____
_____

Say, *"Where do they come from?"*

_____

Say, *"Who are they?"*

_____

Say, *"What is their goal?"*

_____
_____

Based on this information, is there an indication for the treatment of frequent and disturbing auditory hallucinations? ☐ Yes ☐ No

Voice(s) sound like: _____

Onset: Say, *"When did you first start hearing these voices?"*

_____
_____

Psychotic Symptoms—Visual Hallucinations

Say, *"Do you have visions while awake? Do you see things that other people cannot see?"*

_____

If the answer is positive, ask the following:

Say, *"What kind of things?"*

_____
_____

Say, *"What do you think of them?"*

_____
_____

Say, *"Where do they come from?"*

_____
_____

Say, *"Why do you see them?"*

_____
_____
_____

Based on this information, is there an indication for the treatment of frequent and disturbing visual hallucinations? ☐ Yes ☐ No

Vision(s): _____

Onset: Say, *"When did you first start seeing these things?"*

_____
_____

Dysfunctional Core Beliefs

Core beliefs are not just thoughts but long-standing enduring beliefs that are generalized and absolute in nature. Unhealthy negative core beliefs undermine self-esteem, impair the ability to solve problems, and/or cause relational problems.

Say, *"What do you think of yourself?"*

_____
_____

Say, *"What do you think about others?"*

_____
_____

Say, *"What do you think about the world?"*

_____
_____

Say, *"Are any of these core beliefs dysfunctional in that it undermines your self-esteem, impairs your ability to solve problems, and/or causes relational problems?"*

_____
_____

Say, *"If so, please give me some recent examples of that."*

_____
_____
_____
_____

Based on this information, is there an indication for the treatment of dysfunctional core beliefs? ☐ Yes ☐ No

Dysfunctional core belief: _____

Onset: Say, *"When did you first start having this negative belief about yourself?"*

_____
_____

Psychiatric History

Say, *"Have you experienced any psychiatric problems and/or psychiatric hospitalizations?"*

_____
_____

Say, *"If so, how did you experience being admitted?"*

_____
_____

Say, *"Have you been in therapy before? If so, what was it like for you?"*

_____
_____

Say, *"Which medications have you taken in the past?"*

_____
_____

Say, *"Which medications have been prescribed and you are taking at the moment?"*

_____
_____

Say, *"Do you take your medication as prescribed?"*

_____

_____

If not, say, *"Why not?"*

_____

_____

Substance Abuse History

Say, *"Are you currently using any drugs or alcohol?"*

_____

_____

If so, say, *"How much?"*

_____

_____

Then say, *"When did you start using these substances?"*

_____

_____

If not, say, *"In the past?"*

_____

_____

Symptom Selection

Say, *"Considering all that, what current symptoms* (e.g., hallucinations, delusions, core beliefs) *should decrease to help you live a fulfilling life?"*

_____

_____

Note: Make sure a symptom (or a cluster of symptoms) is selected!

The purpose here is to formulate the goal of treatment, *not* to identify relevant life experiences.

Proceed to the Preparation Phase and use either the First, Second, or Third Method Protocol, depending on the selected goal, as listed in Table 3.1.

Table 3.1 Indications and Conceptualization for EMDR in Psychosis

Goal	Target	Method
Reduction of comorbid PTSD symptoms	Memories of traumatic life events that are frequently relived	Standard EMDR Protocol
Reduction of psychotic symptoms	Memories of life events that are directly connected with psychosis	The First Method
	Memories of life events that are indirectly connected with psychosis, because in the patient's view these are "proof" of the negative core beliefs	The Second Method
	Relevant flashforwards or psychosis-related imagery	The Third Method

Note: EMDR, eye movement desensitization and reprocessing; PTSD, posttraumatic stress disorder.

Phase 2: Preparation—In General

Be attentive to factors that influence patients' ability to undergo EMDR. When treating patients with psychosis, stabilizing interventions like medication, a crisis coping plan, and case management have often already been implemented. The authors have good experiences applying this protocol without using additional stabilization techniques like Resource Development and Installation. However, therapists should judge the necessity of developing appropriate resources using their clinical expertise, since there are no data that show clear indications.

> Say, *"Now that we have defined the goal of treatment, it is time to provide you with information on the therapy that I think will help you achieve this goal. This therapy is called Eye Movement Desensitization and Reprocessing; in short: EMDR. We will use eye movements to decrease the emotional load of experiences that have contributed to the problems you are experiencing now. Often, the memories of experiences that are treated with EMDR become less vivid, but what is most important is that the distress and negative influence caused by these memories is decreased. Research has demonstrated that EMDR is highly effective in doing so."*

Provide patients with as much information and explanation as needed, but be aware that postponing the start may increase the stress about what is going to happen.

> Say, *"Addressing these memories can be unsettling, but processing them will help you experience that you have the strength and resilience to cope. I am confident that you will succeed."*

> Say, *"To keep the burden of therapy as low as possible, I will use a very structured way of asking you questions. I request you to answer these questions and digress only when I ask you to. I will interrupt when I think we are going off track, is that OK with you?"*

> Say, *"Do you have any questions so far?"*

Proceed to either the First, Second, or Third Method Protocol (see following section), depending on the selected goal as listed in Table 3.1 (at the end of Phase 1).

Chapter Three: EMDR Therapy for Traumatized Patients With Psychosis   **117**

The First Method

Phase 2: Preparation—The First Method

> Say, *"Now we have to find out what memories are crucial to understand the symptoms we are going to work on. What caused them and what made them worse? When we know what elicited and/or worsened these symptoms, we can use EMDR to disarm these memories by reducing their emotional load. You will not forget these memories, but due to EMDR their interference will wane and* _____ (state the selected symptom) *will decrease."*

> Say, *"From your point of view, what event or events is/are responsible for the onset of the selected symptom?"*

_____
_____

> Say, *"Which event(s) led to this symptom?"*

_____
_____
_____

> Say, *"When was that? How old were you?"*

_____
_____
_____

> Check, say, *"Are you sure you never experienced these symptoms before that event?"*

_____
_____

> Say, *"From your point of view, which event or events is/are responsible for the worsening of the selected symptom?"*

_____
_____
_____

> Say, *"When was that? How old were you?"*

_____
_____
_____

On the *x*-axis of the graph, write down the identified events in the patient's life chronologically. On the *y*-axis, chart the severity of one symptom (e.g., voices) over time to see the correspondence between an event and the increase or decrease in the severity of the symptom. Do a separate graph for each symptom.

> Say, *"I am going to write down these events on a timeline so we can see what it looks like."*

___

> Say, *"Next, we'll have a closer look at how your _____ (state the symptom, e.g., 'voices') were influenced by these events over time. So we are going to graph them on this timeline (draw the y-axis.) The x-axis represents time, the y-axis the severity of _____ (state the symptom). If an event made it worse, we'll see the graph line increase. Do you understand what I mean?"*

___

> Say, *"You weren't born with _____ (state the symptom), right?"*

___

Draw the graph line, starting from the intersection of the axes. The severity is (close to) zero, until the event that caused the symptoms occurred.

> Say, *"Please complete this graph. If an event made it worse, the line rises. Yet, it may very well be that _____ (state symptom) has not been present to the same degree ever since, so the graph may also go down during certain times in your life."*

Note: All relevant memories will be reprocessed in chronological order.

Always start with the memory of the event that is hypothesized to have led to the symptom at first (the conditioning experience), unless there is a good reason to assume that a certain memory very strongly increased a symptom (a striking rise in the graph line, resembling a strong deterioration).

Phase 3: Assessment—The First Method: Event That Caused Psychotic Symptoms to Start

Traumatic Memory

> Say, *"I am sorry that you experienced such terrible things. While these things are in the past, you are still experiencing memories of them. Memories can be very unsettling, but they cannot really harm you* (give an example such as, "Your father used to hit you, but the memory of your father cannot"). *In treatment, we will work through your worst memories. This will help you experience that you have the strength and resilience to cope. I am confident that you will succeed."*

> Say, *"I would like you to describe the incident that caused your current symptoms. You need not go into much detail. Just give a general account of what happened. It's how you remember the incident that is most important, not what actually happened."*

Make sure that the patient tells the entire story, starting where the memory begins to the point where the traumatic experience ends.

___

___

___

Say, *"When you bring up the incident, what is the worst moment for you now?"*

_____
_____
_____

Say, *"Stop the film at that moment so that you can get a snapshot of this part of the incident. The snapshot is not the image of the moment that was most difficult for you then. Describe the image that is the most difficult to see now, looking back. Please describe this image to me in detail."*

_____
_____

Say, *"Where are you in it?"*

_____
_____
_____

If the patient has difficulty understanding, say the following:

Say, *"Imagine that you have a photo album in your mind, and that this photo album contains photos of how you remember the incident and you are present in all the photos. Which photo is the worst for you to look at now?"*

_____
_____
_____

Help the patient to focus by saying the following:

Say, *"What do you see in the image?"*

_____

Say, *"Where are you in the image?"*

_____
_____

A drawing can be made of the image, if desired.

_____

Say, *"Please draw a picture of how this worst moment is represented in your mind."*

Listen for cues about the cognitive domain the NC is in. The narrow categories facilitate connecting of the nodes in the fear network that still need to be processed:

- Responsibility and guilt: "I am guilty" ☐ Yes ☐ No
- Control: "I am powerless/helpless" ☐ Yes ☐ No

- Self-esteem: "I am a bad person," "I am worthless/stupid"   ☐ Yes ☐ No
- Safety in relation to the image: "I am still in danger"   ☐ Yes ☐ No

Check by saying the following:

Say, *"Just to make sure. Is this the image that is the most difficult for you to think about <u>now</u>? Or, is it mainly what was worst for you <u>then</u>?"*

_____

Negative Cognition (NC)

Help the patient to stay in the present!

Say, *"What we need to discover next is why this image is still so disturbing for you, when you bring it up now. This probably has to do with a negative conclusion that you have drawn about yourself in relation to the incident. What conclusion is that?"*

_____

_____

Say, *"What is it that still makes this image so awful for you?"*

_____

If the answer is not at a level of identity, continue to question the following until the patient reaches an "I am..." statement that may serve as an appropriate NC:

Say, *"What words express the negative belief about yourself that go best with the image? How would you describe such a person?"*

_____

Say, *"What does it say about you as a person?"* _____

Say, *"What would you call such a person?"* _____

Say, *"What is this sort of person often called?"* _____

NC: _____

Before going any further, check the NC by noticing if the following criteria are met:

- Dysfunctional?   ☐ Yes ☐ No
- Statement about oneself as a person?   ☐ Yes ☐ No
- Valid in the here and now? (Expressed in present tense!)   ☐ Yes ☐ No
- Emotionally charged?   ☐ Yes ☐ No

Positive Cognition (PC)

Say, *"When you bring up that image again, what would you prefer (like) to think about yourself, instead of _____ (state the NC)?"*

_____

_____

Listen for cues about the cognitive domain the PC is in. Unless the patient objects, the PC is in the same domain as the NC.

- Responsibility and guilt: "I did what I could," or "I am innocent" ☐ Yes ☐ No
- Control: "I can do it," "I can handle it," or "I can manage it" ☐ Yes ☐ No
- Self-esteem: "I'm okay," "I'm worthwhile," "I'm competent," or "I'm fine" ☐ Yes ☐ No
- Safety: "I am safe now" ☐ Yes ☐ No

PC: _____

Validity of Cognition

Say, "When you look at the image, *how true* do those words _____ (repeat PC) *feel to you now? On a scale of 1 to 7, where 1 feels completely false and 7 feels completely true?*"

1   2   3   4   5   6   7

(completely false)   (completely true)

Emotions

Say, "When you bring up the image and those words _____ (state the NC), what emotion(s) do you feel now?"

_____

_____

Subjective Units of Disturbance

Say, "When you bring up the image and you say to yourself _____ (repeat NC), how disturbing does it feel to you now? On a scale of 0 to 10, where 0 is no disturbance or neutral and 10 is the highest disturbance you can imagine, how disturbing does it feel now?"

0   1   2   3   4   5   6   7   8   9   10

(no disturbance)   (highest disturbance)

Location of Body Sensation

Say, "Where do you feel it (the disturbance) in your body?"

_____

Note: Proceed with the desensitization of the target image and installation of the PC, linking the PC with the image (see Phases 4 and 5, and further).

When finished, return to Phase 3/Assessment (see the following section) and repeat the procedure on memories of event(s) that caused symptoms to worsen.

Phase 3: Assessment—The First Method: Event That Caused Psychotic Symptoms to Worsen

Traumatic Memory

Ensure that the patient tells the entire story from where it began to the point where the traumatic experience ended.

Say, *"I would like you to describe the incident that caused your current symptoms to worsen. You need not go into much detail. Just give a general account of what happened. It's how you remember the incident that is most important, not what actually happened."*

_____

_____

_____

Say, *"When you bring up the incident, what is the worst moment for you now?"*

_____

_____

_____

Say, *"Stop the film at that moment so that you can get a snapshot of this part of the incident. The snapshot is not the image of the moment that was most difficult for you then. Describe the image that is the most difficult to see now, looking back. Please describe this image to me in detail."*

_____

_____

Say, *"Where are you in it?"*

_____

_____

_____

If the patient has difficulty understanding, say the following:

Say, *"Imagine that you have a photo album in your mind, and that this photo album contains photos of how you remember the incident and you are present in all the photos. Which photo is the worst for you to look at now?"*

_____

_____

Help the patient to focus by saying the following:

Say, *"What do you see in the image?"*

_____

_____

Say, *"Where are you in the image?"*

_____

_____

A drawing can be made of the image, if desired.

Say, *"Please draw a picture of how this worst moment is represented in your mind."*

Listen for cues about the cognitive domain the NC is in. The narrow categories facilitate connecting of the nodes in the fear network that still need to be processed:

- Responsibility and guilt: "I am guilty" ☐ Yes ☐ No
- Control: "I am powerless/helpless" ☐ Yes ☐ No
- Self-esteem: "I am a bad person," "I am worthless/I'm stupid" ☐ Yes ☐ No
- Safety in relation to the image: "I am still in danger" ☐ Yes ☐ No

Check by saying the following:

Say, *"Just to make sure. Is this the image that is the most difficult for you to think about now? Or, is it mainly what was worst for you then?"*

_____

Negative Cognition

Help the patient to stay in the present!

Say, *"What we need to discover next is why this image is still so disturbing for you, when you bring it up now. This probably has to do with a negative conclusion that you have drawn about yourself in relation to the incident. What conclusion is that?"*

_____

_____

Say, *"What is it that still makes this image so awful for you?"*

_____

If the answer is not at a level of identity, continue to administer the following questions until the patient reaches an "I am _____" statement that may serve as an appropriate NC:

Say, *"What words express the negative belief about yourself that go best with the image? How would you describe such a person?"*

_____

Say, *"What does it say about you as a person?"* _____

Say, *"What would you call such a person?"* _____

Say, *"What is this sort of person often called?"* _____

NC: _____

Before going any further, check the NC by noticing if the following criteria are met:

- Dysfunctional? ☐ Yes ☐ No
- Statement about oneself as a person? ☐ Yes ☐ No
- Valid in the here and now? (Expressed in present tense) ☐ Yes ☐ No
- Emotionally charged? ☐ Yes ☐ No

Positive Cognition

Say, *"When you bring up that image again, what would you prefer (like) to think about yourself, instead of _____ (state the NC)?"*

_____

_____

Listen for cues about the cognitive domain the PC is in. Unless the patient objects, the PC is in the same domain as the NC.

- Responsibility and guilt: "I did what I could," or "I'm innocent" ☐ Yes ☐ No
- Control: "I can do it," "I can handle it," or "I can manage it" ☐ Yes ☐ No
- Self-esteem: "I'm OK," "I'm worthwhile," "I'm competent," or I'm fine" ☐ Yes ☐ No
- Safety: "I am safe now" ☐ Yes ☐ No

PC: _____

Validity of Cognition

Say, *"When you look at the image, how true do those words _____ (repeat PC) feel to you now? On a scale of 1 to 7, where 1 feels completely false and 7 feels completely true?"*

1   2   3   4   5   6   7

(completely false)   (completely true)

Emotions

Say, *"When you bring up the image and those words _____ (state the NC), what emotion do you feel now?"*

_____

_____

Subjective Units of Disturbance

Say, *"When you bring up the image and you say to yourself: _____ (repeat NC), how disturbing does it feel to you now? On a scale of 0 to 10, where 0 is no disturbance or neutral and 10 is the highest disturbance you can imagine, how disturbing does it feel now?"*

0   1   2   3   4   5   6   7   8   9   10

(no disturbance)   (highest disturbance)

Location of Body Sensation

Say, *"Where do you feel it (the disturbance) in your body?"*

___

Note: Proceed with the desensitization of the target image and installation of the PC, linking the PC with the image (Phases 4 and 5 and further).

When finished, return to the assessment and repeat the procedure on the other memories of event(s).

The Second Method

Phase 2: Preparation—The Second Method

List of Dysfunctional Core Beliefs (Obtained in Phase 1)

___
___
___
___
___

Say, *"Core beliefs are basic assumptions about yourself, others, and the world. They are largely based on previous life experiences, predominantly experiences from our childhood. Negative core beliefs commonly arise from experiences such as being bullied, physically abused, blamed, neglected, or sexually abused. These experiences make people believe that their negative core belief is true. When these experiences instinctively/emotionally still prove that the core belief is true, it is very difficult for them to think differently."*

Start with the dysfunctional core belief that is most explicitly related to the symptom(s).

Say, *"What would you like to believe about yourself* (others/the world) *instead of* _____ (state negative core belief)?"

___

Say, *"What we are going to work on is that you will be able to believe that you are ___ (state the positive core belief) wherever you are, whatever you do, and whatever you are thinking of. To allow this to happen, we are going to remove the evidence for your negative core belief. EMDR will be helpful to process the memories of these negative experiences."*

List of Targets Proving the Dysfunctional, Problematic Beliefs

Collect the "proof" for the first dysfunctional core belief by identifying approximately three relevant experiences in the learning history of the patient. This can be a homework assignment, but it is preferably done within the session, at least for the first belief.

Say, *"Which experiences instinctively still 'prove' to you* _____ (state the dysfunctional belief)?"

___
___

Or say, *"What have you experienced that still convinces you that _____ (state the dysfunctional belief)?"*

_____

Or say, *"What made you (start to) think _____ (state the dysfunctional belief)?"*

_____

Note: Often patients provide evidence that is not a single experience but recurrent experiences, or concerning a period of time in life (for instance, bullying). If this is the case, the metaphor of an "archive" in which it is necessary to identify "files" is helpful. Another useful metaphor is that of a Google search in the long-term memory using the negative core belief as a keyword.

Dysfunctional Belief #1: _____
Proof 1.1: _____
Proof 1.2: _____
Proof 1.3: _____

Dysfunctional Belief #2: _____
Proof 2.1: _____
Proof 2.2: _____
Proof 2.3: _____

Dysfunctional Belief #3: _____
Proof 3.1: _____
Proof 3.2: _____
Proof 3.3: _____

Note: Core beliefs and basic assumptions usually evolve in childhood. Sometimes patients only mention recent experiences in relation to their current negative core beliefs (for instance, "I lost my job," or "My wife left me"). If this happens, help patients to look for earlier proof for the targeted belief. It is also possible to work on the later (often confirmatory) experiences, but working on childhood memories will be more effective in reducing the credibility of negative core beliefs in the present.

Phase 3: Assessment—The Second Method: Most Powerful Proof

Say, *"Now, we will have to select the experience we are going to start with. We will start with the experience that emotionally is the strongest proof for _____ (state dysfunctional core belief) now. Which one is that?"*

Most powerful proof:

_____

Say, *"I would like you to describe this incident. You need not go into much detail. Just give a general account of what happened. It's how you remember the incident that is most important, not what actually happened."*

Note: Make sure that the patient tells the entire story, up to the point where the traumatic experience ends.

_____
_____
_____

Say, *"When you <u>bring up</u> the incident, what is the moment that is the most powerful, emotional proof for you <u>now</u>?"*

_____
_____
_____

Say, *"Stop the film at that moment so that you can get a snapshot of this part of the incident. The snapshot is not the image of the moment that was most difficult for you <u>then</u>, but the image that is <u>now</u> proving most clearly to you that your core belief _____ (state the core belief) is true. Please describe this image to me in detail."*

_____
_____
_____

If the patient has difficulty understanding, say the following:

Say *"Imagine that you have a photo album in your mind, and that this photo album contains photos of how you remember the incident and you are present in all the photos. Which photo is the best proof for you now?"*

If necessary, say, *"Which image represents the entire evidence?"*

_____
_____

Help the patient to focus by saying the following:

Say, *"What do you see in the image?"*

_____
_____
_____

Say, *"Where are you in the image?"*

_____

A drawing can be made of the image, if desired.

Say, *"Please draw a picture of how this worst moment of the incident is represented in your mind."*

_____

Listen for cues about the cognitive domain the NC is in. The narrow categories facilitate connecting of the nodes in the fear network that still need to be processed:

- Responsibility and guilt: "I am guilty" ☐ Yes ☐ No
- Control: "I am powerless/helpless" ☐ Yes ☐ No
- Self-esteem: "I am a bad person," "I am worthless/stupid" ☐ Yes ☐ No
- Safety in relation to the image: "I am still in danger" ☐ Yes ☐ No

Check by saying the following:

Say, *"Just to make sure. Is this the image that is representing the most convincing evidence for you to think about now? Or is it mainly what was worst for you then?"*

_____

Negative Cognition

Help the patient to stay in the present!

Say, *"What we need to discover next is why this image is still so conclusive for you now, when you look back on it. This probably has to do with a negative conclusion that you have drawn about yourself in relation to the incident. What conclusion is that?"*

_____

If the answer is not at a level of identity, continue to question the following until the patient reaches an "I am _____" statement that may serve as an appropriate NC.

Say, *"Which words express the negative belief about yourself that go best with the image? How would you describe such a person?"*

_____

Say, *"What does it say about you as a person?"* _____

Say, *"What would you call such a person?"* _____

Say, *"What is this sort of person often called?"* _____

NC: _____

Before going any further, check the NC by noticing if the following criteria are met:

- Dysfunctional? ☐ Yes ☐ No
- Statement about oneself as a person? ☐ Yes ☐ No
- Valid in the here and now? (Expressed in present tense!) ☐ Yes ☐ No
- Emotionally charged? ☐ Yes ☐ No

Positive Cognition

Say, *"When you bring up that image again, what would you prefer (like) to think about yourself, instead of _____ (state the NC)?"*

_____

_____

Listen for cues about the cognitive domain the PC is in. Unless the patient objects, the PC is in the same domain as the NC.

- Responsibility and guilt: "I did what I could" or "I'm innocent" ☐ Yes ☐ No
- Control: "I can do it," "I can handle it," or "I can manage" ☐ Yes ☐ No
- Self-esteem: "I'm OK," "I'm worthwhile," "I'm competent," or "I'm fine" ☐ Yes ☐ No
- Safety: "I am safe now" ☐ Yes ☐ No

PC: _____

Validity of Cognition

Say, "When you look at the image, *how true* do those words _____ (repeat PC) *feel to you now? On a scale of 1 to 7, where 1 feels completely false and 7 feels completely true?*"

1   2   3   4   5   6   7

(completely false)   (completely true)

Emotions

Say, *"When you bring up the image and those words* _____ (state the NC), *what emotion do you feel now?"*

_____

_____

Subjective Units of Disturbance

Say, *"When you bring up the image and you say to yourself:* _____ (repeat NC), *how disturbing does it feel to you now? On a scale of 0 to 10, where 0 is no disturbance or neutral and 10 is the highest disturbance you can imagine, how disturbing does it feel now?"*

0   1   2   3   4   5   6   7   8   9   10

(no disturbance)   (highest disturbance)

Location of Body Sensation

Say, *"Where do you feel it (the disturbance) in your body?"*

_____

Note: Proceed with the desensitization of the target image and installation of the PC, linking the PC with the image (Phases 4 and 5, and further).

When finished, repeat the procedure on the next proof (see earlier).

When finished with all the evidence for this problematic core belief, continue the procedure with the next core belief, and so on.

The Second Method is always part of a more comprehensive treatment. EMDR is integrated or alternated with cognitive and behavioral interventions; for instance, Socratic questioning, probability reasoning, or behavioral experiments. (For more information on CBT, see, for instance: Beck, Freeman, & Davis, 2006; Morrison, Renton, Dunn, Williams, & Bentall, 2004; Wright, Basco, & Thase, 2006).

The Third Method

Phase 2: Preparation—The Third Method

We suggest that you use this method only if patients are aware that their feared scenarios are not fully realistic or that intrusive experiences actually do not deserve that much attention. If there are no doubts about the (psychotic) conviction(s), it is best to start with cognitive and behavioral work first (see Morrison et al., 2004).

Patients can be hesitant or unwilling to execute behavioral experiments or exposure assignments when they fear terrible consequences. If so, desensitizing the worst-case scenario may be helpful; this is also known as using EMDR on flashforwards (see Engelhard et al., 2010, 2011).

Next to reprocessing flashforwards, EMDR can also be helpful when patients experience intrusive imagery, related to the origin, appearance, or content of a psychotic symptom that is not an actual memory of something that has happened. By desensitizing this imagery, emotional involvement and preoccupation can be reduced (van den Berg, van der Vleugel, Staring, de Bont, & de Jongh, 2013).

Intrusive Thoughts or Images (Future Concerns/Psychotic Symptoms Obtained in Phase 1)

_____

_____

In case of feared future events, continue with the Flashforward Procedure (see the following section).

In case of psychosis-related imagery, continue with Visualization of Psychotic Symptom (see later).

Flashforward Procedure

It is important to create a framework that allows and enables the patient's thinking about the impending doom of the worst-case scenario.

> Say, *"What we need to do is figure out is what kind of image is in your mind that makes you anxious about a future confrontation with the thing/the one you fear. What do you fear will happen and will go wrong when you are confronted with the situation you are avoiding now in the worst-case scenario? Basically we should look for your ultimate disaster image."*

_____

_____

To help identify the patient's worst catastrophic fantasy, the therapist may ask additional questions like:

> Say, *"What do you imagine might go wrong if* _____ (state a relevant worst catastrophic fantasy, such as 'Your neighbor will be talking to the police')?"

_____

_____

Say, *"In your worst nightmare, what is the worst thing that could happen to you?"*

_____
_____

Ask the patient to bring up the image of the worst-case scenario.

Say, *"What does the most disturbing image look like to you?"*

_____
_____

Say, *"What is the worst or most awful part of that for you?"*

_____
_____

Use this as a target for processing.
Continue with Phase 3: Assessment—The Flashforward Procedure (see later).
The NC is in the domain of powerlessness or threat and arousal is usually high.
Always, the PC is "I can handle this."

Visualization of Psychotic Symptom

In Phase 1, information was collected about psychotic symptoms like hallucinations and delusional beliefs. Delusions can be primary (e.g., "The CIA is spying on me") or secondary to hallucinations (e.g., "The voice belongs to my former boss, who wants to ruin my life"). If the patient has an image of the perceived origin, appearance, or content of a symptom (i.e., activating event), the Protocol can be used. The target can be an image of the persecutor, for instance, or of the patient with a man next to him yelling nasty things through a loudspeaker. The NC and the PC may belong to any domain.

Psychotic Imagery (take from Phase 1 information):

_____
_____
_____

Continue with Phase 3: Assessment—Imagery and Phase 3: Assessment—The Flashforward Procedure

Worst Moment of Feared Future Event

Say, *"If you anticipate what might happen, what is the worst moment for you now? Stop the film at that moment so that you can get a snapshot of this part of it. The snapshot is not the image of what will be the most difficult for you then. Describe the image that is most difficult for you to see now, while anticipating it in the future. Please describe this image to me in detail."*

_____
_____

Say, *"Where are you in it?"*

_____

If the patient has difficulty understanding, say the following:

Say, *"Imagine that you have a photo album in your mind, and that this photo album contains photos of what will happen and you are present in all the photos. Which photo is the worst for you to look at now?"*

_____
_____

Help the patient focus by saying the following:

Say, *"What do you see in the image?"*

_____

Say, *"Where are you in the image?"*

_____

A drawing can be made of the image, if desired.

Say, *"Please draw a picture of how the worst moment is represented in your mind."*

_____

Check by saying the following:

Say, *"Just to make sure. Is this the image that is the most disturbing for you to think about now?"*

_____

Negative Cognition

Say, *"The fact that this image is so disturbing to you probably has to do with the fear that you will not be able to cope with it. Is that right?"* ☐ Yes ☐ No

Say, *"Is, 'I am powerless,' the negative belief about yourself that goes with the image?"* ☐ Yes ☐ No

Unless the patient objects, the NC is "I am powerless."

NC: _____

Positive Cognition

Say, *"When you bring up that image again, would you prefer to believe 'I can handle it' (the image)?"*

_____

Unless the NC was not formulated as "I am powerless," the PC is "I can handle it."

PC: _____

Validity of Cognition

Say, *"When you look at the image, <u>how true</u> do those words _____ (repeat PC) feel to you now? On a scale of 1 to 7, where 1 feels completely false and 7 feels completely true?"*

1   2   3   4   5   6   7

(completely false)   (completely true)

Emotions

Say, *"When you bring up the image and those words* _____ *(state the NC), what emotion do you feel now?"*

_____

_____

Subjective Units of Disturbance

Say, *"When you bring up the image and you say to yourself, 'I am powerless,' how disturbing does it feel to you now? On a scale of 0 to 10, where 0 is no disturbance or neutral and 10 is the highest disturbance you can imagine, how disturbing does it feel now?"*

0   1   2   3   4   5   6   7   8   9   10

(no disturbance)   (highest disturbance)

Location of Body Sensation

Say, *"Where do you feel it (the disturbance) in your body?"*

_____

Note: Proceed with the desensitization of the target image and installation of the PC, linking the PC with the image (Phases 4 and 5 and further).

Phase 3: Assessment—Imagery

Most Disturbing Psychotic Imagery

Say, *"Which image represents the most disturbing part of this now?"*

_____

_____

Make sure this is a still image (or a photograph)!

If the patient has difficulty understanding, say the following:

Say, *"Imagine that you have a photo album in your mind, and that this photo album contains photos of* _____ *(state psychotic conviction, for instance, 'The people that are out to get you') and that you are present in all the photos. Which photo is the worst for you to look at now?"*

_____

_____

Listen for cues about the cognitive domain the NC is in. The narrow categories facilitate connecting of the nodes in the fear network that still need to be processed:

- Responsibility and guilt: "I am guilty"   ☐ Yes ☐ No
- Control: "I am powerless/helpless"   ☐ Yes ☐ No

- Self-esteem: "I am a bad person," "I am worthless/stupid" ☐ Yes ☐ No
- Safety in relation to the image: for example, "I am still in danger" ☐ Yes ☐ No

Help the patient to focus by saying the following:

Say, *"What do you see in the image?"*

_____

Say, *"Where are you in the image?"*

_____

A drawing can be made of the image, if desired.

Say, *"Please draw a picture of how the worst moment of the incident is represented in your mind."*

_____

Negative Cognition

Say, *"This is not a pretty image, but what we need to discover next is why this image is so awful for you. This probably has to do with a negative conclusion that you have drawn about yourself in relation to this image. What conclusion is that?"*

_____

If the answer is not at a level of identity, continue to question the following until the patient reaches an "I am..." statement that may serve as an appropriate NC.

Say, *"Which words express the negative belief about yourself that go best with the image? How would you describe such a person?"*

_____

Say, *"What does it say about you as a person?"* _____

Say, *"What would you call such a person?"* _____

Say, *"What is this sort of person often called?"* _____

NC: _____

Before going any further, check the NC by noticing if the following criteria are met:

- Dysfunctional? ☐ Yes ☐ No
- Statement about oneself as a person? ☐ Yes ☐ No
- Valid in the here and now? (Expressed in present tense!) ☐ Yes ☐ No
- Emotionally charged? ☐ Yes ☐ No

Positive Cognition

Say, *"When you bring up that image again, what would you prefer (like) to think about yourself, instead of _____ (state the NC)?"*

_____

_____

Listen for cues about the cognitive domain the PC is in. Unless the patient objects, the PC is in the same domain as the NC.

- Responsibility and guilt: "I did what I could" or "I'm innocent" ☐ Yes ☐ No
- Control: "I can do it," "I can handle it," or "I can manage" ☐ Yes ☐ No
- Self-esteem: "I'm OK," "I'm worthwhile," "I'm competent," or "I'm fine" ☐ Yes ☐ No
- Safety: "I am safe now" ☐ Yes ☐ No

PC: _____

Validity of Cognition

Say, "When you look at the image, *how true* do those words _____ (repeat PC) *feel to you now? On a scale of 1 to 7, where 1 feels completely false and 7 feels completely true?*"

1   2   3   4   5   6   7

(completely false)   (completely true)

Emotions

Say, "When you bring up the image and those words _____ (state the NC), *what emotion do you feel now?*"

Subjective Units of Disturbance

Say, "When you bring up the image and you say to yourself: _____ (repeat NC), *how disturbing does it feel to you now? On a scale of 0 to 10, where 0 is no disturbance or neutral and 10 is the highest disturbance you can imagine, how disturbing does it feel now?*"

0   1   2   3   4   5   6   7   8   9   10

(no disturbance)   (highest disturbance)

Location of Body Sensation

Say, "*Where do you feel it (the disturbance) in your body?*"

_____

Note: Proceed with the desensitization of the target image and installation of PC, linking the PC with the image (Phases 4 and 5 and further).

Phase 4: Desensitization

Say, *"From the moment you follow my hand, I want you to act as an observer. Observe what comes up. This can be thoughts, feelings, images, physical responses—all kinds of things. What comes up can be clearly linked to the incident, but it is also possible that it seems to have nothing to do with it at all. Just observe what comes up, without judging, without influencing. Just follow my instructions. When starting the procedure, it is important you have a close look at the image in your mind, but as soon as you start doing the eye movements, there is no need to stick to the image, it is just the starting point. We will go back to the image (how it is stored in your head) every now and then, however, to see how disturbing it is to look at it. It is possible that the image will change. Remember it is impossible to do it wrong, as long as you just observe and follow what comes up. OK?"*

_____

Say, *"Before we start, just one more thing: If anything comes up that is extremely distressing, do not stop the procedure, continue to follow my fingers. Just think of it as a train running through a dark tunnel. If you do not want to be there, you should not pull the emergency brake, for then it will take longer to reach the end of the tunnel. Instead of stopping the train, you would do better to speed up. Do you understand? The best thing you can do is to concentrate on my fingers even more. Think of my fingers as the accelerator. OK? So keep your mind at rest and just follow my fingers with your eyes."*

_____

Hold your hand in front of the patient's eyes.

Say, *"Look at my fingers. Bring up the image, (pause), and say to yourself _____ (repeat the NC)."*

Say, *"Notice the feeling of _____ (repeat emotion) in _____ (repeat location in the body)."*

Allow the patient time to concentrate, and ask, *"OK, have you got it?"*

_____

Say, *"Follow my fingers with your eyes."*
Provide a series of eye movements of approximately 30 seconds.

Say, *"What comes up?"* or, *"What do you get now?"* or, *"What are you noticing now?"*

_____

Do not start a dialogue!

Say, *"Concentrate on that"* (or *"Go/stay with that"*).

Provide a series of eye movements of approximately 30 seconds.

Say, *"What comes up?"* or, *"What do you get now?"* or, *"What are you noticing now?"*

_____

Do not start a dialogue!

Say, *"Concentrate on that"* (or *"Go/stay with that"*).

Repeat this procedure for 5 to 10 minutes (or shorter if there are no changes in associations for several times in a row). Then, go Back to Target by saying the following:

Say, *"Bring up the original image as it is stored in your brain now. When you look at the image, how disturbing does it feel to you now? On a scale of 0 to 10, where 0 is not disturbing at all or neutral, and 10 is the highest disturbance you can imagine, how disturbing does it feel now?"*

0 1 2 3 4 5 6 7 8 9 10

(no disturbance)   (highest disturbance)

Do not proceed with the Installation of the PC if the SUD > 0!
If the SUD > 0, say the following:

Say, *"Look at the image. What aspect of the image makes you feel so distressed?"*

Or, use the number, and say, *"What do you see in the image that is causing the _____ (state the number)?"*

_____

Say, *"Concentrate on that. (Pause) Have you got it?"*

_____

Provide a series of eye movements of approximately 30 seconds.

Say, *"What comes up?"* or, *"What do you get now?"* or, *"What are you noticing now?"*

_____

Do not start a dialogue!

Say, *"Concentrate on that"* or, *"Go/Stay with that."*

Provide a series of eye movements of approximately 30 seconds.

Say, *"What comes up?"* or, *"What do you get now?"* or, *"What are you noticing now?"*

Note: Repeat this procedure as long as needed, and go Back to Target every 5 to 10 minutes, until the SUD = 0. Then proceed with the installation of the PC linked to this image (Phase 5, see the following section).

Phase 5: Installation

Say, *"How does _____ (state the PC) sound?"*

Say, *"When you look at the image, how true do those words _____ (repeat PC) feel to you now? On a scale of 1 to 7, where 1 feels completely false and 7 feels completely true?"*

1 2 3 4 5 6 7

(completely false)   (completely true)

Say, *"Think of the image and hold it together with the words _____ (state the PC)."*

Do a long set of eye movements. Do not ask what comes up!

Say, *"When you look at the image, how true do those words _____ (repeat PC) feel to you now? On a scale of 1 to 7, where 1 feels completely false and 7 feels completely true?"*

       1   2   3   4   5   6   7

(completely false)   (completely true)

Say, *"Think of the image and hold it together with the words* _____ (state the PC)*."*
Do a long set of eye movements. Do not ask what comes up!
Check the VoC and repeat this procedure until VoC = 7.

If VoC < 7 after repeated (> 20) series of eye movements, check for blocking beliefs.

Say, *"What prevents it from being a 7?"*

_____

_____

Say, *"Where did you learn this* (in your life)*?"*

_____

_____

Continue by reprocessing this issue.
Check the VoC of the PC again, with regard to the (original target) image.

Phase 6: Body Scan

Say, *"Close your eyes and keep in mind the target image, as it stored in your brain now, and the positive cognition. Then bring your attention to the different parts of your body, starting with your head and working downward. Any place you find any tension, tightness, or unusual sensation, tell me."*

_____

If a sensation of discomfort is reported, this is reprocessed using eye movements until the discomfort subsides. Finally, the VoC has to be checked.

Note: Check whether the unusual sensation is related to emotional distress rather than motor side effects from antipsychotic medication.

Say, *"When you look at the image, <u>how true</u> do those words* _____ (repeat PC) *feel to you now? On a scale of 1 to 7, where 1 feels completely false and 7 feels completely true?"*

       1   2   3   4   5   6   7

(completely false)   (completely true)

Phase 7: Closure

At the end of every session, consolidate the changes and improvements that have occurred.

Say, *"What is the most positive thing you have learned about yourself in this session with regard to* _____ (state the incident, theme, or image)*?"*

_____

If the answer is not already on an identity level, say the following:

Say *"What does this say about you?"* (*"What kind of person* _____ ?"*)*

_____

Say, *"Concentrate on that/Go with that."*

Install with eye movements until no further positive changes occur.

Say, *"Things may come up, or they may not. If they do, great. It is not unusual and it is a sign of reprocessing. You can use a log to write down what triggers, images, thoughts or cognitions, emotions, and sensations come up. Please write down the positive experiences, too. It is best to not use sedatives afterwards so your brain can do the healing. If it is absolutely necessary, use the lowest dose possible. If negative feelings do come up, try not to elaborate on them. Remember, it is still just the old stuff. Just write it down for next time. Of course you can give me a call if you need to."*

Phase 8: Reevaluation

Ask the patient to focus on the target you have already reprocessed and review the responses. This is to check whether positive results are maintained.

Say, *"When you bring up the image that we were working on last time, on a scale of 0 to 10, where 0 is no disturbance or neutral, and 10 is the highest disturbance you can imagine, how disturbing does it feel now?"*

0   1   2   3   4   5   6   7   8   9   10

(no disturbance)   (highest disturbance)

Based on this reevaluation, decide whether to move on to a new target (if SUD = 0) or to revisit this target for additional reprocessing and integration (return to Phase 4). If the disturbance level has increased, these reverberations need to be targeted or otherwise addressed.

When it appears that the patient still experiences anticipatory fear of confrontations with certain objects or situations, this should alert you to the possibility of unexplored past traumatic events or psychosis-related imagery that remain to be processed. Once these have all been fully resolved, and/or it is not possible to identify any past event that appears to be relevant to the feared future event, it would then be appropriate to use the Flashforward Procedure.

Flashforward: Worst Moment

Say, *"If you think about what might happen, what is the worst moment for you now? Stop the film there so that you can get a snapshot of this part of it. The snapshot is not of what will be the most difficult for you then, but of what is most disturbing for you now, while anticipating it in the future. Please describe this image to me."*

_____

_____

Say, *"Where are you in it?"*

_____

If patient has difficulty understanding, say the following:

Say *"Imagine that you have a photo album in your mind, and that this photo album contains photos of what will happen and you are present in all the photos. Which photo is the worst for you to look at now?"*

_____

_____

Help the patient focus by saying the following:

Say, *"What do you see in the image?"*

_____

Say, *"Where are you in the image?"*

_____

A drawing can be made of the image, if desired.

Say, *"Please draw a picture of how the worst moment of the incident is represented in your mind."*

_____

Check the following:

Say, *"Just to make sure. Is this the image that is the most disturbing for you to think about now?"* ☐ Yes ☐ No

Negative Cognition

Say, *"The fact that this image is so disturbing for you probably has to do with the fear that you will not be able to cope with it. Is that right?"* ☐ Yes ☐ No

Say, *"Is 'I am powerless' the negative belief about yourself that goes with the image?"* ☐ Yes ☐ No

Unless the patient objects, the NC is "I am powerless."

NC: _____

Positive Cognition

Say, *"When you bring up that image again, would you prefer to believe, 'I can handle it (the image)?'"*

_____

Unless the NC was not "I am powerless," the PC is "I can handle it."

PC: _____

Validity of Cognition

Say, *"When you look at the image, how true do those words _____ (repeat PC) feel to you now? On a scale of 1 to 7, where 1 feels completely false and 7 feels completely true? I do not mean in the case this feared event would come true—I just mean with regard to this image in your head."*

1   2   3   4   5   6   7
(completely false)   (completely true)

Emotions

Say, *"When you bring up the image and those words _____ (state the NC), what emotion do you feel now?"*

_____

_____

Subjective Units of Disturbance

Say, *"When you bring up the image and you say to yourself, 'I am powerless'* (repeat the NC), *how disturbing does it feel to you now? On a scale of 0 to 10, where 0 is no disturbance or neutral and 10 is the highest disturbance you can imagine, how disturbing does it feel now?"*

0   1   2   3   4   5   6   7   8   9   10

(no disturbance)   (highest disturbance)

Location of Body Sensation

Say, *"Where do you feel it (the disturbance) in your body?"*

_____

If the patient's flashforward has been fully processed (i.e., the SUD related to the flashforward is zero), and the patient still indicates feeling uncomfortable with future confrontations with certain stimuli or formerly phobic situations, or in case of extensive avoidance behavior, then other procedures need to be used. This includes installing a Future Template. A limited script is provided; for a more elaborated script, see Shapiro (2001, pp. 210–214; 2006, pp. 51–53, or see Appendix A).

Future Template

Ask patients to imagine a future situation that they have avoided, or experienced with a lot of anxiety, or anticipated with anxiety.

Say, *"What situation have you avoided until now, but you are planning to encounter this week?"*

_____
_____
_____
_____

Say, *"Bring up this image, and say to yourself, 'I can handle it.' OK, have you got it?"*

_____

Provide a series of eye movements.

Say, *"Go with that."*

Say, *"Bring up the image again. On a scale of 1 to 7, to what extent do you think you can manage it? Here I really mean the actual event, not just the image."*

1   2   3   4   5   6   7

(completely false)   (completely true)

Repeat the procedure until the VoC = 7, as you do with the installation of the PC.
Note: Do not ask for the SUD score.

Other procedures of additional value are the "mental video" procedure, which is part of Shapiro's Phobia Protocol (see also de Jongh, 2009), and the use of exposure in vivo or "behavioral experiments." It is important for patients to achieve a degree of self-mastery and experience that they are able to handle a certain level of anticipatory anxiety and fear with confidence again. The use of these cognitive behavioral procedures can be indispensable. In the end, patients need to expose themselves to the feared stimulus to learn that their negative expectations actually do not occur. Some patients will do this automatically following EMDR sessions. Others need the structure and rationale of exposure or behavioral experiments. Some need more cognitive work to really challenge their negative beliefs.

Video Check

Say, *"This time, I would like you to imagine yourself stepping into the future. Close your eyes and play a movie from the beginning until the end. Imagine yourself coping with any challenges that come your way. Notice what you are seeing, thinking, feeling, and experiencing in your body. While playing this movie, let me know if you hit any blocks. If you do, just open your eyes and let me know. If you don't hit any blocks, let me know when you have viewed the whole movie."*

_____

_____

If patients encounter blocks and open their eyes, the therapist says the following:

Say, *"Say to yourself, 'I can handle it' and follow my fingers."*

To provide the therapist with an indication regarding patient self-efficacy, have them rate their responses on a VoC scale from 1 to 7. This procedural step may give the therapist feedback on the extent to which patients are capable of in vivo confrontations.

Say, *"When you think of the incident, how true do those words _____ (repeat the PC) feel to you now on a scale of 1 to 7, where 1 feels completely false and 7 feels completely true?"*

1   2   3   4   5   6   7

(completely false)   (completely true)

If patients are able to play the movie from start to finish with a sense of confidence and satisfaction, they are asked to play the movie once more from the beginning to the end, using eye movements, and the PC, "I can handle it" is installed, analogous to a Future Template.

Say, *"Okay, play the movie one more time from beginning to end and say to yourself 'I can handle it.' Go with that."*

_____

_____

Prepare the Patient for In Vivo Confrontations

Say, *"Many people appear to avoid certain activities for so long that they no longer know how to behave and how to feel secure in this situation. To be able to help further alleviate your fears and concerns, it is important that you learn to counter the negative belief that contributes to this sense of threat and anxiety. Therefore, you need to actually test the catastrophic expectations you have that fuel your anxiety in real life. I would like to ask you to gradually confront the objects or situations that normally would provoke a fear response. It may seem odd, but if you have a positive experience and it appears that the catastrophe you fear does not occur, it helps you to further demonstrate—or to convince yourself—that your fear is unfounded."*

Say, *"I want you to understand that nothing will be done against your will during the confrontation with the things that normally would evoke fear. The essence of this confrontation is that it is safe."*

In Vivo Exposure

In Vivo Exposure is done to reduce avoidance and evoke mastery, while observing that no real danger exists. It is essential that therapists help patients to pay attention to the features of the phobic object or situations that are positive or interesting while being exposed to it.

Say, *"Please describe the most notable features of the situation. Are you noticing any interesting elements about _____ (state the phobic object or situation)?"*

_____

_____

To identify negative thought content, say the following:

Say, *"What are you thinking as you pay attention to _____ (state the phobic object or situation)?"*

_____

_____

To cognitively reconstruct the situation, say the following:

Say, *"How would someone who is not afraid of _____ (state the phobic object or situation) view or evaluate this situation?"*

_____

_____

If needed, give advice to help cope with both the situation and the mental and body sensations. It is helpful to make variations with regard to the stimulus dimensions such as action, distance, and time.

Say, *"Isn't it interesting to notice that now that you are confronted with this _____ (state the object or situation) and _____ (state the catastrophe the patient normally would have feared to happen) does not occur?"*

_____

_____

Say, *"Do you notice that your anxiety is not as physically harmful as you might have expected?"*

_____

_____

Say, *"These emotional reactions will subside and fade over time. Therefore, it is important that you continue exposing yourself to the feared stimuli as long as you feel that you have achieved a certain degree of self-mastery. Please note that you are gradually learning to feel that you are capable of handling a certain level of anticipatory anxiety with confidence."*

The therapist should make sure that confrontations are repeated so that the reduction in distress is fully consolidated before moving on.

The results can be checked by assessing the validity of the catastrophe.

Say, *"If you would encounter* _____ (state the phobic object or situation) *again, on a scale of 1 to 10, where 1 feels completely false and 10 feels completely true, how true does it feel you are in danger?"*

0   1   2   3   4   5   6   7   8   9   10

(completely false)   (completely true)

Summary

EMDR is a valuable intervention in the treatment of various mental disorders, especially if symptoms are associated with negative life experiences. In this chapter, the authors describe possible interactions between trauma and psychosis and offer several methods for conceptualizing a case to facilitate the application of EMDR in the treatment of people with psychosis. Clinical experiences, exploratory studies, and emerging scientific proof of effectiveness are promising and defy the long-standing belief that psychosis is a contraindication for trauma treatment. On the other hand, it should also be clear that EMDR alone is usually not comprehensive enough to treat psychotic disorders, so a combination of effective therapies is advocated. Moreover, we stress the importance of therapist competence. EMDR in the treatment of patients with psychosis should be delivered by well-trained therapists who are familiar with psychosis and cognitive behavioral treatment of psychotic symptoms, and who collaborate in multidisciplinary treatment teams.

References

Achim, A. M., Maziade, M., Raymond, E., Olivier, D., Mérette, C., & Roy, M. A. (2011). How prevalent are anxiety disorders in schizophrenia? A meta-analysis and critical review on a significant association. *Schizophrenia Bulletin, 37*(4), 811–821.

Andrade, J., Kavanagh, D., & Baddeley, A. (1997). Eye-movements and visual imagery: A working memory approach to the treatment of post-traumatic stress disorder. *British Journal of Clinical Psychology, 36*, 209–223.

Beck, A. T. (1970). Role of fantasies in psychotherapy and psychopathology. *The Journal of Nervous and Mental Disease, 150*(1), 3–17.

Beck, A. T., & Steer, R. A. (1990). *Manual for the Beck anxiety inventory.* San Antonio, TX: Psychological Corporation.

Beck, A. T., Freeman, A., & Davis, D. D. (2006). *Cognitive therapy of personality disorders.* New York, NY: Guilford.

Birchwood, M., & Chadwick, P. (1997). The omnipotence of voices: Testing the validity of a cognitive model. *Psychological Medicine, 27*(06), 1345–1353.

Blake, D. D., Weathers, F. W., Nagy, L. M., Kaloupek, D. G., Gusman, F. D., Charney, D. S., & Keane, T. M. (1995). The development of a Clinician-Administered PTSD Scale. *Journal of Traumatic Stress, 8*(1), 75–90.

Bora, E., Yucel, M., & Pantelis, C. (2009). Cognitive functioning in schizophrenia, schizoaffective disorder and affective psychoses: Meta-analytic study. *The British Journal of Psychiatry: The Journal of Mental Science, 195*(6), 475–482.

Bradley, R., Greene, J., Russ, E., Dutra, L., & Westen, D. (2005). A multidimensional meta-analysis of psychotherapy for PTSD. *The American Journal of Psychiatry, 162,* 214–227.

Braga, R. J., Mendlowicz, M. V., Marrocos, R. P., & Figueira, I. L. (2005). Anxiety disorders in outpatients with schizophrenia: Prevalence and impact on the subjective quality of life. *Journal of Psychiatric Research, 39*(4), 409–414.

Buckley, P. F., Miller, B. J., Lehrer, D. S., & Castle, D. J. (2009). Psychiatric comorbidities and schizophrenia. *Schizophrenia Bulletin, 35*(2), 383–402.

Croes, C. F., van Grunsven, R., Staring, A. B. P., van den Berg, D. P. G., de Jongh, A., & van der Gaag, M. (2014). Mentale beelden bij psychose: EMDR als een nieuwe interventie bij het behandelen van stemmen en wanen. *Tijdschrift voor Psychiatrie, 56*(9), 568–576.

de Bont, P. A. J. M., van den Berg, D. P. G., van der Vleugel, B. M., de Roos, C., de Jongh, A., van der Gaag, M., & van Minnen, A. (2015). *Prevalence of PTSD: Predictive validity of the Trauma Screening Questionnaire (TSQ) for patients with psychotic disorders.* Manuscript accepted for publication.

de Bont, P. A. J. M., van den Berg, D. P. G., van der Vleugel, B. M., de Roos, C., Mulder, C. L., Becker, E. S.,...van Minnen, A. (2013). A multi-site single blind clinical study to compare prolonged exposure, eye movement desensitization and reprocessing and waiting list on patients with a current diagnosis of psychosis and co-morbid post-traumatic stress disorder: Study protocol for the randomized controlled trial Treating Trauma in Psychosis. *Trials, 14,* 151.

de Bont, P. A. J. M., van Minnen, A., & de Jongh, A. (2013). Treating PTSD in patients with psychosis: A within-group controlled feasibility study examining the efficacy and safety of evidence-based PE and EMDR protocols. *Behavior Therapy.* doi:10.1016/j.beth.2013.07.002

de Jongh, A. (2009). EMDR and specific fears: The Phobia Protocol Single event trauma. In M. Luber (Ed.), *Eye movement desensitization and reprocessing: EMDR scripted protocols, Special populations* (pp. 575–610). New York, NY: Springer.

de Jongh, A., ten Broeke, E., & Meijer, S. (2010). Two method approach: A case conceptualization model in the context of EMDR. *Journal of EMDR Practice and Research, 4*(1), 12–21.

Elofsson, U. O., von Schèele, B., Theorell, T., & Söndergaard, H. P. (2008). Physiological correlates of eye movement desensitization and reprocessing. *Journal of Anxiety Disorders, 22*(4), 622–634.

Engelhard, I. M., van den Hout, M. A., Dek, E. C., Giele, C. L., van der Wielen, J. W., Reijnen, M. J., & van Roij, B. (2011). Reducing vividness and emotional intensity of recurrent "flash forwards" by taxing working memory: An analogue study. *Journal of Anxiety Disorders, 25*(4), 599–603.

Engelhard, I. M., van den Hout, M. A., Janssen, W. C., & van der Beek, J. (2010). Eye movements reduce vividness and emotionality of "flash forwards." *Behaviour Research and Therapy, 48*(5), 442–447.

Foa, E. B., Hembree, E. A., & Rothbaum, B. O. (2007). *Prolonged exposure therapy for PTSD: Emotional processing of traumatic experiences: Therapist guide.* New York, NY: Oxford University Press.

Foussias, G., & Remington, G. (2010). Negative symptoms in schizophrenia: Avolition and Occam's razor. *Schizophrenia Bulletin, 36*(2), 359–369.

Fowler, D. G., Freeman, D., Steel, C., Hardy, A., Smith, B. H., Hackmann, C.,...Bennington, P. E. (2006). The catastrophic interaction hypothesis: How do stress, trauma, emotion and information processing abnormalities lead to psychosis? In *Trauma and psychosis* (pp. 101–124). Hoboken, NJ: John Wiley.

Freeman, D., Garety, P. A., Bebbington, P. E., Smith, B., Rollinson, R., Fowler, D.,...Dunn, G. (2005). Psychological investigation of the structure of paranoia in a non-clinical population. *The British Journal of Psychiatry: The Journal of Mental Science, 186,* 427–435.

Freeman, D., Thompson, C., Vorontsova, N., Dunn, G., Carter, L.-A., Garety, P.,...Ehlers, A. (2013). Paranoia and posttraumatic stress disorder in the months after a physical assault: A longitudinal study examining shared and differential predictors. *Psychological Medicine.* doi:10.1017/S003329171300038X

Frueh, B. C., Grubaugh, A. L., Cusack, K. J., Kimble, M. O., Elhai, J. D., & Knapp, R. G. (2009). Exposure-based cognitive-behavioral treatment of PTSD in adults with schizophrenia or schizoaffective disorder: A pilot study. *Journal of Anxiety Disorders, 23,* 665–675.

Garety, P. A., & Hemsley, D. R. (1987). Characteristics of delusional experience. *European Archives of Psychiatry and Clinical Neuroscience, 236*(5), 294–298.

Garety, P. A., Kuipers, E., Fowler, D., Freeman, D., & Bebbington, P. E. (2001). A cognitive model of the positive symptoms of psychosis. *Psychological Medicine, 31*(2), 189–195.

Gaudiano, B. A., Young, D., Chelminski, I., & Zimmerman, M. (2008). Depressive symptom profiles and severity patterns in outpatients with psychotic vs. nonpsychotic major depression. *Comprehensive Psychiatry, 49*(5), 421–429.

Goodwin, F. K., & Jamison, K. R. (1990). *Manic-depressive illness.* Oxford, England UK: Oxford University Press.

Gracie, A., Freeman, D., Green, S., Garety, P. A., Kuipers, E., Hardy, A.,...Fowler, D. (2007). The association between traumatic experience, paranoia and hallucinations: A test of the predictions of psychological models. *Acta Psychiatrica Scandinavica, 116*(4), 280–289.

Grech, A., van Os, J., Jones, P. B., Lewis, S. W., & Murray, R. M. (2005). Cannabis use and outcome of recent onset psychosis. *European Psychiatry: The Journal of the Association of European Psychiatrists, 20*(4), 349–353.

Gunter, R. W., & Bodner, G. E. (2008). How eye movements affect unpleasant memories: Support for a working-memory account. *Behaviour Research and Therapy, 46*(8), 913–931.

Hackmann, A., Surawy, C., & Clark, D. M. (1998). Seeing yourself through others' eyes: A study of spontaneously occurring images in social phobia. *Behavioural and Cognitive Psychotherapy, 26*(01), 3–12.

Haddock, G., McCarron, J., Tarrier, N., & Faragher, E. B. (1999). Scales to measure dimensions of hallucinations and delusions: The Psychotic Symptom Rating Scale (PSYRATS). *Psychological Medicine, 29*(4), 879–889.

Haltenhof, H., Ulrich, H., & Blanenburg, W. (1999). Themes of delusion in 84 patients with unipolar depression. *Krankenhauspsychiatrie, 10*, 87–90.

Hammersley, P., Taylor, K., McGovern, J., & Kinderman, P. (2010). Attributions for hallucinations in bipolar affective disorder. *Behavioural and Cognitive Psychotherapy, 38*(2), 221–226.

Hardy, A., Fowler, D., Freeman, D., Smith, B., Steel, C., Evans, J.,...Dunn, G. (2005). Trauma and hallucinatory experience in psychosis. *Journal of Nervous and Mental Disease, 193*(8), 501–517.

Kay, S. R., Fiszbein, A., & Opler, L. A. (1987). The Positive and Negative Syndrome Scale (PANSS) for schizophrenia. *Schizophrenia Bulletin, 13*(2), 261–276.

Kelleher, I., Connor, D., Clarke, M. C., Devlin, N., Harley, M., & Cannon, M. (2012). Prevalence of psychotic symptoms in childhood and adolescence: A systematic review and meta-analysis of population-based studies. *Psychological Medicine, 42*(9), 1857–1863.

Kessler, R., Chiu, W., Demler, O., & Walters, E. (2005). Prevalence, severity, and comorbidity of 12-month DSM-IV disorders in the National Comorbidity Survey Replication. *Archives of General Psychiatry, 62*(6), 617–627.

Kim, D., Choi, J., Kim, S. H., Oh, D. H., Park, S. C., & Lee, S. H. (2010). A pilot study of brief eye movement desensitization and reprocessing (EMDR) for treatment of acute phase schizophrenia. *Korean Journal of Biological Psychiatry, 17*(2), 94–102.

Kingdon, D. G., Ashcroft, K., Bhandari, B., Gleeson, S., Warikoo, N., Symons, M.,...Mehta, R. (2010). Schizophrenia and borderline personality disorder: Similarities and differences in the experience of auditory hallucinations, paranoia, and childhood trauma. *The Journal of Nervous and Mental Disease, 198*(6), 399–403.

Krebs, M. O., Bourdel, M. C., Cherif, Z. R., Bouhours, P., Lôo, H., Poirier, M. F., & Amado, I. (2010). Deficit of inhibition motor control in untreated patients with schizophrenia: Further support from visually guided saccade paradigms. *Psychiatry Research, 179*(3), 279–284.

Lockett, S. H., Hatton, J., Turner, R., Stubbins, C., Hodgekins, J., & Fowler, D. (2012). Using a semi-structured interview to explore imagery experienced during social anxiety for clients with a diagnosis of psychosis: An exploratory study conducted within an early intervention for psychosis service. *Behavioural and Cognitive Psychotherapy, 40*(1), 55–68.

Logie, R., & de Jongh, A. (2014). The "Flashforward procedure": Confronting the catastrophe. *Journal of EMDR Practice and Research, 8*, 25–32.

Matheson, S. L., Shepherd, A. M., Pinchbeck, R. M., Laurens, K. R., & Carr, V. J. (2013). Childhood adversity in schizophrenia: A systematic meta-analysis. *Psychological Medicine, 43*(2), 225–238.

McCarthy-Jones, S., Trauer, T., Mackinnon, A., Sims, E., Thomas, N., & Copolov, D. L. (2012). A new phenomenological survey of auditory hallucinations: Evidence for subtypes and implications for theory and practice. *Schizophrenia Bulletin*. doi:10.1093/schbul/sbs156

McGorry, P., Chanen, A., McCarthy, E., Riel, R., McKenzie, D., & Singh, B. (1991). Posttraumatic stress disorder following recent-onset psychosis. An unrecognized postpsychotic syndrome. *The Journal of Nervous and Mental Disorders, 179*(5), 253–258.

Morrison, A. P., Beck, A. T., Glentworth, D., Dunn, H., Reid, G. S., Larkin, W., & Williams, S. (2002). Imagery and psychotic symptoms: A preliminary investigation. *Behaviour Research and Therapy, 40*(9), 1053–1062.

Morrison, A. P., Frame, L., & Larkin, W. (2003). Relationships between trauma and psychosis: A review and integration. *British Journal of Clinical Psychology, 42*(4), 331–353.

Morrison, A. P., Renton, J. C., Dunn, H., Williams, S., & Bentall, R. P. (2004). *Cognitive therapy for psychosis: A formulation-based approach.* New York, NY: Brunner-Routledge.

Mueser, K. T., Goodman, L. B., Trumbetta, S. L., Rosenberg, S. D., Osher, F. C., Vidaver, R.,...David, W. (1998). Trauma and posttraumatic stress disorder in severe mental illness. *Journal of Consulting and Clinical Psychology, 66*(3), 493–499.

Mueser, K. T., Lu, W., Rosenberg, S. D., & Wolfe, R. (2010). The trauma of psychosis: Posttraumatic stress disorder and recent onset psychosis. *Schizophrenia Research, 116*(2–3): 217–227.

Mueser, K. T., Rosenberg, S. D., Goodman, L. A., & Trumbetta, S. L. (2002). Trauma, PTSD, and the course of severe mental illness: An interactive model. *Schizophrenia Research, 53*, 123–143.

Mueser, K. T., Rosenberg, S. D., Xie, H., Jankowski, M. K., Bolton, E. E., Lu, W.,...Wolfe, R. (2008). A randomized controlled trial of cognitive-behavioral treatment for posttraumatic stress disorder in severe mental illness. *Journal of Consulting and Clinical Psychology, 76*(2), 259–271.

National Institue for Clinical Excellence (NICE). (2009). *Clinical guideline 82, schizophrenia—Core interventions in the treatment and management of schizophrenia in primary and secondary care.* London, UK: Author.

Ogden, P. K. M., & Pain, C. (2006). *Trauma and the body.* New York, NY: W.W. Norton.

Perkonigg, A., Kessler, R. C., Storz, S., & Wittchen, H. U. (2000). Traumatic events and post-traumatic stress disorder in the community: Prevalence, risk factors and comorbidity. *Acta Psychiatrica Scandinavica, 101*(1), 46–59.

Read, J., van Os, J., Morrison, A. P., & Ross, C. A. (2005). Childhood trauma, psychosis and schizophrenia: A literature review with theoretical and clinical implications. *Acta Psychiatrica Scandinavica, 112*(5), 330–350.

Romme, M., & Escher, A. (1989). Hearing voices. *Schizophrenia Bulletin, 15*(2), 209–216.

Ronconi, J. M., Shiner, B., & Watts, B. V. (2014). Inclusion and exclusion criteria in randomized controlled trials of psychotherapy for PTSD. *Journal of Psychiatric Practice, 20,* 25–37.

Schulze, K., Freeman, D., Green, C., & Kuipers, E. (2013). Intrusive mental imagery in patients with persecutory delusions. *Behaviour Research and Therapy, 51*(1), 7–14.

Shapiro, F. (2001). *Eye movement desensitization and reprocessing: Basic principles, protocols and procedures.* New York, NY: Guilford Press.

Shapiro, F. (2006). *EMDR: New notes on adaptive information processing with case formulation principles, forms, scripts and worksheets.* Watsonville, CA: EMDR Institute.

Shaw, K., McFarlane, A., & Bookless, C. (1997). The phenomenology of traumatic reactions to psychotic illness. *The Journal of Nervous and Mental Disease, 185*(7), 434–441.

Sheehan, D. V., Lecrubier, Y., Sheehan, K. H., Amorim, P., Janavs, J., Weiller, E.,...Dunbar, G. C. (1998). The Mini-International Neuropsychiatric Interview (M.I.N.I.): The development and validation of a structured diagnostic psychiatric interview for DSM-IV and ICD-10. *Journal of Clinical Psychiatry, 59*(Suppl. 20), 22–33; quiz 34–57.

Spinazzola, J., Blaustein, M., & van der Kolk, B. A. (2005). Posttraumatic stress disorder treatment outcome research: The study of unrepresentative samples? *Journal of Traumatic Stress, 18*(5), 425–436.

Stampfer, H. G. (1990). "Negative symptoms": A cumulative trauma stress disorder? *The Australian and New Zealand Journal of Psychiatry, 24*(4), 516–528.

Stompe, T., Friedman, A., Ortwein, G., Strobl, R., Chaudhry, H. R., Najam, N., & Chaudhry, M. R. (1999). Comparison of delusions among schizophrenics in Austria and in Pakistan. *Psychopathology, 32*(5), 225–234.

Trower, P., & Chadwick, P. (1995). Pathways to defense of the self: A theory of two types of paranoia. *Clinical Psychology: Science and Practice, 2*(3), 263–278.

van den Berg, D. P. G., de Bont, P. A. J. M., van der Vleugel, B. M., de Roos, C., de Jongh, A., van Minnen, A., & van der Gaag, M. (2015). Prolonged exposure versus eye movement desensitization and reprocessing versus waiting list for posttraumatic stress disorder in patients with a psychotic disorder: A randomized clinical trial. *JAMA Psychiatry.* Online First. doi:10.1001/jamapsychiatry.2014.2637

van den Berg, D. P. G., & van der Gaag, M. (2012). Treating trauma in psychosis with EMDR: A pilot study. *Journal of Behavior Therapy and Experimental Psychiatry, 43*(1), 664–671.

van den Berg, D. P. G., van der Vleugel, B. M., Staring, A. B. P., de Bont, P. A. J. M., & de Jongh, A. (2013). EMDR in psychosis: Guidelines for conceptualization and treatment. *Journal of EMDR Practice and Research, 7*(4), 208–224.

van den Hout, M. A., Engelhard, I. M., Smeets, M. A. M., Hornsveld, H., Hoogeveen, E., de Heer, E.,...Rijkeboer, M. (2010). Counting during recall: Taxing of working memory and reduced vividness and emotionality of negative memories. *Applied Cognitive Psychology, 24*(3), 303–311.

Varese, F., Smeets, F., Drukker, M., Lieverse, R., Lataster, T., Viechtbauer, W.,...Bentall, R. P. (2012). Childhood adversities increase the risk of psychosis: A meta-analysis of patient-control, prospective- and cross-sectional cohort studies. *Schizophrenia Bulletin, 38*(4), 661–671.

Vaughan, S., & Fowler, D. (2004). The distress experienced by voice hearers is associated with the perceived relationship between the voice hearer and the voice. *British Journal of Clinical Psychology, 43*(2), 143–153.

Wright, J. H., Basco, M. R., & Thase, M. E. (2006). *Learning cognitive-behavior therapy: An illustrated guide.* Washington, DC: American Psychiatric Press.

SUMMARY SHEET:
EMDR Therapy for Traumatized Patients With Psychosis

3A

Berber van der Vleugel, David van den Berg, Paul de Bont,
Tonnie Staring, and Ad de Jongh
SUMMARY SHEET BY MARILYN LUBER

Name: _____ Diagnosis: _____

Medications: _____

Test Results: _____

☑ Check when task is completed, response has changed, or to indicate symptoms.

Note: This material is meant as a checklist for your response. Please keep in mind that it is only a reminder of different tasks that may or may not apply to your incident.

Introduction

Most prominent psychotic symptoms:

- ☐ Hallucinations: perceptual experiences without corresponding external visual, auditory, olfactory, gustatory, or tactile source.
    - ☐ Auditory Verbal Hallucinations: voices often saying negative things; for example, commands (*"Kill yourself"*), comments (*"He's a moron"*), or threats (*"Let's get rid of him"*).
- ☐ Delusions: convictions that are uncommon in a cultural context and that are maintained despite evidence to the contrary
    - ☐ Paranoid Delusions: characterized by threat appraisals in which others are thought to have malevolent intentions. For instance, thinking that others are spying on you or are out to get you. Delusions often form an explanation for anomalous or unsettling experiences, like hallucinations. They are usually accompanied by preoccupation, anxiety, and safety behaviors.

EMDR Therapy should be within a comprehensive treatment program with a multidisciplinary team: pharmacotherapy, case management, CBT, supported employment, family interventions, and peer support. EMDR Therapy should be used within this comprehensive context.

1. Trauma and Psychosis Are Related (in three different ways):
   - ☐ Even with distinct onsets, PTSD and psychosis symptoms can be mutually reinforcing
   - ☐ The experience of psychotic symptoms can be traumatic and lead to PTSD
   - ☐ Trauma is a substantial risk factor for the development of psychosis
   1.1 *Psychosis and Comorbid PTSD*—the prevalence of comorbid PTSD is high in patients with psychoses and characterized by intrusive experiences, negative symptoms, and avoidance behaviors.
   1.2 *Trauma and Psychosis*—two thirds of women and more than half of men with psychosis report sexual or physical abuse as a child. The more severe the trauma, the greater the risk of developing psychosis and the worse the prognosis.
      1.2.1 *The direct route*—associations between stressful or emotional events and onset of psychotic symptoms or the content or theme of the psychotic symptoms is associated with life events.
      1.2.2 *The indirect route*—negative core beliefs about oneself (e.g., "I am guilty, weak, defenseless") and negative expectations about others (e.g., "Other people are dangerous, untrustworthy, bad") can form a cognitive link between traumatic life experiences and psychosis and may determine the nature of a delusion.
   1.3 *Imagery in Psychosis*—three types most dominant in psychosis:
      - ☐ Images of feared catastrophes (often in paranoia)
      - ☐ Visualizations of the perceived origin or content of a symptom (often in voices)
      - ☐ Images of negative life experiences that are somehow related to the psychotic symptoms (actual memories)

EMDR for Traumatized Patients With Psychosis Script Notes

To enhance diagnostic reliability, use validated standardized measures to assess symptoms and problematic functioning, construct a case formulation, and evaluate treatment effects.

- ☐ Mini-International Neuropsychiatric Interview-Plus (M.I.N.I. Plus)
- ☐ Clinician-Administered PTSD Scale (CAPS)
- ☐ Positive and Negative Syndrome Scale (PANSS)
- ☐ The Psychotic Symptom Rating Scale (PSYRATS)

1. Case Conceptualization Methods
   1.1 *First Method*: Conceptualizing EMDR in the treatment of *DSM-5* disorders, including PTSD. Select the target symptom/cluster of symptoms, after which etiological and subsequent aggravating events are identified and visually summarized on a timeline.

   Process chronologically for symptom reduction.
   1.2 *Second Method:* Identify memories that underlie dysfunctional basic assumptions and target images of experiences leading to the formation of negative beliefs about oneself, others, and the world (proof/evidence).

   Rank them from strong to weak proof and reprocess with the Standard EMDR Protocol.
   1.3 *Flashforwards:* Target unrealistic and fearful expectations or negative imagery related to psychosis. Process the frightening imagery and/or the worst-case scenario.

Use the NC, "I am powerless," as the default NC.
Standard PC: "I am in control (of the flashforward)," or "I can handle it (i.e., the flashforward)."
2. Obstacles and Related Treatment Strategies
    2.1 Adaptation to the EMDR Standard Protocol
        o Always use a still image for assessment
        o NC and PC relate to the image and can be different from the core belief
        o When Back To Target (BTT), ask for the image again to keep the focus
        o During Phase 4, go BTT every 5 to 10 minutes to keep the association chains limited
        o When thoughts and feelings are disorganized, use: *"Stay with that"* or *"Concentrate on that"* instead of *"Go with that"*
        o Domains of NC: distinction between the cognitive domains of self-esteem (e.g., "I am weak") and responsibility (e.g., "I am guilty") to facilitate connecting of the nodes in the fear network that still need to be processed
        o PC to consolidate and reinforce learning
    2.2 Ongoing Traumatization by Psychotic Experiences
        o If patient is continuously feeling unsafe and the SUD is high and not dropping, use a Cognitive Interweave on the blocking belief, but sometimes more cognitive interventions are needed
        o When there is some doubt, EMDR can be used with flashforward followed by behavioral experiments and exposure assignments
    2.3 Cognitive Impairments
        o There is poor concentration and working memory deficits in patients with psychosis
        o Consider adjusting taxing of working memory when dual task is too compelling, by speeding up or slowing down the passes when using Ems or switch to beeps
    2.4 Difficulty With Eye Movements
        o Saccadic eye movements in schizophrenia are found to be impaired; however, the authors do not find Ems a problem
    2.5 Antipsychotic Medications
        o Antipsychotic meds and meds against motor side effects of antipsychotics can affect cholinergic receptors and it is thought that EMDR may work because it activates the cholinergic system in the brain
        o If patient is not responding and is heavily medicated, consider lowering the dosage
    2.6 Low Affective Expression
        o Because patients have flattened affect does not mean that they do not have a high emotional experience; make sure to use the SUDs
    2.7 Unusual Side Effects and Destabilization
        o Predict that psychotic symptoms may increase temporarily in or between sessions and make sure that there is an action plan about what to do
        o Normalize these types of reactions and continue treatment
        o Discuss that dissociation as a defense is possible as well; help patient by reorienting
3. Therapeutic Stance
    ☐ Empathic
    ☐ Goal-oriented
    ☐ Inquisitive
    ☐ Self-confident
    ☐ Addresses trauma as burdensome but harmless

EMDR Therapy for Traumatized Patients With Psychosis Scripted Protocol

Phase 1: Symptom Selection

Current and Future Concerns

Current psychological problems/worries: _____

_____

What you think will happen in the future: _____

_____

What triggers the thoughts: _____

Images about what may happen in the future: _____

What triggers the images: _____

How you feel as a result of these thoughts and images: _____

_____

What is happening in your body as a result of thoughts and images: _____

_____

What you do because of these thoughts and images: _____

_____

What your worst-case scenario is: _____

_____

What is the most likely scenario: _____

_____

Posttraumatic Stress Symptoms

Highs and lows of your life: _____

_____

    ☐ Yes   ☐ No Experienced/witnessed/confronted with event(s) involving actual/threatened death/serious injury of threat to physical integrity of yourself or others?

If so, answer the following:
    ☐ Yes   ☐ No Felt terror, helplessness/horror?
    ☐ Yes   ☐ No Think about or reexperience vivid memories of what happened to you in the past?
    ☐ Yes   ☐ No Sometimes act or feel as if the event were recurring?
    ☐ Yes   ☐ No Distressed when exposed to situations or symbols that resemble the traumatic event (psychologically/physiologically)?

Summary Sheet: EMDR Therapy for Traumatized Patients With Psychosis 153

☐ Yes ☐ No Try to avoid thoughts, feelings, activities, places, or people that are associated with the incident?
☐ Yes ☐ No Pronounced decreased interest in activities that were once important to you?
☐ Yes ☐ No Feeling detached or estranged from others?
☐ Yes ☐ No Feeling flat or down?
☐ Yes ☐ No Do you have a sense that your future will be short?
☐ Yes ☐ No Have you had problems falling or staying asleep?
☐ Yes ☐ No Have you felt especially irritable or showed strong feelings of anger?
☐ Yes ☐ No Have you found it difficult to concentrate on what you were doing or on things going on around you?
☐ Yes ☐ No Have you been especially alert or watchful, even when there was no real need to be?
☐ Yes ☐ No Have you had any strong startle reactions?"

For all of the above symptoms, if the answer is positive, ask the following:

"What is that like?" _____

_____

Onset: *"When did you first start experiencing this symptom?"* _____

_____

Frequency: *"How much of the time in the past week/month did you feel that way?"* _____

_____

Intensity: *"How difficult was that for you? How much does that interfere with your everyday life at the moment?"* _____

_____

Is there an indication for the treatment of frequent and disturbing trauma-related symptom(s)? ☐ Yes ☐ No

Psychotic Symptoms—Delusional Ideas

☐ True ☐ False Others cannot be trusted

☐ True ☐ False Think others are after you/spying on you/want to harm you

☐ True ☐ False Others can read your mind/hear your thoughts or the other way around

☐ True ☐ False Someone is putting ideas in your mind and/or controlling you in some way

☐ True ☐ False Receive messages (on TV, radio/newspapers) conveyed especially to you

☐ True ☐ False You are special in some way/have special gifts

If the above symptoms are true, ask the following:

"What is it like?" _____

"How often does this happen?" _____

"How disturbing is this?" _____

Is there an indication for the treatment of frequent and disturbing delusional ideas? ☐ Yes ☐ No

Psychotic Symptoms—Auditory Verbal Hallucinations

☐ True ☐ False Hear voices/sounds others cannot hear

If true, ask the following:

What they say: _____

What you think of them: _____

Where they come from: _____

Who they are: _____

Their goal: _____

Is there an indication for the treatment of frequent and disturbing auditory hallucinations?
☐ Yes ☐ No

Psychotic Symptoms—Visual Hallucinations

☐ True ☐ False Visions while awake. See things others cannot see

If true, ask the following:

What kind of things: _____

What you think of them: _____

Where they come from: _____

Why you see them: _____

Is there an indication for the treatment of frequent and disturbing visual hallucinations?
☐ Yes ☐ No

Dysfunctional Core Beliefs = not just thoughts but long-standing enduring beliefs that are generalized and absolute in nature. Unhealthy negative core beliefs undermine self-esteem, impair the ability to solve problems, and/or cause relational problems.

What you think of yourself: _____

What you think of others: _____

What you think about the world: _____

Is there an indication for the treatment of dysfunctional core beliefs? ☐ Yes ☐ No

Psychiatric History

☐ Yes ☐ No Experienced any psychiatric problems and/or psychiatric hospitalizations

If so, how did you experience being admitted? _____

_____

☐ Yes ☐ No Prior psychotherapy

If so, what was it like for you? _____

_____

Past Medications

☐ Yes ☐ No Takes medication as prescribed

If not, why not? _____

_____

Substance Abuse History

☐ Yes ☐ No Currently using drugs and alcohol.

How much: _____

If so, when started: _____

If not, in the past? _____

Symptom Selection

Choose current symptoms that should decrease (first) to have a fulfilling life:

- ☐ Hallucinations
- ☐ Delusions
- ☐ Core Beliefs

The First Method

Phase 2: Preparation—The First Method

"Now we have to find out what memories are crucial to understand the symptoms we are going to work on. What caused them and what made them worse? When we know what elicited and/or worsened these symptoms, we can use EMDR to disarm these memories by reducing their emotional load. You will not forget these memories, but due to EMDR their interference will wane and the selected symptom(s) will decrease."

Event/events responsible for onset of selected symptom: _____

_____

Event that led to this symptom: _____

_____

When was that? How old were you? _____

_____

☐ Yes ☐ No You never experienced these symptoms before that event

Event/events responsible for the worsening of the selected symptom: _____

_____

When was that? How old were you? _____

_____

Draw a timeline and put in the identified events. Graph in the severity of the symptom(s) selected for treatment:

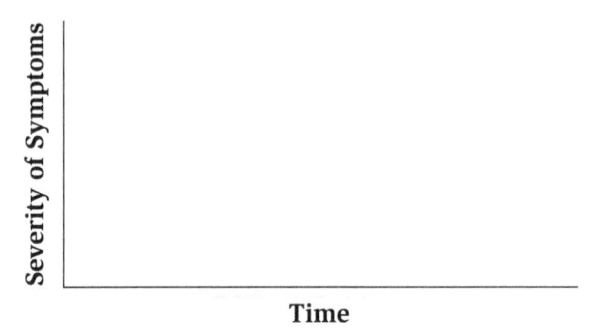

Severity of Symptoms

Time

Reprocess relevant memories in chronological order.

Phase 3: Assessment – The First Method: Event That Caused Psychotic Symptoms to Start

Traumatic Memory: *"I am sorry that you experienced such terrible things. While these things are in the past, you are still experiencing memories of them. Memories can be very unsettling, but they cannot really harm you (give an example, such as, 'Your father used to hit you, but the memory of your father cannot'). In treatment, we will work through some of your worst memories. This will help you experience that you have the strength and resilience to cope. I am confident that you will succeed."*

"I'd like you to describe the incident that caused your current symptoms. You need not go into much detail. Just give a general account of what happened. It's how you remember the incident that is most important, not what actually happened."

Make sure that the patient tells the entire story, starting where the memory begins to the point where the traumatic experience ends.

Worst moment: _____

Most difficult image now: _____

_____

What you see in the image: _____

_____

Where you are in the image: _____

_____

☐ Yes ☐ No Draws image of worst moment

Cognitive domain of NC:

☐ Yes ☐ No Responsibility and guilt ("I am guilty")
☐ Yes ☐ No Control ("I am powerless/helpless")
☐ Yes ☐ No Self-esteem ("I am a bad person; I am worthless/stupid/vulnerable")
☐ Yes ☐ No Safety (in relation to the image—"I am still in danger")

Check: *"Is this the image that is the most difficult for you to think about now? Or is it mainly what was worst for you then?"*

NC: _____

Check the NC meets the criteria:

☐ Yes ☐ No Dysfunctional
☐ Yes ☐ No Statement about oneself as a person
☐ Yes ☐ No Valid in the here and now? (Expressed in the present tense)
☐ Yes ☐ No Emotionally charged

Positive Cognition

PC: _____

Cognitive domain of PC:

☐ Yes ☐ No Responsibility and guilt ("I did what I could/I am innocent")
☐ Yes ☐ No Control ("I can do it/I can handle it/I can manage it")
☐ Yes ☐ No Self-esteem ("I am OK/I am worthwhile/I am competent/I am fine")
☐ Yes ☐ No Vulnerability ("I am strong/I am resilient")
☐ Yes ☐ No Safety ("I am safe now")

Validity of Cognition: _____ /7

Emotions: _____

Subjective Units of Disturbance: _____ /10

Location of Body Sensation: _____

Desensitize the target image and install the PC and link the PC with the image.

When finished, return to assessment and repeat on memories of event(s) that caused symptoms to worsen.

Phase 3: Assessment—The First Method: Event That Caused Psychotic Symptoms to Worsen

Traumatic memory: Ensure that the patient tells the entire story from where it began to the point where the traumatic experience ends.

> *"I'd like you to describe the incident(s) that caused your current symptoms to worsen. You needn't go into too much detail. Just give a general account of what happened. It's about how you <u>remember</u> the incident, not so much about what actually happened."*

Worst moment: _____

Most difficult image now: _____

_____

What you see in the image: _____

_____

Where you are in the image: _____

_____

☐ Yes ☐ No Draws image of worst moment

Cognitive domain of NC:

☐ Yes ☐ No Responsibility and guilt ("I am guilty")
☐ Yes ☐ No Control ("I am powerless/helpless")
☐ Yes ☐ No Self-esteem ("I am a bad person; I am worthless/I am stupid")
☐ Yes ☐ No Vulnerability ("I am weak")
☐ Yes ☐ No Safety (in relation to the image—"I am still in danger")

Check: *"Is this the image that is <u>now</u> the most difficult for you to think about <u>now</u>? Or is it mainly what was worst for you <u>then</u>?"*

NC: _____

Check the NC meets the criteria:

☐ Yes ☐ No Dysfunctional
☐ Yes ☐ No Statement about oneself as a person
☐ Yes ☐ No Valid in the here and now? (Expressed in the present tense)
☐ Yes ☐ No Emotionally charged

NC: _____

Cognitive domain of PC:

☐ Yes ☐ No Responsibility and guilt ("I did what I could/I am innocent")
☐ Yes ☐ No Control ("I can do it/I can handle it/I can manage it")
☐ Yes ☐ No Self-esteem ("I am OK/I am worthwhile/I am competent/I am fine")
☐ Yes ☐ No Vulnerability ("I am strong/I am resilient")
☐ Yes ☐ No Safety ("I am safe now")

Validity of Cognition: _____ /7

Emotions: _____

Subjective Units of Disturbance: _____ /10

Location of Body Sensation: _____

Desensitize the target image and install the PC and link the PC with the image.*

When finished, return to assessment and repeat on other memories of event(s) that caused symptoms to worsen.

The Second Method

Phase 2: Preparation—Second Method

List of Dysfunctional Core Beliefs (Obtained in Phase 1)

_____
_____
_____

> *"Core beliefs are basic assumptions about yourself, others, and the world. They are largely based on previous life experiences, most predominantly experiences from our childhood. Negative (core) beliefs usually arise from experiences such as _____ (name experiences of the patient, such as being bullied, physically abused, blamed, neglected, sexually abused). These*

experiences made you believe that _____ (state the core belief) *is true. No matter how hard you try, it is very difficult to think differently, for these experiences instinctively/emotionally still prove that* _____ (state the core belief) *is true to you."*

Start with the dysfunctional core beliefs that are most explicitly related to problems the patient experiences nowadays.

"What would you like to believe about yourself (others/the world) *instead of* _____ (state core belief)*?"*

_____

"What we are going to work on is that you will be able to believe that you are _____ (state the positive core belief) *wherever you are, whatever you do, and whatever you are thinking of. To allow this to happen, we are going to remove the evidence for your negative core belief. EMDR will be helpful to process the memories of these negative experiences."*

_____

List of Targets Proving the Dysfunctional, Problematic Belief

"What experiences instinctively still 'prove' _____ (state the dysfunctional belief)*?"*

"What have you experienced that still convinces you that _____ (state the dysfunctional belief)*?"*

"What made you (start to) think _____ (state the dysfunctional belief)*?"*

(Fill in below)

Dysfunctional Belief #1: _____
    Proof 1.1 _____
    Proof 1.2 _____
    Proof 1.3 _____

Dysfunctional Belief #2: _____
    Proof 2.1 _____
    Proof 2.2 _____
    Proof 2.3 _____

Dysfunctional Belief #3: _____
    Proof 3.1 _____
    Proof 3.2 _____
    Proof 3.3 _____

Phase 3: Assessment—The Second Method: Most Powerful Proof

Most Powerful Proof _____

_____

Describe the incident—a general account. Tell the entire story, up to the point where the traumatic experience ended. _____

_____

Most powerful emotional proof for you now: _____

Photo of the best proof image now: _____

What you see in the image: _____

Where you are in the image: _____

☐ Yes ☐ No Draws image of worst moment
Check:
☐ Yes ☐ No Image represents the most convincing evidence for you

NC: _____

Cognitive domain of NC:

☐ Yes ☐ No Dysfunctional
☐ Yes ☐ No Statement about oneself as a person
☐ Yes ☐ No Valid in the here and now? (Expressed in the present tense)
☐ Yes ☐ No Emotionally charged

PC: _____

Cognitive domain of PC:

☐ Yes ☐ No Responsibility and guilt ("I did what I could/I am innocent")
☐ Yes ☐ No Control ("I can do it/I can handle it/I can manage it")
☐ Yes ☐ No Self-esteem ("I am OK/worthwhile/competent/fine/I am strong/I am resilient")
☐ Yes ☐ No Safety ("I am safe now")

Validity of Cognition: _____ /7

Emotions: _____

Subjective Units of Disturbance: _____ /10

Location of Body Sensation: _____

Desensitize the target image. Install PC + image.

Note: Proceed with the desensitization of the target image and installation of the PC, linking the PC with the image. When finished, repeat the procedure on the next proof. When finished with all the evidence for this problematic core belief, continue the procedure with the next core belief, and so on.

The Third Method

Phase 2: Preparation—The Third Method

Use this method if patients are aware that their feared scenarios are not fully realistic or that intrusive experiences actually do not deserve that much attention. If there are no doubts about the (psychotic) conviction(s), it is best to start with cognitive and behavioral work first. Patients can be hesitant or unwilling to execute behavioral experiments or exposure assignments when they fear terrible consequences. If so, desensitizing the worst-case scenario may be helpful; this is also known as using EMDR on flashforwards.

Next to reprocessing flashforwards, EMDR can also be helpful when a patient experiences intrusive imagery related to the origin, appearance, or content of a psychotic symptom. By desensitizing this imagery, emotional involvement and preoccupation can be reduced.

Note: The First Method is used to find memories that contributed to the onset/aggravation of, for example, voices. The Third Method works with imagery (not memories of real incidents) related to voices; often this imagery has a later onset than the symptom itself.

Intrusive thoughts or images (future concerns/psychotic symptoms obtained in Phase 1)

_____

_____

_____

Flashforward

It is important to create a framework that allows and enables the patient's thinking about the impending doom of the worst-case scenario.

"What we need to figure out is what kind of image is in your mind that makes you fearful about a future confrontation with the thing/the one you fear. What do you fear will happen and will go wrong when you are confronted with the situation you are avoiding now in the worst-case scenario? Basically we should look for your ultimate disaster image."

Identifying the details of the worst catastrophic fantasy:

What might go wrong: _____

_____

Worst thing that could happen: _____

_____

Bring up the image of the worst-case scenario:

Most disturbing image: _____

Worst/most awful part: _____

_____

Use this as a target for processing.
NC: Domain of powerlessness/threat and arousal is usually high
PC: "I can handle this"

Visualization of Psychotic Symptom

In Phase 1, information was collected about psychotic symptoms like hallucinations and delusional beliefs. Delusions can be primary (e.g., "The CIA is spying on me") or secondary to hallucinations (e.g., "The voice belongs to my former boss, who wants to ruin my life"). If the patient has an image of the perceived origin, appearance, or content of a symptom (i.e., activating event), the Standard EMDR Protocol can be used.

The flashforward can be an image of the persecutor, for instance, or of the patient with a man next to him yelling nasty things through a loudspeaker. The NC and the PC may belong to any domain.

Psychotic imagery (take from Phase 1 information): _____

_____

Phase 3: Assessment—The Flashforward Procedure

Worst Moment of Feared Future Event

> "If you anticipate what might happen, what is the worst moment for you <u>now</u>? Stop the film at that moment so that you can get a snapshot of this part of it. The snapshot is not the image of what will be the most difficult for you <u>then</u>. <u>Describe the image</u> that is most difficult for you <u>to see now</u>, while anticipating it in the future. Please describe this image to me in detail."

_____

_____

Most difficult image now: _____

_____

What you see in the image: _____

_____

Where you are in the image: _____

_____

☐ Yes ☐ No Draws image of worst moment

Check: *"Is this the image that is <u>now</u> the most difficult for you to think about <u>now</u>? Or is it mainly what was worst for you <u>then</u>?"*

Negative Cognition

> "The fact that this image is so disturbing to you probably has to do with the fear that you will not be able to cope with it. Is that right?"   ☐ Yes ☐ No

NC: "<u>I am powerless</u>" (unless patient objects)

Positive Cognition

> "When you bring up that image again, would you prefer to believe 'I can handle it' (the image)?"

PC: "<u>I can handle it</u>" (unless the NC was not formulated as "I am powerless")

Validity of Cognition: _____ /7

Emotions: _____

Subjective Units of Disturbance: _____ /10

Location of Body Sensation: _____

Desensitize the target image and install the PC and link the PC with the image.

When finished, return to assessment and repeat on memories of event(s) that caused symptoms to worsen.

Phase 3: Assessment—Imagery

Most Disturbing Psychotic Imagery

Image of most disturbing part: _____

Worst moment: _____

Cognitive domain of NC:

- ☐ Yes ☐ No Responsibility and guilt ("I am guilty")
- ☐ Yes ☐ No Control ("I am powerless/helpless")
- ☐ Yes ☐ No Self-esteem ("I am a bad person; I am worthless/stupid; I am weak")
- ☐ Yes ☐ No Safety (in relation to the image—"I am still in danger")

What you see in the image: _____

_____

Where you are in the image: _____

_____

- ☐ Yes ☐ No Draws image of worst moment

Negative Cognition

"This is not a pretty image, but what we need to discover now is why this image is so awful for you. This probably has to do with a negative conclusion that you have drawn about yourself in relation to this image. What conclusion is that?" _____

_____

"What it is that makes this image so awful?" _____

_____

NC: _____

Check that the NC meets the criteria:

- ☐ Yes ☐ No Dysfunctional
- ☐ Yes ☐ No Statement about oneself as a person
- ☐ Yes ☐ No Valid in the here and now? (Expressed in the present tense)
- ☐ Yes ☐ No Emotionally charged

Positive Cognition

PC: _____

Cognitive domain of PC:

- ☐ Yes ☐ No Responsibility and guilt ("I did what I could/I am innocent")
- ☐ Yes ☐ No Control ("I can do it/I can handle it/I can manage it")
- ☐ Yes ☐ No Self-esteem ("I am OK/worthwhile/competent/fine; I am strong/I am resilient")
- ☐ Yes ☐ No Safety ("I am safe now")

Validity of Cognition: _____ /7

Emotions: _____

Subjective Units of Disturbance: _____ /10

Location of Body Sensation: _____

Note: Proceed with the desensitization of the target image (Phase 4) and installation of PC (Phase 5), linking the PC with the image.

Phase 4: Desensitization

"From the moment you follow my hand, I want you to act as an observer. Observe what comes up. This can be thoughts, feelings, images, physical responses; all kinds of things. What comes up can be clearly linked to the incident, but it is also possible that it seems to have nothing to do with it at all. Just observe what comes up, without judging, without influencing. Just follow my instructions. When starting the procedure, it is important you have a close look at the image in your mind, but as soon as you start doing the eye movements, there is no need to stick to the image, it is just the starting point. We will go back to the image (how it is stored in your head) *every now and then, however, to see how disturbing it is to look at it. It is possible that the image will change. Remember it is impossible to do it wrong, as long as you just observe and follow what comes up. OK?"*

"Before we start, just one more thing: If anything comes up that is extremely distressing, do not stop the procedure, continue to follow my fingers. Just think of it as a train running through a dark tunnel. If you do not want to be there, you should not pull the emergency brake, for then it will take longer to reach the end of the tunnel. Instead of stopping the train, you would do better to speed up. Do you understand? The best thing you can do is to concentrate on my fingers even more. Think of my fingers as the accelerator. OK? So keep your mind at rest and just follow my fingers with your eyes."

Repeat this procedure for 5 to 10 minutes (or shorter if there are no changes in associations for several times in a row). Then, go Back to Target (BTT): _____ /10
Go BTT every 5 to 10 minutes until the SUD = 0.

Phase 5: Installation (according to Standard EMDR Protocol/EMD Protocol)

PC:_____ ☐ Completed

New PC (if new one is better): _____

VoC: _____ /7

Incident + PC + BLS

Phase 6: Body Scan ☐ Completed

Body Scan—only at the end of processing all targets and memories of event
Original memory + PC + Scan Body

Unresolved tension/tightness/unusual sensation: _____

_____

Do BLS until subsides.
Note: Check whether the unusual sensation is related to emotional distress rather than motor side effects from antipsychotic medication.

Phase 7: Closure

> "What is the most positive thing you have learned about yourself in this session with regard to _____ (state the incident, theme, or image)?"

If the answer is not already on an identity level, say the following:

> "What does this tell us about you?" (What kind of person...)

Install with eye movements until no further positive changes occur.

> "Things may come up, or they may not. If they do, great. It is not unusual and it is a sign of reprocessing. You can use a log to write down what triggers, images, thoughts or cognitions, emotions, and sensations come up. Please write down the positive experiences, too. It is best to not use sedatives afterwards so your brain can do the healing. If it is absolutely necessary, use the lowest dose possible. If negative feelings do come up, try not to elaborate on them, try not to make negative feelings important. Remember, it is still just the old stuff. Just write it down for next time. Of course you can give me a call if you need to."

Phase 8: Reevaluation

SUDS of Incident(s) Processed: _____ /10

New material: _____

Reprocessed necessary targets: ☐ Completed

EMDR helpful in daily life: ☐ Completed

When patient still experiences anticipatory fear of confrontations with certain objects or situations, there may still be unexplored past traumatic events that remain to be processed. Once all memories are resolved, and/or it is not possible to identify any past relevant events to the feared future event, use the Flashforward Procedure.

Flashforward: Worst Moment

WORST MOMENT OF FEARED FUTURE EVENT

> "If you anticipate what might happen, what is the worst moment for you _now_? Stop the film at that moment so that you can get a snapshot of this part of it. The snapshot is not the image of what will be the most difficult for you _then_. _Describe the image_ that is most difficult for you _to see now_, while anticipating it in the future. Please describe this image to me in detail."

Most difficult image now: _____

_____

What you see in the image: _____

_____

Where you are in the image: _____

_____

☐ Yes   ☐ No Draws image of worst moment

Check: "Is this the image that is _now_ the most fearful for you to think about _now_? Or is it mainly what was worst for you _then_?"

Negative Cognition

"The fact that this image is so disturbing to you probably has to do with the fear that you will not be able to cope with it. Is that right?" ☐ Yes ☐ No

NC: "I am powerless" (unless patient objects)

Positive Cognition

PC: "I can handle it" (unless the NC was not formulated as "I am powerless")

Validity of Cognition: _____ /7

Emotions: _____

Subjective Units of Disturbance: _____ /10

Location of Body Sensation: _____

Desensitize the target image and install the PC and link the PC with the image.

When finished, return to assessment and repeat on memories of event(s) that caused symptoms to worsen.

If flashforward is zero and the patient is concerned with future confrontations with certain stimuli or formerly phobic situations, or there is avoidance behavior, then install a future template.

Future Template

Situation avoided until now and plan to encounter this week: _____

Image + "I can handle it" + BLS

VoC: _____ /7 (repeat until VoC = 7/7)

Video Check

"This time, I'd like you to imagine yourself stepping into the future. Close your eyes, and play a movie from the beginning until the end. Imagine yourself coping with any challenges that come your way. Notice what you are seeing, thinking, feeling, and experiencing in your body. While playing this movie, let me know if you hit any blocks. If you do, just open your eyes and let me know. If you don't hit any blocks, let me know when you have viewed the whole movie."

If blocks, say, "I can handle it," and BLS. Repeat until whole movie can be viewed entirely without distress.

VoC: _____ /7

If client can play movie from beginning to end with confidence and satisfaction, play the movie one more time from beginning to end + BLS: ☐ Yes ☐ No

Prepare the Patient for In Vivo Confrontations

"Many people appear to avoid certain activities for so long that they no longer know how to behave and how to feel secure in this situation. To be able to help further alleviate your fears and concerns, it is important that you learn to counter the negative belief that contributes to this sense of threat and anxiety. Therefore, you need to actually test the catastrophic expectations you have that fuel your anxiety in real life. I would like to ask you to gradually confront the objects or situations that normally would provoke a fear response. It may seem odd, but if you have a positive experience and it appears that the catastrophe you fear does not occur, it helps you to further demonstrate—or to convince yourself—that your fear is unfounded."

"I want you to understand that nothing will be done against your will during the confrontation with the things that normally would evoke fear. The essence of this confrontation is that it is safe."

In Vivo Exposure

This is done to reduce avoidance and evoke mastery while observing that no real danger exists. Pay attention to features of the phobic object or situation that are positive or interesting while being exposed to it.

Description of most notable features of the situation: _____

_____

_____

Negative thoughts during in vivo exposure: _____

Thoughts someone who is not afraid would think in the situation:

_____

It is helpful to make variations with regard to the stimulus dimensions "action," "distance," and "time."

> "Isn't it interesting to notice that now that you are confronted with this _____ (state the object or situation) _____ (state the catastrophe the clients normally would have feared to happen) *does not occur?*"
>
> ☐ Yes ☐ No
>
> "Do you notice that your anxiety is not as physically harmful as you might have expected?"   ☐ Yes ☐ No
>
> "These emotional reactions will subside and fade over time. Therefore, it is important that you continue exposing yourself to the feared stimuli as long as you feel that you have achieved a certain degree of self-mastery. Please note that you are gradually learning to feel that you are capable of handling a certain level of anticipatory anxiety with confidence."

Importance of practice.

Check with VoC (0–100%): _____

# EMDR Integrative Group Treatment Protocol© Adapted for Adolescents (14–17 Years) and Adults Living With Ongoing Traumatic Stress

Ignacio Jarero and Lucina Artigas

Introduction

The Eye Movement Desensitization and Reprocessing-Integrative Group Treatment Protocol (EMDR-IGTP; Artigas, Jarero, Alcalá, & López Cano, 2014) for early intervention was developed by members of the Mexican Association for Mental Health Support in Crisis (AMAMECRISIS) to deal with the extensive need for mental health services after Hurricane Pauline ravaged the coasts of the states of Oaxaca and Guerrero in 1997 (Jarero & Artigas, 2009). This protocol combines the Standard EMDR Protocols and Procedures, including the eight phases (Shapiro, 2001), with a group therapy model and an art therapy format, and uses the Butterfly Hug (Artigas & Jarero, 2014a) as a form of self-administered bilateral stimulation.

The present protocol is an adaptation of the EMDR-IGTP for early intervention, based on Ignacio Jarero and Lucina Artigas's many years of experience in both clinical and field work in Latin America, the Caribbean, Europe, and South Asian countries. It is designed specifically to treat the exact moment in which the critical incident happens. For this group format, the critical incident consists of a number of stress-related events that continue over an extended period of time with no *posttrauma safety period for memory consolidation*, as with clients who receive cancer diagnoses or victims of earthquakes, flooding, typhoons, and so on, who experience the continuing stressors that go along with these types of catastrophes that change the client's whole world. This idea was first thought promising for adults living with continued traumatic stress related to the diagnosis of cancer (Jarero et al., 2015) after seeing the parallel between trauma with no posttrauma safety period for victims of man-made and natural catastrophes and the work of Morasso (2002), who "considers people with cancer interconnected to a series of crises that occur during the course of the disease and/or that involve changes in the environmental ecosystem surrounding the patient."

For Jarero and Uribe (2011, 2012), acute trauma situations are related not only to a time frame (e.g., days or months), but also to a posttrauma safety period. They hypothesized that the continuum of stressful events with similar emotions, somatic, sensory, and cognitive information does not give the state-dependent traumatic memory sufficient time to consolidate into an integrated whole. Thus, the memory networks remain in a permanent excitatory state, expanding with each subsequent stressful event in this continuum, like the ripple effect of a stone thrown in the middle of a pond, with the risk of posttraumatic stress disorder (PTSD) and comorbid disorders growing with the number of exposures.

Research

This adapted EMDR-IGTP protocol has been implemented with female cancer patients. Jarero et al. (2015) have done a pilot study on this work and results showed significant main effects for time and group and an overall subjective improvement in the participants, as measured by the Short PTSD Rating Interview (SPRINT; Connor & Davidson, 2001). The authors' clinical observations have shown that one or two applications of the protocol are not enough to achieve the best clinical results. Therefore, they suggested six applications, in an intensive EMDR Therapy treatment format, twice a day on three consecutive days, with fidelity to the protocol and using validated measures to obtain reliable results. After the initial application, each subsequent application should begin with the self-soothing exercises indicated in Phase 2.

This type of intensive administration of the EMDR-IGTP can be a valuable support for cancer patients with PTSD symptoms related to their diagnoses and treatment.

EMDR-IGTP© Adapted for Adolescents (14–17 Years) and Adults Living With Ongoing Traumatic Stress

Script Notes

In Phase 1, history taking for each participant must be obtained through individual interview prior to the group work, according to the Standard EMDR Therapy Protocol (Shapiro, 2001). The EMDR Screening and Data Checklist (Shapiro, 2001, pp. 427–428) is used to screen if the individual is ready to profit from the use of EMDR-IGTP by screening for the following: dissociative disorders; sufficient rapport, ability to use self-control techniques; personal and environmental stability; life supports; sufficient mental and physical resources (other than the diagnosis upon which the group is based); medication needs; drug or alcohol abuse; legal issues; secondary gains; and timing considerations. Informed consent should be obtained during this phase and before starting any activity with participants. In the case of attending minors, their parents or legal guardians must sign the consent. If the participant(s) reported prior unresolved, emotional wounding experiences, or "red flags" (e.g., signs of dissociative disorders, suicide attempts, self-mutilation, substance abuse) that may complicate treatment of the distressing event(s) that will be addressed during the group protocol, these participant(s) will not participate in the group protocol and must receive individual therapy as soon as possible.

In Phase 2, it is important to set up the experience to include a number of different concerns.

Assessment Scale

The SPRINT (Connor & Davidson, 2001; Vaishnavi, Payne, Connor, & Davidson, 2006) is an eight-item interview or self-rating questionnaire with solid psychometric properties that can serve as a reliable, valid, and homogeneous measurement of PTSD, illness severity, and global improvement, as well as a measure of somatic distress, stress coping, and work, family, and social impairment. Each item is rated on a 5-point scale. Scores between 18 and 32 correspond to marked or severe PTSD symptoms, from 11 to 17 to moderate symptoms, and from 7 to 10 to mild symptoms; scores of 6 or less indicate either minimal or no symptoms. SPRINT also contains two additional items to measure global improvement according to percentage of change and severity rating. SPRINT performs similarly to the Clinician-Administered PTSD Scale (CAPS) for the assessment of PTSD symptom clusters and total scores, and it can be used as a diagnostic instrument (Vaishnavi et al., 2006). It should be applied *at least* four times: pretreatment; posttreatment; first follow-up, a week after the treatment; and second follow-up, 3 months after treatment.

Note: This study was done before the publication of the *Diagnostic and Statistical Manual of Mental Disorders, Fifth Edition* (*DSM-5*) and International Classification of Diseases (ICD)-11, therefore, the assessment scales will have to be updated.

If during Phase 2, activities such as mindfulness, yoga, artistic expression, and so on are conducted prior to the EMDR Therapy reprocessing, it is important that the assessment scales be applied first to get a baseline measure before the self-regulatory exercises are utilized. The next application would be the pretreatment assessment after the preparation activities and immediately before the beginning of the group reprocessing sessions.

Emotional Protection Team

A ratio of 1 member of the Emotional Protection Team (EPT) for every 8 to 10 participants is recommended. The EPT members welcome the participants, saying hello in a culturally appropriate manner, in order to establish rapport. The EPT should be interspersed among the participants and accessible to the participants during the course of the intensive.

Logistics

If the team will be working with a small group of adolescents or adults (up to 10), the work area must be equipped with enough chairs for both the EMDR Therapy team members (EPT) and the participants. Chairs *must have an accessory* writing surface to place the paper and the colored pencils (crayons) on, to be used during the protocol. The chairs can be arranged in a circle and the EPT members will sit interspersed among the participants. If there are no suitable chairs or there are a larger number of participants, tables can be placed in rows as in a classroom or in a horseshoe shape.

It is important to have a board or flipchart (a tripod with a large white paperboard) with the appropriate implements for writing on them, several boxes or small packages of tissues, and a box of six to eight crayons for each participant.

Note: Crayons are better than colored pencils because they are stronger and less likely to break.

In Phase 3: Assessment, the crucial adaptation or difference of the IGTP for Adolescents and Adults Living with Ongoing Traumatic Stress and the other IGTP formats for Children and/or Adults is during this phase. The main difference here is a modification in the instruction to the participants. Instead of asking the participants to "*remember what happened during the event* (e.g., hurricane, earthquake)," the team leader asks the participants to close their eyes and "*run a mental movie of everything that happened just before the cancer diagnosis until the present moment.*" The wording for this protocol has been tested in the field many times. There is different wording from the child and adult EMDR-IGTP to address the specific needs of adolescents and adults living with ongoing traumatic stress.

In Phase 5 (Future Vision instead of Installation): After each group reprocessing and/or before the next group reprocessing, the EPT gathers the participants' drawings and reviews them. If the Future Vision drawings—elicited in Phase 5—and/or the title of the drawing indicates/shows some unresolved disturbances, in that case, at the next session, the participants are asked to "*run a mental movie from today to the future . . . and when you have finished, choose to reprocess anything disturbing at this moment.*"

In Phase 8: Reevaluation, the authors observed that one or two applications of the IGTP were not sufficient to achieve the best clinical results; therefore, they suggested four to six applications, in an intensive EMDR treatment format, with fidelity to the protocol and using validated measures to obtain reliable results as mentioned here. After the first application of the IGTP, begin the next applications with the Phase 2 self-soothing exercises.

At the end of the group intervention, the EPT will identify participants needing additional support. This assessment will be determined by taking into consideration the following: the client history; the reports made by the participant´s relatives or friends; the results obtained in the scales; the entire sequence of drawings with the SUD scale ratings (especially the last ones written in the part of the sheet of paper where they write their name and age); the Future Vision drawing and cognition; the body scan; and the EPT report. The

EMDR-trained members of the team can continue treating those who require individual follow-up attention, using this adapted EMDR-IGTP in smaller groups or with the EMDR-Protocol for Recent Critical Incidents (EMDR-PRECI; Jarero & Artigas, 2014) or the Flashforward Procedure (Logie & de Jongh, 2014; see vol. 2 of this book, chapter 1).

Note: The Flashforward Procedure is "a procedure to address clients' irrational fears and anticipatory anxiety responses, which persist after the core memories of past events have been fully processed (flashforward). Even though the client's focus is on the future, the fears are experienced in the present, triggered by negative, irrational thoughts with a catastrophic content. To this end, these are considered to be current fears, suitable for processing in the second prong" (Logie & de Jongh, in press) of the 3-Pronged Protocol.

EMDR-IGTP© Adapted for Adolescents (14–17 Years) and Adults Living With Ongoing Traumatic Stress Script

Phase 1: History Taking

The leader and members of the EPT screen prospective members of the group individually according to the guidelines in Francine Shapiro's 2001 text.

Phase 2: Preparation

The EMDR-IGTP Team Leader introduces _____ (himself/herself) and all the EPT members:

> Say, *"My name is _____ (state name). I want to introduce you to our Emotional Protection Team (EPT). This is _____ (state name) and this is _____ (state name and introduce as many members as there are in the EPT). We are here to help you with the emotional aspects of the experience you are currently living. Thank you for giving us this opportunity to serve you."*

Ask participants to turn off electronic devices:

> Say, *"We would appreciate if you take this opportunity to turn off any electronic devices, in order to enhance the proper functioning of the group work today. (Pause). Thank you."*

Explain the Adaptive Information Processing (AIP) system to the participants and ask about the symptoms they have had. This explanation is simple, using a comparison between the digestive system and the AIP.

> Say, *"We can digest a light meal with no problem, but when we eat heavy food like _____ (give examples of traditional food), it is hard to digest and causes what type of symptoms _____ (ask the participants for examples)?"*

_____

_____

> Say, *"Yes, in the same manner, heavy information such as the experiences you are currently living is difficult for the brain to digest and causes symptoms. For example, what type of symptoms have you noticed since the day of the event until now?"*

_____

_____

_____

Note: It is important not to force anyone to talk. Also, pay attention to the symptoms the participants describe concerning how they are doing in their day-to-day lives and with their basic responsibilities. Particularly pay attention to seriously maladaptive behaviors, such as obsessive–compulsive behavior (such as taking showers many times a day), because they will play an important role in triaging/selecting who will be invited to receive personal attention at the conclusion of the EMDR-IGTP.

When everyone has spoken, the leader normalizes symptoms by saying the following:

Say, *"All the symptoms you have mentioned are normal examples of your brain's processing system trying to assimilate the experience you are living."*

Mention the availability of staff for further help.

Say, *"I also want to remind you that all of us will be available to you after our experience today and at other times. We would be honored to continue to help you—and others you know—in any way that we can."*

Note: The EPT staff does not provide individual EMDR sessions between group reprocessing; they wait until the end of all the reprocessing. Between group sessions, the EPT staff can provide psychoeducation or information on trauma-related symptoms, stress management techniques, and/or attentive listening.

Assessment Scales

If no assessment scales have been administered, say the following:

Say, *"Please answer this questionnaire (or questionnaires). If you have any doubt, a member of the Emotional Protection Team can help you."*

Teach Self-Soothing Exercises

Teach the participants self-soothing exercises:

Say, *"The following exercises you will learn are going to help you to feel better. During the exercise, the EPT members will take care of everything, so you are welcome to relax and close your eyes if you would like to do so."*

One of the EPT members leads the following exercises.

ABDOMINAL BREATHING

Say, *"This is the Abdominal Breathing Exercise. Imagine you have a balloon inside your stomach that inflates when you inhale and deflates when you exhale... focus all your attention in this exercise. If anything distracts you, gently return to the exercise."*

Do this exercise from 3 to 5 minutes.

CONCENTRATION EXERCISE

Say, *"This is called the Concentration Exercise. When you inhale and exhale, mentally repeat: I know I am inhaling... I know I am exhaling... focus all your attention in this exercise. If anything distracts you, gently return to the exercise."*

Do this exercise from 3 to 5 minutes.

PLEASANT MEMORY

Say, *"This exercise is the Pleasant Memory Exercise. Remember a moment when you felt happy or peaceful. Once you have found this memory, put your right hand on the center of your chest. Now, allow those good feelings and positive physical sensations to expand throughout your body. Focus all your attention* on the good feelings and sensations. If anything distracts you, gently return to the exercise."

Do this exercise from 3 to 5 minutes. Use the Five Steps Technique to assist participants in coming out of the exercise smoothly:

Say, "As you continue to think about this pleasant memory, we will begin to come back into the room as I count from 5 to 1. We are at five and you are in that pleasant memory ... Now, we are at four and you start returning to this space ... We are now at three and you can feel the ground with your feet and the chair with your thighs and back ... Now we are at two and when you are ready open your eyes ... Now we are at one and we can stretch comfortably."

Note: At the beginning of each group reprocessing session, practice these three exercises with participants. It only takes around 15 minutes.

Bilateral Stimulation

BUTTERFLY HUG (AN AIP SYSTEM SELF-STIMULATION METHOD)

Say, "Cross your arms over your chest, so that the tip of the middle finger from each hand is placed below the clavicle or the collarbone and the other fingers and hands cover the area that is located under the connection between the collarbone and the shoulder and the collarbone and sternum or breastbone. Hands and fingers must be as vertical as possible so that the fingers point toward the neck and not toward the arms. Now interlock your thumbs (to form the butterfly's body and antennas) and the extension of your other fingers outward will form the butterfly's wings.

Close your eyes or keep them partially opened, focusing on a spot ahead. Next, alternate the movement of your hands, like the flapping wings of a butterfly.

Breathe slowly and deeply (abdominal breathing), while you observe what is going through your mind and body (thoughts, images, sounds, odors, feelings, and physical sensations), without changing, judging, or pushing your thoughts away. You can pretend what you are observing is like clouds passing by."

Do this exercise for 1 minute only.

Say, "Please slowly stop the Butterfly Hug."

The Team Leader asks the participants how they are feeling:

Say, "I would like to know how you are feeling now."

_____

_____

EMDR Protocol Scale

SUBJECTIVE UNITS OF DISTURBANCE SCALE

Introduce the Subjective Units of Disturbance scale (SUDS) to participants:

Say, "The disturbance is characterized by unpleasant or annoying emotions and/or physical sensations. For measuring them, we will use the Subjective Units of Disturbance scale (SUDS). The SUD scale ranges from 0 to 10, with 0 being no disturbance, and 10 being the maximum disturbance you can feel."

On the board or flipchart, one of the EPT members draws a horizontal line with a 0 on the left end and a 10 on the right end, with the numbers 1 to 9 distributed along the line. Also, another way to make this scale more accessible is to draw three faces representing the intensity of the emotions: one for 0, one for 5, and one for 10.

The EPT members hand out white sheets of paper and crayons to each participant.

Say, *"Please write your name and age in the upper left side of the paper. Now, write down what I am going to dictate _____ (dictate the day, month, year, and the time of the day, morning or afternoon)."*

Say, *"Now, turn the sheet of paper to the other side. With a dark crayon draw one vertical line and one horizontal line in the middle of the paper to divide it in four equal parts. Ready? We are going to mark each part of the paper with the letters A, B, C, and D. These letters must be small and in the upper left corner of each part (show how to do it)."*

Note: One of the EPT members draws the four equal parts and the letters on the board or flipchart.

Phase 3: Assessment

The Team Leader says, *"With your eyes closed or partially closed, please run a movie in your mind of everything that happened just before the critical incident _____ (state the type of incident, such as cancer or other severe illness diagnosis and treatment, family violence, war, geopolitical crisis, disaster) until now. Then, open your eyes when you finish."*

When all the participants have finished, the Team Leader says the following:

Say, *"As you make a movie in your mind of the incident, please choose the hardest, most painful or distressing moment of this whole experience. Now observe which emotions and body sensations are part of that memory, NOW, DURING THIS MOMENT."*

_____

> **Note**: For each reprocessing session that follows, say the following:
>
> Say, *"With your eyes closed or partially closed, please run a mental movie of everything that happened just before the critical incident until now. Then, open your eyes when you finish."*
>
> When all the participants have finished, the Team Leader says the following:
>
> Say, *"From the whole movie, please choose the most disturbing memory that remains, now, at this moment in time."*
>
> _____
> _____

The Team Leader continues, *"Take WHATEVER EMERGES from your head to your neck, to your arms, to your hands and finger; and now, take one or more crayons and DRAW it in the square with the letter A."*

When 90% of the participants have finished drawing in Square A, say the following:

Say, *"Please put your crayons down and lower your hands to your thighs.*

Look at your drawing.

Now observe your body.

On a scale where 0 is no disturbance and 10 the maximum disturbance you can feel, how much disturbance are you feeling now? Write this number in the lower right corner of the square."

_____

One of the EPT members writes "SUDS" in the lower right corner of the square on the board or flipchart.

Note: The highest emotional or sensory impact is not always in the first drawing. Sometimes, it is not present until the second or the third drawing.

Phase 4: Desensitization

Once 90% of the participants have finished:

> Say, *"Please put your crayons aside and do the Butterfly Hug while you are looking at your drawing. Observe what is happening to you—without judging or trying to change it—and stop when you <u>feel in your body</u> it is enough and lower your hands to your thighs."*

Note: This takes about 2 or 3 minutes. If after 3 minutes, a participant has not lowered his or her hands to his or her thighs, a member of the EPT will approach and ask him or her kindly to stop.

> Then the Team Leader says, *"Now observe how you are feeling and draw it in Square B."*

When 90% of the participants have finished drawing in Square B:

> Say, *"Please put your crayons down and lower your hands to your thighs.*
>
> *Look at your drawing.*
>
> *Now, observe your body.*
>
> *On a scale where 0 is no disturbance and 10 the maximum disturbance you can feel, how much disturbance are you feeling now? Write this number in the lower right corner of the square."*

One of the EPT members writes "SUDS" in the lower right corner of the square on the board or flipchart.

Once 90% of the participants have finished:

> Say, *"Please put your crayons aside and do the Butterfly Hug while you are looking at your drawing. Observe what is happening to you—without judging or trying to change it—and stop when you <u>feel in your body</u> it is enough and lower your hands to your thighs."*

> Then the Team Leader says, *"Now observe how you are feeling and draw it in Square C."*

When 90% of the participants have finished their drawings in Square C:

> Say, *"Please put your crayons down and lower your hands to your thighs.*
>
> *Look at your drawing.*
>
> *Now observe your body.*
>
> *On a scale where 0 is no disturbance and 10 the maximum disturbance you can feel, how much disturbance are you feeling now? Write this number in the lower right corner of the square."*

One of the EPT members writes "SUDS" in the lower right corner of the square on the board or flipchart. After they have written the number, the Team Leader says the following:

> Say, *"Please put your crayons aside and do the Butterfly Hug while you are looking at your drawing. Observe what is happening to you—without judging or trying to change it—and stop when you <u>feel in your body</u> it is enough and lower your hands to your thighs."*

Then the Team Leader says, *"Now observe how you are feeling and draw it in Square D."*

When 90% of the participants have finished their drawings in Square D:

Say, *"Please put your crayons down and lower your hands to your thighs.*

Look at your drawing.

Now observe your body.

On a scale where 0 is no disturbance and 10 the maximum disturbance you can feel, how much disturbance are you feeling now? Write this number in the lower right corner of the square."

One of the EPT members writes "SUDS" in the lower right corner of the square on the board or flipchart.

After they have written the number, the Team Leader says the following:

Say, *"Please put your crayons aside and do the Butterfly Hug while you are looking at your drawing. Observe what is happening to you—without judging or trying to change it—and stop when you <u>feel in your body</u> it is enough and lower your hands to your thighs."*

Next the Team Leader says: *"Observe all of your drawings carefully and choose the drawing that disturbs you the most. Turn your paper to the other side, and observe how you feel in your body. On a scale where 0 is no disturbance and 10 the maximum disturbance you can feel, how much disturbance are you feeling <u>NOW</u>? Write this number in the upper right corner of the square."*

One of the EPT members writes "SUDS" in the upper right corner of the other side of the paper on the board or flipchart.

Note: The EPT must be aware that the participants do not make the mistake of just copying the SUD of the most disturbing drawing, but write the SUD of the disturbance they are feeling NOW—AT THE PRESENT MOMENT.

Phase 5: Future Vision (Instead of Installation)

Phase 5 (Installation) of the Standard EMDR Protocol cannot be conducted in large groups for the following reasons: each participant may have a different SUD level because some participants cannot go any further; blocking beliefs; previous problems and trauma; or different timing for processing (for some, there is not enough time to follow the four designs format) and reach an ecological level of disturbance.

The Installation Phase can be done during the individual follow-up intervention, as needed (see Phase 8). At this stage of the protocol, work on a Future Vision to identify adaptive or nonadaptive drawings and cognitions that are helpful in the evaluation of the participant at the end of the protocol. An example of a nonadaptive Future Vision would be if the participant did not see a future for himself, as when a 28-year-old man drew a black circle and wrote "I have nothing to do in the future."

Say, *"Now, draw how you see yourself in the future."*

Then say, *"Write a word, phrase, or a sentence that explains what you drew; the TITLE OF THE DRAWING."*

Then say, *"Please put your crayons aside and do the Butterfly Hug while you are looking at your drawing. Observe what is happening to you—without judging or trying to change it—and stop when you <u>feel in your body</u> it is enough and lower your hands to your thighs."*

When everybody has finished, the leader asks the EPT to gather all the drawings and the crayons.

The drawings must be kept in a big envelope with the date and the time of the day (morning or afternoon). At the end of all group sessions, the sheets of each participant must be stapled in chronological order, in order to facilitate data collecting for evaluation and statistical purposes.

Phase 6: Body Scan

The leader says, *"Remember the drawing that disturbed you the most. Close your eyes and observe your body from your head to your feet. Notice if you feel any pleasant or unpleasant sensations. When you have finished, do the Butterfly Hug while observing what is happening to you—without judging or trying to change it—and stop when you feel in your body it has been enough and lower your hands to your thighs."*

Phase 7: Closure

The leader says, *"Choose your favorite self-soothing exercise and do it now and do it for several minutes."*

Do this for about 2 to 3 minutes.

After this, say, *"Breathe deeply and open your eyes."*

Then, the participants are invited to share their reprocessing experiences. The EPT members normalize the reprocessing experiences, explaining that these are normal, and answer questions.

Say, *"If you would like to do so, please share your experiences during the reprocessing. What did you experience?"*

_____

_____

Phase 8: Reevaluation and Follow-Up

In between the administration of the group interventions, if the Future Vision drawings—elicited in Phase 5—and/or the titles of the drawings indicate/show some unresolved disturbances, at the next session, ask the participants to *"run a mental movie from today to the future ... and when you have finished, choose to reprocess anything disturbing at this moment."*

At the end of all the group interventions, the EPT identifies participants needing additional support. This assessment will be determined by taking into consideration: the client history; the reports made by the participant's relatives or friends; the results obtained in the scales; the entire sequence of drawings with their SUD scale ratings (especially the last ones written on the side of the sheet of paper where the participant wrote his or her name); the Future Vision drawing and cognition; the body scan; and the EPT report. The members of the team, or mental health professionals trained as EMDR psychotherapists, can continue treating those who require individual follow-up attention, using this adapted EMDR-IGTP for ongoing trauma in smaller groups or with the EMDR-PRECI (Jarero & Artigas, 2014). The Flashforward Procedure may be indicated as another option for individual treatment at the end of the group sessions.

Additional Individual Support

After the last group processing, the EPT again gathers the participants' drawing and reviews them. If the Future Vision drawing that was elicited in Phase 5 and/or the title of the drawing indicates/shows a "flashforward" (Logie & de Jongh, 2014; see vol. 2 of this book, chapter 1), it is important to have one of the EPT members approach that participant individually and ask the participant to undertake an individual session.

During the individual session, begin with Phase 2: Preparation, as indicated in the following section, when using the Flashforward Procedure.

Phase 2: Preparation

Introduce the process in the following way:

Say, *"We have now dealt with all the events from your past that seem to have been feeding into your current problems and these are no longer distressing you. But, it seems that you are still left with some fear and dread of what might happen in the future, which has been left behind, even after all the past events have been dealt with. So, we are now going to focus on this present trigger of the future, and what it is that you are dreading, using the same procedure as we used for the past events."*

Phase 3: Determine the Flashforward

Step 1: Identify the Catastrophic Event

Say, *"We need to figure out what kind of image is in your head that makes you scared about a future confrontation with what you fear. What is the worst thing you could imagine happening? Basically we should look for your ultimate doom scenario."*

_____

_____

If necessary, the therapist asks additional questions, for example:

Say, *"What do you imagine might go wrong if you* _____ *(state the concern, such as 'Come across a dog,' 'Have a dental treatment,' 'Climb a tower,' etc.)?"*

Say, *"If you had a terrible nightmare about* _____ *(state the concern, such as 'Driving your car to work on a busy road'), what would the most disturbing picture look like?"*

_____

_____

Step 2: Follow the Event to Its Ultimate Conclusion

Say, *"Why would this be so terrible for you?"*

_____

_____

Say, *"What would be the worst thing about that?"*

_____

_____

Repeat as necessary until the client cannot identify anything worse.

Step 3: Make a Detailed Picture of Flashforward

IMAGE

The therapist might then ask the client to make a still picture of this scene. Ask that the picture be as detailed as possible.

Say, "*Exactly what would* _____ (the flashforward identified above) *look like?*"

_____

_____

The rest is the same as in Phase 3 of the Standard EMDR Protocol.

References

Artigas, L., & Jarero, I. (2014a). The butterfly hug. In M. Luber (Ed.), *Implementing EMDR early mental health interventions for man-made and natural disasters* (pp. 127–130). New York, NY: Springer.

Artigas, L., & Jarero, I. (2014b). The EMDR integrative group treatment protocol (IGTP) for adults. In M. Luber (Ed.), *Implementing EMDR early mental health interventions for man-made and natural disasters* (pp. 253–260). New York, NY: Springer.

Artigas, L., & Jarero, I. (2014c). Summary sheet for each participant: The EMDR Integrative Group Treatment Protocol (IGTP) for adults. In M. Luber (Ed.), *Implementing EMDR early mental health interventions for man-made and natural disasters* (pp. 261–262). New York, NY: Springer.

Artigas, L., & Jarero, I. (2014d). Summary sheet for clinicians: The EMDR Integrative Group Treatment Protocol (IGTP) for adults. In M. Luber (Ed.), *Implementing EMDR early mental health interventions for man-made and natural disasters* (pp. 263–266). New York, NY: Springer.

Artigas, L., Jarero, I., Alcalá, N., & López Cano, T. (2014). The EMDR Integrative Group Treatment Protocol (IGTP) for children. In M. Luber (Ed.), *Implementing EMDR early interventions for man-made and natural disasters* (pp. 237–251). New York, NY: Springer.

Connor, K. M., & Davidson, J. R. T. (2001). SPRINT: A brief global assessment of post-traumatic stress disorder. *International Clinical Psychopharmacology, 16*(5), 279–284.

Jarero, I., & Artigas, L. (2009). EMDR integrative group treatment protocol. *Journal of EMDR Practice & Research, 3*(4), 287–288.

Jarero, I., & Artigas, L. (2014). The EMDR protocol for recent critical incidents. In M. Luber (Ed.), *Implementing EMDR early mental health interventions for man-made and natural disasters* (pp. 217–232). New York. NY: Springer.

Jarero, I., Artigas, L., Uribe, S., García, L. E., Cavazos, M. A., & Givaudán, M. (2015). Pilot research study on the provision of the EMDR Integrative Group Treatment Protocol with female cancer patients. *Journal of EMDR Practice and Research, 9*, 1.

Jarero, I., & Uribe, S. (2011). The EMDR protocol for recent critical incidents: Brief report of an application in a human massacre situation. *Journal of EMDR Practice and Research, 5*(4), 156–165.

Jarero, I., & Uribe, S. (2012). The EMDR protocol for recent critical incidents: Follow-up report of an application in a human massacre situation. *Journal of EMDR Practice and Research, 6*(2), 50–61.

Logie, R., & de Jongh, A. (2014). The flashforward procedure: Confronting the catastrophe. *Journal of EMDR Practice and Research, 8*, 25–32.

Logie, R. & de Jongh, A. (in press). Flashforward. In M. Luber (Ed.), *Eye movement desensitization and reprocessing (EMDR) therapy scripted protocols and summary sheets: Treating trauma, anxiety and mood-related conditions.* New York, NY: Springer.

Morasso, G. (2002). Nuove prospettive in psico-oncologia. In *Formazione, psicologia, psicoterapia, psichiatria* (p. 2). Roma, Italy: Grin SRL.

Shapiro, F. (2001). *Eye movement desensitization and reprocessing: Basic principles, protocols, and procedures* (2nd ed.). New York, NY: Guilford Press.

Vaishnavi, S., Payne, V., Connor, K., & Davidson, J. R. (2006). A comparison of the SPRINT and CAPS assessment scales for posttraumatic stress disorder. *Depression and Anxiety, 23*(7), 437–440.

SUMMARY SHEET:
EMDR Integrative Group Treatment Protocol© Adapted for Adolescents (14–17 Years) and Adults Living With Ongoing Traumatic Stress

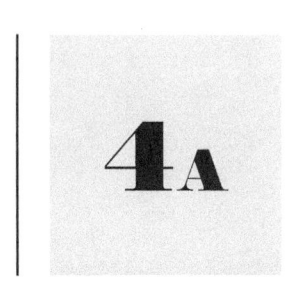

Ignacio Jarero and Lucina Artigas
SUMMARY SHEET BY MARILYN LUBER

Name: _____ Diagnosis: _____

Medications: _____

Test Results: _____

☑ Check when task is completed, response has changed, or to indicate symptoms or diagnosis.

Note: This material is meant as a checklist for your response. Please keep in mind that it is only a reminder of different tasks that may or may not apply to your client.

The EMDR Integrative Group Treatment Protocol for Adults

Phase 1: Client History

Event Date: _____

Event Narrative: _____

_____

_____

_____

_____

AIP-Digestion Metaphor ☐ Completed

Phase 2: Preparation—First Part

Prep

Introduce leader and EPT members: ☐ Completed
Turn off electronic devices ☐ Completed
AIP/Digestion Metaphor ☐ Completed

Notice members not doing well: _____

_____

Normalize traumatic symptoms: ☐ Completed
Mention availability of staff: ☐ Completed
Assessment Instrument Administration: ☐ Completed

Self-Soothing Techniques—introduce
    Abdominal Breathing: ☐ Completed
    Concentration Exercise: ☐ Completed
    Pleasant Memory: ☐ Completed
Bilateral Stimulation—introduce
    Butterfly Hug: ☐ Completed
EMDR Protocol Scale—introduce
    Introduce SUD scale: ☐ Completed

(**Note**: No VoC because there is no Installation Phase)

- ☐ Hand out paper and crayons
- ☐ Write name and age on top left
- ☐ Dictate the day, month, year, and the time of the day, morning or afternoon
- ☐ Divide paper into four parts:
  — Mark each part A, B, C, and D in upper left corner of each part

Phase 3: Assessment

- ☐ Run movie from before the incident until now
- ☐ Hardest, most painful/distressing moment of this whole experience (draw Square A):
  — Emotions and sensations
  — Movie from today into the future and concerns
  — Draw what emerges in square with letter "A"
  — SUDs = _____ /10 in lower right corner

Phase 4: Desensitization

- ☐ Drawing A in Square A:
  — SUDs in Square A: _____ /10
  — BH + Look at Drawing A

- ☐ Drawing B in Square B:
  — SUDs in Square B: _____ /10
  — BH + Look at Drawing B

- ☐ Drawing C in Square C:
  — SUDs in Square C: _____ /10
  — BH + Look at Drawing C

- ☐ Drawing D in Square D:
  — SUDs in Square D: _____ /10
  — BH + Look at Drawing D

- ☐ Look at all drawings. Pick the most disturbing. SUDS: _____ /10 (upper right-hand corner of page).
  SUDs ratings decrease? ☐ Yes ☐ No

Phase 5: Future Vision (Instead of Installation)

Drawing of self in future: ☐ Completed

Is this drawing adaptive? ☐ Yes ☐ No

Word/phrase/sentence about what is drawn: _____
Is this word/phrase/sentence adaptive? ☐ Yes ☐ No

- ☐ Look at Future Drawing + BH:
- ☐ EPT collects drawings and crayons

Phase 6: Body Scan

- ☐ Most Disturbing Drawing + Body Scan + BH (until enough)

Report a disturbing body sensation? ☐ Yes ☐ No

Phase 7: Closure

- ☐ Do favorite self-soothing exercise
- ☐ Breathe deeply and open your eyes
- ☐ Have participants share experiencing
- ☐ Completed

Phase 8: Reevaluation and Follow-Up

At the end of the group intervention, the EPT identifies participants needing further assistance. These participants will need to be thoroughly evaluated to identify the nature and extent of their symptoms, and any co- or preexisting mental health problems. Staff can make this determination by taking into consideration reports made by the participants' relatives and/or friends, whatever valid measure was used (e.g., IES, IES-R), the entire sequence of pictures, the SUD scale ratings, Body Scan, the Future Vision drawing and cognition, and the Emotional Protection Team report.

Participant needs further help ☐ Yes ☐ No

_____

_____

Optional for participant who needs further assistance:

Flashforward:

- ☐ Phase 2: Preparation
- ☐ Phase 3: Determine the Flashforward
  - ☐ Step 1: Identify the Catastrophic Event _____

  _____

  - ☐ Step 2: Follow the Event to Its Ultimate Conclusion _____

  _____

  _____

  - ☐ Step 3: Make a Detailed Picture of the Flashforward _____

  _____

  _____

  _____

Use the Standard EMDR Protocol:

Picture: _____

Negative Cognition: _____

Positive Cognition: _____

Validity of Cognition (VoC): _____ /7

Emotions: _____

Subjective Units of Disturbance (SUD): _____ /10

Location of Body Sensation: _____

ACUTE STRESS DISORDER

Reaching the Unseen First Responder With EMDR Therapy: Treating 911 Trauma in Emergency Telecommunicators

5

Jim Marshall and Sara G. Gilman

I handled the call just like I handle all of them. But when I finished, I went to the bathroom, vomited, and then I took the next call.

—Anonymous 911 Telecommunicator (2012)

Introduction

911 Telecommunicators: Unseen, Underrecognized, and at High Risk

Since the 1970s, mental health researchers and practitioners have extensively addressed the stress-related risks encountered by police and other field responders, in the line of duty. The roles and duties of these emergency responders in serving the public are common knowledge. The psychological risks they face are well established and there is a robust extant literature on treatment intervention and support to address their critical incident stress. Solomon (2013) has recently provided Eye Movement Desensitization and Reprocessing (EMDR) clinicians with in-depth insights into the characteristics of law enforcement officers (LEOs), and made adaptations to the Standard EMDR Protocol and Procedures that enable clinicians to customize and thus enhance treatment.

Within the greater community of emergency response professionals (police, fire, and medical), there exists another special subpopulation largely unrecognized by mental health clinicians: 911 telecommunicators (911 TCs). These 911 TCs are responsible for executing one or both of the two core telecommunication roles crucial to the success of every community's emergency response system:

- *Call taking*: This involves gathering and utilizing information received during 911 calls from the public. Depending on the nature of the call, the 911 TC may be required to personally deliver immediate intervention, such as guiding the delivery of a baby, instructing the caller in administration of cardiopulmonary resuscitation (CPR), or assisting a caller in escaping a sinking vehicle.
- *Dispatching*: This role involves engaging the appropriate emergency field responders (fire, medical, or law enforcement), and informing them (via radio) with critical information gathered from the caller about the emergency.

Safety of field responders and all others on scene may depend on the 911 TC's effective execution of these two roles. In this chapter, the authors provide EMDR clinicians with a greater understanding of the inner world of the 911 TC. This highly underserved population has unique exposure to traumatic events and has responded well when treated with EMDR Therapy.

Clinicians are generally unfamiliar with the 911 TC's unique role, their duties, and their unique work-related stressors. There is a paucity of current scientific research identifying the psychological risks and impacts of 911 work, and mental health interventions have thus far not been designed to target the unique dimensions of these impacts. The adage, *"Out of sight, out of mind"* applies poignantly to 911 TCs who, while never seen or physically present at the scene of our emergencies, are indeed "on scene" psychologically and are profoundly affected by their work. Still, Lilly & Allen (2015) found that 24.6% of 808 telecommunicators from throughout the United States acknowledged symptoms consistent with a diagnosis of posttraumatic stress disorder (PTSD) utilizing civilian cut-off scores on self-report measures. In an earlier preliminary study by Pearce and Lilly (2012), the PTSD rate among 911 TCs had been estimated at 9% to 10%. The earliest published study on 911 stress reported that 16% of telecommunicators reported symptoms consistent with the label of secondary traumatic stress (Troxell, 2008).

Prior to these studies, data showing the degree of 911 TCs' exposure to traumatic events on the job was virtually absent in the established traumatology literature. Lacking such awareness, and perhaps because 911 TCs operate off-scene and remain faceless to the public, the nation's mental health practitioners and scientists had not recognized or strategically addressed the psychological risks faced by these telecommunicators.

911 TCs as the "Very First Responder"

Because 911 TCs are the first to answer emergency calls from the public and to dispatch field responders, they are literally the *Very First Responder* in the worst moments of our lives as citizens. When citizens call 911 sobbing in despair or as they are dying, it is the telecommunicator who hears their distress and immediately intervenes. These first few minutes of any crisis are often the worst; the sounds of raw anguish may have softened or fallen silent by the time the LEOs, firefighters, or medical personnel arrive on scene. While field responders are aided in their mental preparation for the tragedies they will encounter on scene by the advance information provided by the telecommunicator, 911 TCs experience such traumatic events without any warning.

It is an established standard of practice that LEOs and other field responders are provided with critical incident stress management (CISM) support services whenever major tragedies occur, such as mass casualty events or death of an officer. By contrast, police and sheriff departments overseeing 911 typically have no local policy assuring that telecommunicators will join field responders in critical incident debriefing sessions following even the most severe traumatic events in which 911 TCs were involved.

Collectively, 911 TCs represent a subculture within the emergency response culture. They possess group characteristics, including the unique nature of their exposure to traumatic events. They typically share an ingrained cognitive and affect management style impacting how they process traumatic experience, and they struggle with professional identity issues specific to 911. By offering insight about these 911 group characteristics and pertinent guidance in adapting the eight-phase EMDR Protocol, the authors hope to empower EMDR clinicians to achieve a solid treatment alliance, attuned assessment, and optimal clinical outcomes.

The Nature of 911 TCs' Stressors and Exposures to Traumatic Events

911 TCs routinely perform numerous tasks that are stressful. They monitor numerous phone lines, access multiple computer applications, and monitor video and alarm information systems. While handling both 911 and nonemergency calls for service, telecommunicators must perform multiple tasks on each individual incident. Many types of emergencies (e.g., managing calls involving children in peril, a barricaded gunman or suicidal subject, or dispatching for deadly multivehicle accidents or multi-alarm fires) involve a high degree of emotional labor and require the 911 TC to rapidly employ extraordinary judgment and critical decision making. Under such conditions, they are at high risk of stress impacts on their health and

performance. These tasks may be compounded by additional responsibilities assigned to the 911 TC on location at the law enforcement agency (LEA), such as handling warrants, clerical duties, and processing inmates (L. Dodson, personal communication, September 19, 2014).

The *Diagnostic and Statistical Manual of Mental Disorders, Fifth Edition (DSM-5;* American Psychiatric Association, 2013) defines a traumatic event as a stressor in which:

The person has been exposed to a traumatic event in which both of the following have been present:

1. *The person has experienced, witnessed, or been confronted with an event or events that involve actual or threatened death or serious injury, or a threat to the physical integrity of oneself or others.*
2. *The person's response involved intense fear, helplessness, or horror (IFH/H).* **Note**: *In children, it may be expressed instead by disorganized or agitated behavior.*

The common implicit assumption in the history of the 911 industry among members of the law enforcement/emergency response community has been that since telecommunicators are not *physically* on scene (like police, fire, and emergency medical services [EMS] workers), they are therefore not exposed to psychologically traumatic events. However, Troxell found that "in contrast to popular belief, the data confirm that not only can those in helping roles be affected by traumatic information whether physically on the scene or not, but also that they can be affected to the same degree. Physical distance does not protect them" (2008, p. 123).

Troxell showed that about one-half of all 911 TCs among the 496 study participants had, at least once in their careers, experienced IFH/H in response to four call types. These call types are cited in Figure 5.1 along with the corresponding percentage of telecommunicators who experienced these symptoms.

About half of all telecommunicators in Troxell's study had experienced such distress in response to one or more incidents during their careers of calls involving death or severe injury of a child, those struggling with suicide risk, and dispatches in which field responders were injured; nearly 40% reported intense distress prompted by calls from family or friends. Yet, as Troxell confirmed, 911 TCs are impacted not only by the call *types* but also by the sounds of human distress they experience over the phone, irrespective of call type. As one study participant stated: "The fear in her voice was the most horrific thing." Troxell adds: "Another related how he heard in the background a 'heinous, horrifying scream' and 'I had chills running down my body and my hands were shaking'" (2008, p. 123). The clinician treating critical incident stress in telecommunicators will receive requests to resolve traumatic stress related to any of these four call types and related to the 911 TCs' experiences with callers who were extremely escalated emotionally.

New 911 Stressors Facing Telecommunicators

The growth of new technology has resulted in the development of new modes of communication the public can use to report and provide additional information to 911 call centers.

CALL TYPE	PERCENTAGE
Calls involving children with severe injuries	51.4
Death of a child	49.5
Officer/firefighter/EMT injured	48.8
Suicidal caller	46.8

Figure 5.1 **Call types for 911 telecommunicators.**

Availability of this technology has increased expectations for 911 service to citizens and responders. These modes, including texting to 911, and in the near future real-time video input from callers and field, will likely improve access to 911, enrich the volume and type of information received, and potentially help save more lives. Yet, the practical work of adapting to and utilizing this technology also has the potential of psychologically overloading 911 TCs (Marshall, 2011). For example, all 911 TCs may potentially face the expectation of managing a text call from a suicidal individual without the benefit of exchanging spoken words essential to assessing emotional status, conveying empathy, and expediting information exchange. A telecommunicator who receives a live "face-time" video call from a sniper—as he assaults victims in a mass casualty event—will predictably be at increased risk of intensified exposure to such a traumatic event compared to managing the same call via traditional phone connection. Therapists should be prepared to assist 911 TCs in resolving trauma related to such additional stressors associated with managing calls via these new modes of communication.

The 911 TCs' Approach to Dealing With Emotional Distress

For the majority of their history, 911 professionals have been housed within and operated by LEAs—state or city police departments and sheriff departments. Ninety percent of call centers, referred to officially as Public Safety Answering Points (PSAPs), are still operated by LEAs that have traditionally adhered to paramilitary attitudes about how they should self-regulate emotional distress and seek mental health assistance. The authors refer to this attitude and outlook in relating to personal emotional distress as an Emotion Code. It is the internal code, reflected in specific cognitions, that governs the choices an individual makes about how to deal with emotions. The Emotion Code practiced by most LEOs, throughout the history of police operations, was shaped by the demands of their unique role as the responder who is tasked with gaining and maintaining interpersonal control of a crisis scene, along with assisting all others—without registering personal distress, irrespective of circumstances however horrific or dangerous. Roger Solomon (2014) addresses the Emotion Code concept in his chapter, "Early mental health EMDR intervention for the police," from the book, *Implementing EMDR Early Mental Health Interventions for Man-Made and Natural Disasters: Models, Scripted Protocols, and Summary Sheets*. He reminds us that police officers maintain the mind set that they are not allowed to feel angry, scared, or sad while they take control of intense and chaotic situations. They must exercise quick judgment during stressful circumstances. The officers learn how to suppress and compartmentalize their emotions so they can go into situations that most people run away from.

This LEO Emotion Code could be stated as a set of cognitions:

- I must, in appearance and reality, be self-controlled and strong at all times.
- Showing and feeling vulnerable emotion (such as fear or sorrow) is synonymous with losing control: it is therefore weak, unhelpful, and inappropriate.
- I need to avoid feeling and expressing theses emotions.

As adaptive as these cognitions may seem during critical moments of service, their dominance in determining how an officer will relate to difficult emotions can do a disservice to him who, like any person, needs the chance to recognize, validate, and process emotional distress when exposed to critical incidents. Naturally, officers, military personnel, and other field responders—facing similar demands—have been inclined to generalize their application of this suppressive Emotion Code, as their modus operandi, in all domains of personal experience. An inevitable byproduct of living by this Emotion Code has been an historical resistance among LEOs to seeking mental health assistance, placing them at increased risk of stress complications, self-medicating, suicide, and family conflict (Kirschman, 2006). LEOs who have shared this Emotion Code can be considered members of a specific emotional culture in which open sharing and support for emotional struggle are very limited. It is into such a suppressive emotional culture that 911 TCs have often been employed and within which they have sought the acceptance and respect of LEOs. Accordingly, telecommunicators in the United States largely adopted the same Emotion Code as field responders, placing them at similar risks.

In the last 30 years, leading members of the law enforcement community have worked hard to create a healthier emotional culture characterized by the adoption of a more adaptive Emotion Code. In response to police suicides, other violent personal behavior, and significant liabilities and risks produced by compromised performance by personnel, the International Chiefs of Police, assisted by police psychologists, have developed comprehensive guidance to advance mental health support for LEOs (Trompetter, 2011). Police psychologists commonly provide psychological training and peer support to LEAs, and critical incident stress management services are offered routinely to field response personnel. Yet, the transformation of pervasive and deeply embedded beliefs about emotion management, adhered to for generations, is a slow process in any culture. The old paramilitary Emotion Code is still widely practiced, however, unofficially, among the nation's LEAs. Thus, in many PSAPs, where new 911 TCs seek acceptance from their older peers, they learn quickly to suppress distress in response to traumatic events and to internalize fear, horror, and helplessness. Unlike LEOs, however, they typically do so without full access to the range of support services available to field responders.

911 TCs as a Subculture Within LEAs

911 TCs share many traits with the greater LEA culture, not only those just discussed, but also positive traits, including a dedication to service and the compassion satisfaction derived from their work. Yet, these telecommunicators are also members of a subculture joined together by shared problematic perceptions of their relationships with field responders and the public.

Telecommunicators as Subordinates Within LEAs

Many 911 TCs operate in LEAs in which they feel respected by their leaders and field responders and enjoy high job satisfaction and a sense of professional affiliation with officers. Yet, most of the nation's PSAPs are led by 911 administrators who are LEOs who have not "sat the console" as telecommunicators and thus lack the direct experience upon which to form a foundation of empathy in relating to their 911 "frontliners." Historically, many of these administrators, without intending any disrespect, shared the perception that 911 work simply involved answering the phone and performing secretarial tasks. Accordingly, those assigned to 911 call taking and dispatching included females (since typically women were not considered for road patrol), retired officers, or those unable to work the road due to injury, illness, or disciplinary issues. As a result, 911 TCs who began their work in the 1980s and 1990s often developed and harbored feelings of being undervalued and underappreciated by their leaders, and by the road officers, firefighters, and emergency medical personnel they supported. These conditions and attitudes among both parties still prevail today. Approximately 66% of 911 TCs are female, although more men are joining their ranks annually (http://911operatorsalary.com/1/1/salary/911-Dispatcher-Salary).

While 911 TCs' relationships with their field responders are complex and often conflicted, they should not be simplistically characterized as adversarial. Telecommunicators and responders often treat each other much like strong-willed siblings. Most 911 TCs feel an extreme loyalty to serve and protect their field responders, who often acknowledge their dependence on the demeanor of 911 TCs for maintaining their emotional composure on scene. Yet, 911 professionals often do not believe responders reciprocate feelings of respect and appreciation. When the clinician identifies a 911 TC to be entrenched in resentment related to such relationship dynamics, success of treatment may depend on helping to resolve this dilemma.

Frustration With Citizen Demands and Devaluation

911 TCs attempt to respond to all calls from the public with courtesy and respect. Yet, often callers make requests for 911 assistance that telecommunicators consider unnecessary: inappropriate demands for services that originate in entitlement; intent to manipulate the legal system for personal advantage through false reporting; or failure to use common sense.

Managing such calls, while maintaining a high standard of customer service, is emotionally draining and stressful. This challenge is increased by another factor: in contrast to respect shown to LEOs by the public, citizens who call 911 are frequently uncooperative, rude, and demeaning to 911 TCs, as typified by statements such as: "I don't want to talk to you. You're just a dispatcher! I want to talk to an officer who can really help me!"

Stress-Related Medical Conditions

The 911 subculture is also joined by its members' struggle with stress-related medical conditions. This is due to a combination of factors, including the 911 TCs' highly stressful work conditions, their suppressive Emotion Code, and a lack of skills training to boost resilience and enable effective stress management. Lilly and Allen (2015) identified that 54.7% of 911 TCs are obese and 24% acknowledge symptoms consistent with a diagnosis of major depression. Self-medicating behaviors, though not yet formally studied, are suspected to be epidemic among 911 TCs. The 911 industry also struggles with chronic excessive use of sick/medical leave and a low level of employee retention annually. As a result, 911 TCs commonly work excessive mandatory overtime hours and variable shifts, resulting in sleep deprivation (an industry-wide issue), and increased susceptibility to chronic stress and other stress-related problems. Troxell (2008) found that forced overtime contributed to an increased susceptibility to compassion fatigue among telecommunicators.

Accordingly, the clinician should always rule out these conditions and disorders when treating 911 TCs. Careful screening (including the use of standardized screening tools) for depression, sleep disorders, substance abuse, and (when obesity is present) eating behavior is encouraged.

Treating 911 Trauma in Emergency Telecommunicators Protocol Script Notes

Initiating EMDR With 911 TCs

Working within the Standard EMDR Protocol and Procedures is the foundation of EMDR Therapy with the 911 TC. The Adaptive Information Processing model (AIP) guides EMDR Therapy and case conceptualization. The AIP proposes that the presenting symptoms are a result of unprocessed disturbing memories within the memory networks; therefore, reprocessing these memories along with present environmental triggers and future anticipated stressors to an adaptive state will decrease and/or eliminate the posttraumatic stress symptoms. Clinicians must initially ascertain how many sessions they will have to treat the client. The fewer the sessions provided, the more specific the clinician must be in choosing targets to process. Utilizing protocols that zero in on specific recent events, such as the Recent Traumatic Events Protocol (Shapiro, 2001) and the Recent-Traumatic Episode Protocol (R-TEP; Shapiro & Laub, 2014, pp. 193–216), is suggested. The following guidance is offered to optimize the clinician's application of EMDR Therapy—within the context of the Protocol for Recent Traumatic Events—for 911 professionals.

The EMDR clinician who invests time and energy to understand the needs of this special population will secure the most effective treatment outcomes with telecommunicators and find a great deal of satisfaction in fostering their healing. Clinicians who have directly observed 911 TCs at work, during "sit-alongs" in their PSAPs, have reported a greater understanding of their crucial role in emergency response. EMDR therapists are encouraged to pursue these sit-along learning experiences as a first step in building relationships with their local 9-1-1 professionals so deserving of the gift Francine Shapiro has given the EMDR community.

Establishing an Alliance With the Telecommunicator

CONVEY RESPECT FOR THE 911 PROFESSIONAL

The treatment process with a 911 TC can quickly become precarious depending on the extent to which the clinician can convey a basic understanding of, and a respect and empathy for, the telecommunicator's unique role—within the larger emergency response community—and the distinct stressors associated with this role. Such regard by the clinician for the 911 profession addresses a major sensitivity among telecommunicators: traditionally, field responders and the public often have perceived them as playing only a menial role, unaffected by traumatic events. The 911 TC client may expect the therapist to share this diminished view of the profession. The clinician can proactively engage the telecommunicator to diffuse this expectation and build the therapeutic alliance.

DEFUSE TREATMENT ANXIETY

In accord with the Emotion Code adhered to by most 911 personnel, the client may be wary of mental health providers and doubt the value of treatment. Predictably then, premature discussion of vulnerable emotions or details related to the presenting problem may threaten a sense of safety and prompt the 911 TC to project negativity about psychotherapy. However, telecommunicators can be set at ease about accepting mental health assistance by normalizing and inviting skepticism.

Predictable Pitfalls to Therapeutic Alliance

Success in 911 telecommunication requires the 911 TC to possess a highly unusual combination of characteristics, including high-speed cognitive processing dependent upon exceptional common sense, reasoning, and judgment; outstanding affect regulation; and the interpersonal skills to foster homeostasis in callers who are oppositional and/or highly distressed. Telecommunicators must "take charge" with callers, by frequently interrupting and firmly redirecting them. Thus, outside their workplace, others may inaccurately perceive 911 TCs as overly dominant, terse, critical, and impatient. By suspending such negative interpretations of the telecommunicator and reframing these attributes as strengths, the clinician can foster a strong therapeutic alliance and more accurate appraisal of the 911 TC as a person.

911 TCs state that one of the exchanges they most dread is with strangers who, in contrast to minimizing the role of 9-1-1, embrace a glamorized notion of all emergency response work and ask invasive questions. "Oh, you're a dispatcher! Will you tell me what your worst call was?" This inquiry often triggers distress, associated with compassion fatigue and unresolved critical incidents, and therefore prompts defensive feelings such as irritability and annoyance. By conveying empathy for the telecommunicator's perception of such questions as intrusive, the clinician will gain credibility, set the 911 TC client at ease, and build alliance. Discussion of this stressful encounter with the public also affords the therapist the opportunity to prepare the client for inquiry about such incidents, for example, by stating: *"I can assure you that we'll relate more respectfully to difficult 911 experiences you've had. We'll be sure to help you prepare to address them in a way that's manageable—and it will be your choice what you share and don't share."*

Reframing the Presenting Problem and Introducing EMDR Therapy With Analogies Relevant to 911

The 911 TC seeking EMDR is likely to complain of feeling chronically exhausted, while lacking insight about possible underlying compassion fatigue. Or, they may present with symptoms of PTSD, stating, for example: "I don't know what's wrong with me, I just can't seem to shake this call, and it keeps replaying over and over. Why won't it go away? I've had way worse calls." Educating the client about chronic and traumatic stress, memory consolidation, and how EMDR Therapy works can help the telecommunicator with self-acceptance, foster hope that change is possible, and boost receptivity to EMDR. This can be done in the context of the initial history taking and during Phase 2 in the basic EMDR Protocol. Because 911 TCs work extensively with computer systems, using computer analogies to explain the neurobiology of traumatization is a helpful way for 911 TCs to relate to their personal experience of the negative impact of stress and improperly stored life experiences.

Addressing Blocking Beliefs Predictable Among 911 TCs

Blocking Beliefs Related to the Suppressive 911 TC Emotion Code: "Suck It Up!"

In accord with this Emotion Code and related anxiety-based ambivalence about identifying and processing distressing emotions, initially telecommunicators may be impeded in joining with the therapist, and in the assessment and treatment processes.

Blocking Beliefs in 911 Clients Mandated to Counseling

When a 911 TC is struggling in her work performance and the PSAP leader is convinced that this struggle is due to unresolved psychological issues, the leader will often urge or mandate psychological assessment and psychotherapy. Those telecommunicators mandated to counseling are inclined to exhibit strong cynicism toward psychology and therapy. However, initial cynicism displayed by the 911 TC may also reflect more extensive, generalized cynicism about humanity, driven by compassion fatigue. This cynicism is commonly voiced by 911 TCs in extreme statements such as: "You can't trust anybody...nobody cares...most everybody out there is an asshole," and "What's the point: It always turns to crap anyway!" This cynicism is the product of three factors:

1. Repeated exposure to callers in genuine crisis who are deeply distressed and feeling helpless in the face of injustice or tragedy, especially children and the elderly
2. A jaded perception of humanity because of excessive and disproportionate exposure to the most derelict and criminal citizens versus a normal, balanced exposure including more happy, well-adjusted, and appreciative "normal" people
3. Excessive production of stress hormones associated with the chronic stress response, fueling negative emotion and distorted cognition

The clinician can consider inviting the resistant and cynical 911 TC to teach about these factors, and then help normalize the responses.

Dehumanizing Callers

Telecommunicators struggling with compassion fatigue, who have become the most hardened and defensive, may be unable to discuss and resolve critical incident trauma without EMDR because they have adopted dehumanizing attitudes toward citizens by whom they feel emotionally threatened. By steeling against natural compassionate responses, the telecommunicator feels fortified against emotional distress and is better able to tolerate exposure to crises. For example, the 911 TC may have recently received a call from a man in a low-income mobile home community who is seriously threatening suicide. At the onset of feelings of fear and helplessness, when attempting to help prevent the caller's death and in anticipation of hearing the fatal gunshot, the telecommunicator may seek to distance himself emotionally. If the 911 TC can convince himself that this man (and others *"like him"*) is "Sub-human—just another piece of White trash," the 911 professional will feel less empathic attachment and thus less distress, if death ensues. Whereas a telecommunicator might otherwise experience horror if the caller completes the suicide while on the phone, this negative labeling enables the 911 TC to block his distress with a dehumanizing declaration: "Well, at least that's one more piece of trailer-trash off the streets!" The clinician may be inclined to judge such a dehumanizing response, but must see this compassionately as a self-protective strategy in need of replacement with one that is more adaptive and also helps restore the 911 TC's own humanity.

Resource Development With the 911 TC: Tapping Into 911 TC Strengths to Reset Mind, Body, and Spirit

Building skills to reset hyperarousal—as it occurs on the job or elsewhere—is a vital part of career stress management, particularly in emergency response work. Managing heart rate variability through skills that combine strategic breath work and activation of positive emotion can help 911 TCs to reduce and manage hypervigilance (McCraty, Tomasino, Atkinson, & Sundram, 1999).

Developing a positive traits list is also an excellent way to boost client resources. Assisting telecommunicators to identify their positive strengths and skills, on the job and personally, will remind them that they are more than their suffering. The clinician can use this list later in treatment to create cognitive interweaves.

Activating Positive Career Memories

Positive outcomes can follow even the most potentially tragic 911 calls, and the telecommunicator may experience traumatic growth and compassion satisfaction from this role. Most experienced 911 TCs have at least a few emergency calls that stand out as very positive and rewarding. The clinician can ask the clients to complete a homework assignment in which they write down such experiences, including the visual memory (as they imagined the scene), and the emotions and cognitions generated by their recall of these events. These resources can be installed and then drawn on, as needed, later in the EMDR treatment process.

Negative and Positive Cognitions Common Among 911 TCs

Cognitions Related to Responsibility

As the very first responder on scene, the 911 TC job requires shouldering the primary responsibility for preparing field responders with the information they need to assure safety for all on scene. Just as emotional attachment is cemented among soldiers by their interdependence while fighting to survive within a shared danger zone, telecommunicators form deep attachments to their field responders through shared traumatic experiences. 911 TCs' sense of responsibility for field responders' safety is deepened by this attachment.

The inordinate sense of responsibility assumed by telecommunicators for the life and death of their officers, firefighters, and paramedics often becomes ingrained in the 911 TCs' professional identity, and constitutes the chief criterion by which many measure their worth. This responsibility also constitutes an irrational expectation, as its fulfillment would require absolute control over people in emergent circumstances. The EMDR therapist can therefore predict the negative cognitions that 911 TCs may experience after an officer they have dispatched to a dangerous scene is injured or killed. For example:

- "He died (or was injured) because I sent him there."
- "It's my fault: he is down/hurt/dead because of a mistake I made."
- "He would still be OK (or alive) if only I had..."
- "I failed my officer: I am a failure" (note the familial sense of responsibility implied by "my").
- "I must do everything perfectly so my officers don't die, so they come home."

Also, the 911 TCs' inordinate sense of responsibility extends to the citizens who call for assistance related to emergency, medical, police, and fire services. Here are some examples of the types of beliefs that 911 TCs have reported:

- "The baby wouldn't have died if I had... (e.g., guided CPR administration better)"
- "The man wouldn't have committed suicide if only I had..."
- "This house fire tragedy might not have happened if I had gotten the address (sooner/more accurately)."

Cognitions Related to Safety

Although 911 TCs are not physically on scene, following critical incidents they may struggle with cognitions and emotions related to a lost sense of personal safety, because they were psychologically present at scenes in which others were at risk, and, since the human brain does not always differentiate between danger to others and danger to self, during a stress response or subsequent encoding of traumatic information. Therefore, telecommunicators may struggle with negative cognitions about these past events and a related anticipation of future danger. Cognitions may include:

- "I shouldn't be reacting like this (e.g., fear, horror, helplessness): I wasn't even there!"
- "Even though I wasn't there, I can't shake these images in my mind."
- "I just don't feel like I can let my guard down."
- "I'm the 'shit magnet' at our PSAP. It's gonna just keep happening."

911 TCs who identify with these cognitions will benefit from the clinician's assurances that they, while problematic, are a normal response to abnormal circumstances; that physical distance from a trauma scene does not protect the 911 TC from traumatization; and that it is normal to struggle with feeling unsafe in the aftermath of such events.

Cognitions Related to Control

Given that 911 TCs are not physically on the scene of the emergencies in which they are involved, they must perform their duties with a significant lack of information crucial to their performance that is routinely available to field responders. This information deficit contributes to heightened distress and a sense of lack of control. EMDR can help resolve such aspects of their experience including the following:

- *Imaginal perception versus actual visual perception:* 911 TCs must depend on their visual imaginations to "see" what is occurring at the scene. To plan for all possible contingencies, telecommunicators universally default to visualizing the worst possible scenario. This strategy can optimize their effort as communicators to keep those on scene safe, yet it can escalate telecommunicators' feelings of helplessness as they anticipate extreme danger and possible death of their field responders.
- *Incomplete information crucial to disposition:* Callers in distress (suicidal, homicidal, those at risk in domestic violence or mass casualty events, those with language disabilities or barriers, etc.) may be ambivalent about the consequences of speaking up or reporting fully to 911 TCs. Such callers may fail to cooperate in providing their address and other vital information that would assure success in preventing tragedy. This withholding of vital information activates a sense of helplessness and lack of control in the 911 TC. Similarly, such feelings are prompted in 911 TCs when field responders at dangerous scenes are hindered from providing details in real time about their status.
- *Lack of timely closure:* When an officer on scene reports by radio to the 911 TC "Shots fired," the telecommunicator may also hear those shots in her headset. Given the immense sense of responsibility that 911 TCs shoulder for their officers' welfare, the telecommunicator is predisposed to dreading the next possible radio transmission that may report: "Officer down" (indicating an injury or fatality unspecified). When field responders are then unable to radio additional information about their welfare, telecommunicators are often left with uncertainty about whether their officers and other field responders have been seriously injured or killed. While field responders on scene know the outcomes of these tragic events in real time, it may be hours before a telecommunicator dispatching such an emergency knows if there has been a fatality among the emergency response family members. Thus, the clinician assessing a telecommunicator after such an event should help to identify and, as needed, help resolve negative cognitions such as:
- "Even though I know now that he survived, it doesn't feel that way."
- "I can't stand not knowing what's going to happen."
- "I have no control."
- "I dread working the radio (dispatching field responders) now."

Treating 911 Trauma in Emergency Telecommunicators Protocol Script

Initiating EMDR Therapy With 911 TCs: Establishing Rapport

Establishing an Alliance With the Telecommunicator

CONVEY RESPECT FOR THE 911 PROFESSIONAL

The 911 TC client may expect the therapist to share a diminished view of the profession. The clinician can proactively engage the telecommunicator to diffuse this expectation and build the therapeutic alliance.

> Say, *"To help me learn more about your work as a 911 professional, can you tell me: If I were sitting at your console with you, what would I see you doing—what would be happening? Could you just take a few minutes to teach me?"*

_____

_____

_____

Summarize the 911 TC's answer and offer genuine recognition of the demanding nature and value of the work described.

> Say, *"_____ (state understanding of 911 TC's response). I now can truly understand how demanding and important your work is."*

It can also help for the clinician to relate a brief story of any personal encounter with a 911 TC in which the therapist or significant others may have been helped by the 911 TC.

> Say, *"_____ (state any personal encounter or time helped by a 911 TC)."*

_____

_____

Readily acknowledge any limitations in the clinician's knowledge and experience with the 911 profession and invite the 911 TC to teach about this. If appropriate, say the following:

> Say, *"You have given me some really helpful insights about the 911 profession. I hope that as we continue along you will feel free to share any other information I need to know about your work."*

_____

_____

DIFFUSE TREATMENT ANXIETY

In accord with the Emotion Code adhered to by most 911 personnel, the client may be wary of mental health providers and doubt the value of treatment. The therapist can state:

> Say, *"So much is expected of emergency responders, including 911, to always be strong, to suck up emotions and get the job done. So, it's pretty normal to be skeptical of therapy. I just want you to know I actually think being a skeptical consumer of therapy is a smart way to start. Can you relate at all to being skeptical?"*

_____

_____

If yes, the therapist can invite them to share their view and questions related to the field of psychology, and specifically about the clinician's practice organization and approach to therapy.

Say, *"Please let me know your view about the field of psychology even if it's negative. Don't worry—I won't be offended. I also want you to feel comfortable asking anything you want about how I do therapy and about* (name of your organization). *Do you have any questions for me now?"* (**Note:** If client has no questions, add: *"By all means, ask any questions you need to as we continue, OK?"*)

_____

_____

_____

As part of the therapist's effort to build treatment alliance, it will be helpful to consider asking the following questions regarding interpersonal challenges 911 TCs typically find most rewarding *and* distressing in their workplace:

Say, *"What is the relationship like between the 911 telecommunicators at your PSAP and your field responders?"*

_____

_____

Say, *"What's most rewarding/stressful about it?"*

_____

_____

Without allying with the 911 TC against his administration, the clinician can still affirm the importance of telecommunicators receiving the support they need.

Say, *"At your PSAP, what kind of support do they provide for you and your peers after the worst calls?"*

_____

_____

Phase 1: History Taking

Upon taking care to establish an alliance in accord with the guidance offered earlier, gain information about what prompted the 911 TC to seek counseling at this time. The EMDR therapist should seek a brief overview of the critical incident and how the client sees it is impacting her. (A more detailed description will come later.)

Overview of Incident

Say, *"Give me an overview of what happened."*

_____

_____

_____

Say, *"How is this impacting you now?"*

_____
_____
_____

Ask the client to describe the reactions and symptoms he is having and when he began to notice them. Often people have difficulty describing or naming their stress symptoms. Providing prompts can help. For example, the clinician can state:

"What sort of reactions are you having?"

_____
_____
_____

Or say, *"Are you having trouble sleeping?"*

_____
_____
_____

Say, *"Are you having repetitive thoughts?"*

_____
_____
_____

Say, *"Do you have physical shaking?"*

_____
_____
_____

Say, *"Are you irritable?"*

_____
_____
_____

Say, *"Do you have stomach problems or headaches?"*

_____
_____
_____

Say, *"Are you feeling edgy or short-tempered?"*

___

History of Previous Critical Incidents

Ask for a brief history of previous critical incidents, then check on these reports later in treatment.

Say, *"Can you give me a brief overview of other critical incidents that you recall? Just the highlights of significant calls in your career."*

___

Medical and Psychological History

Assess for any underlying co-occurring disorders.

Say, *"Are there any other medical or psychological issues that you are having or being treated for?"*

___

Ask about past and present medical problems.

Say, *"Please tell me about any past medical problems that you have had."*

___

Say, *"Please tell me about present medical problems that you are having."*

___

Family History

Ask about family history and current family status.

Say, *"Can you give me an overview of the family you grew up in and your current family situation?"*

_____
_____
_____

Work Situation

Ask about the client's specific role at work and his employment status at the PSAP.

Say, *"Please tell me about your specific role at work."*

_____
_____
_____

Say, *"Please tell me about your employment status at the PSAP."*

_____
_____
_____

Predictable Blocking Beliefs

In accord with this Emotion Code and related anxiety-based ambivalence about identifying and processing distressing emotions, telecommunicators may initially be impeded in joining with the therapist, and in the assessment and treatment processes. To foster their success in resolving this ambivalence, the clinician can suggest:

Say, *"I know that 911 professionals feel the need to put their own emotions aside to do their job; yet there's also a lot of peer pressure to follow the old paramilitary way of dealing with emotions—you know: 'suck it up' and just keep going. Can you relate to that?"*

_____
_____

If the client affirms, the clinician can read each of the associated blocking cognitions below and invite the 911 TC to indicate if and how much he can relate to them.

Say, *"I would like to ask how much you can relate to each of these beliefs. What about, 'It is not OK to express emotions'?"*

_____
_____
_____

Say, *"Also, how about the belief, 'I will be judged as weak if I do …'?"*

_____
_____
_____

Say, *"Or, to be accepted by our sworn personnel, I can't show if I am distressed by a really bad call."*

_____
_____
_____

Worldview

Excessive production of stress hormones associated with the chronic stress response can fuel negative emotion and distorted cognition. The clinician can consider inviting resistant and cynical 911 TCs to teach her about these factors, and then help normalize the responses.

Say, *"I understand that doing emergency response work and dealing with citizens at their worst can set up telecommunicators to get a bit cynical (he will likely laugh at this point). Is that accurate?"*

_____
_____
_____

If the telecommunicator affirms, ask the following:

Say, *"How do you think you've become more cynical?"*

_____
_____
_____

Follow this question with the following:

Say, *"How do you think that's been helpful or maybe unhelpful for you?"*

_____
_____

Dehumanizing Callers

To explore for the presence of blocking cognitions related to the dehumanizing defense (usually a self-protective strategy in need of replacement with one that is more adaptive), the clinician can inquire by stating the following:

Say, *"You definitely can't pour out empathy in some big way for every caller. There is only so much of you to go around. So, it's normal if you think something like this: 'If I allow myself to feel empathy for this caller, it will suck me dry. I don't want give away any more of myself. So I just learned to shut it off.' Can you relate?"*

_____
_____
_____

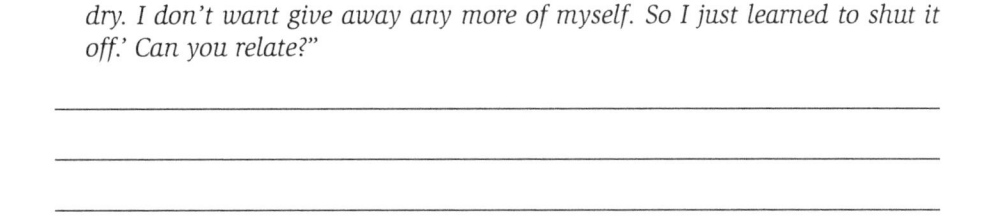

If the client affirms that he can relate strongly to this cognition, the therapist can help the client explore the effects of this choice, without implying that it is wrong or bad, by stating the following:

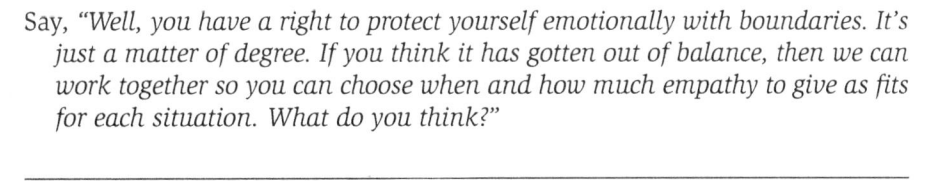

Say, *"Well, you have a right to protect yourself emotionally with boundaries. It's just a matter of degree. If you think it has gotten out of balance, then we can work together so you can choose when and how much empathy to give as fits for each situation. What do you think?"*

_____
_____

Phase 2: Preparation

Reframing the Presenting Problem and Introducing EMDR With Analogies Relevant to 911

EXPLAIN TRAUMATIC STRESS

911 TCs will value the clinician's effort to help them understand the symptoms they are experiencing. Go over the impact of chronic traumatic stress on the mind and body and how EMDR Therapy can help. Consider using the previously mentioned computer analogy to facilitate easy understanding. Allow a brief period for questions to clarify things.

Say, *"Our mind and body systems are like a 'super-computer' that is designed to manage stress and build resilience (mental strength, endurance, and flexibility) over time. However, repeated exposure to traumatic stress can take its toll, even on the strongest system. This toll is like a hard drive running out of storage space and programs not syncing up properly. When this chronic stress impacts the system, our 'super-computer' begins to operate more slowly and inefficiently, losing energy and organization. When this happens we start to see the symptoms you described: fatigue, foggy-thinking, sleep problems, irritability, flashbacks, intrusive thoughts, etc. With proper help, the 'super-computer' can re-boot and restore itself to its prior efficient functioning. Stress management tools along with EMDR Therapy help to reorganize the overloaded mind and body system and clear out what is no longer needed. Once the system is restored, the symptoms significantly diminish or fully disappear."*

EXPLAIN EMDR

Once the 911 TC understands that his symptoms are the result of a system overload and not a weakness of character, he may more readily embrace the process of EMDR.

Say, *"EMDR is a way to achieve that reboot, to activate your natural internal program to help the data to file properly. Once it is re-filed, your symptoms will likely diminish or go away completely."*

EXPLAIN BILATERAL STIMULATION

Say, *"We utilize bilateral stimulation or BLS to engage the brain's right and left hemispheres to activate the whole brain to process information. Just talking about problems may only activate the part of the brain's processing system where the information remains stuck. But we can use BLS to help the system to jump-start its filing program. Have you seen someone perhaps on a TV special on sleep, and their eyes are darting back and forth? That movement is activating the BLS of the brain's hemispheres—and it happens during the REM stages of sleep. So we activate BLS during EMDR to help you process information."*

Resource Development With the 911 TC: Tapping Into 911 TC Strengths to Reset Mind, Body, and Spirit

Positive resource skill building is vital to successful EMDR treatment and to career stress management. The following have been used successfully with 911 TCs: Safe Place, the Container, Heart Rhythm Coherence Training, Positive Traits list, Positive Career Highlights. Additional relaxation skills training will be helpful strategies to decrease the physiological arousal that comes with this job.

SAFE PLACE

Say, *"Imagine a place in nature or somewhere else where you feel calm, protected, and away from any stress. Where would this place be and what does it look like? Describe it in detail with colors, sights, sounds, smells. Allow yourself to be there now and let your body and mind relax in this place."*

THE CONTAINER

An additional tool is the use of an imaginary container to hold any stressful thoughts or feelings of any other old calls and events.

Say, *"Imagine a container that has a lid. With the lid open, please put any thoughts, feelings, and/images into the container. Let me know when you have done that."*

_____

Say, *"Great. Now, it is time to close the lid and lock it down. Anything that is in there can be processed later. The container is so that you can know that everything is safely put away and you do not have to think about it now."*

MANAGING HEART RATE VARIABILITY

Building skills to reset hyperarousal, as it occurs on the job or elsewhere, is a vital part of career stress management, particularly in emergency response work. Skills that combine strategic breath work and activation of positive emotion can help 911 TCs manage heart rate variability to achieve smoother heart-rhythm patterns or "heart coherence." McCraty found that such heart-rhythm coherence training can reduce and foster management of hypervigilance (McCraty et al., 1999).

Say, *"Since the heart is involved in everything we do, we can utilize this powerful organ to help bring us back into balance. Syncing up the heart and the brain is important to an efficiently running system."*

The 911 TC can be advised that skills fostering optimal heart performance and heart–brain synchrony (coherence) can be employed by the client as needed during EMDR sessions, later to manage recall of critical incidents outside sessions, and immediately after managing critical calls at the PSAP.

Say, *"By learning such a skill, you can use it as needed during EMDR sessions and as you need it to manage recall of critical incidents outside our sessions and/or immediately after managing critical calls at the PSAP. If it is OK, I am going to teach the Quick Coherence Technique* (Childre & Martin, 2000). *Is that OK with you?"*

_____

_____

Say, *"Begin with Heart-Focused Breathing: Please focus your attention in the area of your heart. Imagine your breath is flowing in and out of your heart or chest area, breathing a little slower and deeper than usual. You can start by inhaling for 5 seconds and exhaling for 5 seconds, or you can use whatever rhythm is comfortable."*

Say, *"It is helpful to make a sincere attempt to experience a regenerative feeling such as honor or appreciation or care for someone or something in your life. As you notice that positive feeling, you may even feel a smile coming on: breathe that feeling into the center of your chest, into your heart area."*

If the client has difficulty, you can suggest the following:

Say, *"Try to reexperience the feeling you have for someone you love or a pet. You also can focus on feelings of courage, dignity, honor, calm, or ease"* (Institute of HeartMath, 2014).

To encourage reinforcing the positive feelings, say the following:

Say, *"It is often helpful to bring favorite soothing or encouraging photographs and place them near your console, so that you have a focal point for positive emotions throughout your work day, and they can serve as reminders to take deeper breaths as you are able at the beginning, during, and at the end of every call."*

IDENTIFYING POSITIVE STRENGTHS AND SKILLS

Assisting telecommunicators to identify their positive strengths and skills on the job and personally will remind them that they are more than their suffering. You can use this list later in treatment to create cognitive interweaves.

Say, *"After so many years of doing this job, what strengths or positive traits do you know you have? Let's come up with a list."*

_____

_____

_____

_____

Once this is done, read it back to them, and for each trait, ask them the following:

Say, *"For* _____ (state the positive trait), *please generate a positive feeling that represents this trait. Notice it and where you feel this in your body and breathe into that spot."*

_____

_____

The therapist can also ask them to imagine a color that represents any of the positive traits, and then bring something to work of that color to place in view at their console. This provides another anchor to activate a positive emotional state.

Then say, *"Imagine a color that represents _____ (state the trait) and then bring something to work of that color to place in view of your console."*

_____
_____

Go through this exercise for each positive trait on the list.

ACTIVATING POSITIVE CAREER MEMORIES

Positive outcomes can follow even the most potentially tragic 911 calls, and telecommunicators may experience traumatic growth and compassion satisfaction from their role. Most experienced 911 TCs have at least a few emergency calls that stand out as very positive and rewarding. Activation of these memories can be done in the office or as homework.

Say, *"Often, in the most potentially tragic 911 calls, it is possible to have some positive outcomes that result in your sense that you have learned something important and have compassion for yourself in your role as a 911 professional. I hope that you would consider writing down some of these experiences, including how you imagined the scene and the emotions and thoughts that occur when you recall these events. What comes up for you?"*

_____
_____
_____

Use short sets of BLS to install as appropriate.

Say, *"Go with that* (use appropriate BLS).*"*

Past Memories

Phase 3: Assessment

1. Narrative history and identifying

Once the brief overview has been explained, the clinician asks the client to go through the identified incident frame-by-frame and pinpoint any significant moments (worst parts, turning points, or game changers). Take notes of observable body responses; however, wait to do a full body scan until all targets are processed.

Say, *"Let's go through the incident moment by moment, frame-by-frame, from your point of view. This will enable us to identify each significant moment that we will later process with EMDR."*

_____
_____
_____

If the client appears to be stuck in the recall, gently move her along by saying the following:

Say, *"OK, good, then what happened?"*

_____
_____
_____

Use each separate significant moment as a separate target with the full Standard EMDR Procedure and Protocol. Process the material through the installation of the PC. Do a Body Scan after all targets are processed.

Introducing Bilateral Processing

Say, *"We will be doing sets of the bilateral activation. The BLS is important so your whole brain will assist in the refiling of this information. Remember, it is your own brain that is doing the work and you are the one in control. I will ask you to begin by focusing on the target and to follow my fingers (or any other BLS you are using). Just let whatever happens, happen, and when I stop the eye movements we will talk about what came up. Any new information that comes to mind is connected in some way, so you can tell me about whatever comes up. If you want to stop for any reason, just let me know."*

2. Target: most disturbing aspect or moment of the memory

The clinician can either start with the most disturbing moment/frame of the incident or target the moments in chronological order.

Picture

Say, *"Let's target the first stand-out moment of the event and go from there."*

Identify the picture:

Say, *"What picture represents the disturbing moment of the event?"*

_____
_____

If the 911 TC says there's more than one picture or becomes confused, the clinician can help by asking the following:

Say, *"What picture represents the most disturbing moment?"*

_____
_____

If the client is unable to find or pick a picture, the clinician can say the following:

Say, *"OK, just think of the most disturbing part of the event."*

_____
_____

Negative Cognition (NC)

Say, "What words best go with the picture that express your negative belief about yourself now?"

_____
_____

Positive Cognition (PC)

If the 911 TC is unable to come up with a positive statement, the clinician can use a cognitive interweave that includes a positive trait mentioned from the resourcing phase.

Say, "When you bring up that disturbing moment of the event, what would you like to be able to believe about yourself now?"

_____
_____

Validity of Cognition (VoC)

Say, "When you think of the disturbing moment of the event (or picture), how true do those words _____ (clinician repeats the PC) feel to you now on a scale of 1 to 7, where 1 feels completely false and 7 feels completely true?"

   1   2   3   4   5   6   7

(completely false)   (completely true)

Sometimes it is necessary to explain the truth scale further.

Say, "Remember, sometimes we know something with our head, but it feels differently in our gut. In this case, what is the gut-level feeling of the truth of _____ (clinician restates the PC), from 1 (completely false) to 7 (completely true)?"

Emotions

Say, "When you bring up the picture or the disturbing memory of the event and those words _____ (clinician restates the NC), what emotion do you feel now?"

_____
_____

Subjective Units of Disturbance (SUD)

Say, "On a scale of 0 to 10, where 0 is no disturbance or neutral and 10 is the highest disturbance you can imagine, how disturbing does it feel now?"

  0   1   2   3   4   5   6   7   8   9   10

(no disturbance)   (highest disturbance)

Location of Body Sensations

    Say, *"Where do you feel it* (the disturbance) *in your body?"*

_____
_____

    3. Target: remainder of the narrative in chronological order

Repeat Phases 4 through 5 for each segment of the memory until all of the targets have been processed. Phases 6 through 7 are done after the final part of the memory has been processed. The body tensions and sensations will then be able to dissipate more completely.

Picture

    Say, *"Let's target the first stand-out moment of the event and go from there."*

    Identify the picture:

    Say, *"What picture represents the disturbing moment of the event?"*

_____
_____

If the 911 TC says there's more than one picture or becomes confused, the clinician can help by asking the following:

    Say, *"What picture represents the most disturbing moment?"*

_____
_____

If the client is unable to find or pick a picture, the clinician can say the following:

    Say, *"OK, just think of the most disturbing part of the event."*

_____
_____

Negative Cognition

    Say, *"What words best go with the picture that express your negative belief about yourself now?"*

_____
_____

Positive Cognition

If the 911 TC is unable to come up with a positive statement, the clinician can use a cognitive interweave that includes a positive trait mentioned from the resourcing phase.

    Say, *"When you bring up that disturbing moment of the event, what would you like to be able to believe about yourself now?"*

_____
_____

Validity of Cognition

Say, "When you think of the disturbing moment of the event (or picture), *how true do those words* _____ (clinician repeats the PC) *feel to you now on a scale of 1 to 7, where 1 feels completely false and 7 feels completely true?*"

1   2   3   4   5   6   7

(completely false)   (completely true)

Sometimes it is necessary to explain the truth scale further.

Say, "Remember, sometimes we know something with our head, but it feels differently in our gut. In this case, what is the gut-level feeling of the truth of _____ (clinician restates the PC), from 1 (completely false) to 7 (completely true)?"

Emotions

Say, "When you bring up the picture or the disturbing memory of the event and those words _____ (clinician restates the NC), what emotion do you feel now?"

_____

_____

Subjective Units of Disturbance

Say, "On a scale of 0 to 10, where 0 is no disturbance or neutral and 10 is the highest disturbance you can imagine, how disturbing does it feel now?"

0   1   2   3   4   5   6   7   8   9   10

(no disturbance)   (highest disturbance)

Location of Body Sensations

Say, "Where do you feel it (the disturbance) in your body?"

_____

_____

Phase 4: Desensitization

The work in Phase 4 follows the Standard EMDR Protocol.

Introducing EMDR Processing

Say, "We will be doing sets of the bilateral activation. The BLS is important so your whole brain will assist in the refiling of this information. Remember, it is your own brain that is doing the work and you are the one in control. I will ask you to begin by focusing on the target and to follow my fingers (or any other BLS you are using). Just let whatever happens, happen, and when I stop the eye movements we will talk about what came up. Any new information that comes to mind is connected in some way, so you can tell me about whatever comes up. If you want to stop for any reason, just let me know."

Then say, *"Bring up the picture and the words _____ (clinician repeats the NC) and notice where you feel it in your body. Now follow _____ (state BLS)."*

___

___

After all of the targets are reprocessed, go onto visualizing the entire sequence of the event with eyes closed.

4. Rechecking: visualize the entire sequence of event with eyes closed
Have the 911 TC visualize the entire sequence with eyes closed and reprocess it as any disturbance arises. The 911 TC should have a full association, being fully present with the material as it is being reprocessed. Begin by saying the following:

Say, *"Please visualize the entire sequence of the event with your eyes closed. If there is any disturbance, please open your eyes and we will reprocess the material together. Let me know when your disturbance decreases."*

___

___

To check further for disturbances, ask about any sights, sounds, smells the client may have noticed.

Say, *"While you review this event, notice if there are any other sensations in your body, sounds you hear, smells or tastes that show up. Let me know if there is."*

___

___

If disturbance is reported, repeat until the entire event can be visualized from start to finish without emotional, cognitive, or somatic distress. Repeat until the 911 TC can visualize the entire event without disturbance or upset. Once there is no disturbance, the clinician can move on to the following section; visualize the entire sequence of the event with eyes open.

5. Visualize entire sequence of event with eyes open and install PC

Phase 5: Install PC

Have the 911 TC visualize the event from start to finish with *eyes open*, and install the PC.

Say, *"Please visualize the entire sequence of the event with your eyes open and think of _____ (state the PC). Scan the videotape mentally—even though the images will not be clear—and give the stop signal when you are finished. Go ahead with that _____ (or any other BLS you are using)."*

Allow a long set of BLS to enable the client to get through the event.

Phase 6: Body Scan

6. Do the Body Scan
Conclude with Body Scan. Only do Body Scan at the end of the processing of *all* of the targets or moments of the event.

Say, *"Close your eyes and keep in mind the original memory and the _____ (repeat the selected PC). Then bring your attention to the different parts of your body, starting with your head and working downward. Any place you find any tension, tightness, or unusual sensation, tell me."*

If any sensation is reported, do BLS.

Say, *"Go with that."*

_____

_____

If a positive or comfortable sensation is reported, do BLS to strengthen the positive feeling.

Say, *"OK, go with that."*

_____

_____

If a sensation of discomfort is reported, reprocess until discomfort subsides.

Say, *"Go with that."*

_____

_____

911 TCs are highly trained in what they do. They like to know when they are "doing it right." Once processing appears complete, validate their hard work by saying the following:

Say, *"You really stayed with it today. I know it is a lot of work and can be uncomfortable. Great job!"*

Phase 7: Closure—Grounding Is Important

At the end of each session, restore balance and self-regulation as much as possible. It is important to remind the 911 TCs about the type of inner work they are doing and how important it is to "reboot" or "ground" themselves in between sessions, utilizing any of the stabilization skills discussed earlier.

Say, *"You have worked hard today and I wanted to remind you how important it is to 'reboot' or 'ground' yourself in between sessions by using any of the resources we worked on earlier. Do you have any questions about that?"*

_____

_____

Remind the client how to use the imaginary container to hold any stressful thoughts or feelings of any other old calls and events.

Say, *"Imagine a container that has a lid. With the lid open, please put any thoughts, feelings, and/images into the container. Let me know when you have done that."*

_____

_____

Say, *"Great. Now, it is time to close the lid and lock it down. Anything that is in there can be processed later. The container is so that you can know that everything is safely put away and you do not have to think about it now."*

If this is the first experience of EMDR Therapy for the 911 TC, it is important to inform him of what might occur in between sessions.

Say, *"Things may come up or they may not. If they do, great: this is normal. If nothing does, that is normal too. If you are aware of a memory or thought, write it down, and we can check on it next time. If you get any new memories, dreams, or situations that disturb you, just take a good snapshot, make some brief notes. It isn't necessary to record a lot of detail. Just put down enough to remind you so we can target it next time. The same thing goes for any positive dreams or situations. If negative feelings do come up, simply identify them and write them down for next time. You can also toss them into the container and then use any of the relaxation skills that we have worked with. This should help you feel more comfortable in the moment. Even if nothing comes up, make sure to practice the relaxation or heart rate coherence exercises every day and give me a call if you feel stuck or can't shake some discomfort. I can help you reboot over the phone."*

It is possible the 911 TC may have a cascade of "bad" calls surface in between sessions. Making yourself available in between sessions early in treatment, to help the 911 TC apply skills and EMDR treatment principles, can secure treatment outcomes and foster alliance and motivation to remain in therapy.

Phase 8: Reevaluation

The Standard EMDR Protocol and Procedure emphasize the importance of follow-up by the clinician to evaluate the effects of the EMDR processing. Frequently, as time passes, the meaning of the incident to the 911 TC changes and continues to unfold, and further processing may be needed. New details may reveal themselves or other critical incidents will pop up.

Present Triggers

7. Present stimuli or triggers

Experiencing ongoing triggers is simply part of a 911 TC's everyday job. As a part of Phase 8, Reevaluation, the clinician and 911 TC can identify what situation occurred during the week that was a reminder of the incident and if it brought up feelings of fear, vulnerability, or powerlessness. These triggers can occur at work, home, or anywhere.

List the situations that elicit the symptom(s). Examples of situations, events, or stimuli that trigger the 911 TC with a startle response or negative emotion could be the following: another similar trauma, a span of silence over the radio, a child crying, or an officer upset.

Say, *"What are the situations or events that trigger your trauma _____ (state the trauma)? Let's process these triggers one by one."*

Situations, Event, or Stimuli Trigger List

_____

_____

_____

_____

Identify events where the officer is triggered.

Picture

Say, *"What picture represents the situation or event?"*

_____

_____

Negative Cognition

Say, *"What words best go with the picture that express your negative belief about yourself now?"*

_____

_____

Positive Cognition

Say, *"When you bring up that picture, situation, or event where the startle response occurs, what would you like to believe about yourself now?"*

_____

_____

Validity of Cognition

Say, *"When you think of the startle response* (or picture), *how true do those words* _____ (clinician repeats the PC) *feel to you now on a scale of 1 to 7, where 1 feels completely false and 7 feels completely true?"*

1   2   3   4   5   6   7

(completely false)   (completely true)

Sometimes, it is necessary to explain further.

Say, *"Remember, sometimes we know something with our head, but it feels differently in our gut. In this case, what is the gut-level feeling of the truth of* _____ (clinician states the PC), *from 1 (completely false) to 7 (completely true)?"*

1   2   3   4   5   6   7

(completely false)   (completely true)

Emotions

Say, *"When you bring up the picture* (the situation or event where the startle response occurs) *and those words* _____ (clinician states the NC), *what emotion do you feel now?"*

_____

_____

Subjective Units of Disturbance

Say, *"On a scale of 0 to 10, where 0 is no disturbance or neutral and 10 is the highest disturbance you can imagine, how disturbing does it feel now?"*

0   1   2   3   4   5   6   7   8   9   10

(no disturbance)   (highest disturbance)

Location of Body Sensations

Say, *"Where do you feel it* (the disturbance) *in your body?"*

_____

_____

Continue with Phases 4 through 7 for the situation or event that triggers the client. After processing the first situation, check to see if any of the others mentioned are still active; if so, complete processing on those.

Future Templates

8. Create a future template

Future templates are especially important in the treatment of 911 TCs, since they face the probability that the critical incidents they have reprocessed in treatment will occur again. 911 TCs tend to either obsess about or avoid consideration of those call types they most dread handling in the future. The use of future templates not only improves treatment outcomes, but also reinforces a more adaptive coping strategy that can be used as needed to make the 911 TC's work more bearable and rewarding. Using the positive resources from Phase 2 (positive trait list, breathing) will be helpful in the future pacing phase of treatment. The clinician can begin by saying the following:

Say, *"In regard to the incident, what were your moments of strength, moments you feel good about, or positive aspects?"*

_____

_____

Next, assist the client in creating a visualization of a future event, using these positive examples. For example, the 911 TC may imagine a future situation where she dispatches an officer to a dangerous scene.

Say, *"I would like you to imagine yourself coping/performing effectively when* _____ (state the situation that is being mentally rehearsed) *occurs in the future. With the positive belief* _____ (state the positive belief) *and your new sense of* _____ (state the quality: e.g., strength, clarity, confidence, calm), *imagine stepping into this situation."*

"Notice what you see and how you are handling the situation."

"Notice what you are thinking, feeling, and experiencing in your body."

_____

_____

If during this visualization exercise the clinician notices any type of disturbance, it should be checked on. There may be "left-overs" in the memory networks that can be processed. The clinician can also check with the 911 TC.

Say, *"Are there any blocks, anxieties, or fears that arise as you think about this future scene?"*

_____

_____

If yes, say the following:

Say, *"Then focus on these blocks and follow my fingers (or any other BLS)."*

Say, *"What do you get now?"*

_____

_____

If the blocks do not resolve quickly, evaluate if the 911 TC needs any new information, resources, or skills to be able to comfortably visualize the future coping scene. Introduce the needed information or skills.

Say, *"What would you need to feel confident in handling the situation?"*

_____

_____

Or say, *"What is missing from your handling of this situation?"*

_____

_____

If the 911 TC cannot visualize the future confidently and positively and the block remains, the clinician can move into direct questions, float-back, or affect scan. After this is done, it will assist in identifying other targets that may need to be processed. Use the Standard EMDR Protocol to address these targets before proceeding with the template.

When the 911 TC is able to visualize the future scene with confidence and clarity, say the following:

Say, *"Please focus on the image, the positive belief, and the sensations associated with this future scene and follow my fingers (or any other BLS)."*

_____

_____

Process and reinforce the positive associations with BLS. Do several sets until the future template is sufficiently strengthened. Repeating by saying the following:

Say, *"Go with that."*

Then say, *"Close your eyes and keep in mind the image of the future situation and the positive cognition. Then bring your attention to the different parts of your body, starting with your head and working downward. Any place you find any tension, tightness, or unusual sensation, tell me."*

_____

_____

If any sensation is reported, do BLS.

Say, *"Go with that."*

If it is a positive or comfortable sensation, do BLS to strengthen the positive feelings.

Say, *"Go with that."*

If a sensation of discomfort is reported, reprocess until the discomfort subsides. When the discomfort subsides, check the VoC.

Say, *"When you think of the incident* (or picture), *how true do those words* _____ (clinician repeats the PC) *feel to you now on a scale of 1 to 7, where 1 feels completely false and 7 feels completely true?"*

1   2   3   4   5   6   7

(completely false)   (completely true)

You will want to continue the BLS until the VoC is 7 or there is a resolution that is reasonable and ecological.

Building resiliency in the 911 TC is a key to a successful career and fulfilling life. Using the future template techniques with a wide range of future scenarios from their personal and professional lives can enhance resiliency.

Summary

911 TCs are the very first responders to the crises that rock our families, our communities, and our nation. They share values of dedication, loyalty, hard work, and compassion with all other emergency responders. Yet, 911 professionals endure stressors unique to their role, are at high risk of developing stress-related disorders, and are greatly underserved by the mental health profession. EMDR can effectively treat the troubling blocks and traumatic information pile-ups that diminish the quality of life and performance of these very first responders.

Resources

- 911 Wellness Foundation, www.911wellness.com
- EMDR International Association, www.emdria.org
- The Institute of HeartMath, www.heartmath.com
- International Critical Incident Stress Foundation, www.icisf.org
- SafeCallNow.org
- The National Emergency Number Association (NENA), www.nena.org
- The NENA Standard on Acute, Traumatic and Chronic Stress Management

Note: 911 TCs who have experienced critical incident stress are far less likely than field responders to be provided with vital support services that can improve their prognosis for recovery. Thus, they may arrive in the clinician's office without any prior support to cope with traumatic incidents, and without knowledge about resources available to assist 911 professionals to protect their mental health. It is important for the clinician treating 911 TCs to be familiar with and inform the client about the new 911 industry *Standard on Acute, Traumatic and Chronic Stress Management*. This standard was established by the NENA. It states that all PSAPs "shall develop Comprehensive Stress Management Programs (CSMPs) for all personnel." These CSMPs are required to assure telecommunicators access to eight types of resources:

- Training in stress management
- On-site PSAP educational materials and resources about stress-related risks, information about available local and online resources to manage stress
- CISM services, including diffusing and debriefing sessions
- Employee assistance programs
- Identify (and encourage proactive use of) local therapists specializing in treatment of stress and traumatic stress disorders
- Peer support delivered by trained personnel
- Provide comprehensive, ongoing certification training in all emergency call types
- PSAPs are highly encouraged to implement personal health incentivizing programs (NENA, 2013).

By informing telecommunicators about the NENA Standard, they can elect to request that their PSAP administrators implement the full spectrum of psychological support services (including EMDR) now recognized by the 911 industry as essential to protect telecommunicators from the stressors of their work (Marshall, 2013). The client's participation in these CSMP services can also promote the optimal outcomes of the EMDR treatment.

References

American Psychiatric Association. (2013). *Diagnostic and statistical manual of mental disorders* (5th ed.). Washington, DC: Author.

Childre, D., & Martin, H. (2000). *The heartmath solution.* New York, NY: Harper Collins Publishing, Inc.

Kirschman, E. (2006). *I love a cop: What police families need to know.* New York, NY: Guilford Press.

Lilly, M., & Allen, C. (2015). Psychological inflexibility and psychopathology in 9-1-1 telecommunicators. *Journal of Traumatic Stress, 28*, 1–5.

Marshall, J. (2011). *Comment pertaining to 11–153: In the matter of facilitating the deployment of text-to-911 and other NG911 applications: Framework for next generation 911 deployment.* Proceedings of the Federal Communications Commission.

Marshall, J. (2013, November/December). Pursuit of a blueprint for 911 wellness: Resilience takes more than ignoring the stress. *Journal of Emergency Dispatch*, 24–26.

McCraty, R., Tomasino, D., Atkinson, M., & Sundram, J. (1999). *Impact of the heartmath self-management skills program on physiological and psychological stress in police officers.* Boulder Creek, CA: HeartMath Research Center.

National Emergency Number Association (NENA) PSAP Operations Committee, 9-1-1 Acute/Traumatic and Chronic Stress Working Group. (2013, August 5). *NENA Standard on 9-1-1 Acute/Traumatic and Chronic Stress Management* (NENA STA-002). USA: NENA.

Pearce, H., & Lilly, M. (2012). Duty-related trauma exposure in 911 telecommunicators: Considering the risk for posttraumatic stress. *Journal of Traumatic Stress, 25*, 211–215.

Shapiro, F. (2001). *Eye movement desensitization and reprocessing* (pp. 224–227). New York, NY: Guilford Press

Shapiro, E., & Laub, B. (2014). The Recent Traumatic Episode Protocol (R-TEP): An integrative protocol for early EMDR intervention (EEI). In M. Luber (Ed.), *Implementing EMDR early mental health interventions for man-made and natural disasters: Models, scripted protocols, and summary sheets* (pp. 193–215). New York, NY: Springer.

Solomon, R. (2014). Early mental health intervention for the police. In M. Luber (Ed.), *Implementing EMDR early mental health interventions for man-made and natural disasters: Models, scripted protocols and summary sheets* (pp. 383–400). New York, NY: Springer.

Trompetter, P. (2011). Police psychologists: Roles and responsibilities in a law enforcement agency. *The Police Chief, 78*, 52.

Troxell, R. (2008). *Indirect exposure to the trauma of others: The experience of 911 telecommunicators* (Doctoral dissertation). Retrieved from ProQuest Dissertations and Theses. (Accession Order No. AAT 333542).

SUMMARY SHEET:
Reaching the Unseen First Responder With EMDR Therapy: Treating 911 Trauma in Emergency Telecommunicators

5A

Jim Marshall and Sara G. Gilman
SUMMARY SHEET BY MARILYN LUBER

Name: _____ Diagnosis: _____

☑ Check when task is completed, response has changed, or to indicate symptoms or diagnosis.

Note: This material is meant as a checklist for your response. Please keep in mind that it is only a reminder of different tasks that may or may not apply to your client.

The Nature of 911 TCs Stressors and Exposures to Traumatic Events

Tasks:

- ☐ Monitor numerous phone lines
- ☐ Access multiple computer applications
- ☐ Monitor video and alarm information systems
- ☐ Perform multiple tasks on each individual incident
- ☐ Many types of emergencies involve a high degree of emotional labor
- ☐ Rapidly employ extraordinary judgment and critical decision-making

Additional responsibilities may be assigned to the 911 TC on location at the law enforcement agency, such as the following:

- ☐ Handling warrants
- ☐ Clerical duties
- ☐ Processing inmates

The 911 TC's Approach to Dealing with Emotional Distress
This LEO Emotion Code could be stated as a set of cognitions:

- I must, in appearance and reality, be self-controlled and strong at all times.
- Showing and feeling vulnerable emotion (such as fear or sorrow) is synonymous with losing control: it is therefore weak, unhelpful, and inappropriate.
- I need to avoid feeling and expressing theses emotions.

Stress-Related Medical Conditions

Due to combination of factors:
- ☐ Highly stressful work conditions
- ☐ Their suppressive Emotion Code
- ☐ Lack of skills training to boost resilience and enable effective stress management

Symptoms:
- ☐ Obesity
- ☐ Symptoms of major depression
- ☐ Self-medicating behaviors
- ☐ Chronic excessive use of sick/medical leave
- ☐ Low level of employee retention—resulting in forced overtime leading to sleep deprivation, increased susceptibility to chronic stress and other stress-related problems, increased susceptibility to compassion fatigue
- ☐ Important to screen for depression, sleep disorders, substance abuse, and eating behavior

Treating 911 Trauma in Emergency Telecommunicators Protocol Script Notes

Negative and Positive Cognitions Common Among 911 Telecommunicators

Cognitions Related to Responsibility

Inordinate sense of responsibility for life and death of their first responders and how they measure their worth. Responsibility cognitions:

Related to dispatching officers via radio:

- ☐ "He died (or was injured) because I sent him there."
- ☐ "It's my fault: he's is down/hurt/dead because of a mistake I made."
- ☐ "He would still be okay (or alive) if only I had..."
- ☐ "I failed my officer: I am a failure." (Note the familial sense of responsibility implied by "my.")
- ☐ "I must do everything perfectly so my officers don't die, so they come home."

Related to managing calls from citizens regarding emergency medical, police, and fire services:

- ☐ "The baby wouldn't have died if I had... (e.g., guided CPR administration better)"
- ☐ "The man wouldn't have committed suicide if only I had..."
- ☐ "This house fire tragedy might not have happened if I had gotten address (sooner/accurately)."

Cognitions Related to Safety

911 TCs psychologically present at the scene where others at risk. Safety cognitions:

- ☐ "I shouldn't be reacting like this (e.g., fear, horror, helplessness): I wasn't even there!"
- ☐ "Even though I wasn't there, I can't shake these images in my mind."
- ☐ "I just don't feel like I can let my guard down."
- ☐ "I'm the 'shit magnet' at our PSAP: It's gonna just keep happening."

Support: normal response to abnormal circumstances; physical distance from a trauma scene does not protect from traumatization; it is normal to struggle with feeling unsafe afterward.

Cognitions Related to Control

911 TCs are not on the scene and do not have all of the crucial information; that heightens stress and lack of control. EMDR can help resolve such aspects of their experience, including:

- ☐ Imaginal perception vs. actual visual perception
- ☐ Incomplete information crucial to disposition
- ☐ Lack of timely closure

Control cognitions:

☐ "Even though I know now that he survived, it doesn't feel that way."
☐ "I can't stand not knowing what's going to happen"
☐ "I have no control."
☐ "I dread working the radio (dispatching field responders) now."

Treating 911 Trauma in Emergency Telecommunicators Protocol Script

Initiating EMDR With 911 Telecommunicators: Establishing Rapport

Establishing an Alliance With the Telecommunicator

CONVEY RESPECT FOR THE 911 PROFESSIONAL

"To help me learn more about your work as a 911 professional, if I were sitting at your console with you, what would I see you doing—what would be happening? Could you just take a few minutes to teach me?" _____

State understanding of 911 TC's response.

*"I now can truly understand how demanding and important your work is."*_____ (state any personal encounter or time helped by 911 TC).

_____

"You have told me a great deal just now about the 911 profession. I hope that you will continue to let me know—as we go—any more information that I need to know about your work."

DEFUSE TREATMENT ANXIETY

"So much is expected of emergency responders including 911: to always be strong, to suck up emotions, and to get the job done. So, it's pretty normal to be skeptical of therapy. I just want you to know I actually think being a skeptical consumer of therapy is a smart way to start. Can you relate to being at all skeptical?"

Questions about psychology and practice: _____

_____

_____

Relationship between the 911 telecommunicators at your PSAP and field responders: _____

What's most rewarding/stressful about your job: _____

Without allying with the 911 TC against his administration:

"At your PSAP, what kind of support do they provide for you and your peers after the worst calls?"

Phase 1: History Taking

Brief overview of recent critical incident: _____

_____

_____

Symptoms: _____

_____

_____

Impact on TC: _____

_____

_____

_____

_____

Brief history of previous critical incidents: _____

_____

_____

_____

_____

Medical and psychological history: _____

_____

_____

Family history: _____

_____

_____

Work situation: _____

_____

_____

Predictable Blocking Beliefs

In accord with the Emotion Code and related anxiety-based ambivalence about identifying and processing distressing emotions, telecommunicators may be impeded in joining initially with the therapist, and in the assessment and treatment processes. To foster their success in resolving this, the clinician can suggest:

> *"I know that 911 professionals need to put their own emotions aside to do their job; yet there's also a lot of peer pressure to follow the old paramilitary way of dealing with emotions—you know: 'suck it up' and just keep going. Can you relate to that?"* _____

_____

Ask how much 911 TCs can relate to each of these beliefs:

It is not OK to express emotions... _____

_____

I will be judged as weak if I do... _____

To be accepted by our sworn personnel, I can't show if I am distressed by a really bad call.

_____

Worldview

Excessive production of stress hormones is associated with the chronic stress response, fueling negative emotion and distorted cognition. The clinician can consider inviting the resistant and cynical 911 TC to teach about these factors, and then help normalize the responses.

"I understand that doing emergency response work dealing with the public at their worst can set up telecommunicators to get a bit cynical (she or he will likely laugh at this point). *Is that accurate?"* _____

_____

"How do you think you've become more cynical?" _____

_____

"How do you think that's been helpful and maybe unhelpful for you?" _____

_____

Dehumanizing Callers

To explore for the presence of blocking beliefs related to the dehumanizing defense (usually a self-protective strategy in need of replacement with one that is more adaptive), the clinician can inquire by stating the following:

"You definitely can't pour out empathy in some big way for every caller. There is only so much of you to go around. So it's normal if you think something like: 'If I allow myself to feel empathy for this caller, it will suck me dry. I don't want give away any more of myself. So I just learned to shut it off.' Can you relate?" _____

_____

"Well, you have a right to protect yourself emotionally with boundaries. It's just a matter of degree. If you think it has gotten out of balance, then we can work together so you can choose when and how much empathy to give as fits for each situation. What do you think?" _____

_____

Phase 2: Preparation

Explanation of trauma ☐ Completed
Explanation of EMDR ☐ Completed
Explanation of BLS ☐ Completed

Resources Used:
- ☐ Safe Place
- ☐ The Container
- ☐ Managing Heart Rate Variability
- ☐ Identifying Positive Strengths and Skills
- ☐ Activating Positive Career Memories
- ☐ Other _____

Phase 3: Assessment

Past Memories

1. *Narrative History: Frame by Frame*

    Event narrative: _____

    _____

    _____

    _____

    _____

    _____

2. *Target: Most Disturbing Aspect/Moment of the Memory*

    Target/Memory/Image: _____

    NC: _____

    PC: _____

    VoC: _____/7

    Emotions: _____

    SUD: ___/10

    Sensation: _____

3. *Target: Remainder of the Narrative in Chronological Order*

    Target/Memory/Image: _____

    NC: _____

    PC: _____

    VoC: _____/7

    Emotions: _____

    SUD: ___/10

    Sensation: _____

Repeat Phases 4 through 5 for each segment of the memory until all of the targets have been processed. Phases 6 through 7 are done after the final part of the memory has been processed. The body tensions and sensations will then be able to dissipate more completely.

Phase 4: Desensitization

The work in Phase 4 follows the Standard EMDR Protocol.

Introducing EMDR Therapy Processing

> "We will be doing sets of the bilateral activation. The BLS is important so your whole brain will assist in the refiling of this information. Remember, it is your own brain that is doing the work and you are the one in control. I will ask you to begin by focusing on the target and to follow my fingers (or any other BLS you are using). Just let whatever happens, happen, and when I stop the eye movements we will talk about what came up. Any new information that comes to mind is connected in some way, so you can tell me about whatever comes up. If you want to stop for any reason, just let me know."

> "Bring up the picture and the words _____ (clinician repeats the NC) and notice where you feel it in your body. Now follow _____ (state BLS)."

After all of the targets are reprocessed, go to visualizing the entire sequence of the event with eyes closed.

4. *Visualize Entire Sequence of Event With Eyes Closed*
   If disturbance, reprocess.
   Client can view entire event from start to finish, without emotional, cognitive, or somatic distress. ☐ Completed
5. *Visualize Entire Sequence With Eyes Open and Install PC*
   Visualize sequence of events with eyes open + PC + BLS. Stop signal when finished.
   ☐ Completed

Phase 6: Body Scan

6. *Body Scan*—only at the end of processing all targets and memories of event
   Original memory + PC + Scan Body

   Unresolved tension/tightness/unusual sensation: _____

   _____

Do BLS until subsides.

Phase 7: Closure—Grounding Is Important

> "You have worked hard today and I wanted to remind you how important it is to 'reboot' or 'ground' yourself in between sessions by using any of the resources we worked on earlier. Do you have any questions about that?"

Remind the client how to use the imaginary container to hold any stressful thoughts or feelings of any other old calls and events.

> "Imagine a container that has a lid. With the lid open, please put any thoughts, feelings, and/or images into the container. Let me know when you have done that. Great. Now, it is time to close the lid and lock it down. Anything that is in there can be processed later. The container is so that you can know that everything is safely put away and you do not have to think about it now."

> If this is the first experience of EMDR Therapy for the 911 TC, it is important to inform the client of what might occur in between sessions: "Things may come up or they may not. If they do, great: this is normal. If nothing does, that is normal too. If you are aware of a memory or thought, write it down,

and we can check on it next time. If you get any new memories, dreams, or situations that disturb you, just take a good snapshot, make some brief notes. It isn't necessary to record a lot of detail. Just put down enough to remind you so we can target it next time. The same thing goes for any positive dreams or situations. If negative feelings do come up, simply identify them and write them down for next time. You can also toss them into the container and then use any of the relaxation skills that we have worked with. This should help you feel more comfortable in the moment. Even if nothing comes up, make sure to practice the relaxation or heart rate coherence exercises every day and give me a call if you feel stuck or can't shake some discomfort. I can help you reboot over the phone."

It is possible the 911 TC may have a cascade of "bad" calls surface in between sessions. Making yourself available in between sessions early in treatment to help them apply skills and EMDR treatment principles can secure treatment outcomes and foster alliance and motivation to remain in therapy.

Closure: ☐ Completed

Phase 8: Reevaluation

SUDS of Incident: _____/10

New material: _____

_____

Reprocessed necessary targets: ☐ Completed
EMDR helpful in daily life: ☐ Completed

7. Present Stimuli That Trigger the Disturbing Memory/Reaction
   List for Triggering Situations/Events That Are Stimuli for LEOs

1. _____
2. _____
3. _____

Target/Memory/Image: _____

_____

NC: _____

PC: _____

VoC: _____/7

Emotions: _____

SUD: ___/10

Sensation: _____

Triggers: ☐ Completed

Future Template

8. Create a Future Template

IMAGE AS FUTURE TEMPLATE: IMAGINING POSITIVE OUTCOMES
Incorporate a detailed template for dealing adaptively with an appropriate future situation (e.g., coping with a similar situation or coping with present triggers/reminders; see above).

Image of coping effectively with/or in goal in future: _____

PC: _____

New quality/attribute needed: _____

What you see as handling the situation: _____

Thinking, feeling, and experiencing in body: _____

Blocks/anxieties/fears in future scene: _____

1. _____
2. _____
3. _____

Do BLS. If they do not resolve, ask for other qualities needed to handle the situation. Other new information, resources, or skills to comfortably visualize coping in the future:

1. _____
2. _____
3. _____

If blocks are not resolved, identify unprocessed material and process with Standard EMDR Protocol:

1. _____
2. _____
3. _____

Target/Memory/Image: _____

NC: _____

PC: _____

VoC: _____/7

Emotions: _____

SUD: ___/10

Sensation: _____

If there are no blocks, move on.

Future Image + PC + Sensations associated with future scenes + BLS

Do a Body Scan (Close Eyes + Image of Future + PC + Attention to Different Parts of Your Body + Report Tension, Tightness/Unusual Sensation).

If there is a sensation, process until the sensation subsides and the VoC = 7/ecological resolution and move on to the movie as a future template.

VoC: ___/7

Image as Future Template: ☐ Completed

Resources

- 911 Wellness Foundation, www.911wellness.com
- EMDR International Association, www.emdria.org
- The Institute of HeartMath, www.heartmath.com
- International Critical Incident Stress Foundation, www.icisf.org
- SafeCallNow.org
- The National Emergency Number Association, www.nena.org

    The National Emergency Number Association (NENA) developed a new 911 industry *Standard on Acute, Traumatic and Chronic Stress Management.* This standard states that all PSAPs "shall develop Comprehensive Stress Management Programs (CSMPs) for all personnel." These CSMPs are required to assure telecommunicators access to eight types of resources:
    - Training in stress management
    - On-site PSAP educational materials and resources about stress-related risks; information about available local and online resources to manage stress
    - Critical Incident Stress Management services, including diffusing and debriefing sessions
    - Employee Assistance Programs
    - Identify (and encourage proactive use of) local therapists specializing in treatment of stress and traumatic stress disorders
    - Peer support delivered by trained personnel
    - Provide comprehensive, ongoing certification training in all emergency call types
    - PSAPs are highly encouraged to implement personal health incentivizing programs (NENA, 2013)

Reference

National Emergency Number Association (NENA), PSAP Operations Committee, 9-1-1 Acute/Traumatic and Chronic Stress Working Group. (2013, August 5). *NENA Standard on 9-1-1 Acute/Traumatic and Chronic Stress Management* (NENA STA 002). USA: NENA.

EMDR Therapy and Grief and Mourning

Issues of grief and mourning are universal and are reported on a regular basis in our treatment rooms. Whether a loss is expected or a surprise, it reverberates through our lives in many ways. We may not feel it at first but then, in a quiet moment, that song or photograph may transport us into a wave of grief. Even when the loss is distant, when it touches a meaningful place inside us, we can feel the upsurge of distress run through us unless we put it away into the dark recesses in our minds. However, despite our best efforts to silence our feelings, they come out uninvited at times we do not expect.

Depending on our ability to address our pain, we can move through the process of mourning in a fairly smooth and steady manner, or in ways that we deny, avoid, or reject the process until it surges into our lives without our even recognizing the source. EMDR Therapy provides a helpful framework to think about grief and how our past is informing how we experience grief in the present. It assists us in confronting the loss, understanding the effect it has on us, and then helping us in the process of reconnecting with our own lives without the significant other.

Francine Shapiro understood the nature of loss and the intense effect it can have on us. In the normal course of events, when a loved one dies, we grieve our loss and mourn the departure of the person. Over time, we resolve our loss and continue our journey in life without our significant other. Sometimes, for many reasons, the level of suffering and despair is so great that the normal adjustment to the loss is impaired. Through our work with EMDR Therapy, we can assist clients to understand and process these blockages and mourn in a way that is more balanced, and allows for the normal emotions of sadness and grief. EMDR Therapy does not eliminate healthy, appropriate emotions, especially grief, but allows clients to mourn with a greater sense of inner peace.

The protocol for grief and mourning is similar to the Standard EMDR Protocol for trauma. Shapiro set a guideline for using EMDR Therapy with "excessive grief" in her text *Eye Movement Desensitization and Reprocessing: Basic Principles, Protocols and Procedures* (1995, 2001). In the "Protocol for Excessive Grief," she has five steps to access the important issues when a client is suffering from "excessive grief" Step 1—Process the actual events, including the loved one's suffering or death; Step 2—Process any intrusive images that are occurring; Step 3—Process the nightmare images; Step 4—Process any stimuli or triggers associated with the grief experience; and Step 5—Address issues of personal responsibility, mortality, or previous unresolved losses. Ultimately, the goal is for your client to accept the bereavement and think back on his or her life with the significant other that includes both the positive and negative aspects of the relationship.

EMDR Therapy and Grief and Mourning

Roger M. Solomon and Therese A. Rando

Introduction

Grief refers to the process of experiencing reactions to one's perception of loss. In contrast, *mourning* encompasses not only grief, but active coping with the loss through making the personal readjustments necessary to adapt to the world without the deceased, accommodate the loss within one's life, and move forward healthily in the new world (Rando, in press). A major loss can be very distressing, filled with intense anguish and emotional pain. According to the Adaptive Information Processing (AIP) model that guides eye movement desensitization and reprocessing (EMDR) Therapy (Shapiro, 2001), the distressing moments, situations, and memories associated with the loss—with their associated images, thoughts, beliefs, affects, sensations, and perceptions—can become dysfunctionally stored in the brain and can be continually or sporadically triggered. Along with complicating mourning processes, such distress can interfere with assimilation and accommodation of the memories and may prevent other memory networks with positive memories of the loved one from being accessed, experienced, and felt. EMDR Therapy has the ability to facilitate the experiencing and processing of affect and cognitions that are necessary for healthy mourning. Further, EMDR Therapy can treat complicated mourning through its capacity to address frozen or stuck aspects of distressing experiences that interfere with mourning, unblock normal mourning processes, and process emotions that complicate mourning (Solomon & Rando, 2007). Through the use of EMDR reprocessing, impediments are worked through, permitting healthy mourning processes to occur and positive associations/memories with the loved one(s) to emerge (Solomon & Rando, 2007). The emergence of felt, positive memories plays a vital role in the accommodation of loss. These memories link the world with and without the deceased and are the building blocks of an adaptive inner representation. Thus, EMDR Therapy enables the person to progress through mourning, whether uncomplicated or complicated. It is important to note that EMDR Therapy does not eliminate necessary undertakings or dilute appropriate emotions, but serves to process obstacles that complicate appropriate grief and healthy mourning. This chapter focuses on dealing with acute grief and mourning issues, and providing EMDR Therapy to assist the client through the "R" processes, and process the obstacles that can complicate them.

Research

There is limited research specifically on EMDR Therapy and grief and mourning. Sprang (2001) demonstrated the effectiveness of EMDR with mourning, comparing EMDR Therapy and Guided Mourning (GM) for treatment of complicated mourning. Of the five psychosocial measures of distress, four (State Anxiety, Impact of Event Scale, Index of Self-Esteem, and posttraumatic stress disorder [PTSD]) were found to be significantly altered by the type of treatment provided, with EMDR clients reporting the greatest reduction of PTSD symptoms. Data from the behavioral measures showed similar findings. Further, positive memories of the loved one emerged during treatment, which did not occur with GM. Hornsveld, Landwehr, Stein, Stomp, Smeets, and van den Hout (2010) conducted a study wherein participants recalled an aversive experience of loss, holding in mind the image of the most distressing scene, while either performing eye movements, listening to relaxing music, or not performing any dual-attention task (recall only). The eye movement condition was found to be more effective than recall, or recall with relaxation, in decreasing emotionality of the most distressing scene related to loss.

Rando's Conceptualization of Mourning and Traumatic Bereavement

Shapiro and Solomon (1997) describe how EMDR Therapy can be utilized in the treatment of grief and mourning by processing the trauma related to the grief and resolving issues related to responsibility, present safety, and control. However, a broader perspective on using EMDR in the treatment of grief and mourning can be achieved by integrating EMDR Therapy within a comprehensive framework. Rando (1993) has delineated such a structure for dealing with grief and mourning. This framework provides a useful structure for conceptualizing the grief and mourning processes, assessing where the mourner is within the process, monitoring progress, and providing a helpful checklist for evaluating the mourner's status.

Rando (1993) has delineated the six "R" processes of mourning (Table 6.1), which encompass what must be accomplished for the healthy accommodation of a loss.

Table 6.1 The Six "R" Processes of Mourning

1. *Recognize* the loss
   a. Acknowledge the death
   b. Understand the death
2. *React* to the separation
   a. Experience the pain
   b. Feel, identify, accept, and give some form of expression to all the psychological reactions to the loss
   c. Identify and mourn secondary losses
3. *Recollect and reexperience* the deceased and the relationship
   a. Review and remember realistically
   b. Revive and reexperience the feelings
4. *Relinquish* the old attachments to the deceased and the old Assumptive World
5. *Readjust* to move adaptively into the new world without forgetting the old
   a. Revise the assumptive world
   b. Develop a new relationship with the deceased
   c. Adopt new ways of being in the world
   d. Form a new identity
6. *Reinvest*

Source: Adapted from Rando, 1993.

Table 6.2 High-Risk Elements for Traumatic Bereavement

1. Suddenness and Lack of Anticipation
2. Violence
3. Human-Caused Event
4. Suffering (Physical or Emotional) of the Loved One Prior to the Death
5. Unnaturalness
6. Preventability
7. Intent of the Responsible Agent(s)
8. Randomness
9. Multiple Deaths
10. One's Own Personal Encounter With Death
11. Untimeliness
12. Loss of One's Child

Source: From Rando, in press.

The goal of using EMDR Therapy with mourning is to process the dysfunctionally stored memories (both past and recent) and present triggers that interfere with the six "R" processes; process any emotion that requires it; and provide appropriate psychoeducation, resource development, and future templates to enable continued progress through the "R" processes. It is important to assess readiness for EMDR Therapy and provide appropriate stabilization before commencing treatment (Shapiro, 1995, 2001).

Sudden and traumatic death poses a number of specific challenges for the mourner and creates traumatic bereavement. *Traumatic bereavement* is the state of having suffered the loss of a loved one when grief and mourning over the death are complicated or overpowered by the traumatic stress brought about by its circumstances (Rando, in press). Types of traumatic death include accident and disaster; suicide; homicide (including deaths from terrorism and war); and acute natural death, such as deaths caused by catastrophic medical events (for instance, heart attack, stroke, seizure, hemorrhage), acute medical illness (such as acute bacterial or viral infection), or acute syndromes (e.g., Sudden Infant Death Syndrome or Sudden Arrhythmia Death Syndrome). Factors associated with circumstances of a death that bring traumatic bereavement—which are known to add complications to mourning—have been identified by Rando and are delineated in Table 6.2 (Rando, in press).

EMDR and Grief and Mourning Script Notes

The remainder of this chapter delineates how to help a client through the grief and mourning processes, and illustrates how EMDR Therapy can be utilized to overcome obstacles to going through the processes of accommodation to the loss (the "R" processes).

Initial Session

During the initial session, the reason for engaging in therapy is discussed. What has happened? What symptoms are experienced and how are they interfering with the client's ability to function? Are there any factors present that can complicate the loss (see below)? History guidelines provide a direction for gathering necessary information. Not uncommonly, clients will come in with depression or anxiety symptoms that they do not connect with an earlier loss. Or, a previous loss that clients had thought they had adapted to may be an unrecognized cause of present dysfunction. For example, one man came into treatment to deal with his increasing fear of being alone, which had started with the death of his father 3 years earlier and had gotten progressively worse. In initial sessions for the newly bereaved, psychosocial education on common reactions and coping strategies can be quite useful, as acute grief is typically very frightening and clients do not necessarily understand what they are experiencing or why they are experiencing it. A discussion of symptoms and coping strategies is beyond the scope of this chapter, but this information can be obtained from a variety of sources (see, e.g., Rando, 1993). Often, the newly bereaved need reassurance that their distressing feelings and reactions are normal reactions to an intense situation.

Case Conceptualization

Rando's model provides a road map that helps the clinician and client understand where they are in the mourning processes and what has to be done to facilitate the accommodation to the loss. *People do not go through the "R" processes in a linear fashion.* The course of mourning is not linear, but waxes and wanes over time, with movement back and forth between the "R" processes. The clinician needs to assess in which "R" process a client might be "stuck," process past memories and present triggers, and provide future templates—all to facilitate movement through the "R" processes in order to reach accommodation of the loss. Case conceptualization, utilizing the AIP model, comprises History Taking (Phase 1); Preparation (Phase 2); and Phases 3–8, consisting of targeting past memories and present triggers, and providing future templates, according to where the client is stalled. A good place to start is the moment of initial realization of the loss (the past). As necessary, other past memories or present triggers that prevent progressing through the "R" processes can be targeted and future templates can be provided as appropriate.

The framework presented here and the questions posed to assess stuck points and work through them with EMDR Therapy is not a recipe. Indeed, treatment would perhaps be rendered ineffective by routinely following the scripted questions in sequence. Instead, the script that is offered is a way to access the types of questions that are helpful to ask when working with a client who is reacting to loss. The timing of the questions used is at the discretion of the therapist.

It is important to be aware that during treatment, the "R" processes *tend* to segue from one to another, with the earlier "R" processes a prerequisite to the later ones. However, often a client needs to go back and again process issues and stuck points related to earlier "R" processes. Consequently, the clinician has to continually assess client movement through the "R" processes, by assessing in which process he or she may be blocked, and processing relevant memories, present triggers, and future templates relevant to such blocks. The clinician should also be aware that progression through any of the "R" processes can be very painful. Hence, it is crucial to continually attend to the client's affect tolerance, ability to modulate emotion, and capacity to deal with pain.

Timing

- *How soon does one apply EMDR Therapy?* Often the earliest time to think about processing a memory is when the client starts to feel the emotional impact (e.g., the numbness wears off), can stay present with the emotions, and can articulate and reflect on the impact of the loss. For example, a baby was killed in an explosion and the mother was told the baby died of a head wound. In reality, there was no body to show. The mother was stuck on a negative vicarious image of what her baby must have looked like with a head wound, and could not access any other memories of her baby. Two months after the loss, EMDR processing of the trauma was provided (focusing on the negative image), resulting in the other memories arising (e.g., playing with the baby, the baby with the father, and finally the last time she said good-bye to her baby and said "I love you"). However, usually "slower is faster," with the clinician needing to take the time to help clients understand, articulate, and express the emotional impact and meaning of the loss before doing EMDR Therapy.
- *Where to start?* When the time is right, start with the issue/memory that is most predominant, troublesome, or intrusive. Usually this is the moment of realization of the loss (e.g., hearing about the death). This is often a moment of shock and disbelief. However, not uncommonly what is felt and can be a point of entry for EMDR Therapy is a past memory or issue that got triggered (e.g., the loss of my husband is

bringing up awful memories of when my father died). The client's response to the processing and what emerges determines the next step and course of therapy.

Note: The selection and sequencing of targets is determined by clients' progress through the "R" processes, with the scripted questions to determine EMDR Therapy targets aimed toward movement through a blocked process, rather than being a sequenced protocol.

Dealing With Past Unresolved Issues

These are the types of issues that are pertinent to working with patients who are going through the grieving and mourning process.

- *Attachment issues*: There may be unresolved issues with the loved one that have their roots in the mourner's early past and involve deep-seated attachment issues.
- *Trauma issues*: Loss can trigger other earlier trauma-related emotional issues, such as feelings of terror or helplessness or a need to freeze.
- *Conflicts*: Whatever conflicts the mourner had with the loved one that preceded the death do not go away. They are left still to be resolved, although the loved one is no longer here to do so. Consequently, as will be further discussed later, those individuals with significant attachment issues and/or a history of trauma or neglect involving the deceased may have further problems to deal with and resolve, along with grief and mourning issues. For example, a woman whose father had abused her found that his death precipitated significant symptoms related to unresolved relational and trauma issues, which then intermingled with her grief responses.
- *Past and present functioning assessment*: Past trauma and premorbid functioning, along with the impact of the loss on current functioning, must be carefully assessed. Treatment may need to address these long-standing problems if they predominate or complicate the clinical picture.

Note: Though it is beyond the scope of this chapter to address the treatment of pre-death issues, it is important that the clinician be alert for attachment-related problems that have their roots in the past so that they can be addressed appropriately.

The EMDR 8 Phases

During Phase 1, it is very important to identify and assess personal issues, premorbid problems, coping skills and ability, and relevant memories that need to be dealt with. If this is not accomplished before targeting memories directly related to the loss, it must take place at some point during treatment. Many people who seek treatment after a major loss have other personal issues that have been triggered, and a good percentage of them need such problems to be dealt with first.

It is important to understand the context of the loss. As adapted from *The Grief and Mourning Status Interview and Inventory* (Rando, 1993), some of the issues to explore include:

- Circumstances of the death
- Nature of the loss and its meaning to the client
- Reactions of others in the client's life
- Nature of the client's relationship with the loved one
- History of prior loss
- Current issues
- Other difficulties prior to the loss that might be pertinent

When exploring these issues, it is particularly important to assess the attachment history with the deceased, because unresolved attachment issues and conflicts might be compounded by the loss. For example, one woman never felt accepted by her mother. When the mother died, the adult daughter knew she would never get the acceptance she had always wanted, resulting in a *secondary loss* (a loss that goes along with or develops as a consequence of the death; Rando, 1984) that complicated her grief. Hence, along with the loss, attachment issues had to be dealt with. A painful moment that was targeted was when her mother was on her deathbed and the client realized that her mother's total acceptance of her would never happen. Past memories pertaining to this issue were also identified and later processed.

In Phase 2, it is important to recognize that a loss can be devastating and interfere with present functioning. Consequently, a client should be assessed for EMDR Therapy readiness and appropriate resourcing and stabilization strategies ought to be implemented. Provision of psychosocial education regarding the grief and mourning processes is also important. For instance, some clients may need education regarding normal grief symptoms, the particulars of grief and mourning processes, adaptive coping methods, life skills training, and strategies for affect management, among other things, in addition to the EMDR Therapy process.

From the case conceptualization and treatment plan, in Phases 3 to 7, use the targeting sequence plan to target each of the pertinent memories and present triggers with the Assessment based on the six "R" Processes of Mourning. The work in Phase 4 follows the Standard EMDR Protocol and this is used for each of the targets based on the six "R" processes of mourning and the EMDR Therapy three-pronged protocol.

Also, in Phases 3 to 7 (Assessment–Closure), there are several things to keep in mind. Negative Cognitions (NCs) and Positive Cognitions (PCs) may be in the usual themes of responsibility, safety, and control. Examples follow:

- *Responsibility/guilt:* Often when mourners take too much responsibility, the NC is "It's my fault." For example, clients who feel guilty and blame themselves for not being able to do something more, such as the client who was unable to do more for her mother dying of cancer; or a client who was not able to make it to his father's bedside in time to be with him when he died; or the client who thought he was a "bad son" for being the family member who made the decision to turn off the life support system when his mother was brain dead.

    The PC is often "I did the best I could," which fits when the client realizes, "What I could do I did do," or "There was nothing more I could do," or "It was beyond my control."

- *Safety*: There can also be issues of vulnerability when the death of the loved one leaves the client feeling unsafe and thinking NCs such as "I'm vulnerable," or "I am unsafe." The PC can be along the lines of being safe in the present ("I'm safe now") or that clients can deal with the sense of danger ("I can protect myself. I can cope").

- *Control:* Issues of control may arise when mourners feel they should have been able to do something (e.g., prevent the death), or should have done something to mitigate the circumstance, as with the client who watched his loved one deteriorate from an illness over time and felt so powerless (instead of feeling guilt). The NC can be "I'm powerless."

    In this situation, the PC could be "I did the best I could." Also, with the knowledge or realization that clients did what they realistically could do or did all they could do, comes the cognition "I have some control."

- *No cognition*: There are times, however, when there is so much raw, felt affect, that there may be no NC. Clients think of the loved one, have significant emotion, and not a negative thought about themselves. One father was very distraught over his daughter's death in a terrorism attack. He described knowing that it was not his fault; he did not feel in danger, or vulnerable, or powerless; it was just that his daughter was dead and it was awful. In such circumstances, when there is the raw, felt emotion and no negative self-belief (at least initially), it can be helpful to skip the NCs and PCs and continue with the protocol.

Note: This is the exception, as getting the NCs and PCs (which describe the meaning of the situation to the self) facilitates opening up memory networks and subsequent processing. It is worthwhile to take the time when one needs to get appropriate NCs and PCs; but when the raw, felt affect is extremely distressing and the client is very emotional, initiating EMDR processing can help the client get through it even with no cognitions.

During memory reprocessing (Phases 3–7), clients may be blocked. Past memories that "feed" the block or blocking beliefs must be assessed and dealt with through exploration, including floatback and affect scan. For example, one woman whose husband was killed, when targeting the moment she got the news, had the NC: "I can never be happy." Processing became blocked and use of a floatback revealed that her negative belief stemmed from interactions with a depressed mother that resulted in the belief: "If mother is not happy, I cannot be happy." These past memories had to be dealt with in order to clear up the blocks and facilitate her going through the "R" processes.

To aid in using EMDR Therapy with grief and mourning, we delineate questions to ask at each step of the 6 "R" processes. Remember, the questions given here are not a "recipe" to be followed in order. The clinician needs to assess clients for where they are in the "R" processes and provide assistance when progress is blocked or stuck. A variety of questions are provided for each "R" process to assist the clinician in determining what memories or moments of being "stuck" need to be processed. They are suggestions to provide direction for further clinical exploration and discussion, and not all are relevant or necessary.

In Phase 8: Reevaluation, as is usual with EMDR Therapy, at the next session the therapist and client can review what happened between sessions. The clinician can assess whether the results of the last session have maintained and what other memories, difficult moments, and distressing situations have occurred. Further, positive changes that have occurred and progress through the "R" processes can both be monitored. This reevaluation determines the course of the session.

EMDR Therapy and Grief and Mourning Script

A more detailed description of the questions that may be helpful in eliciting EMDR Therapy targets follows. For most "R" processes, the 3-Pronged Protocol is important to keep in mind. Questions having to do with past memories, present triggers, and future concerns are suggested to be used, as needed. Several options are offered, and the reader is cautioned that not all questions may be pertinent.

Note: This is a way to integrate the eight Phases of EMDR Therapy with the six "R" processes of mourning. It is important to remember that clients do not always go linearly through the phases and to keep in mind which phase the client is presenting with so that your intervention matches the client's need.

Phase 1: History Taking

As just described, it is important to assess the context of the client's loss. The following questions can guide the discussion, with the clinician asking appropriate follow-up questions to gather sufficient information to assess where the client is in the "R" processes.

Say, *"What were the circumstances of the death?"*

_____

_____

Say, *"Let's talk about the nature of your loss, and its meaning to you."*

_____

_____

Say, *"What are the reactions of others in your life?"* _____

_____

_____

Say, *"Let's talk about the nature of your relationship with* _____ *(name the person)."*

_____

_____

Say, *"Have you had previous losses in your life?"*

_____

_____

Say, *"What current issues are you experiencing?"*

_____

_____

Say, *"What other difficulties were you experiencing prior to the loss?"*

_____

_____

As the clinician comes to understand the history of the relationship between the client and the deceased, the context of the loss, and the client's history, the following discussion of the "R" processes can guide further assessment and EMDR Therapy target selection.

1. Recognize the Loss
For any person to commence mourning, there first must be a loss that is recognized. Then, there has to be a causal account of the death that makes sense intellectually, regarding what led up to the death and how and why it occurred as it did, even if this account is not emotionally acceptable. The two subprocesses under this "R" process are:

- Acknowledge the death
- Understand the death

EMDR Therapy: It is important to help clients deal with the traumatic or distressing initial impacts of the loss. A place to start is the moment of realization of the loss. This typically is when people first heard about the death, or what they experienced if they were present at the death. For some, however, the moment of realization could be before the death or after. For example, one person said, "When I saw him at the hospital two weeks before he died, I knew we were going to lose him." Another person said that the moment of realization was a month after the loss, which is when she and the loved one would go to the theater and he was not there.

Past Memories

Say, *"When was the moment that you became aware that* _____ *(state the person's name) was dead?"*

_____

_____

Or say, *"When was the worst moment you associate with _____ (state person's name) death?"*

_____
_____

Note: It could be hearing the news or situations before or after the death as just described.

Say, *"Was there anything about the circumstances of _____'s (state the person's name) death (such as anything traumatic, feelings of helplessness, not being able to be present at the death, your imagination about what the loved one experienced, etc.) that is particularly distressing?"*

_____
_____

Say, *"Do you have any unpleasant images, whether personally experienced or imagined, such as what your loved one looked like, felt, or did that continue to disturb you?"*

_____
_____

Present Triggers

Say, *"What are the situations that trigger these negative images or memories?"*

_____
_____

Say, *"Are there current situations that trigger distress or are difficult to deal with?"*

_____
_____

Future Template

Use of the future template: This is applicable to help the client cope with future or anticipated distressing situations in an adaptive way. Future templates may not always be applicable at the time of processing the distress associated with initial realization of the loss.

Say, *"Let's talk about how you would like to manage/handle/cope with the distressing present situations in the future."*

_____
_____

2. React to the Separation

Once the reality of the death has been recognized, the mourner must react to that reality. This entails contending with pain, other psychological reactions to the loss, and secondary losses (e.g., loss of companionship, having to move as a result of economic changes, or loss of a retirement plan). The three subprocesses under this "R" process are:

- Experience the pain

- Feel, identify, accept, and give some form of expression to all the psychological reactions to the loss
- Identify and mourn secondary losses

EMDR Therapy: To utilize EMDR Therapy, identify moments/situations (present triggers) where the person experienced significant distress, and moments where the person experienced secondary loss.

Present Triggers

Sometimes it may be helpful to start with the acute distress (emotional pain) and target when it began.

Say, *"What is the most significant pain you are having now, and when did it start?"*

_____

_____

Say, *"Tell me about what you are currently feeling concerning the loss of _____ (state person's name), and specific moment(s) and situations where your reactions have been particularly strong."*

_____

_____

Say, *"As a result of _____'s (state person's name) loss, what other changes/losses have occurred for you?"*

_____

_____

Say, *"What are the moments where you experienced significant distress over these changes/losses?"*

_____

_____

3. Recollect and Reexperience the Deceased and the Relationship
To make the necessary changes ultimately to accommodate the reality of a significant person's death into one's life, the mourner will have to let go of the previous attachments to the deceased and the old assumptive world that have been rendered obsolete by the death. For this to occur, the emotional investment of the survivor must first be removed from those prior attachments. This requires that in this "R" process the mourner review the attachment, and feel the emotions that go along with the memories associated with it. This is necessary to enable changes to be made in subsequent "R" processes. The two subprocesses under this "R" process are:

- Review and remember realistically
- Revive and reexperience the feelings

EMDR Therapy: EMDR Therapy can be utilized to process painful memories involving the deceased. It is often particularly helpful with this "R" process, as positive memories with associated affect often emerge after the processing of painful moments or memories (Solomon & Rando, 2007).

Past Memories

Say, *"When you review and remember your relationship with _____ (state the person's name), are there any painful memories that are still with you?"*

Say, *"Are there some specific memories concerning problems that were never resolved while _____ (state the person's name) was alive?"*

Say, *"Are there particular memories that are difficult to face because of what _____ (state the person's name) did or did not do?"*

Say, *"Is there unfinished business between you and _____ (state person's name)?"*

Say, *"What specific moments come to mind?"*

Present Triggers

Say, *"What situations in the present are distressing or trigger distressing memories?"*

Future Template

Say, *"What are the difficult situations (e.g., in the context of evoking painful memories/emotions) you anticipate dealing with in the near future?"*

4. Relinquish the Old Attachments to the Deceased and the Old Assumptive World
The world changes significantly with the death of a loved one. The underpinnings of one's life can be irrevocably changed and the mourner must learn to live in a new world that does not include the beloved. To adapt to this new way of living, clients have to let go of old attachments and assumptions that no longer fit. Only in this way will room be made for

Say, *"Are there situations where life difficulties demonstrate how much you want things to be the way they were when your loved one was alive?"*

_____

Example of questions concerning difficulty in developing a new relationship with the deceased:

Say, *"Are there times/situations where you find it difficult to make the transition to loving in absence and being connected to a person who is no longer physically present?"*

_____

Examples of questions concerning difficulty in adopting new ways of being in the world:

Say, *"Are there situations and moments where you find it difficult to adapt to the world without _____ (say the loved one's name)?"*

_____

Say, *"Are there times when you have been frightened about the changes that you have made or have to make?"*

_____

Say, *"Are there moments where you resist making changes so you don't have to realize the implications of your loss?"*

_____

Examples of questions concerning difficulty forming a new identity:

Say, *"Are there situations or moments that evoke guilt/ambivalence/resistance/fear about assuming new roles and behaviors?"*

_____

Say, *"Are there moments/situations where you find it difficult to know who you are in the absence of _____ (say the loved one's name)?"*

_____

Future Template

Note: The future template should be provided when appropriate when presenting challenging situations that reflect the difficulty in adapting to the new world without the deceased. Anticipated future difficulties can also be discussed.

Say, *"What situations do you anticipate will be difficult to deal with/adapt to?"*

_____
_____

6. Reinvest

The last of the mourning processes involves the mourner's reinvesting in a new life without the loved one. The emotional energy formerly directed toward preservation and maintenance of the relationship with the loved one now must be redirected toward emotionally rewarding investments in other people, objects, roles, hopes, goals, and so forth.

EMDR Therapy: Obstacles to moving on can be explored and dealt with. Relevant past memories and present triggers can be identified for processing. The mourner may need new skills, which can be taught and enhanced through the future template.

Past Memories

If past memories are connected to current difficulties, they can be processed first with the Standard EMDR Protocol.

Say, *"Are there any past memories that are still getting in the way of moving forward?"*

_____
_____

Present Triggers

Say, *"When and where are you having difficulty investing in life now?"*

_____
_____

Say, *"What are the situations where it is difficult for you to go forward?"*

_____
_____

Say, *"Are there moments/situations where fear/anxiety regarding the future (including relationships and other involvements) are experienced?"*

_____
_____

Future Template

Note: The future template should be provided for each present trigger relevant to reinvesting in life. In addition, anticipated future difficulties, needed changes, and learning of new skills and building of new resources can be explored.

Say, *"What future difficulties do you anticipate in going forward in life?"*

_____
_____

Say, *"What are some of the changes you would need to make to move forward?"*

_____

_____

Note: Be sure the client has the appropriate skills to go forward before doing the future template.

Say, *"Can you imagine yourself doing this?"*

_____

_____

Say, *"What new skills or resources will you need to reinvest in this new life without your loved one?"*

_____

_____

Phase 2: Preparation

Psychosocial education regarding the grief and mourning process is important. For example, typical reactions involve:

- Emotional reactions (e.g., sadness, anger, guilt, anxiety, numbness)
- Cognitive reactions (e.g., disbelief, denial, confusion, preoccupation with deceased, meaninglessness)
- Physical reactions (e.g., agitation and nervousness, weakness, lack of energy, heart palpitations, headaches)
- Behavioral reactions (e.g., sleep disturbance, appetite disturbance, avoidance behaviors, crying, "searching" for deceased)
- Social reactions (e.g., social withdrawal, decreased interest in relationships, overdependence on others, jealousy of others without loss, boredom)

For a complete list of reactions, see Rando (in press).

Resource Material

Some mourners may not need a lot of stabilization and others may benefit greatly from safe/calm place, resource installation, and other stabilization strategies. Deep breathing exercises, mindfulness, visualization, and other coping strategies may be helpful and provided as needed. Resource material for adaptive coping methods for the grief and mourning process, include Pearlman et al. (2014), Rando (1993, in press), and Worden (2008).

Explanation of EMDR

Say, *"When a trauma occurs, it seems to be locked in the nervous system with the original picture, sounds, thoughts, and feelings. The eye movements we use in EMDR seem to unlock the nervous system and allow the brain to process the experience. That may be what is happening in REM or dream sleep—the eye movements may help to process the unconscious material. It is important to remember that it is your own brain that will be doing the healing and you are the one in control."*

Resources

Deep breathing exercises, mindfulness, visualization, and other coping strategies may be helpful and provided as needed.

Phase 3: Assessment

From the case conceptualization and treatment plan, use the targeting sequence plan to target each of the pertinent memories, with the assessment based on the 6 "R" processes of mourning.

Incident

Say, *"The memory that we will start with today is _____ (select the next incident to be targeted)."*

_____
_____
_____

Picture

Say, *"What picture represents the entire _____ (state the issue)?"*

_____
_____
_____

If there are many choices or if the client becomes confused, the clinician assists by asking the following:

Say, *"What picture represents the most traumatic part of _____ (state the issue)?"*

_____
_____
_____

Negative Cognition (NC)

Say, *"What words best go with the picture that express your negative belief about yourself now?"*

_____

Positive Cognition (PC)

Say, *"When you bring up that picture or _____ (state the issue), what would you like to believe about yourself now?"*

_____
_____

Validity of Cognition (VoC)

Say, *"When you think of the incident* (or picture), *how true do those words* _____ (clinician repeats the PC) *feel to you now on a scale of 1 to 7, where 1 feels completely false and 7 feels completely true?"*

1	2	3	4	5	6	7

(completely false)   (completely true)

Emotions

Say, *"When you bring up the picture or* _____ (state the issue) *and those words* _____ (clinician states the NC), *what emotion do you feel now?"*

Subjective Units of Disturbance (SUD)

Say, *"On a scale of 0 to 10, where 0 is no disturbance or neutral and 10 is the highest disturbance you can imagine, how disturbing does it feel now?"*

0	1	2	3	4	5	6	7	8	9	10

(no disturbance)   (highest disturbance)

Location of Body Sensation

Say, *"Where do you feel it* (the disturbance) *in your body?"*

_____

_____

_____

Phase 4: Desensitization

The work in Phase 4 follows the Standard EMDR Protocol; this is used for each of the targets based on the 6 "R" processes of mourning and the EMDR Therapy 3-Pronged Protocol.

To begin, say the following:

Say, *"Now, remember, it is your own brain that is doing the healing and you are the one in control. I will ask you to mentally focus on the target and to* _____ (state BLS you are using). *Just let whatever happens, happen, and we will talk at the end of the set. Just tell me what comes up, and don't discard anything as unimportant. Any new information that comes to mind is connected in some way. If you want to stop, just raise your hand."*

Then say, *"Bring up the picture and the words* _____ (clinician repeats the NC) *and notice where you feel it in your body. Now follow* _____ (state BLS)."

_____

_____

This procedure is to be repeated until the SUDs = 0. Then the PC is installed. Each traumatic event associated with the problem that is not reprocessed during the normal course of the first target needs to be processed using this protocol until the SUDs reach an ecological 1 or 0 and the PC is installed.

Phase 5: Installation

Say, *"How does _____ (repeat the PC) sound?"*

_____
_____

Say, *"Do the words _____ (repeat the PC) still fit, or is there another positive statement that feels better?"*

_____
_____

If the client accepts the original PC, the clinician should ask for a VoC rating to see if it has improved.

Say, *"As you think of the incident, how do the words feel to you now on a scale of 1 to 7, where 1 feels completely false and 7 feels completely true?"*

1   2   3   4   5   6   7

(completely false)   (completely true)

Say, *"Think of the event and hold it together with the words _____ (repeat the PC)."*

Do a long set of bilateral stimulation (BLS) to see if there is more processing to be done.

Phase 6: Body Scan

Say, *"Close your eyes and keep in mind the original memory and the positive cognition. Then bring your attention to the different parts of your body, starting with your head and working downward. Any place you find any tension, tightness, or unusual sensation, tell me."*

Future Template

For installing the future template, instruct clients by asking them to imagine a future situation that they have avoided. In this situation, the preferred behavior is expressed.

Install the Future Template

Say, *"OK, we have reprocessed all of the targets that we needed to do that were on your list. Now, let's anticipate what will happen when you are faced with _____ (state the fear).*

_____
_____

Say, *"What picture do you have in mind?"*

_____
_____

Say, *"I would like you to imagine yourself coping effectively with _____ (state the fear trigger) in the future. Bring up this picture and say to yourself:*

'I can handle it,' and feel the sensations. OK, have you got it? Follow my fingers (or any other forms of BLS)."

_____

_____

Say: "Bring up the picture again, and rate it on a scale from 1 to 7 where 1 feels completely false and 7 feels completely true. To what extent do you think you can manage to really do it?"

1   2   3   4   5   6   7

(completely false)   (completely true)

Install with sets of eye movements until a maximum level of VoC has been achieved.

If there is a block, meaning that even after 10 or more installations the VoC is still below 7, there are more targets that need to be identified and addressed. The therapist should use the Standard EMDR Protocol to address these targets before proceeding with the template (see Worksheets in Appendix A). Also evaluate whether clients need any new information, resources, or skills to be able to comfortably visualize the future coping scene. Introduce this needed information or skill.

Say, "What would you need to feel confident in handling the situation?"

_____

_____

Or say, "What is missing from your handling of this situation?"

_____

_____

Use BLS. If blocks are not resolved, identify unprocessed material and process with Standard EMDR Protocol.

Future Template as Movie

Say, "This time, I'd like you to imagine yourself stepping into the scene of a future confrontation with the object or the situation for which the future template was meant (e.g., going to a place you both went together). Close your eyes and play a movie of this happening, from the beginning until the end. Imagine yourself coping with any challenges that come your way. Notice what you are seeing, thinking, feeling, and experiencing in your body. While playing this movie, let me know if you hit any blocks. If you do, just open your eyes and let me know. If you don't hit any blocks, let me know when you have viewed the whole movie."

_____

_____

If clients encounter a block and open their eyes, this is a sign for the therapist to instruct clients as follows:

Say, "Say to yourself 'I can handle it' and follow my fingers (introduce a set of eye movements)."

To provide the clinician with an indication regarding the clients' self-efficacy, ask them to rate their response on a VoC scale from 1 to 7. This procedural step may give the clinician feedback on the extent to which the goals are met.

Say, *"As you think of the incident, how do the words feel, from 1 being completely false to 7 being completely true?"*

1   2   3   4   5   6   7

(completely false)   (completely true)

If clients are able to play the movie from start to finish with a sense of confidence and satisfaction, clients are asked to play the movie once more from the beginning to the end, BLS is introduced, and the PC "I can handle it" is installed. In a sense, this movie is installed as a future template.

Say, *"OK, play the movie one more time from beginning to end and say to yourself 'I can handle it.' Go with that."*

_____

_____

Phase 7: Closure

Say, *"Things may come up or they may not. If they do, great. Write it down and it can be a target for next time. You can use a log to write down triggers, images, thoughts or cognitions, emotions, and sensations; you can rate them on our 0 to 10 scale where 0 is no disturbance or neutral and 10 is the worst disturbance. Please write down the positive experiences, too."*

"If you get any new memories, dreams, or situations that disturb you, just take a good snapshot. It isn't necessary to give a lot of detail. Just put down enough to remind you so we can target it next time. The same thing goes for any positive dreams or situations. If negative feelings do come up, try not to make them significant. Remember, it's still just the old stuff. Just write it down for next time. Then use the tape or the Safe Place exercise to let go of the disturbance as far as possible. Even if nothing comes up, make sure to use the tape every day and give me a call if you need to."

Phase 8: Reevaluation

Say, *"Please tell me about any new material from last time and/or the results that you recorded in your log."*

_____

_____

Subjective Units of Disturbance

Say, *"On a scale of 0 to 10, where 0 is no disturbance or neutral and 10 is the highest disturbance you can imagine, how disturbing does it feel now?"*

0   1   2   3   4   5   6   7   8   9   10

(no disturbance)   (highest disturbance)

Check treatment plan to make sure all memories, triggers, and future issues are resolved.

_____

_____

Summary

Any significant loss involves grief (the reaction to the loss), and mourning (the processes required for healthy assimilation of and accommodation to the loss). The six "R" processes are presented as a framework to understand grief and mourning. EMDR Therapy can be utilized to facilitate these processes and to process any obstacles to them.

References

Hornsveld, H. K., Landwehr, F., Stein, W., Stomp, M., Smeets, S., & van den Hout, M. A. (2010). Emotionality of loss-related memories is reduced after recall plus eye movements but not after recall plus music or recall only. *Journal of EMDR Practice and Research, 4,* 106–112.

Pearlman, P. A., Wortman, C. B., Feuer, C. A., Farber, C. H., & Rando, T. A. (2014). *Treating traumatic bereavement: A practitioner's guide.* New York, NY: Guilford Press.

Rando, T. A. (1984). *Grief, dying, and death: Clinical interventions for caregivers.* Champaign, IL: Research Press.

Rando, T. A. (1993). *Treatment of complicated mourning.* Champaign, IL: Research Press.

Rando, T. A. (in press). *Coping with the sudden death of your loved one: A self-help handbook for traumatic bereavement.* Indianapolis, IN: Dog Ear Publishing.

Shapiro, F. (1995). *Eye movement desensitization and reprocessing: Basic principles, protocols, and procedures.* New York, NY: Guilford Press.

Shapiro, F. (2001). *Eye movement desensitization and reprocessing: Basic principles, protocols and procedures* (2nd ed.). New York, NY: Guilford Press.

Solomon, R., & Rando, T. (2007). Utilization of EMDR in the treatment of grief and mourning. *Journal of EMDR Practice and Research, 1*(2), 109–117.

Sprang, G. (2001). The use of eye movement desensitization and reprocessing (EMDR) in the treatment of traumatic stress and complicated mourning: Psychological and behavioral outcomes. *Research on Social Work Practice,* 11, 300–320.

Solomon, R. M., & Shapiro, F. (1997). Eye movement desensitization and reprocessing: An effective therapeutic tool for trauma and grief. In C. Figley, B. Bride, & M. Nicholas (Eds.) *Death and trauma* (pp. 231–247). Washington, DC, Taylor and Francis.

Worden, W. J. (2008). *Grief counseling and grief therapy: A handbook for the mental health practitioner.* (fourth edition). New York, NY: Springer.

SUMMARY SHEET:
EMDR Therapy and Grief and Mourning

6A

Roger M. Solomon and Therese A. Rando
SUMMARY SHEET BY MARILYN LUBER

Name: _____ Diagnosis: _____

Medications: _____

Test Results: _____

☑ Check when task is completed, response has changed, or to indicate symptoms.

Note: This material is meant as a checklist for your response. Please keep in mind that it is only a reminder of different tasks that may or may not apply to your incident.

Rando's Conceptualization of Mourning and Traumatic Bereavement and EMDR Therapy

Six "R" Processes of Mourning (Rando, 1993)

1. Recognize the Loss
    a. Acknowledge the death
    b. Understand the death
2. React to the Separation
    a. Experience the pain
    b. Feel, identify, accept, and give some form of expression to all the psychological reactions to the loss
    c. Identify and mourn secondary loss(es)
3. Recollect and Reexperience the Deceased and the Relationship
    a. Review and remember realistically
    b. Revive and reexperience the feelings
4. Relinquish the Old Attachments to the Deceased and the Relationship
5. Readjust to Move Adaptively Into the New World Without Forgetting the Old
    a. Revise the assumptive world
    b. Develop a new relationship with the deceased
    c. Adopt new ways of being in the world
    d. Form a new identity
6. Reinvest

12 High-Risk Elements for Traumatic Bereavement (Rando, in Press)

- ☐ Suddenness and lack of anticipation
- ☐ Violence
- ☐ Human-caused event
- ☐ Suffering (physical or emotional) of the loved one prior to death
- ☐ Unnaturalness
- ☐ Preventability
- ☐ Intent of the responsible agent(s)
- ☐ Randomness
- ☐ Multiple deaths
- ☐ One's own personal encounter with death
- ☐ Untimeliness
- ☐ Loss of one's child

EMDR Therapy and Grief and Mourning Script Notes

Case Conceptualization and Treatment Planning

The framework presented here, and the questions to assess stuck points and work through them with EMDR Therapy, are not a recipe; treatment would perhaps be ineffective if the clinician followed the scripted questions in sequence. Instead, the script is a way to access the types of questions that are helpful to ask when working with a client who is reacting to loss; the timing of the questions and the questions used are at the discretion of the therapist.

Timing

How soon to apply EMDR?

- ☐ When client feels emotional impact, stays present with emotions, and can articulate and reflect on the impact of the loss
- ☐ "Slower is faster": the clinician should take the time to help clients understand, articulate, and express the emotional impact and meaning of the loss before doing EMDR

Where to start?

- ☐ Most predominant/troublesome/intrusive moment of realization of the loss, or
- ☐ Past memory that triggers another earlier loss

Dealing With Past Unresolved Issues

Issues pertinent to patients grieving and going through the mourning process:

- ☐ Attachment issues
- ☐ Trauma issues
- ☐ Conflicts
- ☐ Assess past and present functioning

Future Template—use in the following situations:

- ☐ A present trigger has evoked significant distress, in which case it can help the client cope with future similar events

☐ Pain has resulted in maladaptive avoidance of situations or activities, in which case it can help the client approach the avoided situation

The future template is not necessarily appropriate in the following circumstance:

☐ Processing the distressing moments when emotional pain was acutely felt

EMDR Therapy and Grief and Mourning Script

History and assessment issues (adapted from *The Grief and Mourning Status Interview and Inventory;* Rando, 1993):

Circumstances of the death: _____

_____

_____

Nature of the loss and its meaning to the client: _____

_____

_____

Reactions of others in the client's life: _____

_____

_____

Nature of the client's relationship with the loved one: _____

_____

_____

History of prior loss: _____

_____

_____

Current issues: _____

_____

_____

Other difficulties prior to the loss that might be pertinent: _____

_____

_____

To further explore where the client is in relation to the "R" processes:

1. Recognize the Loss
(a. Acknowledge the death; b. Understand the death)

Past Memories
Moment aware loved one dead: _____

Worst moment associated with death: _____

_____

Circumstances about death particularly distressing: _____

_____

Unpleasant images (personally experienced/imagined) still disturbing concerning loved one's death: _____

_____

Present Triggers
Situations triggering negative images/memories: _____

_____

Current difficult situations: _____

_____

Future Template
How to manage/handle/cope with distressing present situations in the future: _____

_____

2. React to the Separation
(a. Experience the pain; b. Feel, identify, accept, and give expression to psychological reactions to the loss; c. Identify and mourn secondary losses)

Present Triggers
Most significant pain now: _____

_____

When started: _____

_____

What currently feel about the loss: _____

_____

Other changes/losses after death: _____

_____

Moments of significant distress about these changes/losses: _____

_____

3. Recollect and Reexperience the Deceased and the Relationship
(a. Review and remember realistically; b. Revive and reexperience the feelings)

Past Memories
Painful memories of relationship still with you: _____

_____

Memories of problems never resolved: _____

Memories difficult to face because of something deceased did or didn't do: _____

_____

_____

Unfinished business between you and deceased: _____

_____

_____

Present Triggers
Situations in present distressing or triggering: _____

_____

Future Template
Anticipated difficult situations in the future: _____

_____

4. Relinquish the Old Attachments to the Deceased and the Old Assumptive World

Past Memories
Feelings of giving up assumptions/expectations reminiscent of early situations: _____

_____

_____

Present Triggers

Examples of other times difficult to let go of old connections to loved one: _____

_____

_____

When and what times feel loss strongly: _____

_____

When realized way you thought of present and future changed: _____

_____

Moments you wondered who you are in the world without loved one: _____

_____

Times you still experience you can't live without loved one, etc.: _____

_____

Future Template

Situations where unable/unwilling to make changes to adapt to reality without loved one:

_____

_____

5. Readjust to Move Adaptively Into the New World Without Forgetting the Old

(a. Revise the assumptive world; b. Develop a new relationship with the deceased; c. Adopt new ways of being in the world; d. Form a new identity)

Past Memories

Feelings adjusting to loved one's death reminding you of earlier times in life: _____

_____

Present Triggers

Moments of distress and realize world is not what you expected: _____

_____

Times when life difficulties show you how much you want it to be the way it was: _____

_____

Times when difficult to make transition to loving person in absence and being connected to a person no longer physically present: _____

Times difficult to adapt to the world without loved one: _____

Times frightened about changes you have or had to make: _____

Times resist change so don't have to realize implications of the loss: _____

Situations evoking guilt/ambivalence/resistance/fear about assuming new roles and behaviors: _____

Times when you find it difficult to know who you are in absence of loved one: _____

Future Template

Situations anticipated to be difficult to deal with/adapt to: _____

6. Reinvest

Past Memories

Memories that get in the way of moving forward: _____

Present Triggers

When and where you have difficulty investing in life now: _____

Situations where difficult to go forward: _____
Situations of fear regarding the future: _____

Future Template

Anticipated difficulties in going forward in life: _____

_____

Changes needed to move forward: _____

_____

New skills/resources needed to reinvest in new life without loved one: _____

_____

Other Important Questions:

Other people's reactions to the loss: _____

_____

Other deaths in your life that impacted you: _____

_____

Current issues besides loss: _____

_____

Difficulties before the loss: _____

_____

Phase 2: Preparation

Grief and Mourning Process and Coping Strategies

These are typical reactions in the grief and mourning process as well as coping strategies:

- ☐ Emotional reactions (e.g., sadness, anger, guilt, anxiety, numbness)
- ☐ Cognitive reactions (e.g., disbelief, denial, confusion, preoccupation with deceased, meaninglessness)
- ☐ Physical reactions (e.g., agitation and nervousness, weakness, lack of energy, heart palpitations, headaches)
- ☐ Behavioral reactions (e.g., sleep disturbance, appetite disturbance,
- ☐ avoidance behaviors, crying, "searching" for deceased)
- ☐ Social reactions (e.g., social withdrawal, decreased interest in relationships, overdependence on others, jealousy of others without loss, boredom)

Explanation of EMDR Therapy: *"When a trauma occurs, it seems to be locked in the nervous system with the original picture, sounds, thoughts, and feelings. The eye movements we use in EMDR seem to unlock the nervous system and allow the brain to process the experience. That may be what is happening in REM or dream sleep—the eye movements may help to process the unconscious material. It is important to remember that it is your own brain that will be doing the healing and you are the one in control."*

Resources

- ☐ Deep breathing exercises

☐ Mindfulness
☐ Visualization
☐ Other coping strategies

Phase 3: Assessment

From the case conceptualization and treatment plan, use the targeting sequence plan to target each of the pertinent memories, with the assessment based on the six "R" Processes of Mourning.

Target/Memory/Image: _____

_____

NC: _____

PC: _____

VoC: _____/7

Emotions: _____

SUD: _____/10

Sensation: _____

_____

Phase 4: Desensitization

Apply the Standard EMDR Protocol for all targets.

Phase 5: Installation

Install the PC

Original PC: _____

Use Original PC: _____

Use New PC (if new one is better): _____

VoC: _____/7

Incident + PC + BLS _____

Note: If you have the (new) PC and VoC for the installation, and after stimulation a cognitive association process follows, do not interrupt it by going back to the memory to take the VoC, but follow it until it ends, before going back.

Incident + PC + BLS _____

You may divide the installation of one PC into the checking and installation of two different PCs that clients connect with the event you worked with. These processes seem to be very helpful for some depressive patients.

Second PC: _____/7 _____

Incident + 2nd PC + BLS _____

Phase 6: Body Scan

Unresolved tension/tightness/unusual sensation: _____

_____

Unresolved tension/tightness/unusual sensation + BLS

Strengthen positive sensation using BLS. _____

If there is more discomfort, reprocess until discomfort subsides + BLS. Then repeat Body Scan.

_____

VoC: _____/7

Future Template

Installation of the future template (image)

Image of coping effectively with/or in the fear trigger in the future: _____

PC: (I can handle it) _____

Sensations: _____

+ BLS

VoC (I am able to handle the situation): _____/7 _____
Install until VoC = 7
If continuing to be > 7, there are more targets to be identified and addressed using the Standard EMDR Protocol.
Blocks/Anxieties/Fears in future scene: _____

1. _____
2. _____
3. _____

Do BLS. If they do not resolve, ask for other qualities needed to handle the situation or what is missing.

1. _____
2. _____
3. _____

Use BLS. If blocks are not resolved, identify unprocessed material and process with Standard EMDR Protocol.

1. _____
2. _____
3. _____

Target/Memory/Image: _____

_____

NC: _____

PC: _____

VoC: _____/7

Emotions: _____

SUD: _____/10

Sensation: _____

Video Check (Future Template as Movie)

Say, *"This time, I'd like you to imagine yourself stepping into the future. Close your eyes, and play a movie from the beginning until the end. Imagine yourself coping with any challenges that come your way. Notice what you are seeing, thinking, feeling, and experiencing in your body. While playing this movie, let me know if you hit any blocks. If you do, just open your eyes and let me know. If you don't hit any blocks, let me know when you have viewed the whole movie."*

If block(s), say, "I can handle it," and BLS. Repeat until client can go through the whole movie entirely without distress.

VoC: _____/7

If client can play movie from beginning to end with confidence and satisfaction, play the movie one more time from beginning to end + BLS: ☐ Yes ☐ No

Phase 7: Closure

Say, *"Things may come up or they may not. If they do, great; write it down and it can be a target for next time. If you get any new memories, dreams, or situations that disturb you, just take a good snapshot. It isn't necessary to give a lot of detail. Just put down enough to remind you so we can target it next time. The same thing goes for any positive dreams or situations. If negative feelings do come up, try not to make them significant. Remember, it's still just the old stuff. Just write it down for next time. Then use the tape or the Safe Place exercise to let go of the disturbance as much as possible. Even if nothing comes up, make sure to use the tape every day and give me a call if you need to."*

Phase 8: Reevaluation

New material since last session: _____

_____

Log results: _____

_____

SUDS of incident from last session: _____/10

Target resolved: ☐ Yes ☐ No

Check treatment plan to make sure that memories of relapse, intense craving triggers, and current problems are targeted and reprocessed.

References

Rando, T. A. (1993). *Treatment of complicated mourning.* Champaign, IL: Research Press.
Rando, T. A. (in press). *Coping with the sudden death of your loved one: A self-help handbook for traumatic bereavement.* Indianapolis, IN: Dog Ear Publishing.

Self-Care for Clinicians

This book is for Eye Movement Desensitization and Reprocessing (EMDR) mental health practitioners who are working with clients suffering from trauma, anxiety, and mood-related disorders. As we sit in our offices individually or in a group, we listen, observe, and feel as our clients share with us who they are. They tell us about themselves in so many ways: in whispers or shouting, by gesture or immobility, outright or in metaphor. It is our job to experience them with all of our compassion, our knowledge, and our attention. Our witnessing and experiencing of our clients are essential parts of what make our profession unique and what allow the people who sit in front of us to take the steps that they need to change. Our presence and our expertise as EMDR clinicians are what we cultivate.

It is exhilarating and it is exhausting. It engages us with every ounce of our being even when we are in pain or suffering ourselves. We often push through to honor the contract we have with our clients to give them our expertise and the best of ourselves. Our job is all-encompassing and most of us think of it as an avocation rather than a vocation. We cannot resist our clients' stories and what we can do to help. In the service of our clients, we take courses, go back to school, attend conferences, make speeches, donate our time, talk with our colleagues, stay up late thinking about a particularly delicate or difficult situation. To be a therapist is an all-encompassing experience and commitment.

Who takes care of us? We did not learn how to do that in graduate school. Often, we did not acquire it in our family of origin. If you were to type in "self-care" in the Francine Shapiro Library's EMDR bibliography in February 2015, you would have found only 11 citations! For many of us, it is a puzzle that we have not thought about. For others, we know, but we find it hard to commit to taking care of ourselves. We are too busy, others need us, we will get to it tomorrow—the list of our excuses is infinite.

In trauma response, we are beginning to understand the importance of self-care for our first responders (Jarero & Uribe, 2013) and we now have the Self-Care Standards of the Green Cross Academy of Traumatology (GCAT) for all practitioners. The Self-Care Standards advocate the following:

1. Do no harm to yourself in the line of duty when helping/treating others.
2. Attend to your physical, social, emotional, and spiritual needs as a way of ensuring high-quality services to those who look to you for support as a human being.

Karen Alter-Reid's Trauma Recovery Network (TRN) came up with a plan called "Caring for Our Own Therapists" (Alter-Reid, 2013). Their way was to provide the support as part of the model they used to set up their TRN. When setting up their response to the Newtown,

Connecticut, tragedy, they called on friends, EMDR Humanitarian Assistance Program (HAP) therapists across the country—colleagues who had experience in other disaster situations—to give them support, counsel, consultation, and materials. They gave butterfly hugs (Artigas & Jarero, 2014), did breath work (Kabat-Zinn, 2012), and learned pendulation techniques (Levine, 1997). They emphasized buffering against vicarious trauma, compassion fatigue, and secondary PTSD by promoting proper sleep, exercise, nutrition, family and friend time, body work, stress relief exercises during the meeting, and so on. When they began to think about what they could do, the list of possibilities grew.

In 1999, Derek Farrell (Farrell, 2013) experienced the profound devastation of the Marmara earthquake in Turkey. He was an observer and also part of a team of EMDR practitioners who went into the Marmara earthquake tent cities to treat the survivors. He was so dedicated that he did not realize the reverberation of that devastation inside himself. He was not tending to the signs of his own traumatization:

- Intrusive recollections—flashbacks, bad dreams, nightmares
- Clinical judgment and decision making was impaired
- Profound feelings of over-responsibility, particularly with some of my complex trauma clients
- Overworking in clinical sessions with clients
- Significant imbalance between work and personal life
- Excessive hours of working both at the National Health Service (NHS) and private practice
- Trying to be more active in controlling other people's lives
- Emotional regulation was difficult
- Diminution in confidence and self-esteem
- Quality of personal relationships deteriorated
- Sense of disconnection
- Frequent headaches and migraines
- Loss of meaning, hope, and purpose
- Blame others instead of seeking understanding and productive collaboration
- Increased sensitivity to violence and trauma (p. 510)

He charged forward until he could do so no longer. Luckily, he recognized it himself, and then he sought help. His recognition of his own distress and how he ultimately responded allowed him to create a list of the action points to consider in relation to vicarious trauma:

- If there is a preparedness to bear witness to clients' stories and be open to the multiple layers of narratives that may be involved, then accept the potential for vicarious traumatization as a real occupational possibility
- Obtain, or utilize existing, good-quality and effective clinical supervision/consultation and/or EMDR psychotherapy while at the same time being very clear about the distinction and rationale for both
- Be open and honest with yourself in acknowledging the difficulties you may be experiencing in the present
- Be open to listening to constructive feedback from clinical supervisors, managers, colleagues, friends, family, and loved ones while being mindful to hear the *positives* as well as any potential legitimate, constructive negatives
- Perform the simple things well in taking care of yourself: maintaining a healthy diet, getting regular exercise, and generally making *quality* time for yourself
- Undertake a complete review of your current client caseload, workload balance, clinical supervision/consultation commitments, teaching and learning workload, extracurricular activity, and so on.
- Revisit "old comforts," such as rereading your favorite book, watching your favorite films or television series, visiting your favorite restaurants, listening to music you have not heard for a while
- Give some critical consideration to issues such as work–life balance

- Consider new opportunities for potential inclusion into your life, for example, taking up a new hobby, going on that holiday you always wanted to go on, exploring new friendships, and so on
- Ask yourself about what really is important in your life, what are the areas of real priority?
- "Practice what you preach"—play back the way in which you may assist a client with vicarious trauma and ask yourself whether their treatment should be your treatment?
- Keep a reflective journal, remembering that its benefits are not just for your clients' well-being, as they can be for yours also
- Find physical places and people you can spend some quality time with and make it happen. "A beer with good friends always tastes better"
- Reintroduce yourself and reconnect with social networks and friends
- Practice saying "No" and then feeling OK about it
- Give yourself permission to allow somebody else to take care of you, even if it is just for a while
- Try to find meaning from your experience and ask yourself if there are opportunities for learning, resilience, and posttrauma growth
- Remind yourself why you choose to do what you do, and why doing this work is important to you (p. 517)

The key for Farrell was to make sure, when working with a team, to identify a team member who takes on the responsibility of psychological support for the entire team and to address issues of vicarious traumatization before they take hold. He also devised the "EMDR Positive 'Stay & Go' Scripted Protocol Group Exercise," which emphasizes being part of the EMDR training team, acknowledging the member's contribution to one individual, valuing oneself, focusing on one's needs as an individual, and performing a grounding exercise.

In this section, we have the benefit of Catherine Butler's wisdom through her chapter, "Healer, Heal Thyself: A Commonsense Look at the Prevention of Compassion Fatigue." She suggests that we find out how we are doing concerning our self-care and resiliency by going to the Compassion Fatigue Awareness Project's website (www.compassionfatigue.org) and taking the self-tests available there. She discusses the many names for burnout in our professional literature and then takes us back to graduate school where many of us learned to cultivate what she refers to as "professional perfectionism." She reviews the signs of compassion fatigue and vicarious trauma, and how age, stress, and disease are also part of the picture. She then helps us build our own "personal and healthy compassion fatigue toolkit," emphasizing play and getting help when we need it. This chapter has a companion summary sheet, a CD version for data entry, and a brief exposition of the primary elements of the material.

We have chosen a profession that engages our hearts and souls in the service of others. Do we not deserve to touch our own heart and soul as we do for others?

References

Alter-Reid, K. (2013). Community trauma: A blueprint for support and treatment for trauma recovery network (TRN) responders from the Newtown, CT, tragedy. In M. Luber (Ed.), *Implementing EMDR early mental health interventions for man-made and natural disasters: Models, scripted protocols and summary sheets* (pp. 495–506). New York, NY: Springer Publishing.

Artigas, L., & Jarero, I. (2014). The butterfly hug. In M. Luber (Ed.), *Implementing EMDR early mental health interventions for man-made and natural disasters: Models, scripted protocols and summary sheets* (pp. 127–132). New York, NY: Springer Publishing.

Farrell, D. (2013). Vicarious trauma and EMDR. In M. Luber (Ed.), *Implementing EMDR early mental health interventions for man-made and natural disasters: Models, scripted protocols and summary sheets* (pp. 507–532). New York, NY: Springer Publishing.

Jarero, I., & Uribe, S. (2013). Worst case scenarios in recent trauma response. In M. Luber (Ed.), *Implementing EMDR early mental health interventions for man-made and natural disasters: Models, scripted protocols and summary sheets* (pp. 533–542). New York, NY: Springer Publishing.

Kabat-Zinn, J. (2012). *Mindfulness for beginners*. Boulder, CO: Sounds True.

Levine, P. (1997). *Walking the tiger: Healing trauma*. Berkeley, CA: North Atlantic Book.

Healer, Heal Thyself: A Commonsense Look at the Prevention of Compassion Fatigue

Catherine M. Butler

Self-care is never a selfish act—it is simply good stewardship of the only gift I have.

—Parker Palmer

Introduction

Some very interesting work has come out about the realities of compassion fatigue and burnout, as well as the impact of vicarious trauma (VT) on clinicians and all who work to support and comfort in any capacity. It all seems so sensible and obvious that the burdens generated by working with traumatic situations hour after hour may, at times, build up and overflow. Among professional colleagues, at presentations, it is common to hear, "I know all about this but it's always good to hear it again." Yet, as the confusion, stressors, and conflicts of a troubled world continue to mount, it must be our responsibility as a profession to do more than acknowledge the challenges of the profession; it must be with conscientious intent that we guard against them.

One simple description describes compassion fatigue in the following way: It is like standing out in the hot sun, with no hat, sunscreen, water, or shade and simply willing yourself not to get burned and dehydrated. Eventually, despite mentally commanding yourself to avoid becoming a lobster, it will happen and your body will pay the price. Your clients and your personal life, like the sun, provide the constant exposure to components that can wreak havoc over time on health and well-being. As you continue to work to assist others, the symbolic sun block of self-care needs to be repeatedly reapplied in order to allow you to stay out longer and without damage (Canadian Counseling and Psychotherapy Association, 2014, p. 1).

Take the time to find out what is going on. The Compassion Fatigue Awareness Project (2013) has self-tests available at no charge to help identify the state of your personal union at this moment and then to keep tabs on how it looks over time. The project is dedicated to "educating caregivers about authentic, sustainable self-care and aiding organizations in their goal of providing healthy, compassionate care to those whom they serve." The three assessments are as follows:

- Professional Quality of Life (ProQoL) Self-Test
- The Compassion Fatigue Self-Test
- The Life Stress Self-Test

Once you know what is going on within yourself, you can read this chapter with a different perspective and, hopefully, a new incentive to make the changes you need.

Starting with knowledge and compassion for your state of being is one thing, but taking action to remedy the situation is another. There are many steps in between recognition and resolution, but if left untreated, compassion fatigue can result in the abandonment of a profession, legal issues, substance abuse and addiction, and in a worst-case scenario, self-destructive tendencies and suicide (Panos, 2007, p. 6.)

History and Definitions of Stress Disorders

There may be confusion about the term *burnout*, as there are many words that are used interchangeably, such as compassion fatigue, secondary posttraumatic stress disorder (PTSD), and so on. However, when whatever term you use for burnout occurs, the results are that therapists often are in a state of depersonalization and then provide suboptimal care to their clients. By the nature of their work, caregivers, whether professional or lay people, are exposed to repeated stressors that can rob them of job satisfaction, result in the loss of their personal and professional resiliency, and put them at risk for this condition.

The familiar term *burnout* was coined in the 1970s by American psychologist Herbert Freudenberger and since then it has become part of the language of our culture. Freudenberger (1974) defines *burnout* to be a "state of mental and physical exhaustion caused by one's professional life." Freudenberger and his colleague Gail North created a list of phases of burnout. Tracy (2000) described it as a "general wearing out or alienation from the pressures of work," which can result from "long hours, little down time, and continual peer, customer, and superior surveillance." The symptoms are not experienced solely by clinicians but by the general population as well. The symptoms may not appear sequentially or be clearly noted or identified (Kraft, 2006). *Diagnostic and Statistical Manual of Mental Disorders, Fifth Edition* (*DSM-5*) does not recognize burnout as a term or disorder; however, the International Classification of Diseases-10 (ICD-10; due for release in 2015) recognizes a *"state of vital exhaustion"* (Z73.0) under *"Problems related to life-management difficulty"* (Z73). The U.S. National Library of Medicine notes that there is no consensus of symptoms or even the ability to state that burnout is a disease, but acknowledges that consequences of the stressful activities both inside and outside a job include the following:

- *Emotional exhaustion*: People affected feel drained and exhausted, overloaded, tired and low, and do not have enough energy. Physical symptoms include pain or problems with the stomach or bowel.
- *Alienation from (job-related) activities*: People affected find their jobs increasingly negative and frustrating. They may develop a cynical attitude toward their work environment and their colleagues. They may, at the same time, increasingly distance themselves emotionally, and disengage themselves from their work.
- *Reduced performance*: Burnout mainly affects everyday tasks at work, at home, or when caring for family members. People with burnout regard their activities very negatively, find it hard to concentrate, are listless, and experience a lack of creativity (PubMedHealth, 2013).

Some symptoms of burnout may mask underlying conditions such as depression, and thus treatment may be very different than the recommendation of a few weeks off, or perhaps a change of tasking. A vacation may help exhausted people recover, but if the problem is really depression, more concrete steps must be taken.

Since the early 1990s, the terminology of burnout has expanded and now includes research and practice literature surrounding compassion fatigue (which is also known as secondary traumatic stress, STS), VT, and traumatic countertransference (Figley, 1995a, 1995b, 2002a, 2002b). Figley also discusses the presence of *"compassion stress"* as the "natural behaviors and emotions that arise from knowing about a traumatizing event experienced by another—the stress resulting from helping or wanting to help a traumatized person" (Figley, 1995a, p. xiv).

These are the types of problems that can occur when caretakers are exposed to and/or witness traumatic events:

- *Primary traumatic stress* describes overwhelming traumatic event(s) that are personally experienced. This correlates directly to the criteria listed for Posttraumatic Stress Disorder (PTSD) as a reference point, whether or not PTSD eventually manifests itself or not down the road.
- *Secondary traumatic stress* refers to one witnessing traumatic stress happen to another, and being overwhelmed (Figley & Kleber, 1995). This phenomenon is also known as *compassion fatigue*. *Compassion* is defined by *Merriam-Webster Dictionary* (2013) as "sympathetic consciousness of others' distress together with a desire to alleviate it"; compassion fatigue extends the concept of burnout to another level, as it is a gradual lessening of compassion over time. Those who work directly with trauma victims, such as nurses, clinicians, and first responders, are saturated with pain, loss, and grief and may develop a lack of patience with ongoing and often unresolvable issues. It has been referred to as the "cost of caring" for others who are suffering.
- *Vicarious trauma* is the "phenomenon of the transmission of traumatic stress by bearing witness to the stories of traumatic events" (McCann & Pearlman, 1990). This may occur once to numerous times over a career or lifetime. If the capacity to care is reduced, as with compassion fatigue, VT goes to the core and steals meaning, hope, and the connection to personal spirituality and heart. Since the term was coined, it has since expanded to include clergy, humanitarian workers, social service workers—on the front line—as well as health care providers, journalists, and first responders (McCann & Pearlman, 1990). Additionally, "vicarious traumatization refers to a transformation in the therapist's (or other trauma worker's) inner experience resulting from empathic engagement with clients' trauma material... [Many clinicians are] vulnerable to the emotional and spiritual effects of vicarious traumatization. These effects are cumulative and permanent, and evident in both a therapist's professional and personal life" (Pearlman & Saakvitne, 1995, p. 151).

Primary, secondary, and vicarious trauma are represented in the *DSM-5* criterion for PTSD when one is exposed to real or threatened death, serious injury, or violence. Additionally, Figley notes that "Compassion Fatigue is a more user friendly term for Secondary Traumatic Stress Disorder, which is nearly identical to PSTD, except it affects those emotionally affected by the trauma of another (usually a client or a family member)" (Figley, 2004, p. 7).

The diagnosis has expanded in the 2013 revision to include a new criterion which acknowledges that continued exposure to traumatic events on a regular basis may result in a clinical manifestation of the disorder (American Psychiatric Association, 2013). First responders of all kinds find themselves meeting urgent and emotionally draining events day after day without relief, and sooner or later the brain flips its own switch and says "enough." Eye Movement Desensitization and Reprocessing (EMDR) practitioners are all aware of the negative cognitions, haunting images and feelings, and somatic complaints that get in the way of normal functioning.

Burnout is different from compassion fatigue to the extent that burnout generally refers to general tedium of the workplace, whereas compassion fatigue refers to the consequences of ongoing exposure to client issues such as trauma. This illuminates the fact that there are degrees of exhaustion that can appear with differing values of severity and chronicity over time. The military, for example, makes a distinction that there can be evidence of posttraumatic stress in a veteran as a result of military experience without earning the "D" for disorder. Wherever it falls on the continuum, however, the symptoms are disruptive and potentially dangerous.

Where Does Prevention Begin?

Go Back to School!

From the very beginning, we are taught to recognize the importance of the positive therapeutic alliance and the implementation of measurable treatment goals. This is not the case for compassion fatigue in our professional training. It would make sense for educators and supervisors to specifically focus on discussions about the risks of compassion fatigue from the earliest days of graduate school to reinforce the need for self-care right from the start. As prospective clinicians enter the field in graduate school, they arrive with awareness that they naturally notice how others feel, offer good advice, and are aware that they have a knack for helping others. In a natural progression, as a program evolves, that natural talent or inclination has to fit alongside the risks of legal and ethical issues, transference, countertransference, boundaries, and self-disclosure, among many other things. Suddenly, it is not just about helping people anymore; it is about being legally and ethically responsible, as well as professionally competent. This is a game changer, when the profession becomes real and the burdens become quantifiable as interns are exposed to different kinds of mental illness, intractable personality styles, and the scrutiny of supervisors and licensing boards. Students rapidly realize that it is not just about being a good listener any more.

In an attempt to manage the new material and responsibility, trainees must absorb new information and merge it with techniques that have to come off the textbook pages and transform into real life. Without any real experience, they work hard to look professional and follow all the rules. The clinical tools involving the appropriate setting of boundaries and working with the elements of transference and countertransference imply that compassion fatigue may be held at bay if a new clinician resists joining with or caring about the client's trauma story. However, Charles Figley notes the challenge that emerges as empathy intersects with positive therapeutic change:

> Some would argue that it is wrong for a practitioner to have deep feelings of sympathy and sorrow for their client's suffering. And certainly practitioners must understand their limitations in helping alleviate the pain suffered by their clients.
>
> Yet, most systematic studies of the effectiveness of therapy point to the therapeutic alliance between client and clinician, the ability to empathize to understand and help clients.... If it is not present, it is highly unlikely that therapeutic change will take place. The most important ingredients in building a therapeutic alliance include the client liking and trusting her or his therapist. And these feelings are directly related to the degree to which the therapist utilizes and expresses empathy and compassion. (Figley, 2004, pp. 4–5)

In graduate school, it seemed as if professors/clinical supervisors were more like Disney's Mary Poppins, who was "practically perfect in every way." Perhaps, if students knew what to ask about the effect of a clinical profession on themselves, they would find out more. But is it their responsibility? Should it not be definitively woven into the fabric of their education so that it can gradually become part of their awareness? With so much to learn and master, there may be no space for a frank discussion about the personal toll a career can take on a vibrant spirit unless it is embedded in the curriculum. "I'm going to be a counselor," one young student told this author earnestly. "I can't need therapy!" Seasoned therapists may smile at the naïveté, but know that in fact it is not *if* fatigue will happen, it is *when*. The clincher is to know how to meet and manage it effectively. Students must be involved in the discussion on some level in every class they take, and then in supervision later. Additionally, programs should build in a requirement for students to seek out personal therapy so that they can experience the process from the client side and feel the anxiety their clients may feel. The dual purpose is to help students work through the issues that the course material may elicit in them and help them to experience their own healing as they move forward.

This author coined the term *professional perfectionism*. This refers to the reluctance of new clinicians to reveal any insecurities or concerns about how they appear to their supervisors or clients in order to appear competent and trustworthy. All the insecurities about being in the office with real clients are soon suppressed because interns remain under much scrutiny, both from supervisors and from the clients, and may not want to reveal their feelings for fear of being looked down upon, marked down, or found to be an unsatisfactory intern. If a supervisor is actively open to hearing the worries, there is a much better chance that the intern will view the supervisory process with a more positive approach. Gabor Mate, MD, in his book *When the Body Says No: Exploring the Stress-Disease Connection*, refers to the topic as working with stress and developing emotional competence (Mate, 2003, p. 27). To a great degree, it must be taught, modeled, reviewed, and adapted, if it is to be managed effectively over a lifetime.

School's Out, Now What?

As time goes on and clinicians emerge from the relative safety of the internship, the added concerns of budgets, compliance, stressful cases, and legal matters may start a cycle of wear and tear that sets the stage for clinical sore spots and vulnerabilities. Then, as life continues to unfold and personal landmines get stepped on, the wonderful gifts with which clinicians are wired, such as the ability to naturally care, support, and minister to others, may become dulled—and sometimes disabled. By disregarding their own self-care needs to focus on their clients, opportunities for stress release and renewal may be missed.

Clinicians arrive at licensure with a personal history in tow that includes the good, the bad, and the ugly. As the years go by, professional and personal experiences line up in our memory banks and help define our human experience. All the skills, coping mechanisms, and support networks act as a positive safety net to help navigate through the ups and downs of life. Each individual has unique responses to the emotional challenges that present themselves, as well as individual ways of coping with and transforming the events that unfold. Personal traumatic experiences may walk alongside the stories of the clients very well most of the time, but if something goes sideways, suddenly the view looks very different. There can be observable symptoms that appear where they were not before, and may translate and transfer to many clients and across time.

Although institutions should be caring for the well-being of employees and providing support for the wear and tear the job may deliver, it is the primary responsibility of each person to monitor and address the issues that arise over time, as the work is being undertaken for others who seek help.

The Importance of Clinician Self-Care

The Basics of Compassion Fatigue and Vicarious Trauma

It is true that life may not have a danger music soundtrack that helpfully plays and warns the viewer about trouble ahead, but of course, it certainly does have warning signs. Over a lifetime those signs can change and evolve. With an attentive and mindful approach to our own physical and emotional vulnerabilities, the literal wellspring of energy, reserves, and resiliency can be maintained and replenished to defend against those times when life happens and stress mounts up.

Burnout and compassion fatigue can appear in many professions, but VT is specific to trauma workers and so symptoms will often mirror client symptoms and deliver very specific intrusive imagery, dreams, and other negative consequences stemming from the client's trauma material. The empathetic connection with the client and his or her story takes on a real-life connotation and follows the clinician around in daily life. Essentially, as a result of the trauma story, a worldview can change in a negative way and encroach on personal well-being including the body and the spirit.

Symptoms of Compassion Fatigue and Vicarious Trauma

Having a strong sense of commitment and/or responsibility to those who have been hurt may result in high expectations of oneself that can lead to changes in spiritual, psychological, and physical well-being. Additionally, each person has a unique fingerprint for symptomology that is sourced by individual history, life experiences, and current circumstances. The symptoms for STS and VT are very similar on the surface, but VT has the added elements of *the loss of meaning and hope*. Like a thief in the night, well-being can be replaced quietly by negative emotions, or it can be simply taken down with a well-placed kick that knocks the air out and results in a collapse of the world. Symptoms may include:

- Hopelessness
- Constant feelings of stress
- Negative attitude
- Nightmares, disrupted sleep
- Anxiety
- Tearfulness or irritability
- Lack of enjoyment in normal things
- Decrease in productivity
- Inability to focus
- Feelings of inadequacy or self-doubt
- Cynicism
- Unwillingness to seek support/isolation

The Contributions of Age, Stress, and Disease

The U.S. Army operates on a foundation of self-care by saying, "You are your equipment, and you better maintain it." The premise that no amount of training, equipment, management, or luck will win the day if the human being is failing is fundamental to success in the battlefield or in life. The steps to maintaining and adapting a self-care plan are generally personal but may all be tailored for a perfect fit.

In 2008, the American Psychological Society surveyed practitioners in the United States and found that the median age was 55, two-thirds of whom were working full time. Many held more than one job (American Psychological Association, 2008). Only 10% were 35 years of age or under. Aging alone exacerbates physical and psychological vulnerability and so clinicians who become impacted by chronic illness or deal with other chronic life events must also adapt to the changes in the body over the years. Indeed, every human notes the changes in physical well-being as time goes on, but may avoid taking the steps to minimize the march of time.

The Centers for Disease Control and Prevention (CDC) paints a very dire picture of the cost of stress-related diseases in America today and states that chronic diseases are the leading cause of death. Heart disease, obesity, diabetes, stroke, cancer, and arthritis are the most common, costly, *and the most preventable* of the conditions noted today across the population (CDC, 2014). Financially, each one of the conditions listed is costing the economy billions and billions of dollars each year as the numbers climb and affect more people.

The stressors of the job contribute to the stressors on the body and the cycle begins to loop and facilitate a downward trend. Quality of life is impacted by pain that is both physical and emotional when no regular attention is paid to the contributors of the situation. The behaviors that contribute the most to chronic illness today include lack of physical activity, poor nutrition, tobacco use, and drinking too much alcohol (CDC, 2014).

Dr. Gabor Mate, author of *When the Body Says No: Exploring the Stress-Disease Connection* (2003), states that there is a physiological impact from the emotions we experience, but that it is possible to feel tension without activating the physiological mechanisms of stress such as feelings of nervousness, agitation, or overwhelm. "Physiological stress responses can be evoked when the threat is outside conscious awareness or even when the individual may believe himself to be stressed in a 'good' way" (Mate, 2003, p. 29). Stress affects the hormonal system (changes in the adrenal glands); the immune system (effects on the spleen, thymus, and lymph glands); and the intestinal lining of the digestive system (p. 32). He notes that "emotional competence" must be maintained and developed if we are to protect ourselves from hidden stress that creates a risk to health, and we must regain it if we are to heal. Emotional competence requires:

- Capacity to feel emotions so we are aware when stress occurs
- Ability to express emotions effectively, assert needs, and maintain integrity of emotional boundaries
- Facility to distinguish between present-day reactions to present versus past issues so that our needs today are not linked to unconscious, unsatisfied needs from childhood
- Awareness of genuine needs that require satisfaction, rather than their repression in order to gain acceptance or approval from others (Mate, 2003, p. 38)

A broad conclusion from the research surrounding the cost and consequences of compassion fatigue concludes that often those who report the symptoms are not taking care of their needs and are giving all their personal resources to others and losing their ability to cope.

Okay, It's True. I'm Tired. What Do I Do?

So maybe you admit that you have got a few on the list, or maybe someone you are working with is showing signs as well. While there is no known treatment for the depletion of compassion, there are many recommended self-care and preventative measures. If a vacation or a few days off will clear out the logjam of frustration and overwhelm, then balance is fairly easily maintained. But waking up feeling worse than when you went to sleep or dreading the day or the client line-up tells a much different story.

Clinician Self-Care Basics

The following suggestions are just a few ideas to assist you as you review your personal policies and procedures regarding self-care both in and out of the office.

Ethics and Self-Care

Hippocrates cautioned, "First, do no harm," and all the professional ethical codes say the same thing. If it becomes clear that the ability to provide care is compromised, we are bound ethically to take the necessary remedial steps. The APA Code of Ethics says, "When psychologists become aware of personal problems that may interfere with their performing work-related duties adequately, they take appropriate measures, such as obtaining professional consultation or assistance, and determine whether they should limit, suspend or terminate work related duties" (APA Code of Ethics, Section 2.06: Personal Problems and Conflicts).

In a worst-case scenario and worst nightmare, the discussion may be in front of a judge and jury who have to hear why the decisions made seemed like a good idea at the time and weigh the cost of the damage to the public. In the July/August 2014 edition of *The Therapist*, California's journal for marriage and family therapists, 6 out of 11 actions taken by the disciplinary committee of the Board of Behavioral Sciences or Board of Psychology were directly related to substance abuse issues of some kind and resulted in license revocation as well as civil charges (*The Therapist*, 2014, pp. 65–71). The rest of the actions taken surrounded other results of flawed thinking and resulting behaviors that ran contrary to the "do no harm" basis of the profession. A glance at any professional journal will undoubtedly reveal similar cases that show how personal poor judgment and behaviors extended into the public safety sector, which for all helping professions is unacceptable and entirely avoidable.

As readers review the causes and symptoms of compassion fatigue and vicarious trauma and recognize that it is a well-researched and valid consequence of working with humanity over time, the actionable aspect of prevention becomes very positive and effective—unless, of course, it is ignored. This becomes, in essence, an ethical violation on the one hand, and a possible legal issue on the other.

Build a Personal and Healthy Compassion Fatigue Toolkit

Emotional Considerations

First things first! Complete the three self-assessment measurements listed at the beginning of the chapter. Review the results and pledge to make changes wherever possible. Take the time to design your own personal toolkit that reflects individual needs, situations, and unique stressors. Drawn from an article titled "Running on Empty" by Francoise Mathieu, a Canadian compassion fatigue specialist, answering a series of specific questions can guide the process toward concrete and action-oriented steps to fend off the consequences of compassion fatigue before it becomes overwhelming. Mathieu suggests blending work and life circumstances and answering the following questions:

- What would go in that toolkit?
- What are my warning signs—on a scale of 1 to 10, what is a 4 for me, what is a 9?
- Schedule a regular check in every week—how am I doing?
- What things do I have control over?
- What things do I not have control over?
- What stress relief strategies do I enjoy? (e.g., taking a bath, sleeping well, or going for a massage)
- What stress reduction strategies work for me? Stress reduction means cutting back on things in our lives that are stressful (switching to part-time work, changing jobs, reorganizing your caseload, etc.)
- What stress resiliency strategies can I use? Stress resiliency strategies are relaxation methods that we develop and practice regularly, such as meditation, yoga, or breathing exercises (Mathieu, 2007, p. 4).

Other suggestions include the regular commitment to journaling, listening to music, and maintaining creative pursuits such as artistic, physical, or spiritual interests. It may also be helpful to create a meaningful ritual to help transition yourself from your office to your outside life by taking a step to "clear the decks" of your day and move forward. This author puts her hand on her schedule as she ends her day, and asks for blessings on the people listed there for their safety and well-being. Not unlike handing over the watch to the next person on a ship, it creates a space of confidence and calm so that this author can leave it there and not take it with her into her evening. Maintaining a connection to yourself, your energy level, and your sources of renewal is an important component of self-love and self-care.

Health or Physical Considerations

In addition to building and maintaining an emotional toolbox, a physical review is also in order. Additional items to consider include an honest assessment of the following:

- *Substances*: Review the presence of substances such as alcohol or painkillers in your life and determine if the frequency or quantity has increased. If you have had (or need) surgery, you may be relying more on prescription and/or over-the-counter medications to keep your symptoms at bay. Stress and overwhelm in the day-to-day may increase other sources of physical pain and result in higher or more regular use.
- *Sleep*: Inventory the quality and quantity of sleep being had. Consider the age of your mattress and pillows. Pillows should be replaced every year and if your mattress is over 10 years old, it is time to go shopping, particularly if you wake up in pain. Have you developed a sleep disorder over time, such as snoring, sleep apnea, insomnia, or other issues such as cramping, restless leg syndrome (RLS), or neuropathy? Do you wake up from nightmares or anxiety? Ask yourself what it takes to get a good night's sleep and assess if that is happening or not, and why. Sometimes a late infusion of

caffeine or alcohol, having young children with sleep issues, watching TV too late, using tablets, or just missing your window of sleep is easy to identify; if not, your physician may be able to help improve your sleep hygiene.
- *Appetite and nutrition*: Is there a negative change in appetite? Is there a change in your weight? Eating too much or not enough? Are you forgetting to eat or just eating once a day? Evaluate the nutritional balance of healthy versus convenience foods. Get your blood checked for vitamin deficiencies; the World Health Organization (WHO) states that the top nutritional deficiencies in both undeveloped *and* industrialized countries include anemia at the top, followed by vitamins A, B1, B3, B9, D, and finally, calcium deficiency. These vitamins are critical to well-being and overall health because a deficiency can lead to issues such as cancer and gastrointestinal concerns, among many other things (Blake, 2012). In fact, many of the symptoms of vitamin deficiency mirror the symptoms for depression, anxiety, and compassion fatigue. Additionally, changes in blood sugar, hormones, and other physical changes can directly impact mood and energy levels. A full and proper physical assessment may be the answer to many unresolved symptoms that develop as a result of poor self-care of the body, as well as the mind.
- *Hydration:* Evaluate water intake versus caffeine or soda. Caffeine acts as a diuretic and will remove fluid from the body; that can cause stress over the course of a day. The American Heart Association notes that proper hydration means the heart does not have to work so hard, and helps the muscles to remove waste more easily. An easy check is to notice your urine over the course of a day. The darker it is, the more fluid you need. Additionally, those with diabetes or heart disease must drink more in order to avoid taxing internal organs. If you are thirsty, you are already dehydrated (American Heart Association, 2014).
- *Exercise:* A common loss in a busy life is the time set aside to exercise. A sedentary career can contribute to bone and muscle loss if weight-bearing exercises are missing. Clinicians who make and take the time to organize the day around exercise and other positive self-care items can effectively prevent and be more resilient against the effects of compassion fatigue and VT.

How many people finally take some time off, or prepare for a holiday and find themselves sick in bed for most, if not all, of the vacation? This is not an uncommon result of pushing and extending one's resources and expecting the body to keep up. Essentially, the "fight or flight" resources such as cortisol, glucocorticoids, and adrenaline—that are only supposed to be deployed as a last resort to protect us from danger—end up being used often in order to meet the demands of the job. Consequently, when that long-awaited vacation arrives, and the pressure stops, the body is vulnerable and depleted. Any germ that happens by may just decide to stay, as there are fewer immunity resources to meet it and fend it off. The body becomes more vulnerable to disease over time. Feeling weak, tired, and run down are common symptoms in a hectic life and illness may not be far behind as flu and cold seasons return. Additionally, exposure to a variety of clients every day and travel by any public means may also increase exposure to a variety of illnesses if the immune system is not protected and supported on a consistent basis.

In short, look at what is going on and what options are available to reset the impact of the stressors in a preventative fashion by monitoring your overall health and well-being.

Taking Breaks, Maintaining Support, and Getting Supervision

Clinicians must consciously reflect on day-to-day happenings and seek out consultation to help reset and refocus the lens that they are looking through, if they are having difficulty. Being aware of the ever-changing landscape of life while monitoring the pressures is one of the first steps to maintaining balance and connection to those who are most important at the end of the day. Resiliency is a perishable gift. It does not replenish or get replaced without attention and intention.

It is essential to take breaks (real ones!) and do what it takes to separate from the situation and center again. Breathing exercises, regular exercise, meditating, and leaving the technology inside while you go outside are all great places to start. Staying connected with friends, family, and other outside interests helps contribute to a balanced perspective and will help you to work smarter rather than harder when you return, refreshed.

A wise supervisor once said that if she found herself thinking about her clients too much, it meant that she needed to reach out to her friends and connect with them because she was getting lost in her job. A point well taken, but a solution may not be so clear if talking to a pool of friends feels like more work than play. Confidentiality prevents us from sharing our stories with anyone, and that limitation may result in isolation that is that hallmark of compassion fatigue, VT, and all other mood-related challenges. However, reaching out to trusted friends and family to relax and share the many other aspects of life is the safety net that prevents the slide into darker times. The connection keeps us tied to the other glorious aspects of life and not just the trauma that has beset our clientele. Since you cannot share those details with your loved ones, the final point is about having peer support and solid consultation.

Every clinician should have access to a trusted mentor and/or peer network to help sift through the details of a complicated case or to help clarify thinking and diagnostic impressions. This also boosts resiliency and job satisfaction when treatment plans are enhanced or confirmed to be effective. Confident guidance from a peer consultant will also help maintain clear and professional boundaries, can prevent emotional flooding and ultimately the erosion of the gifts that came with you as your "factory setting" when you came into the world and into the profession. Supervision or consultation is especially beneficial for the management of the cases that do not have a happy ending or a positive prognosis. The knowledge that you brought all your skills to the situation will help maintain perspective and appreciation for the opportunity to assist, even if it was not resolvable at this time.

Play

Elements of playing, resting, getting away, and basic self-care are essential, in general, but often take a back seat and become negotiable when the tempo picks up. Being constantly attentive to the needs of personal and professional life may become a daily grind and an overwhelmingly heavy burden that results in isolation and irritability. Instead of a joyful balance, life becomes an unending cycle of worry and pain, which no one who loves you can understand. Warning signs that may keep clinicians off the playground of their life include a lack of energy or desire to find something fun to do. Extended work hours, preoccupation with client situations or stories, constant monitoring of email and phones during off hours, and a decreased desire for intimacy are some signs that there is no line of demarcation between work and personal life. It is important to build in and then guard the time away from the office so that it becomes a healthy and enjoyable space of time that keeps relationships, both with yourself and with your loved ones, going strong for a lifetime.

Dr. Peter Gray, a research professor at Boston College, studies the value of play and notes that the same elements exist for adults as do for children as they develop. He states that play "is uniquely suited for high-level reasoning, insightful problem solving, and all sorts of creative endeavors" and that all characteristics of play are to do with motivation and mental attitude and are not to do with the overt behavior. In other words, what is fun for someone else may not be enjoyable at all for another (Gray, 2008, pp. 1–2). Also, he points out that adult play is often combined with adult motives combined with adult responsibilities. One perfect example would be attending a professional conference in another city, taking a tour of a local landmark, eating out with a friend or two, and trying to convince oneself that it was a true vacation.

In order to evaluate the role of true play in an adult life, evaluate chosen activities against the following criteria for play and see if the activity holds up or if it really serves another purpose (Gray, 2008, p. 4):

- Self-chosen and self-directed and can be quit at any time
- Activity in which means are more valued than ends

- Structure, or rules, not dictated by physical necessity but emanate from the minds of the players
- Imaginative, nonliteral, mentally removed in some way from "real" or "serious" life
- Active, alert, but nonstressed frame of mind

There are many occasions in which Gray believes people are pawns in someone else's game or activity, and therefore it is not really able to be stopped at any time. Having a "fun" day or activity that is sourced by someone else may not fit the criterion, as the participant really cannot stop it at will or has to hold out until the end. That sounds like the description of many a dinner, birthday, or other events that center around someone else's definition of what is truly removed from "real or serious life." Gray says, "It is through social play that children learn, on their own, with no lectures, how to meet their own needs while, at the same time, satisfying the needs of others. This is perhaps the most important lesson that people in any society can learn" (Gray, 2008, p. 8). The message for adults and clinicians in particular is that *while meeting the needs of others is important, the ability to choose and engage in activities that engage the brain in a personal and self-directed way is paramount to the restoration of well-being and overall satisfaction.*

Psychiatrist Stuart Brown, founder of the National Institute of Play, considers play to be "the gateway to vitality. By its nature it is uniquely and intrinsically rewarding. It generates optimism, seeks out novelty, makes perseverance fun, leads to mastery, gives the immune system a bounce, fosters empathy and promotes a sense of belonging and community" (National Institute for Play, 2014). It makes sense to recognize that goals typically set for clients must also be transferable to professionals who seek to help reestablish joy and satisfaction in life. If play can act as a catalyst for change, then contentment and productivity cannot be far behind.

Knowing how to engage in true personal play may feel like an idea that belonged to a more carefree time in life. How does one figure out what is truly fun in the present stage of life when there are so many competing stressors? Some people are very clear on what that looks like and are dedicated to their hobbies and interests outside of work, but others may feel unmotivated and defeated, choosing to simply stay in old patterns or habits that are run by someone or something else. "We don't lose the need for novelty and pleasure as we grow up," says Scott G. Eberle, PhD, vice president for Play Studies at the National Museum of Play and editor of the *American Journal of Play* (Tartakovsky, 2012, p. 3). Suggestions to help jumpstart the process if it has stalled or needs an infusion of energy may include:

- *Change how you think about play.* Do you really think you have no time for play? Is it frivolous or ridiculous to devote energy to play?
  Note: Play is critical for relationships and creativity, and is therefore a secret weapon for success instead of a time waster.
- *Take a play history.* What did you love to do as a child or young adult? Did you engage in those activities with others or by yourself? Can you still do it now or re-create it today?
- *Surround yourself with playful people.* Select friends who are playful and play with your loved ones.
- *Play with little ones.* Take the time to see it again through their eyes and enjoy that experience again (Tartakovsky, 2012, pp. 15–20).

Finally, consider the influence of your work setting. According to Gray, "What is true for children's play is also true for adults' sense of play. Research studies have shown that adults who have a great deal of freedom as to how and when to do their work often experience that work as play, even (in fact, especially) when the work is difficult. In contrast, people who must do just what others tell them to do at work rarely experience their work as play" (Gray, 2008, p. 10).

EMDR

EMDR as a personal therapeutic tool in a clinician's toolbox is a wonderful and positive addition to the options that move us toward wellness and health. Although there is no research currently to quantify the benefits of EMDR on the elements of compassion fatigue specifically, there is a growing body of evidence to support positive results EMDR has on a multitude of issues such as sleep, pain, childhood abuse and neglect, anxiety, PTSD, single incident trauma, complex trauma, eating disorders, substance abuse issues, and many other topics. The entire collection of research may be found housed in the Francine Shapiro Library at Northern Kentucky University. The growing body of evidence-based research on EMDR reflects the efficacy of EMDR as it is used to heal the past and enhance the ability to live in the present and work toward the future.

Seeking Professional Help and Support

How do clinicians know when they need to seek professional help to relieve the pile-up of symptoms that cloud professional and personal judgment? What about the families who may feel like extensions of the clinical day as they go about the business of growing up and living life with a resident relational expert who sees the worst of the worst? According to Ofer Zur, PhD, in his article examining the effect of clinical practice on individual and family dynamics, the job may certainly hurt the family that surrounds a clinician. He notes that Freud said as early as 1937 that this is an "impossible profession" due to the low efficacy that may result from feelings of frustration, inadequacy, and self-doubt. I recommend a review of this online article to read a literature review and summary of what research there has been over the years surrounding therapists, the challenges that exist, as well as some strategies to balance out the family unit. Zur comments that unlike other helping professions that provide protective gear for the practitioner, a clinician may be considered to be unprotected and isolated in the office setting, often facing hostile, dysfunctional, and demanding patients (Zur, n.d., section 3). The influence of such pain and frustration may be expected to come home at night; even Sigmund Freud's wife barred him from the door of his children's nursery, declaring, "Psychoanalysis stops at the door to the children's room!" (Freud, 1954).

Zur states, "Systems of psychotherapy have bearing on most aspects of therapists' lives, from the personal to the interpersonal, from the emotional to the behavioral aspects of existence. As such, psychology does not stop and cannot be stopped at the end of the clinical hour. It permeates therapists' lives and inevitably impacts their intimate and familial relationships" (Zur, n.d, section 4). He comments that families may be on the receiving end of unsolicited interpretations of their dreams or relationships with others, as well as the reality that after a day of listening, the clinician wants to talk and may not listen effectively to family issues. Alternatively, incessant questioning or analysis may be present even in the most benign discussions and cause alienation. Developmental phases may be minimized or exaggerated, and, perhaps, distance is maintained due to an inability to engage and connect with the emerging needs of a growing and changing family.

It is an active decision to seek out treatment for yourself and be attentive to your own personal and family needs. Just like the safety speech delivered on every airplane as it prepares for departure, the air mask has to go on you first before any help can be effectively delivered to anyone else. If you have a competent and compassionate therapist who is skilled at working with peers and who understands the professional roadblocks that may go up when the client/therapist knows too much about the topic, you have taken the ethical step that the various ethical codes demand: to seek assistance so that nothing gets in the way of delivering appropriate services to the public. If you need a therapist, consider looking on your insurance panel to see if anyone says that treating peers is a specialty, or seek a recommendation from a trusted mentor. It is also prudent to seek out an EMDR clinician who is certified or a consultant, so that you, as a client, are not second-guessing her technique or questioning her skill level.

Recognition of the signs that point you in the direction of seeking support can come from different directions. Here are signals that you are in need of assistance:

- *Trauma overload*: If you are unable to process the trauma stories of your clients and they are replaying over and over in your head, changing your worldview in terms of safety, you are experiencing a trauma overload and your nervous system is telling you it is too hot.
- *Anxiety, depression, and/or mania overload.* If the resulting anxiety, depression, or mania is taking over and getting in the way, it is time to seek some relief.
- *Isolation.* Feeling like no one can listen or understand creates isolation that is a hallmark sign of trouble for a caring person.
- *Normal resources provide no stress relief.* If the things you normally do to alleviate stress and create a peaceful place are not working well, you need to develop other resources.
- *Escapism.* If you are looking for substances or someone to try and create that escape, it is time to look for support.
- *Others notice you are not yourself.* When those whom you love and respect are noticing that you are not yourself, it is clear that the inside feelings have found a way out and others are concerned; reach out and let a skilled EMDR practitioner walk with you and help reprocess the problems you face.

After the Work Is Done, Allow for Transformation

Ultimately, *vicarious transformation* allows for spiritual growth to emerge from the ashes of the pain that can result from VT. As this evolves, the negative can somehow become a positive icon of hope. The embracing of the pain and loss allows each person involved to walk through the circumstances to a different place where connection, meaning, and hope can still be found. It is a process, of course, and not some magical end point where all is forgotten and now all is well. It is not about fending off the pain of others, but embracing it instead. This can result in a greater appreciation for life's gifts and opportunities, instead of a bleak and dismal view of a world without hope or love in it (Dillon, 2011). It may expand our humanity instead of shutting it down, and allow us to walk with trauma survivors to another destination and find a new place for ourselves in the process. Frankl (1963-2007), in his book *Man's Search for Meaning*, said, "Life is never made unbearable by circumstances, but only by lack of meaning and purpose."

Summary

In conclusion, what makes you awesome can burn you out. Simply put, the gifts and talents that you bring to your profession and to your family are perishable if they are not taken care of, nurtured, and replenished regularly. The attention that is paid to the other routine details of private life must be extended to the professional practice of self-care in order to avoid the pitfalls of developing compassion fatigue and VT. Life continues to happen personally as well as professionally and the overlap is to be expected across the lifespan.

The enduring needs and challenges of dealing compassionately hour after hour are identified as a primary ethical and legal issue in which doing no harm to patients is paramount. However, that idea should also be extended to oneself and the important people who populate our hearts and minds every day in the most intimate ways. Recognizing the natural and inevitable impact of constant exposure to others' sadness, tragedy, anxiety, and related emotional and physical injuries on the spirit is the first step to designing a maintenance and recovery plan. The "cost of caring" is measurable, but so is the value of attention to nutrition, sleep, play, ongoing education, and supervision, as well as the maintenance of connection to others who love everything about you and your presence in their lives.

Evaluate the impact of the stressors in your life on a regular basis and adjust accordingly in order to foster a resilient and positive approach to your personal and professional well-being. Assist others in your circle to pay attention as well, and prioritize the culture of self-care among yourselves so that accountability can be valued and encouraged.

At the West Coast Post-Trauma Retreat (WCPR), a residential treatment program for first responders with PTSD, the message to the participants is to reset their priorities off of the all-consuming nature of the job and onto a balanced, loving, satisfying life experience. The clients are guided to rethink the focus that they placed on the career that drove them. They know how much it cost them personally as they review painful memories of multiple critical incidents, fractured relationships, health concerns, and changed options that, upon reflection, were not worth it.

As they leave the retreat to reenter their lives, they are encouraged to mindfully make the changes necessary so that at the end of it all, they can look back over their career and say, "I really liked my job, *but I really love my life!*".

References

American Heart Association. (2014). *Staying hydrated, staying healthy*. Retrieved from http://www.heart.org/HEARTORG/GettingHealthy/PhysicalActivity/FitnessBasics/Staying-Hydrated---Staying-Healthy_UCM_441180_Article.jsp

American Psychological Association. (2008). Retrieved from http://www.apa.org/workforce/publications/08-hsp/

Blake, K. (2012). Nutritional deficiencies (malnutrition). Retrieved from http://www.healthline.com/health/malnutrition#Overview1

Canadian Counseling and Psychotherapy Association. (2014). *Four basic steps for preventing compassion fatigue*. Retrieved from http://www.ccpa-accp.ca/blog/?p=2106

Centers for Disease Control and Prevention. (2014). *Chronic diseases and health promotion*. Retrieved from http://www.cdc.gov/chronicdisease/overview/

Compassion Fatigue Awareness Project. (2013). Retrieved from http://www.compassionfatigue.org/

Dillon, J. (2011). From vicarious trauma to transformation. Retrieved from http://www.jacquidillon.org/1046/blog/reflections/from-vicarious-trauma-to-transformation/

Figley, C. R. (Ed.). (1995a). *Compassion fatigue: Coping with secondary traumatic stress disorder in those who treat the traumatized*. New York, NY: Brunner/Mazel.

Figley, C. R. (1995b). Compassion fatigue as secondary traumatic stress disorder: An overview. In C. R. Figley (Ed.), *Compassion fatigue: Coping with secondary traumatic stress disorder* (pp. 1–20). New York, NY: Brunner Mazel.

Figley, C. R. (Ed.). (2002a). *Treating compassion fatigue*. New York, NY: Brunner-Rutledge.

Figley, C. R. (2002b). Compassion fatigue: Psychotherapists' chronic lack of self-care. *Journal of Clinical Psychology, 58*, 1433–1441. doi:10.1002/jclp.10090

Figley, C. R. (2004). Gift from within: PTSD resources for survivors and caregivers. Retrieved from http://www.giftfromwithin.org/html/What-is-Compassion-Fatigue-Dr-Charles-Figley.html

Figley, C. R., & Kleber, R. (1995). Beyond the "victim": Secondary traumatic stress. In R. Kleber, C. R. Figley, & B. P. R. Gersons (Eds.), *Beyond trauma: Cultural and societal dynamics* (pp. 75–109). New York, NY: Plenum.

Francine Shapiro Library. (2014). Retrieved from http://emdr.nku.edu/

Frankl, V. E. (1963–2007). *Man's search for meaning. An introduction to logotherapy*. Boston, MA: Beacon Press.

Freud, S. (1954). *The origins of psycho-analysis: Letters to Wilhelm Fliess*. New York, NY: Basic Books.

Freudenberger, H. J. (1974). Staff burnout. *Journal of Social Issues* 30(1): 159–165. doi:10.1111/j.1540-4560.1974.tb00706.x.

Gray, P. (2008). The value of play I: The definition of play gives insights. Retrieved from http://www.psychologytoday.com/blog/freedom-learn/200811/the-value-play-i-the-definition-play-gives-insights

ICD-10: International Classification of Diseases (1994). Geneva, Switzerland: World Health Organization. Retrieved from http://www.icd10data.com/ICD10CM/Codes/Z00-Z99/Z69-Z76/Z73-/Z73.0

Kraft, U. (2006, June/July). Burned out. *Scientific American Mind*, 28–33.

Mate, G. (2003). *When the body says no: Exploring the stress-disease connection*. Hoboken, NJ: John Wiley.

Mathieu, F. (2007). Running on empty. Retrieved from http://www.compassionfatigue.org/pages/RunningOnEmpty.pdf

McCann, I. L., & Pearlman, L. A. (1990). Vicarious traumatization: A framework of the psychological effects of working with victims. *Journal of Traumatic Stress, 3*(1), 131–149.

Merriam-Webster Dictionary. (2013). Compassion. Retrieved from http://www.merriam-webster.com/dictionary/compassion

National Institute for Play. (2014). Retrieved from http://www.nifplay.org/opportunities/

Panos, A. (2007). *Understanding and preventing compassion fatigue: A handout for professionals.* Retrieved from http://www.giftfromwithin.org/html/prvntcf.html#diet

Pearlman, L. A., & Saakvitne, K. W. (1995). Treating therapists with vicarious traumatization and secondary traumatic stress disorders. In C. R. Figley (Ed.), *Compassion fatigue: Coping with secondary traumatic stress disorders in those who treat the traumatized* (pp. 150–177). New York, NY: Brunner/Mazel.

PubMedHealth. (2013). *What is burnout syndrome?* Retrieved from http://www.ncbi.nlm.nih.gov/pubmedhealth/PMH0050545/

Tartakovsky, M. (2012). *The importance of play for adults.* Retrieved from http://psychcentral.com/blog/archives/2012/11/15/the-importance-of-play-for-adults/

The Therapist. (2014, July-August). Disciplinary actions. *Magazine of the California Association of Marriage and Family Therapists,* 65–71.

Tracy, S. (2000). Becoming a character of commerce emotion. *Management Communication Quarterly, 14,* 90–128.

West Coast Post-Trauma Retreat. (2014). Retrieved from www.WCPR2001.org

Zur, O. (n.d). Psychotherapists and their families: The effect of the practice on the individual and family dynamics. *Psychotherapy in Private Practice, 13*(1), 69–95. Retrieved from http://www.zurinstitute.com/therapistsfamilies.html

SUMMARY SHEET:
Healer, Heal Thyself: A Commonsense Look at the Prevention of Compassion Fatigue

Catherine M. Butler
SUMMARY SHEET BY MARILYN LUBER

Name: _____ Diagnosis: _____

☑ Check when task is completed, response has changed, or to indicate symptoms or diagnosis.

Note: This material is meant as a checklist for your response. Please keep in mind that it is only a reminder of different tasks that may or may not apply to your client.

Introduction

Compassion Fatigue Description: It is like standing out in the hot sun, with no hat, sunscreen, water, or shade and simply willing yourself not to get burned and dehydrated. Eventually, despite mentally commanding yourself to avoid becoming a lobster, it will happen and your body will pay the price.

The Compassion Fatigue Awareness Project

☐ Professional Quality of Life (ProQoL) Self-Test
☐ The Compassion Fatigue Self-Test
☐ The Life Stress Self-Test

History and Definitions of Stress Disorders

Burnout

Freudenberger (1993): "state of mental and physical exhaustion caused by one's professional life."

Tracy (2000): "general wearing out or alienation from the pressures of work"; can result from "long hours, little down time, and continual peer, customer, and superior surveillance."

ICD-10: Problems Related to Life-Management Difficulty (Z73): State of Vital Exhaustion (Z73.0) (retrieved from http://www.icd10data.com/ICD10CM/Codes/Z00-Z99/Z69-Z76/Z73-/Z73.0).

United States National Library of Medicine acknowledges that consequences of stressful activities inside and outside the job may include the following.

Emotional Exhaustion: People affected feel drained and exhausted, overloaded, tired and low, and do not have enough energy. Physical symptoms include pain or problems with the stomach or bowel.

Alienation From (Job-Related) Activities: People affected find their jobs increasingly negative and frustrating. They may develop a cynical attitude toward their work environment and their colleagues. They may, at the same time, increasingly distance themselves emotionally, and disengage themselves from their work.

Reduced Performance: Burnout mainly affects everyday tasks at work, at home, or when caring for family members. People with burnout regard their activities very negatively, find it hard to concentrate, are listless, and experience a lack of creativity (PubMedHealth, http://www.ncbi.nlm.nih.gov/pubmedhealth/PMH0050545/).

Burnout vs. Depression

- Burnout: vacation helps exhausted people recover
- Depression: more concrete steps than vacation are needed

Figley

- *Compassion Stress*: "natural behaviors and emotions that arise from knowing about a traumatizing event experienced by another—the stress resulting from helping or wanting to help a traumatized person" (Figley, 1995a, pp. xiv).

Types of problems possible when caretakers are exposed to and/or witness traumatic events:

- *Primary traumatic stress* is defined as "direct exposure to, or witnessing of, extreme events and one is overwhelmed by the trauma" (Figley, 1992) and correlates to PTSD criteria as a reference point, whether or not PTSD eventually manifests itself down the road.
- *Secondary traumatic stress (STS)* refers to witnessing traumatic stress happen to another, and one is overwhelmed (Figley & Kleber, 1995) or experiences *compassion fatigue*. *Compassion* is defined as "sympathetic consciousness of others' distress together with a desire to alleviate it" (*Merriam-Webster Dictionary*, 2013). Compassion fatigue extends the concept of burnout to another level, as it is a gradual lessening of compassion over time. Those who work directly with trauma victims can be saturated with pain, loss, and grief and may develop a lack of patience with ongoing and often unresolvable issues and/or the "cost of caring" for others who are suffering.
- *Vicarious trauma (VT)* is the "phenomenon of the transmission of traumatic stress by bearing witness to the stories of traumatic events" (McCann & Pearlman, 1990). Can occur numerous times over a career or lifetime. If the capacity to care is reduced by compassion fatigue, VT goes to the core and steals meaning, hope, and the connection to personal spirituality and heart. The term has expanded to include clergy, humanitarian workers, social service workers on the front line, healthcare providers, journalists, and first responders (McCann & Pearlman, 1990).

Burnout vs. Compassion Fatigue

- Burnout—general tedium of the workplace
- Compassion fatigue—consequences of ongoing exposure to client issues such as trauma

Where Does Prevention Begin?

Go Back To School!

- Professional Perfectionism (Butler, 2010)—the reluctance of new clinicians to reveal any insecurities or concerns about how they appear to their supervisors or clients in order to appear competent and trustworthy.

☐ Role of Supervisor—when the supervisor is actively open to hearing the intern's worries, the intern will view the process more positively and is supported in learning to work with stress and develop emotional competence (Mate, 2003, p. 27).

School's Out, Now What?

It is the primary responsibility of each person to monitor and address the issues that arise over time, as the work is being undertaken for others who seek help.

The Importance of Clinician Self-Care

The Basics of Compassion Fatigue and Vicarious Trauma

Vicarious trauma is specific to trauma workers and mirrors client symptoms.

Symptoms of Compassion Fatigue and Vicarious Trauma

☐ Hopelessness (specific to VT)
☐ Constant feelings of stress
☐ Negative attitude
☐ Nightmares, disrupted sleep
☐ Anxiety
☐ Tearfulness or irritability
☐ Lack of enjoyment in normal things
☐ Decrease in productivity
☐ Inability to focus
☐ Feelings of inadequacy or self-doubt
☐ Cynicism
☐ Unwillingness to seek support/isolation

The Contributions of Age, Stress, and Disease

U.S. Army: "You are your equipment, you better maintain it."

Aging exacerbates physical and psychological vulnerability.

Chronic Illness (heart disease, obesity, diabetes, stroke, cancer, arthritis, etc.)—behaviors contributing to chronic illness today include lack of physical activity, poor nutrition, tobacco use, and drinking too much alcohol.

Physiological Impact from Emotions: stress affects the hormonal system, the immune system, and the intestinal lining of the digestive system.

Emotional Competence Requires:

☐ Feel emotions so aware when stress occurs
☐ Express emotions effectively, assert needs, and maintain integrity of emotional boundaries
☐ Distinguish between present-day reactions to issues and past issues so needs today are not linked to unconscious, unsatisfied needs from childhood
☐ Be aware of genuine needs that do require satisfaction, rather than repressing them to gain acceptance or approval from others (Mate, 2003, p. 3)

Clinician Self-Care Basics

Ethics and Self-Care

Hippocrates: "First, do no harm."

APA Code of Ethics; Section 2.06, Personal Problems and Conflicts: "When psychologists become aware of personal problems that may interfere with their performing work-related duties adequately, they take appropriate measures, such as obtaining professional consultation or assistance, and determine whether they should limit, suspend or terminate work related duties" (retrieved from http://www.apa.org/workforce/publications/08-hsp/).

Build a Personal and Healthy Compassion Fatigue Toolkit

Emotional Considerations

1. Complete self-assessment measures
   - ☐ Professional Quality of Life (ProQoL) Self-Test
   - ☐ The Compassion Fatigue Self-Test
   - ☐ The Life Stress Self-Test
2. Review the results and pledge to make changes wherever possible.
3. Answer Francoise Mathieu's questions from "Running on Empty":
   - ☐ What would go in that toolkit?
   - ☐ What are my warning signs—on a scale of 1 to 10, what is a 4 for me, what is a 9?
   - ☐ Schedule a regular check in every week—how am I doing?
   - ☐ What things do I have control over?
   - ☐ What things do I not have control over?
   - ☐ What stress relief strategies do I enjoy? (e.g., taking a bath, sleeping well, or going for a massage)
   - ☐ What stress reduction strategies work for me? Stress reduction means cutting back on things in our lives that are stressful (e.g., switching to part-time work, changing jobs, reorganizing your caseload, etc.)
   - ☐ What stress resiliency strategies can I use? Stress resiliency strategies are relaxation methods that we develop and practice regularly, such as meditation, yoga, or breathing exercises (Mathieu, 2007, p. 4)
4. Other suggestions concerning regular commitments:
   - ☐ Journaling
   - ☐ Listening to music
   - ☐ Maintaining creative pursuits such as artistic, physical, or spiritual interests
   - ☐ Creating a meaningful ritual to help transition yourself from your office to your outside life

Health or Physical Considerations

Do a physical review and assess the following areas of your life for your relationship with the area:

- ☐ *Substances*
  - Has frequency or quantity increased?   ☐ Yes ☐ No
- ☐ *Sleep*
  - Replace pillows every year   ☐ Yes ☐ No
  - Replace mattress every 10 years   ☐ Yes ☐ No
  - Developed a sleep disorder over times: ☐ Snoring ☐ Sleep apnea/insomnia
    ☐ Restless legs syndrome ☐ Neuropathy
  - Wake up from nightmares or anxiety?   ☐ Yes ☐ No
  - Too much caffeine/alcohol   ☐ Yes ☐ No
  - Young children with sleep issues   ☐ Yes ☐ No
  - Watching TV too late   ☐ Yes ☐ No
  - Just missing your window of sleep   ☐ Yes ☐ No
- ☐ *Appetite and Nutrition*
  - Negative change in appetite?   ☐ Yes ☐ No

- Weight change? ☐ Yes ☐ No
- Eating too much? ☐ Yes ☐ No
- Not eating enough? ☐ Yes ☐ No
- Forgetting to eat/eating once a day? ☐ Yes ☐ No
- Check nutritional deficiencies: ☐ Vitamin A ☐ Vitamin B1 ☐ Vitamin B3
  ☐ Vitamin B9 ☐ Vitamin D ☐ Calcium
- Changes in blood sugar? ☐ Yes ☐ No
- Changes in hormones? ☐ Yes ☐ No
- Other physical changes? ☐ Yes ☐ No

☐ Hydration (If you are thirsty, you are already dehydrated)
- How much water do you drink daily?
- How much caffeine do you ingest daily?

☐ Exercise ☐ Yes ☐ No

Note: When you push and extend your resources beyond your body's capacity, cortisol, glucocorticoids, and adrenaline are used to meet the demands; when a vacation arrives and the pressure stops, the body is depleted and more vulnerable to disease.

Taking Breaks, Maintaining Support, and Getting Supervision

Be aware of daily changes of life while monitoring the pressures

☐ TAKE BREAKS
Breathing exercises ☐ Yes ☐ No
Regular exercises ☐ Yes ☐ No
Meditating ☐ Yes ☐ No
Technology break ☐ Yes ☐ No
Stay connected with family and friends ☐ Yes ☐ No
Have outside interests ☐ Yes ☐ No

☐ MAINTAIN SUPPORT
Reach out to family and friends ☐ Yes ☐ No

☐ SUPERVISION
Peer consultant to address practice questions ☐ Yes ☐ No
Trusted mentor to address practice questions ☐ Yes ☐ No
Supervision/Consultation ☐ Yes ☐ No

Play

Warning signs preventing play:

☐ Lack of energy
☐ Lack of desire to find something fun to do
☐ Extended work hours
☐ Preoccupation with client situations or stories
☐ Constant monitoring of email and phones during off hours
☐ Decreased desire for intimacy

Gray's Criteria for Play—Play "is uniquely suited for high-level reasoning, insightful problem solving, and all sorts of creative endeavors"; all characteristics of play are to do with motivation and mental attitude and are not to do with the overt behavior.

☐ Self-chosen and self-directed and can be quit at any time.
☐ Activity in which means are more valued than ends.
☐ Structure, or rules, not dictated by physical necessity but emanate from the minds of the players.

☐ Imaginative, nonliteral, mentally removed in some way from "real" or "serious" life.
☐ Active, alert, but nonstressed frame of mind (Gray, 2008).

Note: While meeting the needs of others is important, the ability to choose and engage in activities that engage the brain in a personal and self-directed way is paramount to the restoration of well-being and overall satisfaction.

Ways to jumpstart play:

☐ *Change how you think about play*. Do you really think you have no time for play? Is it frivolous or ridiculous to devote energy to play?
Note: Play is critical for relationships and creativity, and is therefore a secret weapon for success instead of a time waster.
☐ *Take a play history*. What did you love to do as a child or young adult? Did you engage in those activities with others or by yourself? Can you still do it now or recreate it today?
☐ *Surround yourself with playful people*. Select friends who are playful and play with your loved ones.
☐ *Play with little ones*. Take the time to see it again through their eyes and enjoy that experience again (Tartakovsky, 2012, paragraphs 15–20).

Note: "Adults who have a great deal of freedom as to how and when to do their work often experience that work as play, even (in fact, especially) when the work is difficult. In contrast, people who must do just what others tell them to do at work rarely experience their work as play" (Gray, 2008).

EMDR

EMDR as a personal therapeutic tool in a clinician's toolbox is a wonderful and positive addition to the options that move us toward wellness and health. Although there is no research currently to quantify the benefits of EMDR on the elements of compassion fatigue specifically, there is a growing body of evidence to support positive results of EMDR on a multitude of issues such as sleep, pain, childhood abuse and neglect, anxiety, PTSD, single incident trauma, complex trauma, eating disorders, substance abuse issues, and many other topics. The entire collection of research may be found housed in the Francine Shapiro Library at Northern Kentucky University (http://emdr.nku.edu).

Seeking Professional Help and Support

Ofer Zur (n.d.) suggestions for balancing the family unit include recognizing the signs that you need support:

☐ *Trauma overload*: If you are unable to process the trauma stories of your clients and they are replaying over and over in your head, changing your worldview in terms of safety, you are experiencing a trauma overload and your nervous system is telling you it is too hot.
☐ *Anxiety, depression, and/or mania overload*. If the resulting anxiety, depression, or mania is taking over and getting in the way, it is time to seek some relief.
☐ *Isolation*. Feeling like no one can listen or understand creates isolation that is a hallmark sign of trouble for a caring person.
☐ *Normal resources provide no stress relief*. If the things you normally do to alleviate stress and create a peaceful place aren't working well, you need to develop other resources.
☐ *Escapism*. If you are looking for substances or someone to try and create that escape, it's time to look for support.

☐ *Others notice you are not yourself.* When those whom you love and respect are noticing that you are not yourself, it is clear that the inside feelings have found a way out and others are concerned; reach out and let a skilled EMDR practitioner walk with you and help reprocess the problems you face.

Note: See Zur, O. (n.d), Psychotherapists and their families: The effect of the practice on the individual and family dynamics. *Psychotherapy in Private Practice, 13*(1), 69–95. Retrieved online from http://www.zurinstitute.com/therapistsfamilies.html.

After the Work Is Done, Allow for Transformation

Vicarious transformation allows for spiritual growth to emerge from the ashes of the pain that can result from VT.

Viktor Frankl (1963–2007) said: "Life is never made unbearable by circumstances, but only by lack of meaning and purpose."

References

Figley, C. R. (Ed.). (1995). *Compassion fatigue: Coping with secondary traumatic stress disorder in those who treat the traumatized.* New York, NY: Brunner/Mazel.

Figley, C. R. & Kleber, R. (1995). Beyond the "victim": Secondary traumatic stress. In R. Kleber, C. R. Figley, and B. P. R. Gersons (Eds.), *Beyond trauma: Cultural and societal dynamics* (pp. 75–98). New York, NY: Plenum.

Frankl, V. E. (1963–2007). *Man's search for meaning: An introduction to logotherapy.* Boston, MA: Beacon Press.

Freudenberger, H. (1993). *American Psychologist, 48*(4), 356–358.

Gray, P. (2008). The value of play I: The definition of play gives insights. Retrieved from http://www.psychologytoday.com/blog/freedom-learn/200811/the-value-play-i-the-definition-play-gives-insights

Mate, G. (2003). *When the body says no: Exploring the stress-disease connection.* Hoboken, NJ: John Wiley.

Mathieu, F. (2007). Running on empty. Retrieved from http://www.compassionfatigue.org/pages/RunningOnEmpty.pdf

McCann, I. L., & Pearlman, L. A. (1990). Vicarious traumatization: A framework of the psychological effects of working with victims. *Journal of Traumatic Stress, 3*(1), 131–149.

Merriam-Webster Dictionary. (2013). Compassion. Retrieved from http://www.merriam-webster.com/dictionary/compassion

Tartakovsky, M. (2012). *The importance of play for adults.* Retrieved from http://psychcentral.com/blog/archives/2012/11/15/the-importance-of-play-for-adults/

Tracy, S. (2000). Becoming a character of commerce emotion. *Management Communication Quarterly, 14*, 90–128.

Zur, O. (n.d.). Psychotherapists and their families: The effect of the practice on the individual and family dynamics. *Psychotherapy in Private Practice, 13*(1), 69–95. Retrieved from http://www.zurinstitute.com/therapistsfamilies.html

Appendix A: Worksheets

Past Memory Worksheet Script (Shapiro, 2001, 2006)

Incident

Say, *"The memory that we will start with today is _____ (select the next incident to be targeted)."*

_____
_____
_____

Say, *"What happens when you think of the _____ (state the issue)?"*

_____
_____
_____

Or say, *"When you think of _____ (state the issue), what do you get?"*

_____
_____

Picture

Say, *"What picture represents the entire _____ (state the issue)?"*

_____
_____
_____

If there are many choices or if the client becomes confused, the clinician assists by asking the following:

Say, "*What picture represents the most traumatic part of* _____ (state the issue)?"

___
___
___

Negative Cognition

Say, "*What words best go with the picture that express your negative belief about yourself now?*"

___
___

Positive Cognition

Say, "*When you bring up that picture or* _____ (state the issue), *what would you like to believe about yourself now?*"

___
___

Validity of Cognition

Say, "*When you think of the incident* (or picture), *how true do those words* _____ (clinician repeats the positive cognition [PC]) *feel to you now on a scale of 1 to 7, where 1 feels completely false and 7 feels completely true?*"

1   2   3   4   5   6   7

(completely false)   (completely true)

Emotions

Say, "*When you bring up the picture or* _____ (state the issue) *and those words* _____ (clinician states the negative cognition [NC]), *what emotion do you feel now?*"

___

Subjective Units of Disturbance

Say, "*On a scale of 0 to 10, where 0 is no disturbance or neutral and 10 is the highest disturbance you can imagine, how disturbing does it feel now?*"

0   1   2   3   4   5   6   7   8   9   10

(no disturbance)   (highest disturbance)

Location of Body Sensation

Say, *"Where do you feel it* (the disturbance) *in your body?"*

_____

Phase 4: Desensitization

To begin, say the following:

Say, *"Now, remember, it is your own brain that is doing the healing and you are the one in control. I will ask you to mentally focus on the target and to follow my fingers* (or any other bilateral stimulation [BLS] you are using). *Just let whatever happens, happen, and we will talk at the end of the set. Just tell me what comes up, and don't discard anything as unimportant. Any new information that comes to mind is connected in some way. If you want to stop, just raise your hand."*

Then say, *"Bring up the picture and the words* _____ (clinician repeats the NC) *and notice where you feel it in your body. Now follow my fingers with your eyes* (or other BLS)."

Phase 5: Installation

Say, *"How does* _____ (repeat the PC) *sound?"*

_____

_____

_____

Say, *"Do the words* _____ (repeat the PC) *still fit, or is there another positive statement that feels better?"*

_____

_____

_____

If the client accepts the original PC, the clinician should ask for a VoC rating to see if it has improved:

Say, *"As you think of the incident, how do the words feel, from 1* (completely false) *to 7* (completely true)?"

1   2   3   4   5   6   7

(completely false)   (completely true)

Say, *"Think of the event and hold it together with the words* _____ (repeat the PC)."

Do a long set of BLS to see if there is more processing to be done.

Phase 6: Body Scan

Say, *"Close your eyes and keep in mind the original memory and the positive cognition. Then bring your attention to the different parts of your body, starting with your head and working downward. Any place you find any tension, tightness, or unusual sensation, tell me."*

_____
_____

Phase 7: Closure

Say, *"Things may come up or they may not. If they do, great. Write it down and it can be a target for next time. You can use a log to write down what triggers images, thoughts or cognitions, emotions, and sensations; you can rate them on our 0 to 10 scale where 0 is no disturbance or neutral and 10 is the worst disturbance. Please write down the positive experiences, too.*

"If you get any new memories, dreams, or situations that disturb you, just take a good snapshot. It isn't necessary to give a lot of detail. Just put down enough to remind you so we can target it next time. The same thing goes for any positive dreams or situations. If negative feelings do come up, try not to make them significant. Remember, it's still just the old stuff. Just write it down for next time. Then use the tape or the Safe Place exercise to let go of as much of the disturbance as possible. Even if nothing comes up, make sure to use the tape every day and give me a call if you need to."

Phase 8: Reevaluation

There are four ways to reevaluate our work with clients.

1. Reevaluate what has come up in the client's life since the last session.

   Say, *"Okay. Let's look at your log. I am interested in what has happened since the last session. What have you noticed since our last session?"*

   _____
   _____
   _____

   Say, *"What has changed?"*

   _____
   _____
   _____

If the client has nothing to say or does not say much, say the following:

Say, *"Have you had any dreams or nightmares?"*

_____
_____
_____

Say, *"What about* _____ *(state symptoms you and client have been working on) we have been working on, have you noticed any changes in them? Have they increased or decreased?"*

_____
_____
_____

Say, *"Have you noticed any other changes, new responses, or insights in your images, thoughts, emotions, sensations, and behaviors?"*

_____
_____
_____

Say, *"Have you found new resources?"*

_____
_____
_____

Say, *"Have any situations, events, or other stimuli triggered you?"*

_____
_____
_____

Use the material from your reevaluation to feed back into your case conceptualization and help decide what to do next concerning the larger treatment plan.

2. Reevaluate the target worked on in the previous session. Has the individual target been resolved? Whether the previous processing session was complete or incomplete, use the following instructions to access the memory and determine the need for further processing.

Say, *"Bring up the memory or trigger of* _____ *(state the memory or trigger) that we worked on last session. What image comes up?"*

_____
_____
_____

Say, *"What thoughts about it come up?"*

_____
_____

Say, *"What thoughts about yourself?"*

_____

_____

Say, *"What emotions do you notice?"*

_____

_____

Say, *"What sensations do you notice?"*

_____

_____

Say, *"On a scale of 0 to 10, where 0 is no disturbance or neutral and 10 is the highest disturbance you can imagine, how disturbing does it feel now?"*

0   1   2   3   4   5   6   7   8   9   10

(no disturbance)   (highest disturbance)

Evaluate the material to see if there are any indications of dysfunction. Has the primary issue been resolved? Is there ecological validity to the client's resolution of the issue? Is there associated material that has been activated that must be addressed?

If you are observing any resistance to resolving the issue, say the following:

Say, *"What would happen if you are successful?"*

_____

_____

If there are no indications of dysfunction, and SUD is 0, do a set of BLS to be sure that the processing is complete.

Say, *"Go with that."*

Say, *"What do you get now?"*

_____

_____

Check the PC.

Say, *"When you think of the incident (or picture), how true do those words _____ (clinician repeats the PC) feel to you now on a scale of 1 to 7, where 1 feels completely false and 7 feels completely true?"*

1   2   3   4   5   6   7

(completely false)   (completely true)

If the VoC is 7, do a set of BLS to be sure that the processing is complete.

Say, *"Go with that."*

Say, *"What do you get now?"*

_____

_____

If there are any signs of dysfunction, such as a new negative perspective(s) or new facets of the event or the SUD is higher than 0, say the following:

Say, *"Okay, now please pay attention to the image, thoughts, and sensations associated with _____ (state the memory or trigger) and just go with that."*

_____

_____

Continue with the Standard EMDR Protocol until processing is complete. If the VoC is less than 7, say the following:

Say, *"What is keeping it from being a 7?"*

_____

_____

Note the associated feelings and sensations, and resume processing.

Say, *"Go with that."*

Continue with the Standard EMDR Protocol through the Body Scan until processing is complete.

If a completely new incident or target emerges, say the following:

Say, *"Are there any feeder memories contributing to this problem?"*

_____

_____

Do the Assessment Phase on the appropriate target and fully process it. It is not unusual for another aspect of the memory to emerge that needs to be processed.

If the client claims that nothing or no disturbance is coming up (or he can't remember what was worked on in the previous session), and the therapist thinks that the work is probably still incomplete and that the client is simply not able to access the memory, say the following:

Say, *"When you think of _____ (state the incident that was worked on) and the image _____ (state the image) and _____ (state the NC), what body sensations do you feel now?"*

_____

_____

Say, *"Go with that."*

_____

_____

Continue processing with the Standard EMDR Protocol.

If the client wants to work on a charged trigger that came up since the last session instead of the target from the previous session, say the following:

Say, "*Yes, this IS important information. Tell me about what came up for you.*"

_____

_____

Then assess the magnitude of the trigger. If it is indeed a severe critical incident, then proceed accordingly, using the Assessment Phase to target the new material and return to the original target when possible.

If it is not, then say the following:

Say, "*Yes, this is important, however, it is important that we finish our work on* _____ (state what you are working on) *before moving to another target. It is like what happens when you have too many files open on your computer and it slows down, or finishing the course of antibiotics even if you feel okay* (or any other appropriate metaphor for your client)."

Fully reprocess each target through the Body Scan and Reevaluation before moving on to the next in order to ensure optimal results.

3. At various critical points in treatment (before moving on to the next symptom, theme, goal, etc.), reevaluate what has been effectively targeted and resolved and what still needs to be addressed.

Say, "*Now that we have finished this work, let's reevaluate our work so far.*"

"*Remember* _____ (state the work you have done). *On a scale of 0 to 10, where 0 is no disturbance or neutral and 10 is the highest disturbance you can imagine, how disturbing does it feel now?*"

0   1   2   3   4   5   6   7   8   9   10

(no disturbance)   (highest disturbance)

If the SUD is higher than 0, evaluate what else needs to be done by continuing to work with the disturbance in the framework of the Standard EMDR Protocol.

Also evaluate whether the client has been able to achieve cognitive, behavioral, and emotional goals in his life.

Say, "*Have you accomplished all of the goals that we had contracted to work on such as* _____ (read the list of agreed-upon goals)?"

_____

_____

_____

If not, evaluate what still needs to be targeted, such as feeder memories.

Say, "*Please scan for an earlier memory that incorporates* _____ (state the NC). *What do you get?*"

_____

_____

_____

Use the Standard EMDR Protocol to process any feeder memories. Check if previously identified clusters of memories remain charged.

Say, "*Are there any memories left concerning* _____ (state the cluster of memories previously worked on)?"

_____
_____
_____

If so, work on the memory(ies), using the Standard EMDR Protocol. Make sure to incorporate the positive templates for all previously disturbing situations and projected future goals. See the Future Template Worksheet Script.

4. Before termination, reevaluate targets worked on over the course of therapy and goals addressed during treatment.

Say, "*Before we end our treatment, let's reevaluate our work to make sure that all of the targets are resolved and goals are addressed. Are there any PAST targets that remain unresolved for you?*"

_____
_____
_____

Or say, "*These are the past targets with which we worked; do any of them remain unresolved? What about the memories that we listed during our history taking and over the course of treatment?*"

_____
_____
_____

Check with the SUDs for any disturbance.

Say, "*On a scale of 0 to 10, where 0 is no disturbance or neutral and 10 is the highest disturbance you can imagine, how disturbing does it feel now?*"

0   1   2   3   4   5   6   7   8   9   10
(no disturbance)   (highest disturbance)

Check the major NCs to see if there are any unresolved memories still active.

Say, "*These are the main negative cognitions with which we worked. Hold* _____ (state one of the cognitions worked with) *and scan for any unresolved memories. Does anything surface for you?*"

_____
_____

If there is more unresolved material, check with BLS to see if the charge decreases. If not, use the Standard EMDR Protocol.

Say, "*Now scan chronologically from birth until today to see if there are any other unresolved memories. What do you notice?*"

_____
_____

If there is more unresolved material, check with BLS to see if the charge decreases. If not, use the Standard EMDR Protocol.

Progressions can occur during other events or during the processing of a primary target; use your clinical judgment as to whether it is important to return and reevaluate these memories.

Clusters are related memories that were grouped together during treatment planning and can be scanned to identify any memories that were not involved through generalization of treatment effects.

Say, *"Let's check the _____ (state the cluster) we worked on earlier. When you think about it, are there any other memories that were not involved that you are aware of now?"*

_____

_____

If there is more unresolved material, check with BLS to see if the charge decreases. If not, use the Standard EMDR Protocol.

Participants are significant individuals in the client's life who should be targeted if memories or issues regarding them remain disturbing.

Say, *"Let's check if there are any remaining concerns or memories concerning _____ (state whoever the client might be concerned about). Is there anything that still is bothering you about _____ (state the person's name)?"*

_____

_____

If there is more unresolved material, check with BLS to see if the charge decreases. If not, use the Standard EMDR Protocol.

Say, *"Are there any PRESENT or RECENT triggers that remain potent?"*

_____

_____

_____

Say, *"Are there any current conditions, situations, or people that make you want to avoid them, act in ways that are not helpful, or cause you emotional distress?"*

_____

_____

If there is more unresolved material, check with BLS to see if the charge decreases. If not, use the Standard EMDR Protocol.

Say, *"Are there any future goals that have not been addressed and realized?"*

_____

_____

_____

Make sure to use the future template for each trigger, new goal(s), new skill(s), issues of memory, or incorporating the client's new sense of himself. See Future Template Worksheet Script in this appendix.

Present Trigger Worksheet Script

Target and reprocess present triggers identified during history taking, reprocessing, and reevaluation. Steps for working with present triggers are the following.

1. Identify the presenting trigger that is still causing disturbance.
2. Target and activate the presenting trigger using the full assessment procedures (image, NC, PC, VoC, emotions, SUD, sensations).
3. Follow Phases 3 through 8 with each trigger until it is fully reprocessed (SUD = 0, VoC = 7, clear Body Scan) before moving to the next trigger.

Note: In some situations a blocking belief may be associated with the present trigger, requiring a new Targeting Sequence Plan.

4. Once all present triggers have been reprocessed, proceed to installing future templates for each present trigger (e.g., imagining encountering the same situation in the future; see future template protocols).

Present Stimuli That Trigger the Disturbing Memory or Reaction

List the situations that elicit the symptom(s). Examples of situations, events, or stimuli that trigger clients could be the following: another trauma, the sound of a car backfiring, or being touched in a certain way.

Say, *"What are the situations, events, or stimuli that trigger your trauma* _____ (state the trauma)? *Let's process these situations, events, or stimuli triggers one by one."*

Situations, Events, or Stimuli Trigger List

_____

_____

_____

_____

Target or Memory

Say, *"What situation, event, or stimulus that triggers you would you like to use as a target today?"*

_____

_____

Picture

Say, *"What picture represents the* _____ (state the situation, event, or stimulus) *that triggers you?"*

_____

_____

If there are many choices or if the client becomes confused, the clinician assists by asking the following:

Say, "What picture represents the most traumatic part of the _____ (state the situation, event, or stimulus) that triggers you?"

_____

_____

When a picture is unavailable, the clinician merely invites the client to do the following:

Say, "Think of the _____ (state the situation, event, or stimulus) that triggers you."

_____

_____

Negative Cognition

Say, "What words best go with the picture that express your negative belief about yourself now?"

_____

Positive Cognition

Say, "When you bring up that picture or the _____ (state the situation, event, or stimulus) that triggers you, what would you like to believe about yourself now?"

Validity of Cognition

Say, "When you think of the _____ (state the situation, event, stimulus, or picture that triggers), how true do those words _____ (clinician repeats the PC) feel to you now on a scale of 1 to 7, where 1 feels completely false and 7 feels completely true?"

1   2   3   4   5   6   7

(completely false)   (completely true)

Sometimes, it is necessary to explain further.

Say, "Remember, sometimes we know something with our head, but it feels different in our gut. In this case, what is the gut-level feeling of the truth of _____ (state the PC), from 1 (completely false) to 7 (completely true)?"

1   2   3   4   5   6   7

(completely false)   (completely true)

Emotions

Say, *"When you bring up the picture* (or state the situation, event, or stimulus) *that triggers you and those words* _____ (state the NC), *what emotion do you feel now?"*

_____

Subjective Units of Disturbance

Say, *"On a scale of 0 to 10, where 0 is no disturbance or neutral and 10 is the highest disturbance you can imagine, how disturbing does it feel now?"*

0   1   2   3   4   5   6   7   8   9   10

(no disturbance)   (highest disturbance)

Location of Body Sensation

Say, *"Where do you feel it* (the disturbance) *in your body?"*

_____

Continue to process the triggers according to the Standard EMDR Protocol.

Future Template Worksheet (Shapiro, 2006)

The future template is the third prong in the Standard EMDR Protocol. Work with the future template occurs after the earlier memories and present triggers are adequately resolved and the clients are ready to make new choices in the future concerning their issue(s). The purpose is to address any residual avoidance and any need for further issues of adaptation, to help with incorporating any new information, and to allow for the actualization of client goals. It is another place, in this comprehensive protocol, to catch any fears, negative beliefs, inappropriate responses, and so forth; to reprocess them; and also to make sure that the new feelings and behavior can generalize into the clients' day-to-day lives.
There are two basic future templates:

1. Anticipatory Anxiety
   Anticipatory anxiety needs to be addressed with a full assessment (Phase 3) of the future situation.

2. Skills Building and Imaginal Rehearsal
   These do not need a full assessment of target and can begin directly with "running a movie."

Future Template Worksheet Script (Shapiro, 2001, pp. 210–214; 2006, pp. 51–53)

Check the Significant People and Situations of the Presenting Issues for Any Type of Distress

It is helpful to check to see if all the material concerning the issue upon which the client has worked is resolved or if there is more material that has escaped detection so far. The future template is another place to find if there is more material that needs reprocessing.

Significant People

When the client's work has focused on a significant person, ask the following:

> Say, "*Imagine yourself encountering that person in the future* _____ (suggest a place that the client might see this person). *What do you notice?*"

_____

_____

_____

> Watch the client's reaction to see if more work is necessary. If a client describes a negative feeling in connection with this person, check to see if it is reality based.

> Say, "*Is* _____ (state the person's name) *likely to act* _____ (state the client's concern)?"

_____

_____

If the negative feeling is not matching the current reality, say the following:

> Say, "*What do you think makes you have negative feelings toward* _____ (state the person in question)?"

_____

_____

If the client is unsure, use the Float-Back or Affect Scan to see what other earlier material may still be active.

If the negative feelings are appropriate, it is important to reevaluate the clusters of events concerning this person and access and reprocess any remaining maladaptive memories. (See Past Memory Worksheet.)

Significant Situations

It is important to have the client imagine being in significant situations in the future; this is another way of accessing material that may not have been processed.

> Say, *"Imagine a videotape or film of how* _____ (state current situation client is working on) *and how it would evolve* _____ (state appropriate time frame) *in the future. When you have done that let me know what you have noticed."*

_____

_____

If there is no disturbance, reinforce the positive experience.

> Say, *"Go with that."*

Do BLS.

Reinforce the PC with the future situation using BLS, as it continues the positive associations. For further work in the future, see below.

If there is a disturbance, assess what the client needs: more education, modeling of appropriate behavior, or more past memories for reprocessing.

> Say, *"On a scale of 0 to 10, where 0 is no disturbance or neutral and 10 is the highest disturbance you can imagine, how disturbing does it feel now?"*

0   1   2   3   4   5   6   7   8   9   10

(no disturbance)   (highest disturbance)

Anticipatory Anxiety

When the SUD is above 4, or when the desensitization phase is not brief, the clinician should look for a present trigger and its associated symptom and develop another Targeting Sequence Plan using the 3-Pronged Protocol. (See worksheets on Past Memories and Present Triggers.)

When there is anticipatory anxiety at a SUD level of no more than 3 to 4 maximum, it is possible to proceed with reprocessing using the future template. The desensitization phase should be quite brief.

> Say, *"What happens when you think of* _____ (state the client's anticipatory anxiety or issue)?*"*

_____

_____

_____

> Or say, *"When you think of* _____ (state the client's anticipatory anxiety or issue), *what do you get?"*

_____

_____

_____

Picture

Say, "What picture represents the entire _____ (state the client's anticipatory anxiety or issue)?"

_____
_____
_____

If there are many choices or if the client becomes confused, the clinician assists by asking the following:

Say, "What picture represents the most traumatic part of _____ (state the client's anticipatory anxiety or issue)?"

_____
_____
_____

Negative Cognition

Say, "What words best go with the picture that express your negative belief about yourself now?"

_____
_____

Positive Cognition

Say, "When you bring up that picture or _____ (state the client's anticipatory anxiety or issue), *what would you like to believe about yourself now?*"

_____
_____

Validity of Cognition

Say, "When you think of _____ (state the client's anticipatory anxiety or issue) *or picture, how true do those words* _____ (repeat the PC) *feel to you now on a scale of 1 to 7, where 1 feels completely false and 7 feels completely true?*"

| 1 | 2 | 3 | 4 | 5 | 6 | 7 |

(completely false)   (completely true)

Emotions

Say, *"When you bring up the picture or* _____ *(state the client's anticipatory anxiety or issue) and those words* _____ *(state the NC), what emotion do you feel now?"*

_____

Subjective Units of Disturbance

Say, *"On a scale of 0 to 10, where 0 is no disturbance or neutral and 10 is the highest disturbance you can imagine, how disturbing does it feel now?"*

0   1   2   3   4   5   6   7   8   9   10

(no disturbance)   (highest disturbance)

Location of Body Sensation

Say, *"Where do you feel it* (the disturbance) *in your body?"*

_____

_____

Phase 4: Desensitization

To begin, say the following:

Say, *"Now remember, it is your own brain that is doing the healing and you are the one in control. I will ask you to mentally focus on the target and to follow my fingers (or any other BLS you are using). Just let whatever happens, happen, and we will talk at the end of the set. Just tell me what comes up, and don't discard anything as unimportant. Any new information that comes to mind is connected in some way. If you want to stop, just raise your hand."*

Then say, *"Bring up the picture and the words* _____ *(repeat the NC) and notice where you feel it in your body. Now, follow my fingers with your eyes (or other BLS)."*

Continue with the Desensitization Phase until the SUD = 0 and the VoC = 7.

Phase 5: Installation

Say, *"How does* _____ *(repeat the PC) sound?"*

_____

Say, *"Do the words* _____ *(repeat the PC) still fit, or is there another positive statement that feels better?"*

_____

If the client accepts the original PC, the clinician should ask for a VoC rating to see if it has improved.

Say, *"As you think of the incident, how do the words feel, from 1 (completely false) to 7 (completely true)?"*

1   2   3   4   5   6   7

(completely false)   (completely true)

Say, *"Think of the event and hold it together with the words _____ (repeat the PC)."*

Do a long set of BLS to see if there is more processing to be done.

Phase 6: Body Scan

Say, *"Close your eyes and keep in mind the original memory and the positive cognition. Then bring your attention to the different parts of your body, starting with your head and working downward. Any place you find any tension, tightness, or unusual sensation, tell me."*

_____

_____

Make sure that this anticipatory anxiety is fully processed before returning to the future template.

The future template for appropriate future interaction is an expansion of the Installation Phase; instead of linking the positive cognition with the past memory or trigger, the PC is linked to the future issues. Once the client's work has been checked and the other known issues in the past and present have been resolved, each client has the choice to do a more formal future template installation. The first option is to work with the situation or issue as an image.

Image as Future Template: Imagining Positive Outcomes

Imagining positive outcomes seems to assist the learning process. In this way, clients learn to enhance optimal behaviors, to connect them with a PC, and to support generalization. The assimilation of this new behavior and thought is supported by the use of BLS into a positive way to act in the future.

Say, *"I would like you to imagine yourself coping effectively with or in _____ (state the goal) in the future. With the positive belief _____ (state the positive belief) and your new sense of _____ (state the quality: i.e., strength, clarity, confidence, calm), imagine stepping into this scene. Notice what you see and how you are handling the situation. Notice what you are thinking, feeling, and experiencing in your body."*

_____

_____

_____

Again, here is the opportunity to catch any disturbance that may have been missed.

Say, *"Are there any blocks, anxieties, or fears that arise as you think about this future scene?"*

_____

_____

_____

If yes, say the following:

> Say, *"Then focus on these blocks and follow my fingers (or any other BLS)."*
>
> Say, *"What do you get now?"*

_____

_____

If the blocks do not resolve quickly, evaluate if the client needs any new information, resources, or skills to be able to comfortably visualize the future coping scene. Introduce needed information or skills.

> Say, *"What would you need to feel confident in handling the situation?"*
>
> Or say, *"What is missing from your handling of this situation?"*

_____

_____

If the block still does not resolve and the client is unable to visualize the future scene with confidence and clarity, use direct questions, the Affect Scan, or the Float-Back Technique to identify old targets related to blocks, anxieties, or fears. Remember, the point of the 3-Pronged Protocol is not only to reinforce positive feelings and behavior in the future but again to catch any unresolved material that may be getting in the way of an adaptive resolution of the issue(s). Use the Standard EMDR Protocol to address these targets before proceeding with the template (see Worksheets in this appendix). If there are no apparent blocks and the client is able to visualize the future scene with confidence and clarity, say the following:

> Say, *"Please focus on the image, the positive belief, and the sensations associated with this future scene and follow my fingers (or any other BLS)."*

_____

_____

Process and reinforce the positive associations with BLS. Do several sets until the future template is sufficiently strengthened.

> Say, *"Go with that."*

_____

Then say, *"Close your eyes and keep in mind the image of the future and the positive cognition. Then bring your attention to the different parts of your body, starting with your head and working downward. Any place you find any tension, tightness, or unusual sensation, tell me."*

_____

If any sensation is reported, do BLS.

Say, *"Go with that."*
If it is a positive or comfortable sensation, do BLS to strengthen the positive feelings.

Say, *"Go with that."*
If a sensation of discomfort is reported, reprocess until the discomfort subsides.

Say, *"Go with that."*
When the discomfort subsides, check the VoC.

Say, *"When you think of the incident* (or picture), *how true do those words _____* (repeat the PC) *feel to you now on a scale of 1 to 7, where 1 feels completely false and 7 feels completely true?"*

1	2	3	4	5	6	7
(completely false)				(completely true)		

Continue to use BLS until reaching the VoC = 7 or there is an ecological resolution. When the image as future template is clear and the PC true, move on to the movie as future template.

Movie as Future Template or Imaginal Rehearsing

During this next level of future template, clients are asked to move from imagining this one scene or snapshot to imagining a movie about coping in the future, with a beginning, middle, and end. Encourage clients to imagine themselves coping effectively in the face of specific challenges, triggers, or snafus. Therapists can make some suggestions in order to help inoculate clients with future problems. It is helpful to use this type of future template after clients have received needed education concerning social skills and customs, assertiveness, and any other newly learned skills.

Say, *"This time, I'd like you to close your eyes and play a movie, imagining yourself coping effectively with or in _____* (state where client will be) *in the future. With the new positive belief _____* (state positive belief) *and your new sense of _____* (strength, clarity, confidence, calm), *imagine stepping into the future. Imagine yourself coping with ANY challenges that come your way. Make sure that this movie has a beginning, middle, and end. Notice what you are seeing, thinking, feeling, and experiencing in your body. Let me know if you hit any blocks. If you do, just open your eyes and let me know. If you don't hit any blocks, let me know when you have viewed the whole movie."*

_____

_____

If the client hits blocks, address as above with BLS until the disturbance dissipates.

Say, *"Go with that."*

If the material does not shift, use interweaves, new skills, information, resources, direct questions, and any other ways to help clients access information that will allow them to move on. If these options are not successful, usually it means that there is earlier material still unprocessed; the Float-Back and Affect Scan are helpful in these cases to access the material that keeps the client stuck.

If clients are able to play the movie from start to finish with a sense of confidence and satisfaction, ask them to play the movie one more time from beginning to end and introduce BLS.

Say, *"Okay, play the movie one more time from beginning to end. Go with that."*
Use BLS.

In a sense, you are installing this movie as a future template.

After clients have fully processed their issue(s), they might want to work on other positive templates for the future in other areas of their lives using these future templates.

Appendix B: EMDR Therapy Summary Sheet and EMDR Therapy Session Form

The Eye Movement Desensitization and Reprocessing (EMDR) Summary Sheet and EMDR Therapy Session Form are helpful tools in keeping the important data, issues, and information pertinent to your client easily accessible.

The EMDR Therapy Summary Sheet creates a place to record the presenting problem(s), demographics, relevant health issues, and attachment concerns in an easily visible format.

Write down the presenting problem in an abbreviated form along with all of the relevant information pertaining to that problem, such as: the worst part; the negative image; irrational belief, feelings, sensations; and urges.

The 3-Pronged Protocol is addressed by including *past memories* such as the touchstone event and places to record pertinent adverse life experiences from birth through adulthood as needed, as well as proof memories for irrational negative beliefs; providing places for *present triggers* and flashforwards; and allocating an area to write in concerns about the future to assist in developing the *future template*.

There is a section to record present resources, such as the safe place, positive attachment figures, mastery experiences, and a category for "other." Recording relevant major themes that arise to use for negative cognitions and cognitive interweaves concerning issues of safety/survival; self-judgment/guilt/blame (responsibility); self-defectiveness (responsibility); choices/control; and other concerns is helpful when formulating the case conceptualization and treatment plan with your client.

The Clinical Impressions section is a place to summarize your impression of the client, record a diagnosis, write down the results of assessment measures, assess the client's ability to regulate affect, and record your subjective response to the client. There is also a quick and easy scale (Elan Shapiro, personal communication, 2007) to rate the severity of the problem, your client's motivation, your client's strengths, and your client's level of functioning on a 1 to 5 scale (where 1 = low and 5 = high) according to the client's intake responses and your clinical impression.

The EMDR Therapy Session Form is set up to record each individual EMDR Therapy session so that you have a running record of all of the EMDR Therapy targets worked on, including the date, presenting problem/image, negative and positive cognitions, Validity of Cognition (VoC) scale, emotions, Subjective Units of Disturbance (SUDs) scale, location of body sensations, and the ending rating of the SUDs (2SUDS) and the VoC (2VoC). In this way, you will have easy access to each of the EMDR targets you have worked on, and the ability to see if it has been completed or not.

EMDR Therapy Summary Sheet

Name: _____ Diagnosis: _____

PRESENTING PROBLEM(S)
_____
_____

Goals: _____

DEMOGRAPHICS
Age: _____ Gender: ☐ Male ☐ Female   *Highest Education _____
Family Status: ☐ Single ☐ Married ☐ Partnered ☐ Widower ☐ Separated ☐ Divorced
Work Status: ☐ Employed ☐ Unemployed ☐ Student ☐ Retired
Living Situation: ☐ Lives Alone ☐ Lives With Others _____

HEALTH
Health in General: ☐ Excellent ☐ Good ☐ Poor
Specify: _____
_____

Mood: _____
Medications: _____

Addictions: _____
Accident(s): _____
Hospitalizations: ☐ YES ☐ NO

Specify: _____
Chronic Pain: ☐ YES ☐ NO _____
Previous Psychological Treatment: ☐ YES ☐ NO   Hospitalization(s): ☐ YES ☐ NO

Specify: _____
Past Trauma: ☐ YES ☐ NO
Specify: _____

ATTACHMENT
Nuclear Family Issues: _____
Mother: _____
Father: _____
Sibs: _____
_____

Major Loss(es): _____
_____

Positive Attachment Figures: _____
_____

Attachment Style/Predominant States: _____
Social Stigma Issues: _____
Violent Behavior in Family: _____

PRESENTING PROBLEM(S)

Problem

1. _____ 2. _____ 3. _____ 4. _____

Worst Part of the Problem

A. _____ B. _____ C. _____ D. _____

Negative Image Associated With Problem

A. _____ B. _____ C. _____ D. _____

Irrational Negative Beliefs Associated With Problem

A. _____ B. _____ C. _____ D. _____

Feelings Associated With Problem

A. _____ B. _____ C. _____ D. _____

Sensation/Uncomfortable Internal Negative Experience/Location

A. _____ B. _____ C. _____ D. _____

Urge Associated With Problem

A. _____ B. _____ C. _____ D. _____

PAST MEMORIES   TOUCHSTONE EVENT

A. _____ B. _____ C. _____ D. _____

Birth—12 years of age (Childhood)

1. _____ 1. _____ 1. _____ 1. _____
2. _____ 2. _____ 2. _____ 2. _____
3. _____ 3. _____ 3. _____ 3. _____

13 years through 19 years (Adolescence)

4. _____ 4. _____ 4. _____ 4. _____
5. _____ 5. _____ 5. _____ 5. _____
6. _____ 6. _____ 6. _____ 6. _____

20 years and higher (Adulthood)

7. _____ 7. _____ 7. _____ 7. _____
8. _____ 8. _____ 8. _____ 8. _____
9. _____ 9. _____ 9. _____ 9. _____
10. _____ 10. _____ 10. _____ 10. _____

PROOF MEMORIES
(For irrational negative beliefs—How do you know the negative belief is true?)

1. _____ 1. _____ 1. _____ 1. _____
2. _____ 2. _____ 2. _____ 2. _____
3. _____ 3. _____ 3. _____ 3. _____

PRESENT TRIGGER(S)

1. _____ 1. _____ 1. _____ 1. _____
2. _____ 2. _____ 2. _____ 2. _____
3. _____ 3. _____ 3. _____ 3. _____

FLASHFORWARD (Worst case or doom scenario)

1. _____ 1. _____ 1. _____ 1. _____

FUTURE TEMPLATE/ANTICIPATORY ANXIETY

1. _____ 1. _____ 1. _____ 1. _____
2. _____ 2. _____ 2. _____ 2. _____

PRESENT RESOURCES

Safe Place

1. _____ 1. _____ 1. _____ 1. _____
2. _____ 2. _____ 2. _____ 2. _____

Positive Attachment Figures

1. _____ 1. _____ 1. _____ 1. _____
2. _____ 2. _____ 2. _____ 2. _____

Mastery Experiences

1. _____ 1. _____ 1. _____ 1. _____
2. _____ 2. _____ 2. _____ 2. _____

Other

1. _____ 1. _____ 1. _____ 1. _____

MAJOR THEMES/NEGATIVE COGNITIONS/COGNITIVE INTERWEAVES

Safety/Survival

1. _____ 1. _____ 1. _____ 1. _____
2. _____ 2. _____ 2. _____ 2. _____

Self-Judgment/Guilt/Blame (Responsibility)

1. _____ 1. _____ 1. _____ 1. _____
2. _____ 2. _____ 2. _____ 2. _____

Self-Defectiveness (Responsibility)

1. _____ 1. _____ 1. _____ 1. _____
2. _____ 2. _____ 2. _____ 2. _____

Choice/Control

1. _____ 1. _____ 1. _____ 1. _____

Other Concerns

1. _____ 1. _____ 1. _____ 1. _____

CLINICAL IMPRESSIONS

Clinical Impressions: _____
_____

Diagnosis: _____

Affect Regulation (Identify, Differentiate, Manage): ☐ Good ☐ Adequate ☐ Poor
(Explain): _____

Do you like this client? : ☐ YES ☐ NO

Specify: _____

Do you dislike this client? ☐ YES ☐ NO

Specify: _____

S = Severity: (Low)   1 2 3 4 5 (High) Ratings based on all information
M = Motivation: (Low)   1 2 3 4 5 (High) and clinical impression
S = Strengths: (Low)   1 2 3 4 5 (High)
LoF = Level of Functioning: (Low) 1 2 3 4 5 (High)

EMDR Therapy Session Form:

Name: _____ Resources: _____ Safe Place: _____ EM ____ Tones ____ Tapping ____ TAC ____

Date	Presenting Problem/Image	Negative Cognition/PC	VOC	Emotions	SUDS	Location	2SUDS	2VOC